HANDLIST OF SOMERSET PROBATE INVENTORIES AND ADMINISTRATORS' ACCOUNTS, 1482–1924

ADRIAN JAMES WEBB

SOMERSET RECORD SOCIETY
c/o Somerset Heritage Centre, Brunel Way, Norton Fitzwarren, Taunton, TA2 6SF
2019

Handlist of Somerset Probate Inventories and Administrators' Accounts, 1482–1924
by Adrian J. Webb
Taunton, Somerset Record Society, 2019

ISBN 978 0 901732 46 0

The Somerset Record Society, founded in 1888, has a charitable object of:

The advancement of education and learning and the promotion of public interest in local history and the preservation of ancient manuscript records relating to the county of Somerset by their transcription and publication so that their contents may be made generally available.

Set in Times New Roman

Produced by 4word Ltd, Bristol

CONTENTS

ACKNOWLEDGEMENTS

In 1995, in the introduction to my *Index of Somerset probate inventories* my acknowledgements were given as follows: I gratefully acknowledge the help given to me by Mary Siraut for suggestions regarding the format of the text and to Dr Dunning for his comments on the introduction and the indexing. Thanks are due to the staff of the Somerset Record Office and the Public Record Office at Chancery Lane, also to Harry Galloway, Stan Howard, Peter Kidner, Marek Lewcun, Mrs. M.M. Rowe (Devon County Archivist), Suzy Turner and Mr. J.S. Williams (Bristol City Archivist). A special note of thanks goes to Mr. & Mrs. Steer of Romford for the facilities provided by them.

For this updated and much revised version of 2019 I further acknowledge the help of David T. Hawkings for his encouragement, checking references and for assisting with identifying further inventories. Philip Ashford, David Bromwich and William Hancock for their interest in this handlist and encouragement. Liz Grant of the Somerset Heritage Centre (S.H.C.) has been particularly helpful, as have her colleagues Andy, Eve, Kate, Rob and Simon. I am grateful to Steve Hobbs for reading my introductory text and for his comments. Harry Galloway and I published the 1995 edition but since then the names of the Somerset Record Office, Public Record Office, Devon Record Office and Bristol City Archives have changed, details of which are included in this volume. I would also like to thank Dr Andrew Butcher and Dr Robert Dunning for accepting my proposal to publish this volume. Further thanks go to Robert for his encouragement, comments on the text and for references to the origins of inventories in the diocese of Bath and Wells. Also to Mark McDermott for letting me use his transcripts of Somerset probate inventories.

NOTES ON TRANSCRIPTION AND EDITING

All surnames have been kept as their original spelling. All place-names have been modernised where possible. Some place-names have not been identified and have been left as they appear either in the original or on the index card in the repository concerned and '(*sic*)' added after the name. It should be noted that some of the places given in the card indexes to inventories at The National Archives are doubtful and have therefore been cross referenced. Some have been deleted, especially where the wrong county was assumed by the person filling in the card. Any mistakes in transcribing from the indexes are my own, although every effort has been made to avoid any errors.

Some surnames, occupations and places are given with a question mark following them. This usually means that the information has been derived from evidence within the inventory, but cannot be totally relied upon. The date given has been copied from the catalogue, list or card index, without checking each document. It is not always clear whether dates have been modernised or not. If the date should prove to be incorrect it is hoped an electronic version of this publication can be corrected and published on the internet to include such anomalies.

The use of dots has been adopted to show words and letters that are partially missing or illegible *e.g.* ....ton. Where a place-name has not been given, or is illegible, the term '[no place]' has been used. Where a Christian or surname has not been given, or is illegible, the term '[missing]' has been used. Many of the damaged documents in this handlist have been examined to try and establish more information about the person whose inventory was exhibited. Any relevant information has been added to this handlist and is not on the corresponding online catalogue. Sometimes this is only a note of less common types of goods or belongings indicating a particular occupation, in others the name of the parish of the appraisers has been identified.

In the transcripts of documents included in the introduction, any contractions have been silently expanded. The spelling in a transcript has been faithfully reproduced. Any Latin text is shown in italics. Interlined text is shown in angular brackets. Editorial text is in square brackets. Text that is crossed through is as it appears in the original.

INTRODUCTION

The creation of an inventory was the second of two processes administered by church courts that followed a death. Probate, the first stage, was the acknowledgement that the wishes of the deceased expressed in writing (a will) or by verbal declaration (nuncupative) was, indeed, both the last and genuine will and the testament covering the disposal of assets. Having been proved both genuine and acceptable, an inventory of those assets, whether moveable goods, leases or debts to be called in, was to be made by appointed neighbours, usually two or more, occasionally as many as seven, and duly submitted to the appropriate authority. Such a process dated back at least to the middle of the 13th century.[1]

Inventories of the goods and chattels of deceased people contain a wealth of information – their names and occupations, their properties owned or leased, their personal possessions, merchandise, crops, goods, furniture, kitchen paraphernalia and any outstanding debts. They also give an insight into the types of buildings inhabited. However, as valuations they should be interpreted with caution. From medieval times the purpose of the inventory was to list and value the personal goods and chattels of the deceased soon after death as a defence against theft, especially of the property of priests: 'for the instinct of the malicious is ... to invade his property, reap his corn, if it is in the ear, or pull up his root crops'.[2] Inventories were no longer required after 1782, unless called for by an interested party,[3] As a consequence this volume contains only 267 entries dating between 1783 and 1924.

In 1995, in the introduction to my *Index of Somerset probate inventories*, I wrote that 'I have been able to locate some 6,100 inventories ... more may yet come to light'.[4] The prophecy has proved to be correct. The present volume lists over 7,600 documents, including some duplicates, an addition of over 550 inventories and a collection of over 850 administrators' accounts. It also contains some 'out' county inventories, mainly found in family papers at the Somerset Heritage Centre. Those have been included as the people involved appear to have an immediate Somerset connection. Inventories of testators dying in Somerset have also been included.

For probate purposes. the diocese of Bath and Wells, almost co-terminous with the ancient county of Somerset, was divided between the archdeaconries of Bath, Wells and Taunton and smaller areas know as 'peculiars' belonging to Wells cathedral and many of the members of its chapter. As a general rule the will of a deceased person whose goods were to be found solely within one of those areas was proved in its court. Should the goods be found in more than one but still within the diocese, responsibility passed to the bishop, before the 16th century to his officer called the commissary-general and later direct to the diocesan consistory court. The commissary-general's court moved across the whole diocese. The consistory met at Wells. Should the deceased be particularly prominent, probate might be claimed by the bishop in person; and should the estate be found in more than one diocese, the right of probate would be claimed in the southern province by the archbishop of Canterbury in his London-based court known as the Prerogative Court of Canterbury

(P.C.C.).[5] Inventories compiled by authority of the appropriate court presumably found their way, with the associated will, to the court's own repository, and the varied sources of inventories listed in this volume are a measure of the variety of courts ecclesiastical in the diocese of Bath and Wells. An example of this apparently complicated system at work along medieval lines in the 18th century concerned the will of George Walter of Mark dated 12 March 1770. His executor and trustee, William Harden, obtained probate in a court at Wells, probably the peculiar court of the dean. Walter's estate, however, lay in 'diverse dioceses' and for that reason so late as 14 May 1776, presumably after complaints from dissatisfied legatees, the archbishop of Canterbury ordered the dean to transfer the will to the P.C.C. Harden claimed ignorance of the rules; what the dean thought is not recorded.[6]

Many inventories for Somerset residents have survived in collections held outside the county because at least two adjoining dioceses held probate jurisdiction over some Somerset parishes. Wambrook, for instance, was part of the peculiar of the prebendary of Chardstock in Salisbury cathedral; and an inventory of a Dunster mariner is to be found among the records of Bristol diocese.[7] Thus 144 inventories and administrators' accounts either at Bristol Archives or the Wiltshire and Swindon History Centre have been included in this volume. Wills proved and estates administered by the P.C.C account for a total of 1,414 items. A more detailed description of the main collections of inventories and accounts is to be found below.

The survival of inventories in the courts associated with the diocese of Bath and Wells is fortunate. Many were evidently lost three centuries before the main collection of probate records was sent to Exeter and was destroyed by enemy action in 1942. The Bath and Wells diocesan registrar in the 1630s, Mark Tabor, left detailed notes about the probate process and how the documents generated for that purpose were filed away at Wells. He noted how to process inventories and administrators' accounts:

> ... if dayes beegoven for bare idlnous within the peculiers to passe their accompts or to exhibite their Inventaries be carfull to sett downe the dayes in the third booke of Accompts And att the day caull them or send a new processe for them if they doe not appeare, but in any case fayle not in the greete vacacion once a yeare or sooner if you wisse any wills bonds or Inventaryes to sett them downe particulerly in the same manner as they are nowe inserted in the second booke of Addicons that the executors or Administrators may theruppon presently bee Cited to supply the same.
>
> In the end of the yeare in the great vacacion when you right upp the Office, if you finde any wills Inventoryes or bonds which ar not rightly philed or bundelled hange they uppon the right phile yf you cannot without much labour fynde the right fyle or bundle then hang them uppon the phile of scatterd Wills Inventarys & bonds and afterwards calender them in the booke of scatterd Wills made for that purpose. And soe likewise of accompts.

It is likely that Tabor had come across inventories and/or accounts that had not been 'rightly philed or bundelled' at Wells, hence his advice, or instruction. Part of the confusion with the incorrect arrangement of the inventories and other types of probate records was caused by John Meeres. Tabor noted on the 27 August 1636:

> Wills Inventaries and bands left unperfected by John Meeres when hee went from mee which was about the 24th of December 1634 which afterwards I delivered againe unto

> him and hee promised mee to putt them in order, but hee afterwards brought them to mee againe mixt altogether, And those wills that have bands and Inventaries ar philed and calendered in the yeere 1634 or 1635. The other who have neither bands nor Inventaries are philed uppon the last phile of scattered wills, and soe likewise are the bands and Inventaries uppon the phile of scattered bands and Inventaries.

Tabor drew up a list of cases involving inventories and bonds that were not completed, partially thanks to Meeres, adding a further cache he found that had been left 'unperfected' by William Androwes.[8] It is unfortunate that Tabor's highly organised record keeping was not kept intact but left to rot in damp conditions in Wells over two hundred years later.[9] However, his 'phile of scattered bands and Inventaries'[10] may explain the survival of some of the inventories that made their way to the Somerset County Record Office (S.C.R.O.), currently having a reference starting with D/D/ct/1 in this handlist.

Some idea of the number that were once extant for one court can be deduced from a list of inventories for the jurisdiction of the dean's peculiar court of Wells for the period 1660–1697. In this list there are 561 inventories, roughly equating to approximately 15 per year (if the two incomplete years of 1660 and 1697 are disregarded).[11] If this figure is applied across the period 1560–1782, then there might have been as many as 3,195 inventories for the dean's peculiar alone, although the reality was probably a much lower figure. Nevertheless this does give some indication of the number of losses at Exeter in 1942, which makes the surviving inventories more valuable to historians. It also appears that each inventory may have been given an individual number and then stored in yearly bundles rather than inside the will it related to. This may also explain why some of the inventories have survived in the diocesan collection and were, thankfully, not sent to Exeter.[12]

The date when making an inventory of an individual's goods was introduced in the diocese of Bath and Wells is something that had been established before *c*.1258.[13] Examples of orders to make an inventory can rarely be found in the bishops' registers: in one of 1410, John Tyssebury, commissary-general of Nicholas, bishop of Bath and Wells,[14] ordered William Gosse, Robert Vele, William Newtone and William Kingestone to take possession of all the goods and chattels of William Whittok of Ilchester, deceased, intestate, to compile an inventory of them and to render an account of them when requested.[15] Another example survives from 1445/6, when the inventory of Alice Somerey of Dunster, whose will was proved on 16 February 1445/6 at Monksilver by the official of the archdeacon of Taunton, was exhibited at Dunster four days later in the archdeacon's court.[16]

A case in the court of the dean of Wells in 1637 shows something of the practice, which could have been widespread, of reducing the number of items recorded in an inventory. This practice meant the value of the deceased's goods would have been reduced for probate purposes. Subsequently this could have meant paying a lower fee to have it exhibited in the dean's court,[17] and a lower share of the estate enjoyed by beneficiaries. The case of Grave alias Hooke *contra* Knight, brought in the dean's court in 1637, mentions an inventory in a dispute concerning the value of a deceased's estate and how the figure was calculated.

The deceased mentioned in the case was William Hooke alias Grave of Bridgwater.[18] He was buried on 3 May 1636 at Bridgwater (within the archdeaconry of Taunton).[19] The administrator was his son-in-law, John Knight, husbandman of Broomfield, a peculiar in the diocese of Bath and Wells attached to the deanery.[20] Knight had married William's daughter Grace on 13 October 1628 at Bridgwater[21] and the newly-weds moved in with William and his wife Jane. Domestic matters appear to have been cordial to start with. One of the deponents in the case, Robert Shattock of Dunwear, formerly of West Bagborough, said that at the time of their marriage William became bound unto John in a bond of £60. The bond ensured William would provide them, and any of their children, with 'necessarie howseroome, and meate, and drinck, or six pounds per annum in lewe thereof'; this type of arrangement is rarely recorded, especially for people of the lower ranks of society. John allegedly helped himself to Hooke's livestock to cover the cost of this arrangement.[22] Grace may have been quite young, as John was appointed executor of William's will during her 'minority', but the Bridgwater parish register contains a baptism for a Grace on 11 October 1601.[23] This indicates that her 'minority' referred to her status as a married woman who was not allowed to be an administratrix whilst her husband was still alive.

Much of the case involved establishing how much William's estate was worth. John Hobbs, husbandman, stated William was indebted to him for a bond of £6 4s 9d, which he received from John Knight who was administrator of Grace (as executrix of Hooke's will). William's widow Jane, aged 44, stated that her husband's funeral cost 5s 3d and at the time of his death 'owed by bill' and bonds to Thomas Bennett of Bridgwater 21s, to John Hobbs of North Petherton £6 4s 9d, to Joane Huett widow of Othery £10, to Joane Sealie widow and Edward Sealie of Bridgwater 18s, to Humphrie Pitts of Bridgwater 8s 2d, and to John Daniell of Bridgwater 9s 6d. On his death bed William admitted he owed his son-in-law John Knight £4 5s. All the people who were owed money had received it in full since Hooke's death, suggesting part, or all, of William's estate had been sold off to cover those debts.

Other people deposed other debts. John Daniel of Bower in Bridgwater, husbandman, stated that John Knight, administrator of William, paid him 32s 1d and 23s 1d to cover the cost of the funeral for flesh meat costing 11s 2d, for a shroud and candles 5s 11d, for two bushells of malt 6s, and 9s for an outstanding debt due to Daniel; in total the funeral cost over £3. Thomas Popham of North Bower in Bridgwater, husbandman, laid out 42s towards the cost of the funeral but had also been repaid by John Knight. James Bartlett, husbandman of Broomfield, aged 48, confirmed the information concerning the debts, as did George Towill, tanner of Broomfield (formerly of Enmore and North Petherton). However, William's widow, Jane, deposed that she did not witness any such documentation, but the debts do not appear to have been further contested.

Jane claimed she had married William about five years before the case was heard, about 'St James tyde' and lived with him ever since. This may have been a contributory factor to the dispute. As Grace was a blood relative and Jane was not, was this dispute over the rights of a widow over her husband's estate, rather than those rights being vested in her step-daughter? She stated that during his life time he owned the following goods, which she valued for the benefit of the court proceedings:

> Imprimis one malte mill or Querne worth iijs iiijd. Item one felting trowe worth in this Deponents Judgment xijd Item a parcell of shides att the hare howse end, but worth she cannot depose; Item fower windowes of glasse about the howse, one of which had a Cassment, which windowes of glasse weare made fast with smale nailes, all worth in this Deponents Judgment some fower or five shillings, which glasse windowes are there still remeyning aboute the house the deceased dyed in; Item three lettice windows worth in this deponent Judgment xijd there still remeyning and as she remembreth they containe in the whole twelve lightes. Item seaven doares of the said howse besides the streate doare and back doare worth at least five shillinges: Item one brewing trowe worth sixe pence. Item three pailes worth two shillinges: Item one

> chaire worth in this Deponents Judgment and opinion eight pence; Item dishes and trenches worth sixe pence. Item one table cloath of aboute three yards worth three shillinges fower pence. Item one peck and three senes worth xijd. Item one woollen turne worth xiiijd. Item one bacon rack but what worth well she knoweth not but beleiveth worth eight pence: Item one Holberd worth in this Deponents opinion and Judgment twelve pence: Item two Ladders worth two shillinges: Item the herbadg of the hedland and the Crofte the backsides orchard and gardens all conteyning aboute three acres worth three pownds, and as this Deponent remembreth she this Deponent gave the defendant John Knight the administrator soe much for it, for the tyme he was to hold itt by virtue of his administration of the goods of the said William Hooke alias Grave deceased.

But whether any of the items she listed were left out of her husband's inventory, for some strange reason, she did not know but referred to the inventory exhibited in court. She also told the court that her husband died possessed of 'one acre and halfe of wheate, two acres of beanes and of the halfendeale of seaven yard of pease'. Jane paid John Knight, in his capacity as administrator, £10 10s for these and the peas were 'well worth sixteene shillinges'. She made her mark at the end of her deposition but the result of the case, or any further depositions are lost. Presumably the goods she mentioned in her deposition were not included in the inventory.[24]

It is worth pointing out that normally the value of the item listed in an inventory was only an estimated value. The actual value of the item, in most cases, was only realised after it had been sold. Therefore an inventory was a way of undervaluing an estate and may not represent the full amount the beneficiaries received. A good example of this can be found in the accounts kept by John Bampfylde, Thomas Gerard and John Bois, executors of John Sydenham (1589 – 10 Mar. 1626/7) of Brympton. At Brympton his sheep were valued in the inventory at £140 but were later sold for £149 7s 9d; similarly horses valued at £42 were sold for £43 6s 6d, 'rother beasts' at £116 sold for £122 13s 4d, and pigs at £8 sold for £10 17s. At Combe Sydenham 'rother beasts' valued at £26 13s 4d sold for £30 9s and horses valued at £18 sold for £18 8s.

The livestock was a straightforward matter that was easily dealt with. The subject of disposing of his crops was a different matter. Of the corn that was sold the executors recorded two entries relating to Sydenham's inventory:

> Item received of John Nowis late Servant unto Mr Sydenham in parte payment of Lxj^{li} viij^{s} viij^{d} for the Wheat Rye and Barley which was in Mowes and in the Barnes at Brimpton at Mr Sydenhams death being all Inventaryed at 40^{li} [*total*] xxx^{li}

> Item received more of the said John Nowis in parte of payment of One Hundred poundes for some of the Corne groweng upon Mr Sydenhams Land at the tyme of his death, All which was Inventaryed at Lxx^{li}, the residue of the said 100^{li} stands Chargable upon the said John Nowis Accompts [*total*] L^{li}[25]

Nowis (d.1645)[26] was steward to John Sydenham and was later appointed Receiver to the Committee of the lands and body of John Sydenham, a King's ward, from 1629 until 1640. As steward he would have taken overall responsibility for all the farming matters involved at the time the inventory was taken. The executors' account shows that it was easier to estimate the value of livestock, but the same cannot be said of the crops. The true value of some of the corn was more than 50% higher than estimated in the inventory and was only known after it had been gathered and processed.

Another discrepancy could occur if some of the deceased's goods came to light after the inventory had been exhibited. Sydenham's executors noted in their accounts the discovery of £370 15s 1d in cash in Brympton House. However, when they drew up the inventory of Sir John's estate some time earlier they only included £366 11s. The reason for the discrepancy between the two is that the 'Inventary of his Goodes exhibited into the Prerogative Court of the Arches in St Pawles London' was made before £4 4s had been discovered, and, presumably, was never declared to the court.[27] The records for this period for the Court of Arches are lost,[28] but, nevertheless, the accounts clearly show Sydenham's goods were worth more than stated in his inventory.[29]

Studies of probate inventories for other counties have revealed evidence for a standard pricing system for certain types of goods, suggesting that appraising goods was a relatively straightforward task. The process of probate became problematic when an inventory was not made. An interesting case in 1622, brought before Quarter Sessions by William Panter, Nathaniel Saunders, Clement Cogswell and Edmond Sands, overseers of the poor for Keynsham, shows how one such problem arose. They stated that Thomas Carter and his wife died intestate, which meant their six children were chargeable to the parish. Carter's goods were then taken by William Byde, overseer, until probate could be granted. Byde then began to sell the goods, but he then died leaving no inventory or accounts of the Carters' goods and money. Instead of being brought before an ecclesiastical court the matter hinged upon the maintenance of a family of six orphans. This was something which Quarter Sessions dealt with as it was a matter within the limits of the Elizabethan Poor Law.[30] The fact there was no inventory of the Carters' goods was the cause of a problem that ended up being a burden for the parish rate payers.

Inventories were not always made, or appraised, immediately following the death of an individual, as can be seen by comparing burial entries in parish registers with the dates on the inventories. There was also another obvious delay between the date of the inventory and the date it was exhibited. Margaret Steig quotes a case in the archdeaconry of Taunton that shows the problem. In an attempt to obtain probate a widow 'admitted her husband's death and after an interval exhibited an inventory of his goods, formally renouncing administration, and was dismissed with a 12 pence fee for the renunciation, and a 4 pence court fee'.[31] How common this was cannot be established for all the courts in the diocese. However, it is possible to obtain the data for a large number of inventories proved in the archdeacon's court at Taunton. The vast majority of inventories were annotated with the date they were exhibited, as well as the names of the officials involved,[32] which can be compared with burial dates in parish registers.

Another example of the time taken between the different probate stages involving inventories can be seen in a case concerning the will of James Lock of West Hatch. On 6 April 1810, George Lock and William Lock, the lawful nephews and next of kin of the late James Lock of the parish of West Hatch, were ordered to be sworn in as faithful executors and administrators of the last will and testament of the said James Lock. On the 23rd of the same month George and William were ordered to compile an inventory of the property and possessions of the late James Lock. Then, less than two weeks later, on 5 May, authority was given to George and William to execute and administer the will.[33] On the whole this appears to have been a very quick and efficient process.

Settling a deceased's estate was often more problematic and time consuming. Following the death of Jonathan Radcliffe, vicar of East Brent, some time after May 1663 (and before the 13th of December),[34] his administrator, Mr Thomas Bell of St Martins, Ludgate in the City of London, merchant taylor, had to deal with his debts. Radcliffe owed £25 to William Peirs D.D., archdeacon of Taunton, and £30 to Arthur Mattocke, gentleman. Piers and Mattocke wanted their money. As Radcliffe's administrator, Bell was able to claim the profits of the vicarage of East Brent to the tune of £60, a figure that would have conveniently paid off Radcliffe's two debts. Bell used his attorneys, sometime after 1 October 1664, to settle the matter, but how long the archdeacon had to wait for his money is not clear.[35] One Elizabethan administrators' account appears to have been compiled in 1575 but not exhibited until 1588.[36] Whether the date is a copyist's mistake or not may never be proven. But the deceased had died before 1581,[37] therefore suggesting the 13 year hiatus was correct.[38]

Despite the above, making an inventory was relatively straightforward, but it had to be paid for. The appraisers, the costs of exhibiting the document in the appropriate probate court and making any copies, all cost money. In the P.C.C. in the 1630s, Tabor noted the following fees were applied:

> For dispensacion for an Inventory and accompt wher the executor and administrator will enter into band to pay all debts and legacies withoute takeing benefitt of the Inventory and accompt 33s 4d.
> For coppies of Inventaries for every presse 8d
> For coppies of accompts and orders everie every [*sic*] sheete 8d
> For exhibiting the Inventaries after the day 2s
> For ingrossing of Inventaries for every presse of parchment ijs
> For ingrossing of Accompts for every presse of parchment 3s 4d
> For drawing of Accompts more or lesse according to the labor not exceeding 12d the sheete 12d

Tabor also noted the fees charged during the time Parliament had effectively done away with the local courts in the 1650s. Of note was the cost 'for parchment to duble write the will and Inventory – 16d',[39] which again is more evidence for the creation of copies. After the Interregnum, when the local probate courts were restored, a table of fees charged in the dean of Wells's court, in the 1670s, shows they were the same for any ecclesiastical court. Those inventories valued £40 to £100 were charged one shilling, from £100 to under £500 charged six shillings, from £500 to under £1,000 charged twelve shillings and from £1,000 or above charged one pound two shillings.[40]

Also included in this handlist are details of administrators' accounts. Most of those, like the inventories, date from the 1580s through until 1740s, with a few exceptions. They can contain some fascinating information and one includes details of costs incurred 18 years before it was approved in 1705.[41] Many contain details of educating and maintaining the deceased's children, business and travel costs, debts and property holdings.

Just as an executor of a will had to provide accounts to show that he or she had settled a testator's estate, paid any outstanding bills and distributed the legacies left by the deceased, so administrators' accounts were a necessary requirement following the death of a person dying intestate. This type of document was the last stage in the process of settling an intestate's affairs, and it had to set out all the money received by way of debts, rents or sales and all the expenses incurred by the administrator during the process of dealing with the estate. Most importantly, it had to record a final balance which, when approved by whichever ecclesiastical court oversaw the process, meant that the administrator was freed from any further liability. As proof of his fair dealing the administrator was required to keep receipts for any sum of money over 40/- that he either received or disbursed and such receipts were handed over to the court in evidence, although the survival rate of these is very poor.

Any issues concerning administrators' accounts, like the inventories themselves, were dealt with by the bishop's court.[42] The surviving accounts within the diocese of Bath and Wells indicate that those from the archdeacon of Taunton's court date from 1637 to 1756. Whereas before that period accounts for people living within the archdeaconry of Taunton can be found in the diocesan collection (see below under D/D/Cta); these were processed at Wells. It is far from clear whether 1637 was the date when the business of administrators' accounts was split between Taunton and Wells. Why this geographical overlap occurred may have been due to the fact that the deceased had financial interests in both archdeaconries. Therefore, as Wells was a higher authority they dealt with such cases.[43]

It was also not unusual for an individual to refuse to be an administrator of an estate, for any number of reasons. On 20 October 1752, Martha James of Bristol, widow and next of kin of Thomas Dando late of Chelwood, deceased and intestate, renounced the administration of his estate. She appointed Robert Holloway, a proctor, to present her renunciation in the bishop's consistory court at Wells and to arrange the appointment of George Hodges of High Littleton esquire as the administrator in her place.[44]

Not all inventories were made for probate purposes. There are many examples of inventories made in order to settle outstanding debts.[45] Some can be found amongst the records of the court of Quarter Sessions. For example, the inventory of the estate and effects of John Newton, late of Montacute, linen weaver, who was a prisoner for debt in the sheriff's ward at Ilchester, was made on New Year's day 1742/3.[46] Because of the involvement of the sheriff some inventories can be found in the papers of men who served this office. One collection, from 1720, survives in the papers of Jepp Clarke of Nynehead;[47] the subject of distraint is not within the scope of this volume. Inventories are also sometimes with title deeds, listing the furniture in particular rooms. These are not strictly probate inventories, more schedules of goods that are included in a sale or lease of a property, but, nevertheless, are particularly useful for establishing how rooms were furnished.

Occupations[48]

In this handlist a description is given in just over 3,000 documents of an occupation, married status, or title; of the last two categories there are 7 baronets, 3 knights, 103 esquires, 106 spinsters, 37 bachelors, 691 widows and widowers, 213 gentlemen and two gentlewomen. As the vast majority of inventories in this handlist were exhibited in the archdeaconry court of Taunton covering the west of the county, it is not surprising that Frome, Wells and Shepton Mallet are poorly represented in the following list. Approximately 2,000 people are named with occupations, from which some observations can be made. Starting with the more obscure occupations, which appear only once, are a 'Batchelor of Physick' who lived in Taunton in the 1680s, a 'Barber and perickmaker' of Minehead, a bargeman of Lyng, a bishop of Bath and Wells, a brickmaker of Bridgwater, a carver of Durston, a cheesemonger of Bleadon, a clockmaker in Taunton, a 'coffeeman' of Bath, a cook of Langford Budville, a curate of Trull, a drugget maker of Rode, an edge tool maker of Bedminster, an Excise officer of Crewkerne, a fisherman of Stogursey, a flax dresser of Bridgwater, a gallipot maker of Brislington, a girth-web weaver of Winsham, a glassmaker of Bedminster, a groom of Kingston St Mary, a hatter of Taunton, a headmaster of Bishops Hull, a helliar of Bridgwater, an ironmonger of Langport, a leather cutter of Taunton, a linen weaver of South Petherton, a locksmith of Taunton, a 'Mendipman' of East Harptree, a pilot of Abbots Leigh, a poulterer of Bath, a purser and a roper both of Minehead, a rough mason of Horsington, a sail cloth weaver of East Chinnock, a shear grinder of Taunton, a silk thrower of Shepton Mallet, a skinner of Minehead, a tallow chandler of Frome Selwood, a tipler of Porlock, a toy man of Bath, a waggoner and a watchmaker both of Taunton, a wheelwright of North Petherton, a white yarn washer of Crewkerne, a woolman of Taunton, and a yarnworker of Crewkerne. Many of these were specialist occupations that were predominantly based in urban areas, such as Bath, Bedminster, Bridgwater, Crewkerne, Minehead and Taunton.

Of those occupations that appear more than once, some observations can be made which help describe how the majority of trades in the county were distributed, geographically, from the late 16th century until the middle of the 18th century. Of those trades that were involved with the higher end of society there appears to have been a trend towards them being located in urban areas, such as a watchmaker and a clockmaker in Taunton. There were ten apothecaries, all of whom were men who lived in substantial towns, as did the four goldsmiths who lived in Bath, Crewkerne and Taunton. Similarly physicians were in Bath, Bridgwater, Chaffcombe, Crewkerne, Nynehead, Taunton, and Wiveliscombe and a 'surgeon and apothecary' in Crewkerne and Dunster. The physician based in Nynehead was close to the wealthy Sanford family at Nynehead Court and the town of Wellington. Supporting such medical men was a gallipot maker at Brislington who made apothecary pots for the Bristol market, which is one of the rarest of occupations found in Somerset. Carriers at Chard, Compton Bishop, Frome and Milverton show the importance of also basing such a business in a town on a main road through the county. Similarly tobacconists are found in Crewkerne and Bridgwater. The Industrial Revolution can account for a small number of specialist occupations (an edge tool maker, braziers, and a glassmaker) in urban areas such as the hinterland of Bristol, Frome, Glastonbury and Taunton. The decline in the number of inventories produced after the 1750s explains why there are not greater numbers of occupations reflecting industrialisation.

Outside those areas the parishes of Abbots Leigh, Bridgwater, Dunster, Easton in Gordano and Minehead could account for the majority of mariners and shipwrights, however there were a few living elsewhere. Most of the sailors, or mariners, living away from the coast were associated with the Royal Navy, such as those at Shepton Mallet and Somerton. Those living in Bath were of higher rank, such as a captain, and a commander. The total of men connected directly with the sea is 54, approximately 3% of those whose occupation was recorded.

As Somerset was predominantly an agricultural county in the 16th and 17th centuries it is not surprising that the number of agricultural occupations is so high. Yeomen and husbandmen are the largest number involved in agricultural trades with 500 and 407 respectively, to which can be added 5 farmers. On their own these three occupations roughly account for nearly half of all the 1,988 occupations. As so many documents do not record an occupation it is likely that this figure could have been much higher. Reading through many of the inventories with no stated occupation, it is clear that a very high percentage had some involvement with agriculture. For example, testators owned small numbers of cows or sheep, and/or tools used for agricultural work; those inventories that specifically mention husbandry tools have been given the occupation of husbandman in this handlist. Although it has not been possible to check every inventory, the scale of agricultural workers compared to other trades must have been much higher than the 50% recorded in this handlist. Again the figures could also have been slightly skewed by the survival of documents in such large numbers for the archdeaconry of Taunton. This area covers the west and south of Somerset (forming a triangular area from Bridgwater to Crewkerne to Exmoor) which was predominantly involved in agriculture and clothmaking.

It is worth noting that the goods that were appraised and listed in inventories were only a brief snapshot in time. Because a man or a woman had tools of a particular trade in their house it did not necessarily mean they were practising that specific trade. For example, the inventory of Henry Vincent, a potter of Wanstrow, was drawn up in 1633. If the inventory's preamble did not include his trade as a 'potter' it would not be possible to deduce this from the list of his possessions. Like countless other people his goods were appraised and show nothing out of the ordinary. He owned crops in fields, a beast, cheese, butter, bacon, wood, a cheese press, furniture of the basic sort, and 'some bords in the shoppe'. No mention is made of any of the tools or paraphernalia of his trade, or the value of any clay or finished pots, unless they were insignificant enough to be described as 'Smalle things not yet seene nor Remembred' valued at five shillings. The total of his inventory came to £18 5s and, without the reference to being a potter, it could easily be possible to deduce that he may have been a cheesemaker. The likelihood is that he had more than one source of income, that is pottery production, cheese making and growing crops, which he may have sold or used for his own consumption. As the inventory makes no mention of any pottery, or earthenware, does this also suggest that Henry Vincent was an employee and the pots he made were elsewhere in his employer's possession? Perhaps the 'bords' in his shop[49] were used to display pieces of pottery he made.

Of the trades that relied upon agriculture for their raw materials, the cloth industry has many occupations associated with it in this handlist. Some 296 occupations are connected to the industry, including 15 fullers, 26 mercers, 33 people involved with serge, 39 weavers, accounting for approximately 15% of the whole. This figure does not include 21 merchants, as it is not always possible to be confident that any commodities, or goods, they dealt with were always reflected in their inventories. Of the other trades involved in the basic staple functions in village and town life, there were 10 bakers, 41 blacksmiths, 25 butchers, 41 carpenters and joiners, 33 cordwainers and shoemakers, 52 innkeepers, 6 labourers, 7 maltsters, 15 masons, 29 millers, 3 potters, 4 sadlers, 6 soapboilers and soapmakers, 28 tanners, 6 thatchers and 11 victuallers. A total of 306 occupations equates to approximately 15% of the whole. In addition to this are 83 clerks (most of whom were clerics), 6 vicars, a bishop, an archdeacon, a sub-dean, a canon and a doctor of divinity, who provided a spiritual and religious input into daily life. These percentages show that between about 1580 and 1750 over half the work force in the county was, potentially, involved with agriculture. Between the cloth industry, agriculture and those general occupations (listed above), approximately 82% of the people whose trades are recorded in this handlist can be accounted for. With 4% classed as clergy and 3% as maritime, this leaves 3% in the slightly less frequent occupations, some of which, apart from labourers, were highly skilled. But these figures are inevitably skewed, as the number of inventories and accounts for labourers of any description (only six), miners (only one) and other physically demanding low paid jobs are almost non-existent. Every parish in the county was home to agricultural labourers, suggesting thousands were too poor to have had an inventory made after their death.

Collections of probate inventories and administrators' accounts

Inventories at the Somerset Heritage Centre

Owing to the destruction of most of the Bath and Wells diocesan probate material in 1942, during a German bombing raid on Exeter, there remain very few inventories for the archdeaconries of Bath, Wells, and for most of the Peculiar courts. The largest single collection of probate inventories for Somerset is that of the archdeaconry of Taunton (see below under DD/SP). The reverse can be said for the survival of administrators' accounts. The S.H.C. is the main location of probate material handled by the courts within the diocese of Bath and Wells.

D/D/Cta, 1577–1748. is a large series of administrators' accounts, with some inventories, for the whole diocese of Bath and Wells, covering the whole of the ancient county of Somerset. This collection includes records for a large number of peculiars, as well as the archdeaconries of Bath and of Taunton. The accounts (1,005) survive in much greater numbers than the inventories (37). 90 documents have no place associated with them and there are some duplicate accounts.[50] Evidence for the creation of these duplicates can be seen in these accounts in payments to apparitors for organising copies of them. Where an account and an inventory appear in this handlist the year of the inventory has been given; the year of the account is sometimes of a later year for obvious reasons.

There are some 'out' county documents in this collection, for example the administrator's account for John Longe of Compton Abbas, Dorset of 1598.[51] Those that fall into the archdeaconry of Taunton and the archdeaconry of Bath are predominantly, but not exclusively, from the period before the Interregnum. This may suggest that the records may have been stored elsewhere.

Those documents were sorted in the early 20th century when those that had no obvious parish, or personal names were put into a bundle marked 'Blank'. In that bundle there are 53 documents, three of which are separated parts of one account.[52] Many have no details of any worth, except for a date and a few names. However, it is likely that some of the fragments may be missing pages from accounts elsewhere in this collection and prove to be of value. Matching the fragments together will be a long and difficult task, but nevertheless worthwhile. One undated fragment in the lettered series contains a great deal of information about the administration of a cloth merchant's business, but the heading and preamble is missing. Although it does not give a name, place or date it is possible to establish these facts by reading the account. Due to the rarity of such an account, its location and date makes this type of document worthy of further research.[53]

The condition of the Cta series is described in the S.H.C. catalogue as 'poor' but nevertheless it is a valuable archival survival. Those documents for surnames starting with the letter N have been expertly conserved. The rest are in desperate need of conservation and there are many gems of information amongst those damaged records. For example, for the family historian one account mentions four children, a kinsman, an uncle and 'Stephen Winter of Compton Martin who married a Cosen German of the Children by the mothers side'.[54] Another records the details of a marriage settlement of £50 for the deceased's daughter in the 1630s.[55]

D/D/Cti, 1705–1750. Some 107 inventories separated into a series of their own before they were transferred to the S.C.R.O., now stored amongst the Bath and Wells diocesan deposit.

This series contains inventories for parishes across the diocese, as it includes Old Cleeve, Bridgwater and Norton Fitzwarren (to name a few) that are in the archdeaconry of Taunton.

D/D/ct/1, 1575–1640. Approximately 1,750 wills and 195 inventories predominantly proved in the diocese of Bath and Wells consistory court. These are now arranged in volumes by the surname of the deceased, with a typescript list of its contents in the front; all the documents have been conserved. There are wills and inventories for some places in this collection for parishes in the archdeaconry of Taunton such as Taunton, and Creech St Michael. There are also wills from peculiars such as St Decumans, Mark and North Curry. It thus appears this series also covers the whole diocese, but like other series it is probably correct to surmise that a deceased person with financial interests in more than one archdeaconry and/or peculiar, had to have their probate dealt with in Wells. The covering dates in the S.H.C. series description reflects the main body of documents, but the inventories cover the period 1539–1682. The inventory of John Fysher alias Fessher of Portbury, of 1539, is an oddity, as most inventories date from the 1570s through to the mid 1640s.[56]

If an inventory has an associated will in this collection it has not been recorded in this handlist. In a few instances there are two copies of an inventory. Because of these two factors some of the inventories are described with variant spellings of the same surname, which have been taken from both the will and the inventory. As of 2018 the documents in this collection are being listed on the S.H.C. online catalogue.[57]

DD/SP, *c*.1609–1755. For the archdeaconry of Taunton some 4,382 inventories and administrators' accounts have survived amongst the Sheppard collection, which was once housed at Taunton Castle. Whilst it was there it suffered from damp and there is evidence to suggest this happened in the 19th century before the records became of interest to antiquarians. In the 1930s Lt-Col. H.R. Phipps worked his way through the accumulation of probate material and produced many useful lists, consequently some of the inventories bear his familiar hand. He usually noted the year and the names of the person whose inventory was being exhibited on the outside of the document. The inventories were expertly repaired, flattened and arranged by year in volumes[58] in the 1950s by staff at the former S.C.R.O..[59]

The cause of so much damage, partly from the effects of damp and poor handling, can, in part, be blamed on the clerks who filed the documents. The clerks' practice involved gathering inventories into bundles, then making a hole in them so that a piece of string could be used to hold them together. Unfortunately the hole was often made at the top of each inventory near the heading, or preamble. When the documents became affected by damp, the hole made by the clerk was the weakest point. Hence large chunks are missing from some inventories, leaving only a few details of who the inventory belonged to.

The document reference numbers for the inventories in the DD/SP collection were coped by the editor, in 1995, from a modern manuscript calendar loaned to him by the S.C.R.O.. Revisiting this in 2018 threw up many anomalies, including missing inventories in the calendar that are now marked as 'damaged' in the online catalogue. Working through these 'damaged' inventories it has been possible to add some useful information to about 50% of the entries. Some now have the names of the appraisers, from which it was possible to examine other sources, mainly parish registers (held at the S.H.C.) and the Protestation Returns,[60] to identify the name of the parish where the deceased lived. Details of the sources consulted can be found in the notes field in this handlist. Where possible the anomalies have been rectified in this handlist.

One anomaly in this series is a volume containing the earliest inventories, including may that have 'no date'. Until recently those undated inventories had a reference 'DD/SP/undated/' followed by a number. To accommodate those in the online catalogue they were given a new reference of 'DD/SP/1632/' followed by a number. This suggests that the undated inventories are from the year 1632, which is not entirely correct. For this present handlist the date of the undated inventories has been given as '1630s', unless the date has been identified from other sources.

The other sources used include Edward Alexander Fry's, *Calendar of wills and administrations in the court of the Archdeacon of Taunton (Parts I and II, Wills only), 1537–1799*, published by the British Record Society in 1912, and T.L. Stoate and A.J. Howard's, *Somerset Protestation return and lay subsidy rolls, 1640–1641*, published by Stoate in 1975. Although Fry's volume rarely gives information concerning the occupation of the deceased, it gives the place of residence and the date of the will, or when it was proved. Fry's volume was prepared using the 'old calendars' and, helpfully, even though in 1909 many wills could not be found, their details were included. Frustratingly Fry's volume shows just how many wills and administrations were extant for the archdeaconry of Taunton before the losses in Exeter.

A card index to selected subjects in the DD/SP inventory series from 1625–1640, compiled by staff at the (former) Somerset County Record Office (now the S.H.C.), that was seen in 1995 has not been located. The range of subjects is vast, from architecture to wheelwrights and is worth consulting if considering any type of study based on those records.[61] An analysis of the details contained within inventories from this collection, for the period 1729–1747, was made by Thelma Munckton in 1971.[62]

The administrators' accounts only survive for the period 1637–1759. They are also held at the S.H.C. under the reference DD/SP/442. There are only 87 accounts (including duplicates).

<u>Miscellaneous, 1482–1924.</u> Over 350 inventories located in parish and private deposits are included in this handlist. Many of the references to records held at the S.H.C. were taken from the 'subject' cards meticulously maintained for many, many years by Paula Lewis and Sue Berry. However, some inventories, mainly those attached to wills, were not indexed under 'Inventories' in the old card catalogue but in the 'Office Wills Index'; these have not been included in this handlist. All of this has been supplemented with a trawl of the S.H.C. online catalogue, which has added dozens more entries to this handlist. Entries in the Sandford (DD/SF) and Wyndham (DD/WY) collections that have been re-catalogued since 1995, have been amended to show their new reference (as well as their former reference in the notes field in this handlist).

The 'Office Wills Index', held on index cards, is arranged by surname and there is no index to places or occupations, but some of the larger collections have been indexed in *Somerset wills index: printed & manuscript copies* by Sir Mervyn Medlycott, Bt., that was published in 1993. Medlycott records details of inventories with the will.[63] Information about inventories identified by Medlycott has not been included in this handlist. His pioneering work, and years of research, unearthed records in some obscure locations and publications. However, it is not always clear that a full transcript of an inventory has survived with the will, only that a will has survived and the total amount of the inventory was recorded. For this reason they have not been included in this handlist.

Another location of inventories is those transcripts made by record agents operating before World War II. Inventories extracted by record agents, such as Miss Olive Moger, for their clients, were often only abstracts, normally recording the names and value of leases, along with any unusual items. An example is the inventory of Mr Robert Colthurst of Huntworth (in North Petherton) appraised by John Herne and John Mogridge, dated 1 November 1715.[64] This method of abstracting appears to have been the case in the majority of transcripts made by record agents. Some inventories that were published, or included in typescript family histories, were often full transcripts and are helpfully listed by Medlycott.

Inventories at The National Archives (formerly the Public Record Office)

The majority of probate inventories and accounts held at T.N.A. are contained within the class of records described as the Prerogative Court of Canterbury (P.C.C.). They are in several different series. Those included in this handlist are listed below with the series code underlined. Many inventories are also cross-referenced to the will in another series, usually PROB 11, many of which are available on the internet. As the inventories in PROB 4 are described as 'office copies' there is some duplication with those in other PROB series, therefore any duplicate copies have been included in this handlist. The references prefixed PROB were on the whole taken from a card catalogue, except for those for PROB 5 listed in the List & Index Society volume (see PROB 5 below). Some of the entries on the cards were incorrectly assigned to the county of Somerset, and these have not been included in this volume.

PROB 2, 1417–1660. Termed 'Series I'. This series contains the oldest probate inventories at T.N.A.. Inventories in this series were still being repaired and listed in 1995 when the initial survey was undertaken. There were only 23 relating to Somerset, the earliest being for Walter Mayow of Croscombe in 1482. However, they are particularly valuable due to their early date. A search in 2018 revealed 26 inventories covering the period 1482–1660.

PROB 3, 1702, 1718–1782. Termed 'Series II'. Only 135 inventories relating to Somerset are in this series, the majority of which date from 1718 to 1735. After 1735 they peter out with only ten between 1750 and 1782.

PROB 4, 1660-*c*.1720. Termed 'Office' copies. Some 780 Somerset inventories are in this series. It contains the largest number of Somerset inventories in the PROB class.

PROB 5, 1661-*c*.1725. Original paper inventories, a list of which was published as *Principal Probate Registry Prerogative Court of Canterbury paper inventories 1661-c.1725* by the List & Index Society in 1978, as volume 149 in its main series of publications. There are 104 relating to Somerset.

PROB 31, 1722–1858. Some 353 Somerset inventories contained amongst court exhibits. To order a document in this class the year must be converted into a bundle number using the list at T.N.A..

PROB 37, 1783–1858. Only 15 Somerset inventories have been found with these Cause Papers.

Numerous uncatalogued series of probate and other types of records at The National Archives (T.N.A.) include details of the estate of many Somerset people. For further information concerning sources for the value of an individual's estate, see the website of The National Archive under 'Wills and Probate before 1858'. Classes containing relevant records include PROB 8, 9, 12, 14, 16, 32, 38 and 46, some of which date back to the 16th century. For example, PROB 16 covers the period from 1611 to 1858 and is a series of muniment books containing some inventories; all are indexed by surname at the end of each volume. Any Somerset inventories in the PROB 16 series are not included in this handlist.

Inventories at Bristol Archives (formerly Bristol Record Office)

Inventories predominantly for St George (Easton in Gordano) and Abbots Leigh, listed in *A Guide to the Probate Inventories of the Bristol Deanery of the Diocese of Bristol 1542–1804* by E. and S. George (Gloucester, 1988) are included in this handlist. Inventories (just under half of which also have a will) from this volume for other places in Somerset, namely Bedminster, Clapton, Combhay, Dunster, Keynsham, Long Ashton, Portbury and Wellington are also included in this handlist. This diversity of places in Somerset is a reflection of Bristol's maritime and commercial connections, such as an inventory of a mariner from Dunster.

The Bristol Record Society published three volumes of probate inventories from this collection based on transcripts prepared by Edwin and Stella George. However, those volumes concentrate on those inventories from the city only and not for the outlying areas, some of which are in the ancient county of Somerset.[65] Several other inventories found in other collections at Bristol Archives have also been included in this handlist.

Inventories at Lambeth Palace Library

One inventory in the Library catalogue has been identified for Thomas Morgan of Failand in Wraxall, dated 1567. This has survived as his will was disputed and other papers survive dated 1573; the reference is CM III/6. The Court of Arches records are held at Lambeth. Sadly little survives before 1660 but recent cataloguing now provides greater access to the disputes which concern probate business after this date.

Inventories at the Wiltshire and Swindon History Centre (formerly Wiltshire County Record Office)

The jurisdiction of the bishopric of Salisbury included the prebend of Chardstock and Wambrook, the peculiar of the precentor or chanter, the peculiar court of the perpetual vicar of Corsham, the consistory court of Salisbury and the archdeaconry of Salisbury. Inventories exhibited in those courts of Somerset interest are included in this handlist, with a few other inventories in general collections, totalling 62 entries. Therefore inventories relating to Yarnfield in Maiden Bradley have been included. As Yarnfield was in the Hundred of Norton Ferris (in the county of Somerset) I have included any inventories in this handlist. It has been noted whether any other relevant documents are included with the inventory, such as a will, in the notes field in this handlist.

Using this handlist

The inventories listed in this volume are sorted into alphabetical order by surname, followed by forename, then the date of the inventory or of the account. Each inventory has been given a unique number to aid with finding them when using the indexes. The index to place-names includes parishes, counties and countries. All references are for documents at the Somerset Heritage Centre unless prefixed by an abbreviation for a different location, such as B.A., D.H.C., G.A., L.P.L., T.N.A, W.S.H.C., etc. Where the notes relating to a document are verbose, they start on the line below the entry, otherwise any notes are in the right hand column.

Further research
Surprisingly there has been no major study undertaken on the content of this important group of records and how they specifically relate to Somerset. The opportunities are vast as they cover both urban and rural areas. Many have been consulted for the numerous volumes of the Victoria County History of Somerset. More recently, those for Dunster are being used by vernacular historians researching the development of Dunster houses. Thanks to the publication of this handlist it is now a relatively straightforward task to compile a volume of Elizabethan probate inventories, or one for an urban centre such as Taunton, or Bridgwater, to compare, for example the layout of domestic and semi-industrial buildings. Agricultural regions ought also to be studied, noting differences and developments. A study of the administration of the probate courts in the diocese of Bath and Wells is also needed; the annotations on the inventories provide a view into this unrecorded world.

An example how inventories can be used, which relates to Somerset, can be seen in *West Country households 1500–1700*. This volume 'considers the full range of household goods ... in West Country houses' and includes references to published probate inventories. It contains interesting lists of 'Ceramic cups in West Country probate inventories, 1581–1700' and 'Ceramic jugs, cruses and gorges from West Country probate inventories, 1581–1700'. Although neither list includes any examples from Somerset inventories they show how the information can be tabulated to show the frequency of particular types of items in households.[66] To add to those lists from the unpublished Somerset inventories in this

Table 1. Some examples of pottery vessels from Somerset probate records, 1602–1676

Description	***Place***	***Date***	***Source***
Second greatest crock	Wellington	1602	Webb, 114
Chests Coffers Boards and all other utilences of Wood and earthen vessels	St Michaelchurch	1630s	DD/SP/1632/32
Five pewter dishes, fourteen pewter table pleates, six pewter porengers two pewter flagons, four fine earthen sessers	Curry Mallet	1630s	DD/SP/1632/33
Crocks	Taunton St Mary Magdalene	1630s	DD/SP/1632/35
Great porridge jugge	North Petherton	1637	Siraut, 279
One stone Jugge embost with sylver	Thornfalcon	1642/3	Siraut, 55
Great crock	Taunton Archdeaconry	1676	Webb, 103

Sources:
DD/SP – Collection of probate inventories at the S.H.C.
Siraut – M. Siraut, ed., *Somerset wills. Extracted by A.J. Monday*, S.R.S. 89 (2003). The number refers to the page number in the volume.
Webb – A.J. Webb, ed., *Somerset wills II extracted by Olive M. Moger*, S.R.S. 94 (2008). The number refers to the calendar number in the volume.

handlist and other probate sources would take a long time but could be enlightening. For example, a few references to pottery and earthenware in contemporary sources are tabulated above. The references to crocks are tantalising and should not be relied upon. Many wills refer to brass or pewter crocks, but also to unspecified types of 'crocks'. So can it have been the case that those that did not distinguish the type of material they were made from were made of clay?

Further reading

Many excellent volumes of probate inventories have been edited and published by organisations across the county. The following is not a complete list but a useful start for anyone considering transcribing and editing some of the inventories listed in this volume. The website http://www.buildinghistory.org/wills.shtml lists those volumes published prior to 2013. Others can be found by searching the British Library catalogue, www.bl.uk.

N.W. Alcock and N. Cox, eds, *Living and working in seventeenth century England: an encyclopaedia of Drawings and descriptions from Randle Holme's original manuscripts for the Academy of Armory, 1688* (London, 2000).

Anon., *Principal Probate Registry Prerogative Court of Canterbury paper inventories 1661–c.1725*, List & Index Society vol. 149 (1978).

Anon., *Probate Records*, information leaflet number 31, Public Record Office (London, June 1985).

M. Cash, *Devon inventories of the sixteenth and seventeenth centuries*, D.C.R.S. new series 11 (1966).

J. Cox, *Wills, inventories & death duties. A provisional guide*, Public Record Office (London, 1988).

E. & S. George, *A guide to the probate inventories of the Bristol Deanery of the Diocese of Bristol 1542–1804* (Gloucester, 1988).

J.S. Moore, ed, *The goods and chattels of our forefathers: Frampton Cotterell and district probate inventories 1539–1804* (Chichester, 1976).

J.S. Moore, ed, *Clifton and Westbury probate inventories,* 1609–1761, University of Bristol (Bristol, 1981).

M. Overton, J. Whittle and A. Hann, *Production and consumption in English households, 1600–1750* (London, 2004).

P. Spufford and A.L. Erickson, *Index to the probate accounts of England and Wales*, British Record Society *volumes 111 and 112* (1999).

F.W. Steer, *Farm and cottage inventories of mid-Essex 1635–1749* (Chelmsford, 1950).

Abbreviations

ac. = account.
ad.ac. = administrator's account.
admon. = administration.
B.A. = Bristol Archives, 'B' Bond Warehouse, Smeaton Road, Bristol, BS1 6XN.
B.A.L. = Bath Abbey Library.
B.C.R.O. = Bath City Record Office, Guildhall, Bath, Avon, BA1 5AW.
B.R.S. = British Record Society.
C.C.E.d. = Clergy of the Church of England database.
com. = commission.
d. = died.
D.C.R.S. = Devon and Cornwall Record Society.
D.H.C. = Devon Record Office, Castle Street, Exeter, Devon, EX4 3PU.
ed. = edited.
ex. = exhibited.
G.A. = Gloucestershire Archives, Alvin Street, Gloucester, GL1 3DW.
H.T. = R. Holworthy, ed., *Hearth Tax for Somerset 1664–5. With indices. Copied from the original rolls in the Public Record Office* (Fleet, 1916).
inv. = inventory.
L.P.L. = Lambeth Palace Library, London, SE1 7JU.
n.d. = no date.
p. = page.
P.C.C. = Prerogative Court of Canterbury.
P.R. = T.L. Stoate and A.J. Howard, eds, *Somerset Protestation Returns and lay subsidy rolls, 1641–1642* (Almondsbury, 1975).
PROB = Prerogative Court of Canterbury Archive at the National Archives, Kew.
pvd = Proved.
Reg. = Parish registers held at S.H.C.
S.C.R.O. = Somerset County Record Office (now the Somerset Heritage Centre).
S.D.N.Q. = *Somerset & Dorset Notes and Queries*.
S.H.C. = Somerset Heritage Centre (formerly the Somerset County Record Office).
S.R.S. = Somerset Record Society.
T.C.W. = Edward Alexander Fry, ed., *Calendar of Wills and Administrations in the Court of the Archdeacon of Taunton (parts i and ii, wills only), 1537–1799*, British Record Society (1912).
T.N.A. = The National Archives, Kew, London.
vol. = volume.
W.C.A. = Wells Cathedral Archive
W.C.L. = Wells Cathedral Library
W.S.H.C. = Wiltshire and Swindon History Centre, Cocklebury Road, Chippenham, Wiltshire, SN15 3QN.

Sample transcripts

Probate inventory transcripts

1. The probate inventory of William Coffin, fuller of Dunster, 1669.
Reference: S.H.C., DD/SP 1669/2.

An Inventary of all the goodes & C......[67] of William Coffin of Dunster in the County of Somerset Fuller lately deceased taken and apprised the Three & Twentyeth day of March Anno domini 1668 as followeth

	£	s	d
Inprimis wearing Apparrell	2	0	0
In the Hall one Table Board & one Forme one Little Chaire one Livery Cubbard & Three Iron Crookes Two paire of pothookes one Gridiron one paire of Tonges one Fire pann one paire of Andirons one paire of Little grates one spitt one Brandiron one flesh pyke	0	18	0
In the Inner Roome one Cubbard Fower brasse pottes Three old Kittles Two little Brasse skillettes Eighteene pole of pewter six sawcers one goblett one baker & pewter salt Two pewter Candlestickes three Brasse Candlestickes one brasse Skymer one dozen of Trenchers Two brasse morters & Iron pestles one paire of brasse scales	3	1	0
In his Lodginge Chamber Two halfe head bedsteades one Trundle bedstead one Chest two Coffers three boxes one little deske one Table board Two flocke bedes two Feather boulsters two feather peeles two flock boulsters three old Coverlettes two paire of old Blankettes one brasse watch	2	18	4
In the Hall Chamber one halfe head bedstead Three old Coffers one little Stoole one Amorye one Flock bed & one boulster one paire of Blankettes & one old Coverlett	0	16	0
In the Parlour one Chest one presse one Warping Barr two old Turnes and a skarme	0	0	10
In the kitching one little old kittle three Tubbs one barrell	0	5	6
In the buttery one selting Trough one selting Tubb and Two Barrelles & a horse to putt beare on	0	9	0
In the shop Five paire of Clothiers sheires Two sheere boardes one stage of handles one paire of skales one burling board	1	1	2
Item one barrow pigg	0	15	0
The lynnen in house	0	10	0
Three old Cushions	0	1	0
Lumber Stuffe & other thinges not herein expressed	0	5	0
Summa totalis	14	0	0

Apprizers
[*signed*] John Cox
[*signed*] Edmound Brunton
[*signed*] Robert Macknes
[*signed*] George Atwill alias Clark

Exhibited 26 March 1669

2. The probate inventory of John Evet of Dunster, 1668/9.
Reference: S.H.C., DD/SP 1669/8.

An Inuentory of all and Singular the goods Chattles and Creditts of John Evet late of Dunster in the County of Somerset desessed valleud taken and apprised by John housgood Andrew hobs William Harris & James Wilkins the Second day of March in the yeare of oure lord god one thousand Six hundred and Sixty Eight.

	li	s	d
In the Chamber ouer the shope			
Emprimes his Warring apparrill	02	00	00
Item one trockell bedsted and one bed and furnituere belonging theareunto	01	10	00
Item one Chest & to Coffers and one box	00	10	00
Item one Chear and a parsell hoops	00	04	00
Item more small things	00	01	00
Item for the hay	00	01	00
In the Chamber ouer the shope [*sic*]			
Item one bed stead and feather bed and bolster and furniture theareunto belonging	02	00	00
Item more one trockell bed sted and bolster and the furniture theare vnto belonging	00	13	04
Item one Chest and three formes & fouer stooles	00	05	06
in the hall			
Item fower brase kettells & to brase pans one brase pott one brase Chaffing Dish and 2 bras skillitts one stemer	02	00	00
Item one press and one bord and one Forme and to Chares and one stoolle	00	17	00
Item 12 Pewter Diches & 2 flagons & 2 sacers and one Candell stick & one bolle	01	10	00
Item for woode and turfs	00	03	00
Item for barrils and vates and tubes and other tember stuffe	01	00	00
Item for Bacon	00	06	00
Item for one pice of woolling Cloth	01	00	00
Item for one Mare and sadell and paniers	01	00	00
in the shop			
Item for Canuis[68]	02	00	00
Item for Dowles	09	00	00
Item for Bodies	00	10	00
Item for holland	01	15	00
Item for India taffaty	01	00	00
Item for Ribens	01	00	00
Item for Cotten tape and Gallure	00	12	00
Item for Made ware	00	10	00
Item for tamony and Baies	00	10	00
Item for fustion and tafter[69] holland	00	03	00
Item for Siluer lace and bonne lace	00	10	00
Item for lyncy wolcy and blew lyning	00	05	00
Item for thred	00	15	00
Item for manchester tape and Jul..ll	00	12	00
Item for Gaff tring and felliting	00	06	00
Item for laces	00	04	00

Item for pins	00	05	00
Item for wosterd lace	00	04	00
Item for waites and other small things	00	10	00
Item For 2 frin pans and one gredill with all Ier stuffe and all other goods that is nott Mention ned [*sic*]	00	10	00
Item for 2 Chest and one amery and one pare of hampers and three boxes	01	00	00
Item for small debts	00	05	00
For one ness of boxes	00	01	06
The Wholle Sume of the Inuentory is	36	08	04

the marke of John **+** Hosgood
Andrew **H**obs[70]
the marke of William **W** Harris
[*signed*] James Wilkins

Exhibited 22 April 1669

3. The probate inventory of Mary Sharpe, widow of Milverton, 1697.
Reference: S.H.C., DD/SP 1698/3.

A True and perfect Inventory of all and singular The goods and Chattles of Mary Sharpe late of the parish of milverton in the County of Somerset Widdow prized and valued the Eight day of December in the yeare of our lord god 1697 by Robert Major John Comer and Thomas gamlin and Joan major as followeth

	li	s	d
Inprimis her Waring Apparill & money in purse	4	0	0
Item Twenty four sheep	10	0	0
Item two Cows and two heifers	12	0	0
Item two horses and one Colt	5	0	0
Item six swines	3	1	0
Item two wheaten mows	13	12	0
Item one Barley mow	4	0	0
Item one parcell of oats	0	10	0
Item two peices of wheat in ground	7	2	6
Item for hay	4	2	6
Item for hay and straw together	1	10	0
Item one Wood Rick	2	5	0
Item for plough stuff and horse Tackling	1	5	0
Item one syder wring with his purtinances	2	0	0
Item one Bed and bedstead with the furniture one Chest and one Coffer in the kitchin Chamber	3	0	0
Item two Beds and bedsteads with the furniture & one Chest in the Entry Chamber	4	0	0
Item in the hall Chamber one old Bed and bedstead and fleeses of wooll	3	0	0
Item in the hall one table board six Joyne stooles two Chaires and one Cubboard and one settle & one furme	3	0	0
Item in the parlor 3 fats & three tubbs	1	2	6
Item in the Buttry or seller seaven Barrills one trendle two standards or saltters	2	2	6
Item in the kitchin one Cheeswring & one furnace	1	10	0
Item seaven pewter dishes 6 Brasse panns 2 kittles & three pottage potts 2 skillets 5 tinn dishes	3	5	10

Item four hogsheads	0	18	0
Item one silver Beaker two silver spoons & one pewter dish more	1	11	0
Item one Bittle and six wedges & one Ireon barr	0	7	0
Item one spitt 3 Chimney Crooks one frying pann one sarieing Ire two paire of pott hangings one grid Ireon one driping pann 2 fire doggs one paire of fire tongs	0	10	6
Item six Baggs & one wimsheet	0	6	0
Item for husbandry tooles	0	10	0
Item for timber & lumber and things forgotten	0	10	0
the totalle sume is	96	11	4

[*signed*] John Comer
[*signed*] Robert Major
[*signed*] Tho: Gamlyne
the mark of Joan **I** Major

Exhibited 3 May 1698

4. Probate inventory of John Burd, yeoman of Milverton.
Reference: S.H.C., DD/SP 1713/23.

A True & perfect Inventory of ye Goods Chattles & Credits of John Burd of Milverton in ye County of Sumerset yeoman late deceased made & taken ye 13th day of August Anno que Domini 1713 by William Sprite and Thomas Handford aprizers as Followes

	li	s	d
Imprimis His Weareing aperill & money in purse	5	0	0
Item one Chattle Lease	160	0	0
Item two Cows	7	10	0
Item two yearlings & two Calves	6	0	0
Item one Nagg one Mare & three Sheep	10	0	0
Item three Swine Hogs	2	0	0
Item pultrey about ye house	0	3	4
Item Seven Acres of Wheat three Acres of Barly & one acre & halfe of pease Growing in Ground on Bickly	34	0	0
Item thirteene Acres of Wheat & Barly Growing in Cockland	13	0	0
Item twenty three pewter dishes & one pie plate	2	1	4
Item one dusen of pewter plates	0	7	6
Item one pewter Flaggon two Candle sticks & on salt	0	3	4
Item the moyity of one brass furnis	1	0	0
Item three Brass Chittles	1	3	4
Item tenne Brass pans	2	3	4
Item three Brass potts two Skillits & A Warming pan	2	3	4
Item Hay in Reeke & House	3	0	0
Item one Feather Bed & Bedsteed performed standing in ye parler Chamber	4	0	0
Item on Chest one Coffer two boxes two trunks & one Liverey table standing in ye parler Chamber	0	13	4
Item one pare of fire dogs fire pan & tongs	0	2	0
Item one Feather Bed & Bedsteed performed standing in ye butterey Chamber	3	0	0
Item one Feather bed & Bedsteed performed standing in ye porch Chamber	3	13	4
Item on Coffer on box on disk & on stooll in ye same	0	6	8
Item on Hanging press on table board on reeding Chare & three fleeses of Wooll in ye Hall Chamber	2	0	0

Item on feather Bed & bedsteed performed in ye outer Chamber	2	10	0
Item on Flock Bed & bedsteed performed standing in ye same	1	6	8
Item twenty nyne Cheeses & shelfs in ye Cheese Chamber	1	10	0
Item four Mouse Snaps	0	1	0
Item two table Boards nyne Chares two Joyned stoolls standing in ye parlor	1	6	8
Item Table Lining	0	13	4
Item on pare of anjrons & on Fowlling Gun	1	0	0
Item on Settle & one table board & form in ye Hall	0	18	0
Item on Clocke & on Jack	1	10	0
Item two pare of anjrons three Spits & on dripeing pan	0	15	0
Item other Chimney Implements belonging to ye hall Chim [*sic*]	0	6	8
Item on Screan on old Cubard on Salt Coffer and one Cradle in ye hall	0	10	4
Item two Corne Screans & A Grinding Stone & Krooks	1	2	6
Item two Pare of Small Scales and one pare of Large Scales & ye Weights thereunto	0	8	4
Item A Malt Mill	1	1	0
Item 3 fatts on trie & Eight tubs of all sorts	1	0	0
Item two Cheese Wrings Seven Cheese fatts one Breake board & one side board in ye wash house	1	1	4
Item on Dish Cage & Shelfs in ye same house	0	3	4
Item Hogheads	3	10	0
Item Beare Barols & pails	1	10	0
Item two side boards two Jebs bottles & bottle racks in ye buttrey	0	10	0
Item Juggs Putchers & Glasses & a pastle & morter	0	3	4
Item Selver plate in house	1	10	0
Item dishes transhers & spoons in house one [*blank*]	0	1	6
Item one Apple Wring & Mill	3	10	0
Item one Corne Hutch & other Vessels for ye keeping of Corne	1	5	0
Item Winoing Sheets Baggs & other Winoing Implements	0	15	0
Item one Trindle & three Salting fatts	1	5	0
Item Horse tackling Plow tackling & Husbandry toolls	8	0	0
Item Lumber stuff	0	13	4
Item in things unseen & out of Mind	0	6	8
The Whole sume is	303	14	10

[*Signed*] Wm: Spreat
[*signed*] Tho: Handford

Exhibited 14 August 1713

Transcripts of administrators' accounts

5. Administrator's account for John Zellacke of Elworthy, 1588.
Reference: S.H.C., D/D/Cta/Z1.
Editorial note: The account is written in one hand, except for the last three entries starting 'Summa Totalis allocac' which all appear in three different hands.

[*Preamble missing*]

some of one hundred fowerscore and eleven pounds fowre pence of lawfull money for the full and whole pryse and valewe of all and singuler the goods Cattells and debtes of the said John Zellacke comprysed and spired[1] in one Inventarye thereof made and indifferentlye valued and praysed and by these accomptants in the vertue of their othe into this Courte exhybited		Clxxxx^{s}	iiij^{d}
More these accomptaunts doe charge them selves with the some of sixe powndes of lawfull monye by them receaved of Mr Henrye Beamente for a debte due to John Zellacke	vj^{li}		
More the saide accomptaunts doe charge them selves with the some of iij^{li} xiij^{s} iiij^{d} of lawfull monye by them receaved of Christofer Saunders in parte of paymente of a debte due to the said testator	iij^{li}	xiij^{s}	iiij^{d}
Item more the said Accomptaunts doe Charge them selves with the some of nynteene shillings Two pence of lyke lawfull monye by them encreased synce their last accompte made before the worshipfull Mr Doctor Jones xij^{o} Julij		xix^{s}	ij^{d}
Item more this accomptaunts doe charge themselves with the some of three pownds ten shillinges in the hands of the Executors of John Zellacke, of Ellworthye and syxe shillings eight pence in the hawnds of Christofer Sawnders which ar debts due unto the said John Zellacke and yet unpayed and dowtfull to be rembered	iij^{li}	xvj^{s}	viij^{d}
Summa totalis onis	CCv^{li}	ix^{s}	vj^{d}

Allowances[2]		
Inprimis layde out for a shrowde for hym at his buriall	iiij^{s}	viij^{d}
Item for Candells		ix^{d}
Item geven and bestowed at his buriall	xxj^{s}	
Item for fishe and breade at his buriall	v^{s}	
Item for butter and egges the same tyme	...j^{s}	
Item delivered to goodwife Sellacke which she did geave to.... people	xij^{s}	
Item payed to John Cappe for worke donne before his deathe		viij^{d}
Item for a payre of shues for John Sellacke		x^{d}
Item payed to John Tammey for one quarters wages and a payre of hose clothe	xv^{s}	viij^{d}
Item payed to Agnes Browne for wages	x^{s}	iiij^{d}
Item for pytche to signe the sheepe with		viij^{d}
Item for the rentes of parkes and for amercements	vj^{s}	ix^{d}
Item payde of for the rente of the farme	xx^{s}	

[1] This may be a transcription error by the scribe for the word 'prised'.
[2] This word is a heading that appears in the margin.

Item for expenses at wells the first tyme that we travayled for the administracion		iiij^{s}	
Item for a letter of administracion graunted unto Andrewe Jefferye clearke Robert Olliver William Sullye alias Dyer and Roger Wollcotte		v^{s}	
Item for an obligacion for the same			xij^{d}
Item for the Apparitor and for waxe			viij^{d}
Item for a letter of Colligend		vj^{s}	viij^{d}
Item for a Comission graunted by Mr Rychard Lambert Clarke to admininster their othe		v^{s}	
Item for a caveat		v^{s}	
Item spente at Milverton			xiiij^{d}
Item for the second administracion and expenses travaylinge for the same		xxij^{s}	ij^{d}
item for a payre of bodyes of Chamlett and for lyninge to the same		iiij^{s}	v^{d}
Item for vj payre of shues for the children		ij^{s}	ij^{d}
Item for mockadoe to make bodyes for the Children		v^{s}	vj^{d}
Item for ij yardes of hollan for the Children		ij^{s}	viij^{d}
Item for foure yardes of Crescloth		ij^{s}	viij^{d}
Item for an elle of Canvas		iiij^{s}	iiij^{d}
Item payde to Alice Sellacke that she had bestowed			xvj^{d}
Item for the mortuarye to the parson		x^{s}	
Item payde to the parson for tythe fruite		iiij^{s}	
Item payde to the Hooper for dressinge the hoggs hedds			viij^{d}
Item two geldinge coults for the heriottes valued at	v^{li}	xiij^{s}	iiij^{d}
Item payed to Thomas Venne for dyinge of clothe		vj^{s}	viij^{d}
Item payed to Thomas Wollcotte for tuckinge of clothe			xviij^{d}
Item payed to John Ingram for makinge of clothes for the Children		iiij^{s}	vj^{d}
Item payed to goodwife Zallacke that she bestowed at sundrye tymes on the Children		x^{s}	
Item spente at Millverton when we weare summoned to exhibite and Inventorye			xviij^{d}
Item to John Wiche of Crocombe of debts	vj^{li}		
Item payed to John Webber of debte	v^{li}		
Item payed to Willam Sullye of debte		xlv^{s}	
Item payed to John Hancocke of debte	iij^{li}		
Item payed for gatherynge of masce		iij^{s}	
Item payed to Edward Sellacke of debte		xx^{s}	
Item payed for v payre of shues for the Children		iij^{s}	xj^{d}
Item for threed mayted and spices			xviij^{d}
Item spent at Willscombe fayre			vj^{d}
Item payed for lether and thonges			vij^{d}
Item for the fyndinge of iiij Children for one whole yeare after the deathe of their father	x^{li}	viij^{s}	
Item payed to Henrye Towse for James table for one whole yeare and 44 weekes	iij^{li}	iij^{s}	
Item for the nursinge of Agnes for two yeares and an halfe at viij^{d} the weeke	iiij^{li}	vj^{s}	viij^{d}
Item payed to Margarett Sellacke for a flanninge		ij^{s}	iiij^{d}
Item payed for a shirte for John			xx^{d}
Item for iij payre of shues for the Children			xvij^{d}
Item payed to Henrye Washer for weavinge of Cloathe		iiij^{s}	
Item payed for ij yards and halfe of karsye		iij^{s}	xj^{d}

Item paide for two flanninges		iiij^{s}	
Item payed for two payre of hoses			xvij^{d}
Item for ij smockes		ij^{s}	iiij^{d}
Item for threshinge of corne		xxvj^{s}	viij^{d}
Item payed for two reade hatts			v^{d}
Item for iij payre of shues			xiij^{d}
Item for a Coate cloathe for John Zellacke		iij^{s}	vj^{d}
Item for a payre of hose clothe for hym			xvij^{d}
Item for a dublett cloathe for hym			xvij^{d}
Item payed for the makinge of his coate hose and doblett			xv^{d}
Item payed unto Henry Towse for soape for Joane			xij^{d}
Item ij payre of shues iij aprons and a payre of hose for the said Joane		ij^{s}	vj^{d}
Item for iij yardes of fryse to make her a cassocke		iij^{s}	iiij^{d}
Item for makinge the same cassocke and for lace			vj^{d}
Item for two smocks two partletts and the makinge		ij^{s}	viij^{d}
Item payde to Roger Wollcotte for the fyndinge of ij children for iij yeares		xl^{s}	
Item payed to Christofer Fowreacre for one childes table		xx^{s}	
Item payed to Thomas Warman for his travayle the first yeare		xiij^{s}	iiij^{d}
Item payed to the same Thomas for fyndinge of two children		iiij^{s}	
Item for hoses and shues for Joane and mendinge her cassocke		ij^{s}	ij^{d}
Item geven by thes accomptants to Mr John Busshopp one of the proctors of the courte and consistorye of Wells for his counsell concerninge this accompte		iij^{s}	iiij^{d}
Item more to hym for his fee			xij^{d}
Item for drawinge the accompte made xij^{o} July 1575 before Mr Doctor Hues		vj^{s}	viij^{d}
Item for thes accomptants charges in comynge to Wells for them selves and their horses to render and give upp this accompte 12 July 1575		xiij^{s}	iiij^{d}
Item delivered to Phillipp Gillett for the porcion of Alice Gillet the dawghter of the said John Zellacke and nowe his wiefe	xxij^{li}	xvij^{s}	iij^{d}
Item delivered to Robert Baker for the porcion of Eliz Baker his wiefe and one of the dawghters of the said John Zellacke	xxiij^{li}	vj^{s}	viij^{d}
Item delivered to John Dybble for the porcion of Thomasyne Dybble his wiefe one other of the dawghters of the said John Zellacke	xxiij^{li}		
Item delivered to Christofer Zellacke for his porcion	xxiij^{li}		
Item geven by thes accomptants to Mr William Watkyns one of the proctors of this courte for his Councell concerninge this accompte		iij^{s}	iiij^{d}
Items to him for his fees for iij dayes		iij^{s}	
Item for iij acts			xij^{d}
Item for a proxye by hym exhibited unto this Courte for Roger Wollcotte one of these accomptaunts			xvj^{d}
Item for the exhibitinge theareof			iiij^{d}
Item for the drawinge and engrossinge this accompte		vj^{s}	viij^{d}
Item for the Copye theareof		iij^{s}	iiij^{d}
Item the said accomptants doe praye allowance of the severall somes of vij^{li} iij^{s} iiij^{d}, xv^{s} ij^{d}, xlvj^{s} viij^{d}, iij^{s} iiij^{d} being parcell of the goods and Cattells comprysed in the inventoryes of the said John Zellacke and of iij^{li} x^{s} and vj^{s} viij^{d} for so many severall debtes due to the said John Zellacke by the partyes remayninge yet unpayed and dowtfull to be receaved	xliij^{li}	v^{s}	ij^{d}

Item these accomptaunts doe praye to be allowede of the somme of xxiij^{li} for the porcion of Joane Zellacke one of the dawghters of the said John Zellacke Remayninge yet unpayed and remayninge in there hands	xxiij^{li}		
Item thes accomptaunts doe praye allowance of the somme of xxiij^{li} for the porcion of Agnes Zellacke one other of the Children of the said John Zellacke alsoe remayninge unpayed and remayninge in their hands	xxiij^{li}		
Item these accomptaunts doe praye to be allowed of x^{s} iiij^{d} for the fees of lettres testimoniall uppon this accompte		x^{s}	iiij^{d}
Item these accomptaunts praye allowance for their Charges expended in the accompte		vj^{s}	viij^{d}
Summa Totalis allocac	CCxiiij^{li}	vij^{s}	x^{d}
So these the accomptaunts have disbursed more then came to theire hands the some of viij^{li} xviij^{s} iiij^{d}	viij^{li}	xviij^{s}	iiij^{d}

There was exhibited an account under the abovementioned oath in the episcopal counting house of Wells on the xvi day of April 1588 before the venerable master John Daye doctor of laws, official, in the presence of me, Robert Owen, notary public and letters of discharge were decreed to him thereon to be made.[71]

6. Administrator's account for Richard Webb the elder of Bathford, Somerset, 1639. Reference: S.H.C., D\D/cta/W1.

[*f.1*] 15 October 1639 Bathford Richard Webb senior defunctus[72]
The True accompte of John Akerman Administrator of all and singular the goodes, rightes, credites and chattels of Richard ~~Ca~~ Webbe the elder, late whiles he lived of the parish of Bathfford in the Countie of Somerset and diocesse of Bath and Wells, deceased dureinge the minoritie of Richard Cary alias Webbe executor or prime legatarie of and in the last will, and testament nuncupative of the sayd Richard Webbe the elder deceased made and declared in open Courte before the worshippfull Richard Long master of artes surrogate to the right worshippfull Aurthur Ducke Doctor of Lawes, vicar generall, and Officiall principall to the right reverend father in God William by gods providence Lord Bishopp of Bath and Wells on the fivetenne day of October last anno domini 1639.

The Charge.

Inprimis this accountant doth onerate and charge himselfe with the summe of fouretie pounds and tenne shillinges of Lawfull English money beinge the totall summe and true value of all and singular the goodes, Chattels rightes and credits of the sayde Richard Webb deceased comprised and contained in one Inventarie of them into this ...... all readie exhibited, as by the sayde Inventarie it doth and may more <att> large appeare	xl^{li}	x^{s}	

The discharge

This accountant craveth allowance of the summe [of][73] twentie shillinges and five pence layde out .... the funerall of the sayd deceased, and ..... [wri]teinge, sendinge, and exhibitinge ..... of the sayd deceased his goodes into this Courte by Mr. John Warner, and others, ~~into this Courte~~ and for other necessarie charges, in, and aboute the same		xxj^{s}	v^{d}

[*f.2*] Item this accountant craveth allowance of the summe of seventenne shillinges and tenn pence by him layde out for the letters of Administration of all and singular the goodes of the sayd deceased dureinge the minoritie of the sayd Richard Cary, the legatary aforesayde, and for dubble writeinge the Inventarie of the sayde deceased his goodes and for a commission procured, had, and obtayned, and directed for the takeinge of the oaths of the witnesses subscribed to the will nuncupative of the deceased aforesayd, and for the procurator his fees in desireinge and obtayninge the sayd commission and letters of administration and for advise and counsell aboute the same, and for the iudge his seale apposed to the sayd commission and letters of administration and for the produxion and sweareinge of the witnesses aforesayd, and for an Appariter his fees in returninge the commission and reportinge the letters of administration aforesayde for Proctors fees in procureing the said Commission and Administration		xvij^{s}	x^{d}
Item this accountant craveth allowance of the summe of foure shillings by him payde to two poore women in certayne old cloathes and other small househoulde implementes [and] attendinge the sayd deceased in the time of his sickness		iiij^{s}	
Item this accountant craveth allowance of the summe of foure shillinges by him payde to a procurator at Sarum for writeinge, drawinge, and penninge the renuntiation of John Webbe brother of the said deceased and for the assignment of his se.. made and given to this accountante ….. ….. sayd letters of administration ….. ….. Proctors advise about the same		iiij^{s}	
Item this accountante craveth allowance of two shillinges by him payde and layd out, for the entertaynment of the sayd John Webbe brother of the sayde deceased and his freindes and thiere horses for one nighte		ij^{s}	
[*f.3*] Item this accountante craveth allowance of the summe of twelve poundes <and sixtenne shillinges> of lawful English money by him payde unto one John Paynter of the Devizes in the Countie of Wiltes for debte of the sayde deceased due upon bande	xij^{li}	16^{s}	
Item this accountante craveth allowance of the summe of tenne poundes and twelve shillinges of Currante English money by him payde unto one James Biggs of the parish of Bath=fford, for debte of the sayd deceased due uppon bande	x^{li}	xij^{s}	
Item this accountant craveth allowance of the summe of thirtie shillinges of lawfull Englishe money by him to be payde unto one Alice Bigge of Wilfforde in the countie of Wiltes for debte of the sayd deceased, due by bill obligatorie		xxx^{s}	
Item this accountante craveth allowance of the summe of thirtie ~~eighte~~ shillinges of lawfull English money by him layde out for his owne expenses his horse hyre and horse meate in traveillinge to Salisbury and Wantage in the countie of Wiltes, and to Bathfford and to Wells sixtenne or seventenne dayes about the procureinge and obtayneinge the commission and administration aforesayde, and other necessary expenses in and about the same		xxx^{s}	
Item this accountante craveth allowance of the summe of two shillinges and three pence by him payde to a essenger for certifyinge and bringeinge unto him [th]is accountante worde of the proclaymation or inti….. forth out of the Courte, aboute the ….. ….. of the letters of administration graunted ….. …..tante		ij^{s}	iij^{d}

Item this accountante craveth allowance of one shillinge and sixpence by him layd out for carryinge of certayne houshould stuffe and preserveinge and disposinge the same to its best benefit	i^{s}	vi^{d}
Item this accountante craveth allowance of the summe of six shillinges one penny and halfe penny for the Lords rente due frome the sayde deceased for his Coppy=holde Tenement payable at Michaelmas last ….. payd by this accountant	vi^{s}	i^{d} i^{ob}
[*f.4*] Item this accountante craveith allowance of the summe of six shillinges one penny and halfe penny for the Lords rente aforesayd to be payde by this accountant at the feast of the anuntiation of our virgin Mary	vi^{s}	i^{d} i^{ob}
Item this accountante craveth allowance of eighte shillinges and sixe pence by him payde unto one Richard Summerill for the dyet and keepinge of Richard Cary the legatary aforesayd for a paire of shoes	viij^{s}	vj^{d}
Item this accountante craveth allowance of the summe of ninetenne shillinges of lawfull English money for debte of the sayd deceased due unto this accountante	xix^{s}	
Item this accountante craveth allowance of the summe of one and twentie shillinges and foure pence by hime payde for writinge and penninge of this accompte, for advise and counsel aboute the same for letters testimoniall ~~for~~ uppon passinge this accompte for a coppy of this accompte to bee had from the Register of this Courte, for the Judges seale, wax, the Apparitor his fees and other necessary thinges in and aboute the same	xxj^{s}	4^{d}
Item this accountante craveth allowance <of> the summe of three and twentie shillinges by him layd out, and expended in Proctors fees in this Court, and for travellinge hither to pass this accompte for his horse meate and horse hire and other nessessary charges about the same	xxiij^{s}	
[Item this ac]countante craveth allowance of the summe [of ten shilli] nges being the value of the golde wei….. expressed in the Inventorie of the sayd deceased his goodes and of certayne moneys specified therin to be left in the house of the sayd deceased, which never came to this accountants hands	x^{s}	
Item this accountante craveth allowance of fourtenne shillinges and sixpence for desperate debtes where with this accountante standeth charged in the sayde Inventorie, and which he cannot receive	14^{s}	6^{d}
[*f.5*] Item this accountante craveth allowance of the summe of three shillinges by him payd or to bee payde for rates to the Kinge, and towardes the releife and sustentation of the poore of Bath=fforde afforesayd by reason of the profittes of the executor y^{e} yeare issuinge out of the coppy=holde aforesayd	iij^{s}	

The sum total allocated xxxiiij^{li} xiij^{s}
So remains to be administered v^{li} xvij^{s}[74]

References

[1] F.M. Powicke and C.R. Cheney eds, *Councils and synods, with other documents relating to the English Church*, I (Oxford, 1964), 618.
[2] E.F. Jacob, 'The Archbishop's Testamentary Jurisdiction' in *Medieval Records of the Archbishops of Canterbury* (London, 1962), 37.
[3] S. Colwell, *Dictionary of genealogical sources in the Public Record Office* (London, 1992), 34.
[4] A.J. Webb, *Index of Somerset probate inventories* (Weston-super-Mare, 1995).
[5] Calendars of wills proved in P.C.C. from 1383 to 1558 have been published by the Somerset Record Society in volumes 16 (1901), 19 (1903), and 21 (1905), all edited by Rev. F.W. Weaver. Volume 21 (1903) also contains wills proved in person by successive archbishops of Canterbury between 1363 and 1491.
[6] W.C.A., DC/ADM/3/1 (s) Order from the Archbishop of Canterbury, 14 May 1776.
[7] E. and S. George, *A guide to the probate inventories of the Bristol Deanery of the Diocese of Bristol 1542–1804* (Gloucester, 1988).
[8] S.H.C., D/D/Ctp/4 lists of probate documents recorded by Mark Tabor, diocesan registrar, 1614–1650.
[9] The general condition of the diocesan records, including those wills, inventories and accounts that have not been conserved is very poor, which was caused by damp.
[10] S.H.C., D/D/Ctp/4 lists of probate documents recorded by Mark Tabor, diocesan registrar, 1614–1650.
[11] S.H.C., D/D/ol/47 dean's peculiar licence book, 1681–1717.
[12] S.H.C., D/D/Cti and D/D/ct/1.
[13] Powicke and Cheney, *Councils and synods*, 618.
[14] Replace the text in note 14 to read: T.S. Holmes ed., *The register of Nicholas Bubwith*, vol.1, S.R.S. 29 (1914), 3–4.
[15] S.H.C., D/B/il/1/102 instruction to compile an inventory, 1 April 1410.
[16] S.H.C., DD/L/P8/2/193 will of Alice Somerey, 25 December 1445.
[17] S.H.C., D/D/Ca/345 fees for exhibiting inventories, 1677.
[18] S.H.C., D/D/Cd 51 deposition book for the dean of Wells' peculiars, 1616–1639.
[19] S.H.C., D/P/bw.m/2/1/1 Bridgwater St Mary parish register, 1558–1653.
[20] S.H.C., D/D/Cd 51 deposition book for the dean of Wells' peculiars, 1616–1639.
[21] S.H.C., D/P/bw.m/2/1/1 Bridgwater St Mary parish register, 1558–1653.
[22] S.H.C., D/D/Cd 51 deposition book for the dean of Wells' peculiars, 1616–1639.
[23] S.H.C., D/P/bw.m/2/1/1 Bridgwater St Mary parish register, 1558–1653.
[24] S.H.C., D/D/Cd 51 deposition book for the dean of Wells' peculiars, 1616–1639. William's will does not appear in the calendar of wills proved in the archdeaconry court of Taunton, but this does not mean it was not proved. As the dispute was heard in the Dean's Court, this suggests the will was proved in his court and not at Taunton (E.A. Fry, *Calendar of wills and administrations in the Court of the Archdeacon of Taunton (parts i and ii, wills only), 1537–1799*, British Record Society (1912)).
[25] S.H.C., A/AHT/176 account book of the executors of the will of John Sydenham of Brympton, deceased, 1626/27–1629.
[26] His memorial is in the churchyard at Brympton (https://historicengland.org.uk/listing/the-list/list-entry/1263241, accessed 28 October 2018).
[27] S.H.C., A/AHT/176 account book of the executors of the will of John Sydenham of Brympton, deceased, 1626/27–1629.
[28] Lambeth Palace Library website, http://www.lambethpalacelibrary.org/content/arches, accessed 28 October 2018.
[29] S.H.C., A/AHT/176 account book of the executors of the will of John Sydenham of Brympton, deceased, 1626/27–1629.
[30] S.H.C., Q/SR/41/218 petition, 1622.
[31] M. Steig, *Laud's laboratory, the Diocese of Bath and Wells in the early seventeenth century* (London, 1982), 240.
[32] S.H.C., DD/SP probate inventories.
[33] W.C.A., DC/E/12/80 (a) probate papers concerning the will of James Lock, 1810.
[34] C.C.E.d. under East Brent.
[35] W.C.A., DC/E14/18, 1 October 1664.
[36] S.H.C., D/D/cta/Z1 administrator's account for John Zellacke of Elworthy. Unfortunately the parish registers and the calendar of wills for this date have not survived to verify this lengthy hiatus.

[37] A.J. Webb, ed., *Two Tudor subsidy assessments for the county of Somerset: 1558 and 1581–82*, S.R.S. 88 (2002), 117.

[38] S.H.C., D/D/cta/Z1 administrator's account for John Zellacke of Elworthy. Unfortunately the parish registers and the calendar of wills for this date have not survived to verify this lengthy hiatus.

[39] W.C.L., 262 F. Clerke, *Praxis in Curiis Ecclesiasticis* (1596).

[40] S.H.C., D/D/Ca/345 fees for exhibiting inventories, 1677.

[41] S.H.C., D/D/cta/R23 administrators' accounts for Richard Robins, 1707.

[42] For an example see S.H.C., D/D/ca/41 ex-officio Diocesan Court act book, 1569–1570.

[43] For a more detailed explanation of the system of returning administrators' accounts and the layout of the documents see http://familyrecords.dur.ac.uk/nei/NEI_account.pdf. I am grateful to Sue Berry for bringing this to my attention. See also *SDNQ*, March 2019 for a paper based upon an administrator's account from the 1630s.

[44] W.C.A., DC/ADM/3/1 (k) Renunciation by Martha James of Bristol, 20 October 1752.

[45] S.H.C., DD/DP/23/3 Thornfalcon, 1747.

[46] S.H.C., Q/SR/312/52 inventory, 1 January 1742/3.

[47] S.H.C., DD/SF/15/2/35 inventories taken for debt purposes, 1720.

[48] A very small number of individuals were thought to have more than one occupation. For the purpose of the following analysis I have only selected the first occupation that was given.

[49] S.H.C., D/D/Ct/V17 inventory of Henry Vincent, 1633.

[50] S.H.C., D/D/cta/M2 and M3 administrators' accounts for Thomas Masters of Ilchester, 1620.

[51] S.H.C., D/D/cta/L29 administrator's account for John Long of Abbas and Temple Combe, 1598.

[52] S.H.C., D/D/cta/undated/parts 3, 15 and 20.

[53] S.H.C., D/D/cta/Z1 administrator's account for John Zellacke of Tolland, 1588.

[54] S.H.C., D/D/cta/F1 administrators' account for Samuel Filor, 1663.

[55] S.H.C., D/D/cta/F1 administrators' account for ..... Harris, 1632.

[56] S.H.C., D/D/ct/1/F/7 inventory of John Fysher alias Fessher, 1539.

[57] Ex inf Liz Grant, 31 August 2018.

[58] For a link to the online catalogue see http://somerset-cat.swheritage.org.uk/records/DD/SP/443.

[59] See, for example, the back of the earliest volume in this series that has a label stating it was repaired in 1959.

[60] T.L. Stoate and A.J. Howard, eds, *Somerset Protestation return and lay subsidy rolls, 1640–1641* (Almondsbury, 1975).

[61] Information kindly supplied by Sue Berry in 1994.

[62] *Studies in Somerset history*, Bristol University Department of Extra Mural Studies (Bristol, 1971).

[63] Sir M. Medlycott, *Somerset wills index: printed & manuscript copies* (Weston-super-Mare, 1993).

[64] S.H.C., DD/MGR Box 1 published in A.J. Webb, ed., *Somerset wills II extracted by Olive M. Moger*, S.R.S. 94 (2008).

[65] See volumes 54, 57 and 60 in the Bristol Record Society series.

[66] J. Allan, N. Alcock and D. Dawson, eds, *West Country households 1500–1700* (Woodbridge, 2015), 1–5, 378–9, 385.

[67] The missing word is likely to be 'chattles' but it is lost due to the document being damaged.

[68] Canvas.

[69] The word 'tafter' has been inserted above the line.

[70] It is not clear whether this is his signature, or the bold H may be his mark.

[71] This paragraph of text is in a different hand to the main document

[72] This line of text appears in the left-hand margin in a different hand to the main document.

[73] The document is damaged but the top of the letter 'f' is visible.

[74] The last two lines were written by a different person to the previous two hands.

No.	Description	Date	Reference	Notes
1	John ...... alias POWELL of Enmore	1637	DD/SP/1637/60	
2	Joane .....WER, Widow of Orchard Portman	1638	DD/SP/1638/43	Damaged
3	[missing] ....ARD of Curry Rivel	1638	DD/SP/1638/57	
4	[missing] ....THE of Drayton	1643	DD/SP/1643/49	Damaged
5	[missing] ...ARD, Widow of Curry Rivel	1638	DD/SP/1638/57	Damaged
6	... the elder, Husbandman ? of West Monkton	1635	DD/SP/1635/126	
	Note: Appraised by Edward FICHE and Humfry PUDDYE			
7	...... and Catherine his wife of [no place]	1646	DD/SP/1646/93	Damaged
8	[missing] [missing] of [no place]	1590	D/D/cta/Blank/41	Damaged ad.ac.
9	[missing] [missing] of Sampford ?	1592	D/D/cta/S43	Ad.ac.
10	[missing] [missing] of [no place]	1596	D/D/cta/Blank/28	
	Note: Damaged ad.ac.; mentions Thomas VIMPENY, William CLEEVDON and Bristol			
11	[missing] [missing] of Blagdon ?	1600	D/D/cta/Blank/52	
	Note: Damaged ad.ac.; mentions 'Mr Dr BISSE parson of Blagudon'			
12	[missing] [missing] of [no place]	1602	D/D/cta/Blank/10	Damaged ad.ac.
13	[missing] [missing] of Hatch Beauchamp ?	1602	D/D/cta/Blank/16	Damaged ad.ac.
14	[missing] [missing] of [no place]	1604	D/D/cta/Blank/6	
	Note: Damaged ad.ac.; mentions a wife and five children			
15	[missing] [missing] of Taunton	1609	DD/SP/1609/1	Tenement or inn known as the Black Spread Eagle
16	[missing] [missing] of Wincanton	1623	D/D/cta/Blank/29	Damaged ad.ac.
17	[missing] [missing] of [no place]	1625	DD/SP/1625/10	
	Note: First page missing, goods bequeathed to John PIYAM, proved at Taunton			
18	[missing] [missing] of [no place]	1628	DD/SP/1628/17	Top part missing; proved at Taunton
19	[missing] [missing] of Easton in Gordano	1629	D/D/cta/Blank/19	
	Note: Damaged ad.ac.; mentions a son John			
20	[missing] [missing] of Taunton ?	1635	DD/SP/1635/102	
	Note: Appraised by Francis SMYTH, Henry APLEN and Robert FOWLER; damaged (*T.C.W.*, Reg)			
21	[missing] [missing] of [no place]	1635	DD/SP/1635/122	Top missing; damaged
22	[missing] [missing], Husbandman ? of Curry Rivel	1635	DD/SP/1635/14	
	Note: Appraised by Robert PODGER, William HAWKER, Andrew OWSLEY and Henry BAKER; damaged (*P.R.*)			
23	[missing] [missing] of South Petherton ?	1635	DD/SP/1635/22	

	Note: Appraised by Nicholas GUNDRY, Thomas WILLS, John PORTER and Richard STUCKEY; damaged (*P.R.*)			
24	[missing] [missing], Husbandman ? of [no place]	1635	DD/SP/1635/29	Damaged, top missing
25	[missing] [missing], Husbandman ? of West Monkton ?	1635	DD/SP/1635/30	Damaged, top missing
26	[missing] [missing] of [no place]	1635	DD/SP/1635/45	Damaged, top missing
27	[missing] [missing] of [no place]	1635	DD/SP/1635/60	Female; damaged
28	[missing] [missing], Husbandman ? of Brompton Regis or Exton	1635	DD/SP/1635/70	
	Note: Appraised by men from Brompton Regis and Exton; damaged			
29	[missing] [missing], Husbandman ? of Monksilver	1635	DD/SP/1635/71	
	Note: Appraised by John BIRDE and William SULLY; damaged			
30	[missing] [missing] of [no place]	1635	DD/SP/1635/82	Female; damaged
31	[missing] [missing], Husbandman ? of Crewkerne ?	1635	DD/SP/1635/83	
	Note: Appraised by George MERIFIELD the elder, John CROCKER, Henry TAYLOR and Nicholas BRAGG; damaged (*P.R.*)			
32	[missing] [missing] of Bridgwater	1635	DD/SP/1635/84	
	Note: Male; mentions metal working goods in shop; damaged			
33	[missing] [missing] of Staplegrove ?	1635	DD/SP/1635/89	Mentions the advowson of Staplegrove; damaged
34	[missing] [missing], Blacksmith ? of Bridgwater ?	1635	DD/SP/1635/96	
	Note: Appraised by Thomas TRUMAN, William TAYLER, Henry PILCORNE and Richard HORLOCK; damaged (*P.R.*)			
35	[missing] [missing] of [no place]	1636	DD/SP/1636/2	Damaged
36	[missing] [missing] of [no place]	1636	DD/SP/1636/22	Mentions 'Court ground'; damaged
37	[missing] [missing] of [no place]	1636	DD/SP/1636/53	
	Note: Executors Thomas and Elizabeth BODMAN and Joanna MOSKE?; damaged			
38	[missing] [missing] of [no place]	1638	DD/SP/1638/16	Damaged
39	[missing] [missing] of Porlock ?	1638	DD/SP/1638/17	
	Note: Appraised by Richard RIDLER and John ERME; damaged (Reg.)			
40	[missing] [missing], Miller ? of Elworthy ?	1638	DD/SP/1638/18	
	Note: Appraised by William RICHARDS, David SELLECKE, William MARTIN, William EXTON and John EDWARDS; damaged (Reg.)			
41	[missing] [missing] of [no place]	1638	DD/SP/1638/2	List of debts; damaged
42	[missing] [missing] of [no place]	1638	DD/SP/1638/21	Exhibited at Taunton; damaged
43	[missing] [missing] of Milverton ?	1638	DD/SP/1638/22	
	Note: Appraised by Thomas KINGDON, John WEBBE, John PHELIPS and John STAPEL; damaged (*P.R.*)			
44	[missing] [missing] of Milverton	1638	DD/SP/1638/25	

	Note: Appraised by John PARRIS, Thomas SPRETE and Nicholas FARMOR; damaged (*P.R.* and Reg.)			
45	[missing] [missing], Husbandman ? of [no place]	1638	DD/SP/1638/26	Damaged
46	[missing] [missing], Husbandman ? of [no place]	1638	DD/SP/1638/27	Damaged
47	[missing] [missing] of [no place]	1638	DD/SP/1638/3	Mentions a brew house; damaged
48	[missing] [missing] of [no place]	1638	DD/SP/1638/32	Damaged
49	[missing] [missing] of [no place]	1638	DD/SP/1638/34	Mentions a grinding stone; damaged
50	[missing] [missing] of Hatch Beauchamp	1638	DD/SP/1638/35	
	Note: Appraised by Revd Hugh BAUNTON, rector, 1621–1639, Richard DYNHAM and John WALE (C.C.E.d.)			
51	[missing] [missing], Husbandman ? of [no place]	1638	DD/SP/1638/36	Male; damaged
52	[missing] [missing] of [no place]	1638	DD/SP/1638/39	Damaged
53	[missing] [missing] of [no place]	1638	DD/SP/1638/40	
	Note: Appraised by John WEST and John ROWSWELL; damaged			
54	[missing] [missing] of [no place]	1638	DD/SP/1638/41	Damaged
55	[missing] [missing] of Lydeard St. Lawrence	1638	DD/SP/1638/44	Damaged
56	[missing] [missing] of [no place]	1638	DD/SP/1638/45	Damaged
57	[missing] [missing] of [no place]	1638	DD/SP/1638/46	Damaged
58	[missing] [missing], Husbandman ? of Creech St. Michael ?	1638	DD/SP/1638/47	
	Note: Appraised by William WAKELY, Stephen CHEED and Richard HEARNE; damaged (Reg.)			
59	[missing] [missing] of [no place]	1638	DD/SP/1638/49	Damaged
60	[missing] [missing] of [no place]	1638	DD/SP/1638/50	Damaged
61	[missing] [missing] of Over Stowey	1638	DD/SP/1638/52	Appraised by Edward GOVER; damaged
62	[missing] [missing] of [no place]	1638	DD/SP/1638/53	
	Note: Appraised by William CHAPLINE and James HENBURROW; damaged			
63	[missing] [missing] of [no place]	1638	DD/SP/1638/6	
	Note: Appraised by John GIBBS and William ILLETT; damaged			
64	[missing] [missing], Husbandman ? of Stogumber	1638	DD/SP/1638/60	Damaged
65	[missing] [missing], Husbandman ? of [no place]	1638	DD/SP/1638/65	Damaged
66	[missing] [missing] of Porlock ?	1638	DD/SP/1638/66	Damaged
67	[missing] [missing] of [no place]	1638	DD/SP/1638/67	Damaged
68	[missing] [missing] of Dunster	1638	DD/SP/1638/68	
	Note: Appraised by John CLEMENT, Silfester ALLERCOTT, Henry RIDLER and Robert PROWLE; damaged (*P.R.* and Reg.)			
69	[missing] [missing] of [no place]	1638	DD/SP/1638/69	Mentions a malt house; damaged

70	[missing] [missing], Husbandman ? of [no place]	1638	DD/SP/1638/7	Exhibited at Crewkerne; damaged
71	[missing] [missing] of [no place]	1638	DD/SP/1638/9	
	Note: Appraised by William COMBE and William COMBE the younger; damaged			
72	[missing] [missing], Husbandman ? of Kilve ?	1639	DD/SP/1639/4	
	Note: Appraised by William BURNALL, Robert COLES, John SHURTE and Hugh SHURTE; damaged (Reg.)			
73	[missing] [missing] of High Littleton	1640	D/D/cta/Blank/13	
	Note: Damaged ad.ac.; two men of Littleton mentioned			
74	[missing] [missing] of [no place]	1640	D/D/cta/Blank/27	
	Note: Damaged ad.ac.; mentions Richard BANCKES			
75	[missing] [missing], Husbandman ? of [no place]	1640	DD/SP/1640/113	Damaged
76	[missing] [missing] of [no place]	1640	DD/SP/1640/132	Damaged
77	[missing] [missing] of [no place]	1640	DD/SP/1640/147	Damaged
78	[missing] [missing] of Cudworth ?	1640	DD/SP/1640/149	
	Note: Appraised by Nicholas WELMAN; damaged (*P.R.*)			
79	[missing] [missing] of Isle Brewers	1640	DD/SP/1640/31	Appraised by Thomas BOWERMAN; damaged
80	[missing] [missing], Weaver ? of Minehead	1640	DD/SP/1640/74	Mentions wool and looms; damaged
81	[missing] [missing] of Crewkerne ?	1640	DD/SP/1640/90	
	Note: Appraised by George DOWNE, Edward SCEYNE and William LAWRENCE; damaged (*P.R.* and Reg.)			
82	[missing] [missing], Brewer ? of [no place]	1640	DD/SP/1640/96	Damaged
83	[missing] [missing] of [no place]	1641	DD/SP/1641/11	
	Note: Appraised by Richard HARE, Stephen MEAD and Thomas HAWKER; damaged			
84	[missing] [missing] of [no place]	1641	DD/SP/1641/17	Damaged
85	[missing] [missing], Carpenter ? of Milverton ?	1641	DD/SP/1641/18	
	Note: Appraised by William SPREATT, Robert TAYLER and John OWEN; damaged (*P.R.*)			
86	[missing] [missing] of Skilgate ?	1641	DD/SP/1641/19	
	Note: Appraised by Robert YENDALL, Thomas YENDALL and John HURLEY; damaged (*P.R.*)			
87	[missing] [missing] of [no place]	1641	DD/SP/1641/25	Exhibited at Dunster
88	[missing] [missing], Husbandman ? of Tintinhull ?	1641	DD/SP/1641/31	
	Note: Appraised by John MABBARD, John Quick, John PAWGUS and Thomas BOND			
89	[missing] [missing] of Exton	1641	DD/SP/1641/39	Wife Joan; damaged
90	[missing] [missing] of Milverton	1641	DD/SP/1641/40	Damaged
91	[missing] [missing], Weaver of South Petherton ?	1641	DD/SP/1641/42	

	Note: Appraised by William BAKER, Mathew BAKER and Richard HEBDITCH; damaged (*P.R.*)			
92	[missing] [missing], Yeoman of Combe Florey	1641	DD/SP/1641/47	Damaged
93	[missing] [missing], Yeoman? of [no place]	1641	DD/SP/1641/50	
	Note: Mentions leases held of the MOOHNE, TRELAWNEY, VYVIAN and COURTENEY families; damaged			
94	[missing] [missing] of [no place]	1641	DD/SP/1641/52	Female mentions list of bonds; damaged
95	[missing] [missing] of [no place]	1641	DD/SP/1641/56	Mentions list of debts; damaged
96	[missing] [missing] of [no place]	1641	DD/SP/1641/58	Damaged
97	[missing] [missing] of [no place]	1641	DD/SP/1641/59	
	Note: Leases mention 'Churchouse Barne one close called Lingford', one from Mr Nicholas DOWNE of Barnstaple called 'Skinners Close' and a grant from Mr LUTTRELL esquire of 'Linch Barne'; damaged			
98	[missing] [missing] of Luxborough ?	1641	DD/SP/1641/60	
	Note: Appraised by John TURELL and Nicholas SNOW; damaged (*P.R.*)			
99	[missing] [missing] of Milverton or Bathealton	1641	DD/SP/1641/61	
	Note: Appraised by Richard CHURLY and John CHORLEYE and exhibited at Milverton; damaged (*P.R.*)			
100	[missing] [missing] of [no place]	1641	DD/SP/1641/64	Damaged
101	[missing] [missing] of [no place]	1641	DD/SP/1641/65	Damaged
102	[missing] [missing] of [no place]	1641	DD/SP/1641/66	Damaged
103	[missing] [missing] of Taunton	1641	DD/SP/1641/69	
	Note: Appraised by Walter CLIFFE and George HOLCOMBE; damaged (*P.R.*)			
104	[missing] [missing] of [no place]	1641	DD/SP/1641/7	Damaged
105	[missing] [missing] of [no place]	1641	DD/SP/1641/70	Numerous rooms listed; damaged
106	[missing] [missing], Husbandman ? of [no place]	1641	DD/SP/1641/71	Damaged
107	[missing] [missing] of [no place]	1641	DD/SP/1641/72	Damaged
108	[missing] [missing] of Brushford	1641	DD/SP/1641/79	Appraised by Richard PULSFORD; damaged
109	[missing] [missing] of Selworthy	1641	DD/SP/1641/8	Damaged
110	[missing] [missing], Husbandman ? of Luxborough	1641	DD/SP/1641/80	
	Note: Appraised by Augustine WINTER, Thomas HURFORD, Thomas WEBBER and John WINTER; damaged (*P.R.*)			
111	[missing] [missing], Husbandman ? of Buckland (*sic*)	1641	DD/SP/1641/9	Damaged
112	[missing] [missing], Thatcher ? of Hillfarrance	1641	DD/SP/1641/91	
	Note: Appraised by George BINDON mentioning a lease of 'Wenniper and Baarstile'; damaged (*P.R.*)			
113	[missing] [missing] of [no place]	1641	DD/SP/1641/93	Damaged

114	[missing] [missing] of [no place]	1641	DD/SP/1641/94	Damaged
115	[missing] [missing] of [no place]	1641	DD/SP/1641/95	Damaged
116	[missing] [missing] of [no place]	1641	DD/SP/1641/96	Damaged
117	[missing] [missing], Husbandman ? of Winsford	1641	DD/SP/1641/97	
	Note: Appraised by Anthony ROOKE, William LEA, George LEA and William SLOWLY; damaged (*P.R.*)			
118	[missing] [missing] of Hinton St. George	1641	DD/SP/1641/98	
	Note: Appraised by Adam HELLIAR and John PLETFORD; damaged (*P.R.* and Reg.)			
119	[missing] [missing] of Ashbrittle	1642	DD/SP/1642/17	Damaged
120	[missing] [missing], Husbandman ? of Kilve	1642	DD/SP/1642/2	Damaged
121	[missing] [missing] of [no place]	1642	DD/SP/1642/22	Mentions cloths of different types; damaged
122	[missing] [missing] of [no place]	1642	DD/SP/1642/23	Damaged
123	[missing] [missing], Husbandman ? of Dulverton	1642	DD/SP/1642/3	Damaged
124	[missing] [missing], Sheep Farmer of Clatworthy ?	1642	DD/SP/1642/5	
	Note: Male inv. appraised by Arthur BUTTELL, Giles THORNE and James BRYANT; damaged (*P.R.* and Reg.)			
125	[missing] [missing] of Taunton ?	1643	DD/SP/1643/50	
	Note: Joanna relict; appraised by Richard BRYER, John MICKEL and William WRENTMORE; damaged (*P.R.* and Reg.)			
126	[missing] [missing] of Hillfarrance	1645	DD/SP/1645/15	Damaged
127	[missing] [missing] of Middleney, Drayton	1645	DD/SP/1645/30	
	Note: Appraised by seven men and includes details of bequests; damaged			
128	[missing] [missing] of Dunster	1645	DD/SP/1645/46	
	Note: Appraised by Thomas BEARD and Hugh TAILLER; damaged			
129	[missing] [missing], Husbandman of Compton Durville, South Petherton	1645	DD/SP/1645/64	Damaged
130	[missing] [missing], Innholder of Taunton	1645	DD/SP/1645/70	Damaged
131	[missing] [missing], Fuller ? of [no place]	1646	DD/SP/1646/15	
	Note: Appraised by Christopher GARDNER, Richard STEARE and William WIE (?); damaged			
132	[missing] [missing] of [no place]	1646	DD/SP/1646/22	Damaged
133	[missing] [missing] of [no place]	1646	DD/SP/1646/3	
	Note: Male's inv. appraised by John COTTRELL, John CARD, William HEMBURY and William B.....; damaged			
134	[missing] [missing], Husbandman ? of Durston or West Monkton?	1646	DD/SP/1646/57	
	Note: Mentions Durston and West Monkton leases; damaged			

135 [missing] [missing] of Dunster 1646 DD/SP/1646/89 Damaged

136 [missing] [missing] of [no place] 1647 DD/MI Box 3

137 [missing] [missing] of Staplegrove 1648 DD/SP/1648/33 Damaged

138 [missing] [missing] of [no place] 1658 DD/SP/1658/11 Damaged

139 [missing] [missing] of [no place] 1661 D/D/cta/Blank/18
Note: Damaged ad.ac.; mentions a debt to Thomas SEYMORE esquire; corn sold at market

140 [missing] [missing] of Otterhampton ? 1667 DD/SP/1667/58
Note: Mentions lease held of William HODY esquire for land in Otterhampton; damaged

141 [missing] [missing] of Lydeard St. Lawrence 1667 DD/SP/1667/95

142 [missing] [missing], Husbandman ? of Brompton Ralph ? 1669 DD/SP/1669/25
Note: Appraised by Humphry SEALY, Joseph SHORNWAY, George SKINNER and John WOOD; damaged (Reg.)

143 [missing] [missing], Gentleman of Durleigh 1669 DD/SP/1669/96
Note: Appraised by John HILL, David BIFFEN and Zachias DORSE; damaged

144 [missing] [missing], Husbandman of Merriott 1673 DD/SP/1673/31
Note: Appraised by Thomas BECKE, Anthony DAWE, Thomas DAYMOND and John SKYNNER; damaged (Reg.)

145 [missing] [missing], Husbandman ? of Curry Rivel 1673 DD/SP/1673/43
Note: Mentions a lease in Aller Moor; appraised by Stephen MAN vicar, Jeffery ANDREWES and Thomas YOUNG; damaged; Man was vicar of Curry Rivel from 1666–1686 (C.C.E.d.)

146 [missing] [missing] of Drayton ? 1673 DD/SP/1673/44
Note: Appraised by George TREVILIAN, Martin PYKE, Edmund DAWE senior and Thomas HOPTKIN; damaged (*H.T.*)

147 [missing] [missing] of [no place] 1677 DD/SP/1677/88 Damaged

148 [missing] [missing] of Dunster or Minehead ? 1681 DD/SP/1681/116
Note: Appraised by Gabriel BROWNE, Henry CLEMENT and Samuel HOPKINS; damaged (Reg.)

149 [missing] [missing], Clothier [or] Sergemaker of Taunton 1681 T.N.A., PROB 4/25861 Will, mentions stock in trade and a list of debtors

150 [missing] [missing] of [no place] 1685 DD/SP/1685/111c
Note: Appraised by Thomas YEANDELL, John SELLICK and William SURRIDGE; damaged

151 [missing] [missing] of [no place] 1689 D/D/cta/Blank/31
Note: Damaged ad.ac.; mentions Richard THOMAS and Robert THOMS gentleman

152 [missing] [missing] of Taunton ? 1690 DD/SP/1690/19
Note: Mentions being taken at the Lamb which had a room with a 'billerd' table; damaged

153 [missing] [missing] of [no place] 1690 DD/SP/1690/91 Damaged

154 [missing] [missing] of Wootton Courtenay? 1692 DD/SP/1692/38

	Note: Elizabeth relict, appraised by Thomas RIDLER and John WITHYCOMBE; damaged (Reg.)			
155	[missing] [missing] of [no place]	1692	DD/SP/1692/40	Damaged
156	[missing] [missing] of [no place]	1697	DD/SP/1697/55	
	Note: Mentions a lease from Henry WALROND esquire, appraised by Richard FARRELL and John JENT; damaged			
157	[missing] [missing] of Crewkerne and Martock	1705	T.N.A., PROB 4/25938	Sworn by Constance ARDEN. Admon.
158	[missing] [missing] of Mells	1706	D/D/cta/Blank/22	
	Note: Damaged ad.ac.; administered by her sister			
159	[missing] [missing] of [no place]	1711	D/D/cta/Blank/12	Damaged ad.ac.
160	[missing] [missing] of [no place]	1730	D/D/cta/Blank/34	Damaged ad.ac.
161	[missing] [missing] of [no place]	1733	D/D/cta/H9	Ad.ac.
162	[missing] [missing] of [no place]	1740	DD/SP/1740/8	Damaged
163	[missing] [missing], Householder of Thornfalcon	1747	DD/DP/23 OB3	
164	[missing] [missing] of Wells	*c*.1611	D/D/cta/Blank/2	Damaged ad.ac.;
165	[missing] [missing] of Weston ?	*c*.1621	D/D/cta/Blank/3	
	Note: Damaged ad.ac.; executor a minor, mentions Westonzoyland and Street, Agnes BAND married William BLAKE of Pitminster. Pages numbered 5 to 8.			
166	[missing] [missing] of [no place]	*c*.1663	D/D/cta/Blank/38	
	Note: Damaged ad.ac.; the estate of a minor?			
167	[missing] [missing] of [no place]	*c*.1711	D/D/cta/Blank/14	
	Note: Damaged ad.ac.; account for a minor including schooling			
168	[missing] [missing] of [no place]	n.d.	D/D/cta/Blank/15	
	Note: Damaged ad.ac.; pages 13 to 17 of D/D/cta/blank/3 above			
169	[missing] [missing] of Yeovil ?	n.d.	D/D/cta/Blank/17	
	Note: Damaged ad.ac.; debts in the Yeovil area			
170	[missing] [missing] of [no place]	n.d.	D/D/cta/Blank/20	
	Note: Damaged ad.ac.; pages 9 to 12 of D/D/cta/blank/3 above			
171	[missing] [missing] of [no place]	n.d.	D/D/cta/Blank/21	Damaged ad.ac.
172	[missing] [missing] of [no place]	n.d.	D/D/cta/Blank/23	Damaged ad.ac.
173	[missing] [missing] of South Petherton	n.d.	D/D/cta/Blank/24	
	Note: Damaged ad.ac.; relict Mary; mentions Sir George RODBARD of the same parish			
174	[missing] [missing] of [no place]	n.d.	D/D/cta/Blank/25	Damaged ad.ac.; debts mentioned
175	[missing] [missing] of [no place]	n.d.	D/D/cta/Blank/26	
	Note: Damaged ad.ac.; mentions Thomas LYE			

176	[missing] [missing] of [no place]	n.d.	D/D/cta/Blank/30	
	Note: Damaged ad.ac.; mentions Stoke St. Gregory, Milverton and Chelton			
177	[missing] [missing] of Stogursey	n.d.	D/D/cta/Blank/32	
	Note: Damaged ad.ac.; sons Richard and George			
178	[missing] [missing] of Woolavington	n.d.	D/D/cta/Blank/33	Damaged ad.ac.
179	[missing] [missing] of [no place]	n.d.	D/D/cta/Blank/35	Damaged ad.ac.
180	[missing] [missing] of [no place]	n.d.	D/D/cta/Blank/36	Damaged ad.ac.
181	[missing] [missing] of [no place]	n.d.	D/D/cta/Blank/37	
	Note: Damaged ad.ac.; mentions John BAYLIE Doctor of Law, John HANCOCK, Sarah KEARLE and John HEMBRY			
182	[missing] [missing] of [no place]	n.d.	D/D/cta/Blank/39	Damaged ad.ac.
183	[missing] [missing] of [no place]	n.d.	D/D/cta/Blank/4	
	Note: Damaged ad.ac.; debts with people from Martock, Yeovil, Montacute, Manchester, London, Dorchester and Lyme, Dorset; bequest to Mr Monkley vicar; rent owed to Thomas FREEKE esquire			
184	[missing] [missing] of [no place]	n.d.	D/D/cta/Blank/40	
	Note: Damaged ad.ac.; mentions Humphry WYNDHAM of Wiveliscombe (d.1622)			
185	[missing] [missing] of [no place]	n.d.	D/D/cta/Blank/43	
	Note: Damaged ad.ac.; mentions Maurice COLES, Walter DEACON, Peter WALTER and Mr Edmund DAWES			
186	[missing] [missing] of [no place]	n.d.	D/D/cta/Blank/44	Damaged ad.ac.
187	[missing] [missing] of [no place]	n.d.	D/D/cta/Blank/45	Damaged ad.ac.
188	[missing] [missing] of South Cadbury ?	n.d.	D/D/cta/Blank/46	
	Note: Damaged ad.ac. for a cleric mentioning Corton and South Cadbury			
189	[missing] [missing], Sheep Farmer ? of [no place]	n.d.	D/D/cta/Blank/47	Damaged ad.ac.
190	[missing] [missing] of [no place]	n.d.	D/D/cta/Blank/49	Damaged ad.ac.
191	[missing] [missing] of [no place]	n.d.	D/D/cta/Blank/5	
	Note: Damaged ad.ac.			
192	[missing] [missing] of Barrow ?	n.d.	D/D/cta/Blank/50	
	Note: Damaged ad.ac.; mentions Richard ROWLANDSON of Barrow			
193	[missing] [missing] of [no place]	n.d.	D/D/cta/Blank/53	
	Note: Damaged ad.ac.; mentions Thomas CRAB of 'Hannons mill, Gloster'			
194	[missing] [missing] of North Petherton ?	n.d.	D/D/cta/Blank/7	Damaged ad.ac.
195	[missing] [missing] of Shepton Mallet ?	n.d.	D/D/cta/Blank/8	Damaged ad.ac.; Mary relict
196	[missing] [missing] of Huntspill	n.d.	D/D/cta/I6	Ad.ac.
197	[missing] [missing] of [no place]	n.d.	D/D/cta/R16	Ad.ac. missing 6/9/2018

198	[missing] [missing] of Banwell?	n.d.	D/P/ban/17/3/1	Man killed at Banwell Mills
199	George [missing] of Curry Rivel	1640	DD/SP/1640/134	Damaged
200	J...... [missing] of Winsford	1641	DD/SP/1641/24	
	Note: Appraised by William E...... of Clatworthy and John NETHERCOT; damaged			
201	James [missing], Carpenter of Dunster	1646	DD/SP/1646/95	Damaged
201a	Joan NO SURNAME of Stogursey	n.d.	D/D/cta/S8	Ad.ac.
202	Joane [missing] of [no place]	1636	DD/SP/1636/47	Mentions husbandry goods; damaged
203	John [missing] of Elm ?	1601	D/D/cta/Blank/48	
	Note: Damaged ad.ac.; mentions Richard ROOKE of Elm			
204	John [missing], Husbandman ? of Kilve ?	1641	DD/SP/1641/32	
	Note: Appraised by William SEALIE, John THARSSER and Henry PAYNE; damaged (*P.R.*)			
205	John [missing] of Stawley ?	1641	DD/SP/1641/46	
	Note: Appraised by John WILLS and John CHAPPLE alias FARMER; damaged (*T.C.W.*)			
206	John [missing], Brewer ? of Nynehead	1647	DD/SP/1647/15	Damaged
207	Jone [missing] of Drayton	1648	DD/SP/1648/69	Damaged
208	Ma... [missing] of Staplegrove	1670	DD/SP/1670/103	Female; damaged
209	Margaret [missing] of Durleigh	1639	DD/SP/1639/33	Damaged
210	Nicholas [missing], Husbandman ? of North Petherton	1641	DD/SP/1641/51	
	Note: Appraised by Samuel GALLER (?) and William GYLLARD; damaged			
211	R...... [missing], Clothmaker ? of Kilve ?	1636	DD/SP/1636/8	
	Note: Appraised by Samuel WADE and William STANFAST junior; damaged (*P.R.* and Reg.)			
212	Robert [missing] of Staplegrove ?	1641	DD/SP/1641/63	
	Note: Appraised by Richard POYER, Richard MOORE and Thomas DUDDRIGE; damaged (*P.R.*)			
213	Symon [missing], Husbandman ? of [no place]	1641	DD/SP/1641/73	Appraised by Henry WESCOMBE; damaged
214	Thomas [missing] of [no place]	1644	DD/SP/1644/57	Damaged
215	Thomas [missing] of [no place]	1645	DD/SP/1645/69	
	Note: Appraised by ...... WARMAN and John .....; damaged			
216	William [missing], Husbandman ? of South Petherton ?	1647	DD/SP/1647/2	
	Note: Appraised by Josias BAKER; damaged (*P.R.* and Reg.)			
217	Elizabeth ABBOT of Butleigh	1679	DD/S/BT/6/5/6	
218	Robert ABBOT, Husbandman of Crewkerne	1640	DD/SP/1640/127	
219	Thomas ABBOT of Queen Charlton	1714	DD/GS/4 (85)	
220	Agnes ABBOTT of Butleigh	1670	DD/S/BT/11/1/22	

221	John ABBOTT, Innholder of Bruton	1734	D/D/Cti 2	
222	Peter ABBOTT of East Chinnock	1707	D/D/cta/A13	Ad.ac.
223	Robert ABBOTT senior of [no place]	1698	D/D/cta/A10	Ad.ac.
224	Samuel ABBOTT of Queen Charlton	1745	DD/SAS/H143/21	See DD/SAS/C795/PR/337
225	Samuel ABBOTT of Queen Charlton	1746	DD/SAS/FA/166	See DD/SAS/C795/PR/337
226	John ABRAHAM, Husbandman of West Bagborough	1684	DD/SP/1684/51	
227	John ABRAHAM, Gentleman of Purtington, Winsham	1688	T.N.A., PROB 4/5231	Admon
228	William ABRAHAM, Esquire of Bathwick	1804	T.N.A., PROB 31/1804/1223	
229	Sir Alexander ACLAND-HOOD of [no place]	1892	DD/AH Box 58/3	
230	Susanna ACOURT of Frome Selwood	1684	T.N.A., PROB 4/17377	Will also extant
231	Thomas ACOURT of Frome Selwood	1606	D/D/cta/A14	Ad.ac.
232	Henry A'COURT, Carpenter and Widower of Burnett formerly of Northumberland Street, Middlesex	1821	T.N.A., PROB 31/1821/931	
233	David ADAMS of Minehead	1698	DD/SP/1698/24	
234	Joan ADAMS of Chewton Mendip	1635	D/D/cta/A5	Ad.ac.
235	Joan ADAMS of Huish (*sic*)	1751	DD/GS 4 (85)	Clothes only
236	John ADAMS of Taunton St. James	1697	DD/SP/1697/3	
237	John ADAMS of West Chinnock	n.d.	D/D/cta/A12	Ad.ac.
238	Judith ADAMS, Widow of Frome Selwood	1723	T.N.A., PROB 3/22/171	
239	Juliana ADAMS of Baltonsborough	1669	T.N.A., PROB 5/2004	Will T.N.A., PROB 11/591
240	William ADAMS the elder, Husbandman of Over Stowey	1684	DD/SP/1684/117	
241	John ADDAMS of Over Stowey	1637	DD/SP/1637/27	
242	John ADDAMS of Castle Cary	1643	D/D/cta/A15	Ad.ac.
243	William ADDAMS of Bridgwater	1640	DD/SP/1640/81	
244	William ADDICOTT, Tanner of Brushford	1691	DD/SP/1691/46	
245	John AISH, Blacksmith of Stogursey	1678	DD/SP/1678/45	
246	Thomas AISH, Yeoman of North Petherton	1714	DD/SP/1714/24	
247	Peter AISHCOMBE of Taunton St. Mary Magdalene	1698	DD/SP/1698/12	
248	Thomas AISHCOMBE, Husbandman of Milverton	1680	DD/SP/1680/47	
249	Thomas AISHCOMBE of Milverton	1685	DD/SP/1685/81	
250	Henry AISHMAN of Kilmersdon	1706	D/D/cta/A16	Ad.ac.
251	Nicholas AISHTON of Bickenhall	1681	DD/SP/1681/98	
252	Thomas ALBEN of Bruton	1641	D/D/cta/A18	Ad.ac.

253	John ALBURT, Husbandman of Luccombe	1640	DD/SP/1640/2	
254	Louisa Maria ALDER, Spinster of Keynsham	1838	T.N.A., PROB 31/1838/490	
255	George ALDERMAN, Bachelor of Chipstable	1735	T.N.A., PROB 31/1735/341	With ad.ac.
256	John ALDERMAN of Taunton St. Mary Magdalene	1620	D/D/cta/A9	Ad.ac.
257	Joseph ALEINE, Gentleman of Taunton	1669	T.N.A., PROB 4/18464	Will also extant
258	Martin ALEXANDER of Baltonsborough	1600	D/D/cta/A20	Ad.ac.
259	Agnese ALFORD, Widow of West Monkton	1632	DD/SP/1632/21	
260	Joseph ALFORD of Whitestaunton	1682	T.N.A., PROB 4/8637	Admon
261	Mary ALFORD, Widow of Hinton St. George	1635	DD/SP/1635/78	See *T.C.W.*
262	Robert ALFORD of Curry Rivel	1700	DD/SP/1700/6	
263	Samuel ALFORD of Taunton St. Mary Magdalene	1693	DD/SP/1693/31	
264	William ALFORD of Taunton St. Mary Magdalene	1684	DD/SP/1684/62	
265	Philip ALLANSON of the Liberty of St. Andrew, Wells	1768	T.N.A., PROB 31/1768/225	With ad.ac.
266	Abraham ALLEN of Alcombe, Dunster	1731	DD/SP/1731/1	
267	Ann ALLEN of Bedminster	1680	T.N.A., PROB 5/2014	
268	James ALLEN of Thurloxton	1693	DD/SP/1693/53	
269	Joan ALLEN of Stogumber	1685	DD/SP/1685/105	
270	John ALLEN, Yeoman of South Petherton	1638	DD/SP/1638/48	
271	John ALLEN, Husbandman of Dunster	1675	DD/SP/1675/47	
272	Richard ALLEN of Huntspill	1594	D/D/cta/A21	Ad.ac.
273	Richard ALLEN of Stogumber	1731	DD/SP/1731/42	
274	Robert ALLEN, Husbandman of Beercrocombe	1667	DD/SP/1667/87	
275	Simon ALLEN, Yeoman of Dinnington	1720	DD/SP/1720/17	
276	Thomas ALLEN of [no place]	1623	D/D/cta/A2	Ad.ac.
277	William ALLEN of Dunwear, Bridgwater	1683	D/D/cta/A17	Ad.ac.
278	Anne ALLEN alias FOOTE of 29 New King Street, Bath	1857	T.N.A., PROB 37/1752	
279	John ALLERCOTT of Dunster	1646	DD/SP/1646/81	
280	Sylvestor ALLERCOTT of Dunster	1669	DD/L/2/35/2	
281	John ALLEYN, Clerk of Brewham	1725	T.N.A., PROB 3/24/171	
282	William ALLOWAY the elder of Minehead	1686	T.N.A., PROB 4/2776	Will also extant
283	William ALLWOOD of Glastonbury	n.d.	D/D/cta/A19	Ad.ac.
284	John ALLYN of Beercrocombe	1635	DD/SP/1635/9	
285	George ALMSWORTHY of Exford	1690	DD/SP/1690/67	

286	[missing] ALSOP of Shepton Mallet	1712	D/D/cta/A11	Ad.ac.
287	Thomas ALYN of Banwell	1496	T.N.A., PROB 2/125	Will T.N.A., PROB 11/11/5
288	Joane AMBROSE, Widow of North Petherton	1682	DD/SP/1682/1	
289	William AMBROSE, Husbandman of Otterhampton	1680	DD/SP/1680/64	
AMBROSE see COLLICK				
290	George AMERY of Ashbrittle	1685	DD/SP/1685/84	
291	Hugh AMERY of Taunton St. James	1667	DD/SP/1667/56	
292	John AMERY, Husbandman of Trull	1672	DD/SP/1672/29	
293	[missing] AMES of Taunton ?	1692	DD/SP/1692/39	
	Note: Mentions a brother Ames and son Samuel, appraised by William DURSTON, Thomas DANBERY and John FORD; damaged (Reg.)			
294	Benjamin AMORY, Esquire of Bath formerly of St. Christopher, West Indies	1823	T.N.A., PROB 31/1823/397	
295	John AMORY of Stogumber	1639	D/D/cta/A8	Ad.ac.
296	John AMORY of Stogumber	1664	DD/SP/1664/18	
AMRY see PRIOR				
297	Thomas AMSWORTHY of Exford	1640	DD/SP/1640/141	
298	Brereton ANCKUTELLE, Esquire of Taunton and Gray's Inn, Middlesex	1663	T.N.A., PROB 4/13525	Will 1661. ex. 1663
299	Jane ANDERDON, Widow of Bridgwater	1694	DD/SP/1694/11	
300	John ANDERDON of Ilchester	1685	T.N.A., PROB 4/8365	Will also extant
301	John ANDERSEY of Curry Rivel	1672	DD/SP/1672/19	
302	Tamzen ANDERSEY of Drayton	1683	DD/SP/1683/85	
303	Laurence ANDERSIE, Husbandman of Curry Rivel	1684	DD/SP/1684/45	
304	Dorothy ANDREWES, Widow of Stogumber	1678	DD/SP/1678/34	
305	Joan ANDREWES of North Petherton	1677	DD/SP/1677/37	Wife of Henry
306	Thomas ANDREWES of Kingsdon	1640	D/D/cta/A23	Ad.ac.
307	Thomas ANDREWES alias WILCOX of Chewton Mendip	1604	D/D/cta/A24	Ad.ac.
308	Agnes ANDREWS, Widow of London, Old Cleeve	1680	DD/X/MG/1	
309	John ANDREWS of Knapp, North Curry	1590	D/D/ct/1/A/42	
310	Henry ANNERLY of Yarnfield, Maiden Bradley	1673	W.S.H.C., P2/A/261	Inv. and will
311	Margery ANNIS, Widow of Middlezoy	1611	D/D/cta/A22	Ad.ac.
312	Ruben ANSTICE of Norton Fitzwarren	1669	DD/SP/1669/6	
313	John ANSTIE, Yeoman of Dulverton	1636	DD/SP/1636/39	

314	James AP MORGAN of Stogursey	1580	T.N.A., PROB 2/413	
315	Nicholas APLEY alias PITT, Husbandman of Crowcombe	1683	DD/SP/1683/54	
316	David APLIN, Miller of North Petherton	1700	DD/SP/1700/22	
317	James APLIN, Husbandman of Wembdon	1673	DD/SP/1673/10	
318	Thomas APLIN of Taunton St. James	1726	T.N.A., PROB 3/25/46	
APPLEDORE see JENNINGS				
319	Thomas Lewes APPRICE of Old Cleeve	1607	D/D/cta/K10	Ad.ac.
APRISE see LEWIS				
320	John ARDEN, Goldsmith of Crewkerne	1704	T.N.A., PROB 4/25399	
321	John ARDEN, Goldsmith of Crewkerne	1705	T.N.A., PROB 5/4702	
322	George ARENFILD of Withiel Florey	1639	DD/SP/1639/7	See *T.C.W.*
323	George ARMESTRONGE of Bridgwater	1669	DD/SP/1669/64	
324	Robert ARMESTRONGE, King's Service of Bridgwater	1697	DD/SP/1697/28	
325	Mary ARMFELD of Withiel Florey	1635	DD/SP/1635/31	See *T.C.W.*
326	John ARMY alias HANKINE (HAWKINS) of Curry Rivel	1646	DD/SP/1646/63	See *T.C.W.*
327	Nicholas ARNAM of Ansford	1623	D/D/cta/A1	Ad.ac.
328	Robert ARNAM of Frome Selwood	1682	T.N.A., PROB 4/19280	Will also extant
329	Andrew ARNELLS of Stoke Pero	1680	DD/SP/1680/32	
330	John ARNOLD, Woolcomber of Luxborough	1699	DD/SP/1699/9	
331	Margaret ARNOLD of The Liberty, Wells and Wokingham, Berkshire	1775	W.S.H.C., 873/108	Inv. and will
332	Edmund ARNOLL of Hutton	1626	D/D/cta/A3	Ad.ac.
333	John ARNOLL of Selworthy	1693	DD/SP/1693/37	
334	Edward ASH of Trull late of Barbados, West Indies	1672	T.N.A., PROB 4/21032	Will ex. 1672
335	Edward ASHCOMBE of Bradford	1635	DD/SP/1635/108	See *T.C.W.*
336	Grace ASHE of Westcombe, Batcombe	1654	W.S.H.C., 118/108	Will and inv.
337	John ASHE of North Petherton	1560	D/D/B.reg.44 Box 138	
338	Margaret ASHE of Stogumber	1639	DD/SP/1639/8	
339	John ASHELFORD, Yeoman of Lopen	1697	DD/SP/1697/6	
340	James ASHMAN, Worsted Comber of Coleford, Kilmersdon	1714	T.N.A., PROB 5/3279	
341	Edward ASHTON of Ashill	1748	DD/BD/24	
342	Thomas ASHTON of Buckland St. Mary	1731	DD/SP/1731/38	
343	William ASHTON of Ashill	1689	DD/SAS/C59/2	

344	William ASHTON of Dundry	1736	D/D/Cti 3	
345	James ASTON of Beckington	1694	T.N.A., PROB 4/25646	Admon
346	Mary ATCASTLE alias PROCTER alias MATHEW of West Monkton	1666	DD/SP/1666/52	
347	Thomas ATKENS of Stoke St. Mary	1645	DD/SP/1645/2	
348	William ATKINGS, Husbandman of Dulverton	1674	DD/SP/1674/65	
349	Abraham ATKINS, Bachelor of Chard	1675	T.N.A., PROB 4/18694	Admon
350	Mr Alexander ATKINS of Bridgwater	1680	T.N.A., PROB 4/20941	Admon. ex. 1681
351	Edward ATKINS of Taunton St. Mary Magdalene	1679	DD/SP/1679/52	
352	Elizabeth ATKINS, Widow of Chard	1684	T.N.A., PROB 4/2783	Will 1685. ex. 1685
353	John ATKINS of Chard	1681	T.N.A., PROB 4/8345	Will 1681
354	John ATKINS, Yeoman of Dulverton	1683	DD/SP/1683/58	
355	Leonard ATKINS, Labourer of Dulverton	1639	DD/SP/1639/59	
356	Michael ATKINS, Clothier of Bruton	1685	T.N.A., PROB 4/10538	Will 1686. ex. 1686
357	Richard ATKINS of Dunster	1666	DD/SP/1666/38	
358	Robert ATKINS, Clothier of Chard	1682	T.N.A., PROB 4/5237	Admon. ex. 1683
359	William ATKINS, Husbandman of Woolavington	1637	D/D/cta/A4	Ad.ac.
360	John ATKYNS of Castle Cary	1589	D/D/cta/A27	Ad.ac.
361	John ATMORE of Trull	1687	DD/SP/1687/19	
362	John ATMORE of Trull	1698	D/D/cta/A26	Ad.ac.
363	John ATTHAYES of Chewton Mendip	1638	D/D/cta/A6	Ad.ac.
364	Thomas ATTKINS the elder of Bathampton	1635	D/D/cta/A7	Ad.ac.
365	Hugh ATTMORE, Yeoman of Trull	1682	DD/SP/1682/64	
366	John ATWAY, Husbandman of Chedzoy	1680	DD/SP/1680/92	
367	Tomasin ATWAY, Widow of Chedzoy	1690	DD/SP/1690/8	
368	George ATWILL, Clothier of Minehead	1685	DD/SP/1685/34	
369	Nathaniel ATWOOD of Taunton	1681	T.N.A., PROB 4/21717	Admon 1682
370	John ATYOE, Yeoman of Dunwear, Bridgwater	1670	DD/SP/1670/15	
371	Thomas AUSLY of Dulverton	1721	DD/SP/1721/26	
372	John AUSTELL, Canon of Wells	1497	T.N.A., PROB 2/131	Will T.N.A., PROB 11/11/29
373	Edward AUSTEN of Durston	1646	DD/SP/1646/62	
374	John AUSTEN of North Petherton	1681	DD/SP/1681/34	
375	John AUSTIN of [no place]	1691	T.N.A., PROB 4/26011	Admon. ex. 1691

376	Christopher AUSTINE of Glastonbury St. John	1604	D/D/cta/A28	Ad.ac.
377	Benjamin AVERY of Frome Selwood	1676	T.N.A., PROB 4/644	Will also extant
378	William AVERY, Yeoman of Yatton	1681	T.N.A., PROB 4/4191	Will also extant
379	John AWBREY, Clothier of Frome Selwood	1730	T.N.A., PROB 3/29/11	
380	Nicholas AX, Comber (Camer) of Tintinhull	1684	T.N.A., PROB 4/7419	Will also extant
381	Thomas AXE, Gentleman of Orchard Portman	1700	T.N.A., PROB 5/5155	
382	Aaron AXFORD, Grocer of Bath City	1731	T.N.A., PROB 3/30/79	
383	Jacob AXFORD, Brazier of Bath	1734	D/D/Cti 1	
384	James AYSH, Esquire of South Petherton	1681	T.N.A., PROB 4/10407	Admon. ex. 1682
385	John AYSHFORD, Esquire of [no place]	1690	DD/SF/11/1/101	Formerly DD/SF/370
386	Raph AYSHFORD of North Petherton	1637	DD/SP/1637/18	
387	Joan BAB, Spinster of Trull	1677	DD/SP/1677/49	
388	Dorothy BABB, Spinster of Trull	1664	DD/SP/1664/39	
389	Elinor BABB, Widow of Wembdon	1649	DD/SP/1649/76	
390	George BABB of Pitminster	1664	DD/SP/1664/13	
391	John BABB, Yeoman of Cutsey, Trull	1640	DD/SP/1640/19	
392	Robert BABB of Middleney, Drayton	1693	DD/SP/1693/43	
393	Elizabeth BABER, Widow of Sutton Court, Chew Magna	1676	DD/SH/79/9 c/2480	
394	Mrs Elizabeth BABER, Widow of Chew Magna	1676	T.N.A., PROB 4/13002	Will 1675
395	Elizabeth BABER of Sutton Court, Stowey	*c.*1672	DD/SF/11/1/72	Formerly DD/SF/898
396	Richard BABOR, Yeoman of Newton St. Loe	1651	DD/GL/47	
397	Mary BACKER, Spinster of South Petherton	1641	DD/SP/1641/81	
BACKER see BAKER				
398	Henry BACKWELL, Mercer of Wrington	1664	T.N.A., PROB 4/19645	Will also extant
399	Joan BACKWELL, Widow of Wrington	1675	T.N.A., PROB 4/8799	Will. ex. 1676
400	Paul BACKWELL of Wrington	1673	T.N.A., PROB 4/21839	Admon
401	Paul BACKWELL, Clothier of Wrington	1674, 1677	T.N.A., PROB 5/3720–2	
402	Samuel BACKWELL, Mercer of Wrington	1680	T.N.A., PROB 4/1320	Will also extant
403	Amy BACON of Stogumber	1646	DD/SP/1646/25	
404	Francis BACON, Husbandman of North Petherton	1677	DD/SP/1677/32	
405	George BACON of Langford Budville	1690	T.N.A., PROB 4/20027	Will 1691
406	Joseph BACON of Stogursey	1729	DD/SP/1729/63	

407	Margaret BADEN of Wembdon	1604	D/D/cta/B106	Ad.ac.
408	John BADMAN of Congresbury	1602	D/D/cta/B97	Ad.ac.
409	John BADMAN of Wrington	1735	D/D/cta/B57	Ad.ac. and inv.
410	William BAGG of Bridgwater	1721	DD/SP/1721/19	
411	Philip BAGNALL of Wells	1676	T.N.A., PROB 4/10549	Admon. ex. 1679
412	Agnes BAGWELL of Winsham	1662	DD/SAS/FA/161/30	
413	Roger BAGWELL of Cricket St. Thomas	1633	D/D/cta/B64	Ad.ac.
414	John BAILIE of Bath	1612	D/D/cta/B38	Ad.ac.
415	William BAILIE, Tailor of Taunton	1644	DD/SP/1644/56	Shown as BAYLIE on second inv.
BAILIE see PYLE				
416	John BAILY of North Petherton	1713	DD/SP/1713/43	
417	Sarah BAILY, Widow of Croft, Hinton St. George	1675	DD/SP/1675/83	
418	[missing] BAKER of [no place]	1666	DD/SP/1666/24	
419	Amy BAKER of Stogumber	1641	DD/SP/1641/53	
420	Bartholomew BAKER of Milverton	1674	DD/SP/1674/32	
421	Charetie BAKER, Spinster of St. Michaelchurch	1666	DD/SP/1666/27	
422	Christopher BAKER senior of Shepton Beauchamp	1647	DD/SP/1647/4	
423	Edward BAKER of Upton Noble	1798	T.N.A., PROB 31/1798/890	
424	Elesebeth BAKER of Wootton Courtenay	1635	DD/SP/1635/3	
425	Elizabeth BAKER of Taunton	1642	DD/SP/1642/28	
426	Ellinor BAKER, Widow of Upton	1681	DD/SP/1681/51	
427	Francesse BAKER of Nynehead	1635	DD/SP/1635/36	
428	George BAKER of Withypool	1648	DD/SP/1648/46	See *T.C.W.*
429	Henry BAKER, Yeoman of Curry Rivel	1669	DD/SP/1669/67	
430	Hugh BAKER, Pewterer of South Petherton	1646	DD/SP/1646/16	
431	James BAKER of East Quantoxhead	1675	DD/SP/1675/4	
432	Joan BAKER of Taunton St. Mary Magdalene	1683	DD/SP/1683/48	
433	Joane BAKER, Spinster of Trull	1684	T.N.A., PROB 4/10202	Will also extant
434	John BAKER of Portishead	1638	D/D/cta/B23	Ad.ac.
435	John BAKER, Gentleman of Oake	1670	DD/SP/1670/25	
436	John BAKER, Yeoman of Kingswood, Hardington Mandeville	1673	T.N.A., PROB 4/7930	Admon. ex. 1677
437	John BAKER, Yeoman of Morland, Stoke St. Gregory	1675	T.N.A., PROB 4/8063	Will. ex. 1681
438	John BAKER of Treborough	1685	DD/SP/1685/37	

439	John BAKER of Middlezoy	1687	D/D/cta/B58	Ad.ac.
440	John BAKER, Barber of Crewkerne	1704	DD/SP/442/53	Ad.ac.
441	John BAKER, Yeoman of Curry Rivel	1729	DD/SP/1729/48	
442	John BAKER the elder, Yeoman of Withypool	1682	DD/SP/1682/11	
443	John BAKER the elder, Gentleman of Hardington, Wells	n.d.	T.N.A., PROB 4/2661	Admon
444	Jonas BAKER, Husbandman of Isle Abbotts	1675	DD/SP/1675/37	
445	Jonas BAKER, Husbandman of Isle Abbotts	1676	DD/SP/1676/18	
446	Joseph BAKER of Marsh, Hardington Mandeville	1687	T.N.A., PROB 4/7733	Will also extant
447	Judith BAKER, Widow of Bridgwater	1693	DD/SP/1693/51	
448	Mary BAKER of South Petherton	1673	DD/SP/1673/4	
449	Mary BAKER, Widow of Timberscombe	1686	T.N.A., PROB 4/19047	Will. ex. 1687
450	Mathew BAKER of Isle Abbotts	1685	DD/SP/1685/52	
451	Nicholas BAKER, Yeoman of Somerton	1600	DD/MI Box 18/77	Hanged himself in May 1600
452	Philip BAKER of Bridgwater	1691	DD/SP/1691/1	
453	Philip BAKER, Mason of Abbots Leigh	1717	B.A., 1717/2	
454	Richard BAKER of Dulverton	1640	DD/SP/1640/130	
455	Richard BAKER, Husbandman of North Petherton	1664	DD/SP/1664/22	
456	Richard BAKER of Minehead	1664	DD/SP/1664/29	
457	Richard BAKER, Yeoman of Hardington Mandeville	1695	T.N.A., PROB 4/19989	
458	Robert BAKER of Drayton	1646	DD/SP/1646/75	
459	Thomas BAKER of Bradford	1667	DD/SP/1667/72	
460	Thomas BAKER, Husbandman of Stocklinch Magdalene	1677	DD/SP/1677/42	
461	Thomas BAKER of Huish Champflower	1703	DD/SP/442/49	Ad.ac.
462	Thomas BAKER of South Petherton	n.d.	D/D/cta/B40	Ad.ac.
463	William BAKER of [no place]	1585	D/D/cta/B1	Ad.ac.
464	William BAKER, Yeoman of Upcott	1664	DD/SP/1664/48	Listed as Hapcott
465	William BAKER, Sergemaker of Taunton St. Mary Magdalene	1683	T.N.A., PROB 4/8778	Admon
466	William BAKER of Wellington formerly of Manchester Square, Middlesex and of Portland Town, Middlesex	1826	T.N.A., PROB 31/1826/160	
467	Phillip BAKER alias CROOKE of Taunton St. James	1670	DD/SP/1670/22	
468	George BALCH, Gentleman of Bridgwater	1696	DD/SP/1696/16	
469	Habron BALCH of [no place]	1646	DD/SP/1646/87	
470	Robert BALCH of Somerton	1600	D/D/cta/B27	Ad.ac.

471	Thomas BALCH, Vicar of Dulverton	1648	DD/X/WHI/4	
472	John BALCHE, Yeoman of Stoke sub Hamdon	1640	D/D/cta/B49	Ad.ac.
473	Charles BALDWIN, Widower of West Crowcombe, Crowcombe	1825	T.N.A., PROB 31/1825/445	
474	John BALE, Yeoman of Bridgwater	1640	DD/SP/1640/9	
475	Joane BALE alias LEE of Taunton St. James	1668	DD/SP/1668/34	
476	George BALL of Minehead died at Merchant ship *Gibraltar* at Jamaica	1740	T.N.A., PROB 31/1740/787	
477	James BALL, Widower and Bastard of Taunton	1827	T.N.A., PROB 31/1827/1164A	
478	James BALL senior, Worsted Comber of Pitminster	1672	DD/SP/1672/15	
479	John BALL of Kilmersdon	1619	D/D/cta/B86	Ad.ac.
480	John BALL of Trull	1684	DD/SP/1684/119	
481	John BALL, Clerk of Heathfield	1685	DD/SP/1685/103	
482	John BALL of Trull	1685	DD/SP/1685/9	
483	John BALL of Isle Brewers	1687	DD/SP/1687/25	
484	Robert BALL, Yeoman of Thurlbear	1686	DD/SP/1686/7	
485	Thomas BALL of Creech St. Michael	1693	DD/SP/1693/70	
486	William BALL of West Monkton	1591	D/D/cta/B55	Ad.ac.
487	William BALL of Norton Malreward	1641	D/D/cta/B52	Ad.ac.
488	William BALL, Husbandman of Bishops Hull	1697	DD/SP/1697/54	
489	Phillipp BALLAM, Husbandman of North Petherton	1637	DD/SP/1637/33	
490	John BALLER of Curry Mallet	1665	DD/SP/1665/49	
491	William BALLER of West Pennard	1662	D/D/cta/B43	Ad.ac.
492	John BALLETT, Rector of Raddington	1684	DD/SP/1684/175	
493	Susanna BALLETT of Raddington	1691	DD/SP/1691/44	
494	Thomas BALLETT, Minister of Whitestaunton	1670	DD/SP/1670/30	
495	William BALLOR of Abbots Leigh	1669	B.A., 1669/7	
496	William BALMUNT, Miller of Withypool	1679	DD/SP/1679/33	
497	Katherine BALSTONE, Widow of Misterton	1679	DD/SP/1679/34	
498	Amias BAMPFIELD of Weston Bampfylde	1681	T.N.A., PROB 5/4435	
499	Amyas BAMPFIELD, Gentleman of [no place]	1678	T.N.A., PROB 4/2645	Admon. ex. 1679
500	Joan BAMPFIELD of Bath St. Peter and Paul	1668	D/D/cta/B48	Ad.ac.
501	John BAMPFIELD of Hardington Mandeville	1745	T.N.A., PROB 31/1745/574	With ad.ac.

502	Ames BAMPFYLDE of Weston Bampfylde	1686	T.N.A., PROB 4/13120	Admon
503	John BAMPFYLDE of Hestercombe, Cheddon Fitzpaine	1750	DD/SAS/C795/PR/46	
504	Thomas BANBURY, Gentleman of Long Sutton	1752	T.N.A., PROB 31/1752/433	With ad.ac.
505	William BANBURY of South Petherton	1646	DD/SP/1646/13	
506	Samuel BANCKES, Husbandman of Portbury	1629	D/D/ct/1/B/32	Top of inv. missing
507	Robert BAND of North Petherton	1666	DD/SP/1666/40	
508	William BAND alias WRENTMORE of Bridgwater	1647	DD/SP/1647/8	
509	Roger BANDE of Taunton	1637	DD/SP/1637/69	
510	Thomas BANFILL, Husbandman of Bradford on Tone	1700	DD/SP/1700/18	
511	Henry BANGER, Husbandman of North Petherton	1687	DD/SP/1687/30	
512	Henry BANISTER, Yeoman of Abbots Leigh	1641	B.A., 1641/1	Will also extant
513	James BARBER, Yeoman of Clevedon	1669	T.N.A., PROB 4/4666	Will 1670
514	John BARBER of Nynehead	1643	DD/MY/28	
515	John BARBER of Nynehead	1663	DD/MY/28	
516	Richard BARBER the elder of Nynehead	1635	DD/SP/1635/111	
517	William BARBER, Rector of Beercrocombe	1697	DD/SP/1697/1	
518	John BARBY, Weaver of Stawley	1667	DD/SP/1667/59	
519	John BARKER of Dunster	1645	DD/SP/1645/67	
520	John BARKSDALE, Yeoman of Kilmersdon	1719	W.S.H.C., P2/B/1386	Inv. and will
521	John BARLOW, Yeoman of Wookey Hole, Wookey	1674	T.N.A., PROB 4/7904	Will also extant
522	Richard BARNALL, Husbandman of Dulverton	1699	DD/SP/1699/1	
523	Isaac BARNARD of Stoke St. Michael	1738	D/D/cta/B60	Ad.ac. and inv.
524	Nathaniel BARNARD, Gentleman of Fivehead	1684	T.N.A., PROB 4/5316	Admon
525	Jane BARNE, Widow of Oare	1677	DD/SP/1677/22	
526	John BARNE of Winsford	1645	DD/SP/1645/29	
527	John BARNE of Oare	1681	DD/SP/1681/68	
528	George BARNES senior of Taunton St. James	1675	DD/SP/1675/58	
529	Henry BARNES, Carpenter of East Quantoxhead	1684	DD/SP/1684/32	
530	Richard BARNES of North Cadbury	1608	D/D/cta/B99	Ad.ac.
531	Thomas BARNES of Backwell	1666	D/D/cta/B46	Ad.ac.
532	William BARNESBY of Durleigh	1693	DD/SP/1693/8	
533	David BARRATT, Yeoman of Congresbury	1690	T.N.A., PROB 4/9175	Will also extant
534	John BARRATT, Yeoman of Kewstoke	1683	T.N.A., PROB 4/16492	Will also extant

535	Christopher BARREL of West Bagborough	1627	D/D/ct/1/B/38	
536	Elizabeth BARRELL, Widow of Kingstone	1685	DD/SP/1685/79	
537	Martha BARRELL, Widow of Compton Dando	1736	D/D/Cti 4	
538	William BARRELL, Husbandman of West Bagborough	1669	DD/SP/1669/45	
539	Thomas BARRETT of Frome Selwood	1701	D/D/cta/B61	Ad.ac.
540	John BARRINGTON the elder of Lyng	1644	DD/SP/1644/52	
541	John BARRON of Cricket St. Thomas	1675	DD/SP/1675/51	
542	Christopher BARRY of Tickenham	1638	D/D/cta/B22	Ad.ac.
543	Gyles BARRY, Gentleman of Pitminster	1636	DD/SP/1636/27	
BARSTABEL see BASTABLE				
544	Majory BARSTABLE, Widow of Thorne St. Margaret	1693	DD/SP/1693/60	
545	James BARTHOLOMEW of Norton Fitzwarren	1714	DD/SP/1714/17	
546	William BARTHOLOMEW of Norton Fitzwarren	1694	DD/SP/1694/29	
547	William BARTHOLOMEW, Yeoman of Hillfarrance	1697	DD/SP/1697/2	
548	Bartholomew BARTLETT of Dodington	1687	DD/SP/1687/37	
549	Hannah BARTLETT, Widow of Adber, Trent	1767	T.N.A., PROB 31/1767/63	
	Note: With account; widow of Jonathan BARTLETT, yeoman			
550	John BARTLETT of Wick, Stogursey	1620	D/D/cta/B3	Ad.ac.; see *T.C.W.* and burial register for 1620
551	Nicholas BARTLETT of Dunster	1669	DD/SP/1669/36	
552	Thomas BARTLETT of Stolford, Stogursey	1645	DD/SP/1645/63	
553	Thomas BARTLETT, Weaver of Kilton	1693	DD/SP/1693/47	
554	Thomas BARTLEY of West Quantoxhead	1681	DD/SP/1681/96	
555	John BARTOLL of Crewkerne	1640	DD/SP/1640/26	
556	John BARTON, Innholder of Taunton St. Mary Magdalene	1679	DD/SP/1679/20	Reference to the Rose and Crown inn
557	James BARWICK of Minehead	1630s	DD/SP/1632/27	
	Note: Undated; appraised by Thomas HILL, Thomas WILSEN, William SAFFING and Edward DOBBINS			
558	Henry BASELEY, Husbandman of Halse	1685	DD/SP/1685/98	
559	Ann BASTABLE of North Petherton	1639	DD/SP/1639/23	
560	Francis BASTABLE of Lyng	1681	DD/SP/1681/39	
561	George BASTABLE of North Petherton	1675	DD/SP/1675/50	
562	Henry BASTABLE, Husbandman of North Petherton	1639	DD/SP/1639/24	
563	Jane BASTABLE, Widow of Lyng	1684	DD/SP/1684/35	

564	Ralph BASTABLE, Husbandman of North Petherton	1674	DD/SP/1674/29	
565	Ralph BASTABLE of North Petherton	1608	D/D/cta/B95	Ad.ac.
566	Walter BASTABLE of [no place]	1720	DD/SF/15/2/35	Formerly DD/SF/3888
567	Frances BASTONE, Widow of Minehead	1720	DD/SP/1720/23	
568	William BAT, Husbandman of North Petherton	1672	DD/SP/1672/26	
569	Elias BATCHELOR of Kilve	1687	DD/SP/1687/34	
570	Charles BATH, Yeoman of Wrington	1721	T.N.A., PROB 3/20/134	
571	John BATH of Whitmill, Wells St. Cuthbert	1757	T.N.A., PROB 31/1757/246	
572	Richard BATH of Wells	1638	G.A., D4018/F48	
573	Charles BATHE of Wrington	1721	T.N.A., PROB 5/3519	
574	John BATHE of Wrington	1662	D/D/cta/B42	Ad.ac.
575	Agnes BATT, Widow of Leigh on Mendip	1639	D/D/cta/B25	Ad.ac.
576	Alice BATT, Widow of Chedzoy	1639	DD/SP/1639/51	
577	Andrew BATT of North Petherton	1668	DD/SP/1668/61	
578	Elizabeth BATT, Widow of North Petherton	1683	DD/SP/1683/97	
579	James BATT of North Petherton	1638	DD/SP/1638/20	
580	Joseph BATT of Taunton St. Mary Magdalene	1719	DD/SP/442/67	Ad.ac.
581	Nicholas BATT of Lyng	1688	DD/SP/1688/15	
582	Pleasance BATT of North Petherton	1683	DD/SP/1683/93	
BATT see LANGLIE				
583	Alice BATTEN of St. Michaelchurch	1689	DD/SP/1689/11	
584	Henry BATTEN, Yeoman of St. Michaels (*sic*)	1686	T.N.A., PROB 4/2806	Will also extant
585	John BATTEN of North Petherton	1685	T.N.A., PROB 4/10621	Will also extant
586	Richard BATTEN the elder of Lyng	1685	DD/SP/1685/49	
587	William BATTEN of Portishead	1619	D/D/cta/B103	Ad.ac.
588	William BATTEN of Hatch Beauchamp	1669	DD/SP/1669/43	
589	Elizabeth BAULCH, Widow of Broadway	1634	DD/SP/1634/14	
BAULCH see BALCH				
590	Thomas BAUNTON the elder of West Camel	1622	D/D/cta/B9	Ad.ac.
591	Charles BAVE, Gentleman of Bath City	1695	T.N.A., PROB 4/8233	Will 1698
592	John BAWDON of Spaxton	1610	D/D/cta/B82	Ad.ac.
593	John BAWDON of Spaxton	1611	D/D/cta/B81	Ad.ac.
594	Giles BAWDRIP of North Petherton	1691	DD/SP/1691/89	

595	Thomas BAWDRIPP of Raddington	1674	T.N.A., PROB 4/19858	Admon. ex. 1675
596	Richard BAYLEE of Shepton Mallet	1630	D/D/cta/B59	Ad.ac.
597	Francis BAYLEY of North Petherton	1680	DD/SP/1680/1	
598	George BAYLEY, Bachelor of Wells	1811	T.N.A., PROB 31/1811/400	
599	Jane BAYLEY, Widow of Nailsea	1767	T.N.A., PROB 31/1767/919	
600	John BAYLEY of Dodington	1670	T.N.A., PROB 4/5270	Admon. ex. 1671
BAYLEY see BAILIE				
601	William BAYLIE, Tailor of Taunton	1666	DD/SP/1666/73	
BAYLIE see BAILIE, PYLE				
602	Edward BAYLY, Husbandman of Otterhampton	1669	DD/SP/1669/60	
603	Joane BAYLY of Stockland Bristol	1674	DD/SP/1674/12	
604	Thomas BAYLY, Cordwainer? of [no place]	1670	T.N.A., PROB 4/6570	Admon. ex. 1671
605	William BAYLY, Yeoman of Kilton	1673	DD/SP/1673/1	
606	Thomas BAYNARD of Wanstrow, Somerset and East Chickerel, Dorset	1684	T.N.A., PROB 4/11321	Will 1684. ex. 1687
607	John BAYNHAM, Clerk of Stogumber	1690	T.N.A., PROB 4/16847	Will 1689
608	Anne Catherina BEACH, Spinster of Bath	1804	T.N.A., PROB 31/1804/317	
609	George BEACHAM, Glover of [no place]	1715	T.N.A., PROB 4/22790	
610	George BEACHAM, Glover of Yeovil	1715	T.N.A., PROB 5/3193	
611	Edmund BEACON of Congresbury	1592	D/D/cta/B93	Ad.ac.
612	John BEADON of Stogumber	1634	DD/SP/1634/11	See *T.C.W.*
613	John BEADON, Tanner of Hillfarrance	1645	DD/SP/1645/4; A/BFP/1	Photocopy in T/PH/plr/1
614	Rebecca BEADON of Dunster	1778	T.N.A., PROB 31/1778/43	
615	Robert BEADON of Brushford	1688	T.N.A., PROB 4/454	Will 1688
616	William BEADON of Crowcombe	1634	DD/SP/1634/21	
BEADON see BELLRINGER				
617	Robert BEAGE senior, Husbandman of Selworthy	1681	DD/SP/1681/89	
618	Grace BEAGUE of Selworthy	1730	DD/SP/1730/18	
619	Joane BEAKE of Weston (*sic*)	1599	D/D/cta/B30	
	Note: Ad.ac.; possibly Westonzoyland based on parish register evidence			
620	Walter BEAKE of Curry Rivel	1640	DD/SP/1640/123	Proved by William BEAK natural son; damaged
BEAKS see VICERY				

621	Ambrose BEALE of Chewton Mendip	1625	D/D/cta/B15	Ad.ac.
622	Henry BEALE of Huntspill	1665	D/D/cta/B61a	Ad.ac.
623	Henry BEALE of Huntspill	1665	D/D/cta/V4	Ad.ac.
624	John BEALE, Doctor of Divinity of Yeovil	1683	T.N.A., PROB 4/18474	Admon, intestate
625	Thomas BEAMOND of Moorlinch	1590	D/D/cta/B83	Ad.ac.
BEARD see TRATT				
626	Benjamin BEATH, Gentleman of Upton Noble	1744	T.N.A., PROB 31/1744/363	
627	John BEATON of Wells St. Cuthbert	1612	D/D/cta/B37	Ad.ac.
628	Thomas BEATON of Mudford	1588	D/D/cta/B50	Ad.ac.
629	William BEATON, Tailor of Wheathill, Lovington	1588	D/D/cta/B54	Ad.ac.
630	William BEATON, Glover of Bridgwater	1635	DD/SP/1635/103	
631	Elizabeth BECK, Widow of Dinnington	1632	DD/SP/1632/24	
632	Robert BECKE, Husbandman of Kingstone	1684	DD/SP/1684/20	
633	John BEDFORD, Innholder of Bath City	1723	T.N.A., PROB 3/22/118	
634	John and Jane BEENEY of Clevedon	1590	D/D/cta/B84	Ad.ac.
635	Francis BEER, Maltster of Taunton St. Mary Magdalene	1695	DD/SP/1695/38	
636	Elizabeth BEERE, Widow of Taunton St. Mary Magdalene	1714	DD/SP/1714/9	
637	William BELL, Gentleman of London died at Bath	1723	T.N.A., PROB 3/22/201	
638	William BELL of Bath formerly of Highgate, Hornsey, Middlesex	1786	T.N.A., PROB 31/1786/623	
639	John BELLAMY of North Petherton	1696	DD/SP/1696/39	
640	Thomas BELLETT, Bachelor of Sampford Arundel and Bucklersbury, London	1825	T.N.A., PROB 31/1825/347	
641	John BELLRINGER of Chilton, Bridgwater	1680	DD/SP/1680/20	
642	Richard BELLRINGER of [no place]	1644	DD/SP/1644/54	
643	Margaret BELLRINGER alias BEADON of Thornfalcon	1665	DD/SP/1665/41	
644	Richard BENDYSHE, Esquire and Widower of Walcot	1826	T.N.A., PROB 31/1826/116	Ad.ac. 1826/686
645	Samuel BENIGOE, Vicar of Minehead	1693	DD/SP/1693/2	
646	Elizabeth BENNET of Claverton	1685	T.N.A., PROB 4/589	Will 1685
647	[missing] BENNETT of [no place]	1643	DD/SP/1643/51	Damaged
648	Agnes BENNETT, Widow of Chaffcombe	1641	DD/SP/1641/84	
649	Dorothy BENNETT, Widow of North Petherton	1649	DD/SP/1649/75	
650	Elizabeth BENNETT, Widow of Bath formerly of Middleton,			

	Cork, Ireland	1813	T.N.A., PROB 31/1813/63	
651	John BENNETT of Taunton St. James	1676	DD/SP/1676/27	
652	John BENNETT, Innholder of Minehead	1681	DD/SP/1681/16	
653	John BENNETT, Gentleman of Milverton	1688	DD/SP/1688/51	
654	John BENNETT, Cordwainer of Street	1736	D/D/Cti 5	
655	Margaret BENNETT of Stawley	1635	DD/SP/1635/121	
656	Marie BENNETT of Lyng	1644	DD/SP/1644/53	
657	Mary BENNETT, Spinster of Chard	1732	T.N.A., PROB 3/31/71	
658	Rachel BENNETT, Widow of Minehead	1682	DD/SP/1682/26	
659	Richard BENNETT of Norton Fitzwarren	1684	DD/SP/1684/126	
660	Roger BENNETT of Stawley	1690	DD/SP/1690/2	
661	Stephen BENNETT of Chelvey	1729	DD/S/ST/40	
662	Thomas BENNETT, Public Notary of Lyng	1631	DD/SP/1631/19	
663	Thomas BENNETT, Baker of Christchurch, Spitalfields, Middlesex formerly of Lyncombe and Widcombe, Somerset	1821	T.N.A., PROB 31/1821/736	
664	Daniel BERIMAN of Buckland St. Mary	1637	DD/SP/1637/61	
665	William BERIMAN of Minehead	1684	DD/SP/1684/154	
666	Jaell BERKELEY of Yarlington	1706	T.N.A., PROB 4/22270	Will 1706?
667	Edith BERKINS, Widow of Bridgwater	1678	DD/SP/1678/15	Relict of Richard BERKINS, fuller
668	Samuel BERRAT of Litton	1601	D/D/cta/B98	Ad.ac.
669	William BERRIDGE, Sergemaker of Taunton St. James	168–[?]	T.N.A., PROB 4/21981	Admon
670	Henry BERRIMAN of Dunster	1667	DD/SP/1667/75	
671	Henry BERRIMAN senior of Alcombe, Dunster	1671	DD/SP/1671/49	
672	Benjamin BERRY, Clerk of Pitminster	1677	T.N.A., PROB 4/18918	Admon
673	Elizabeth BERRY, Widow of Cothelstone	1666	DD/SP/1666/69	
674	William BERRYMAN, Yeoman of Carhampton	1668	T.N.A., PROB 4/13361	Will 1668
675	Richard BEST of Lopen	1677	DD/SP/1677/30	
676	Eleaner BETTEY, Widow of Barrington	1713	DD/SP/1713/7	
677	Jervice BETTIE of Barrington	1638	DD/SP/1638/4	
678	John BETTIE of Hatch Beauchamp	1634	DD/SP/1634/28	
679	Edmund BETTY, Cordwainer of Curry Rivel	1696	DD/SP/1696/12	
680	John BETTY, Blacksmith of Hatch Beauchamp	1737	DD/SP/1737/40	
681	John BEUES of [no place]	1651	DD/SP/1651/6	

682	Edward BEVIS of Bishops Hull	1639	D/D/cta/B24	Ad.ac.
683	Jonathon BEZANT of Milverton	1698	DD/SP/1698/2	
684	Francis BICKHAM of Bridgwater	1681	DD/SP/1681/100	
685	George BICKHAM of Bridgwater	1664	DD/SP/1664/9	
686	George BICKHAM of Spaxton	1667	DD/SP/1667/48	
687	George BICKHAM of Luccombe	1691	DD/SP/1691/85	
688	John BICKHAM, Husbandman of Ashbrittle	1672	DD/SP/1672/51	
689	John BICKHAM, Mason of Winsford	1679	DD/SP/1679/47	
690	Katherine BICKHAM, Spinster of Kingston	1665	DD/SP/1665/21	
691	Nicholas BICKHAM, Husbandman of West Bagborough	1666	DD/SP/1666/4	
692	Thomas BICKHAM of Langford Budville	1676	DD/SP/1676/32	
693	William BICKHAM, Merchant of Minehead	1662	DD/SP/1662/25	
694	Frances BICKHAM alias CREECH of Kingston	1685	DD/SP/1685/1	Wife of John
695	John BICKLEY of [no place]	1669	DD/SP/1669/44	
696	John BICKLEY of Rendy..., Oake	1765	DD/SAS/HV/38	
697	Ursula BICKLEY, Widow of Nynehead	1685	DD/SP/1685/14	
698	William BICKLEY of Heathfield	1684	DD/SP/1684/168	
699	Ann BICKNELL of Creech St. Michael	1690	DD/SP/1690/55	Wife of Henry, deceased
700	Avice BICKNELL, Widow of Isle Brewers	1639	DD/SP/1639/43	
701	Elizabeth BICKNELL, Widow of Bathealton	1646	DD/SP/1646/42	
702	John BICKNELL, Gentleman of Bradford	1828	T.N.A., PROB 37/674	
703	Joseph BICKNELL of Crewkerne	1741	DD/SP/1741/9	
704	Nicholas BICKNELL of Trent	1659	DD/BRC/24	
705	Sarah BICKNELL, Spinster of Bridgwater	1695	DD/DN/5/2/1	
706	[missing] BIDGOOD of Lyng	1646	DD/SP/1646/58	Proved by Maria BIDGOOD, Widow
707	Ann BIDGOOD of Lyng	1635	DD/SP/1635/46	
708	George BIDGOOD of [no place]	1677	T.N.A., PROB 4/5307	Admon
709	James BIDGOOD, Maltster of Taunton St. Mary Magdalene	1742	DD/SP/1742/15	
710	Robert BIDGOOD of Dunwear, Bridgwater	1636	DD/SP/1636/13	
711	William BIDGOOD, Yeoman of Pitminster	1646	DD/SP/1646/59	
712	David BIFFIN of Bridgwater	1669	DD/SP/1669/94	
713	Joane BIFFIN of Otterhampton	1648	DD/SP/1648/29	
714	John BIFFIN of Fiddington	1677	DD/SP/1677/51	

715	Richard BIGG of Wellow	1622	D/D/cta/B10	Ad.ac.
716	Joane BIGGOOD of North Petherton	1695	DD/SP/1695/8	
717	William BILLETT of Curland	1684	DD/SP/1684/144	
718	John BILLING of Chillington	1634	D/D/cta/B20	Ad.ac.
719	John BILLING of Chillington	1634	D/D/cta/B21	Ad.ac.
720	Richard BILLINGE, Carpenter of Buckland St. Mary	1637	DD/SP/1637/34	
721	Edith BINDON, Widow of Hillfarrance	1675	DD/SP/1675/48	
722	James BINDON, Yeoman of Dulverton	1746	DD/SP/1746/30	
723	Joane BINDON of Winsford	1665	DD/SP/1665/48	
724	Joseph BINDON of Taunton St. Mary Magdalene	1679	DD/SP/1679/30	
725	Robert BINDON of Hillfarrance	1697	DD/SP/1697/52	
BINDON see CROCKER, John (1675)				
726	Ludovic BINEHAN of Kilton	1692	DD/SP/1692/11	
727	George BINFORD, Mariner of Minehead	1673	DD/SP/1673/404 and 40b	
728	Walter BINFORD of Minehead	1677	DD/SP/1677/11	
729	William BINFORD, Merchant of Williton, St. Decumans	1678	T.N.A., PROB 5/5797	
730	Edith BINGHAM alias SWEETE, Widow of North Cheriton	1684	T.N.A., PROB 4/16148	Admon, intestate
731	Jeffrey BINNING, Widower of Bridgwater	1828	T.N.A., PROB 31/1828/1287	
732	Charles BIRD, Yeoman of Dundry	1683	T.N.A., PROB 4/6920	Will also extant
733	George BIRD of Chaffcombe	1684	T.N.A., PROB 4/20207	Will 1684
734	John BIRD of [no place]	1635	DD/SP/1635/123	
735	Richard BIRD, Free-mason of Bristol, Gloucestershire died at Bedminster	1681	T.N.A., PROB 4/448	Will 1681
736	Anthony BIRKING of [no place]	1645	DD/SP/1645/22	
737	William BISGOOD of Lyng	1680	DD/SP/1680/35	
738	Richard BISHEPE of Winsford	1661	DD/SP/1661/17	
739	James BISHOP of Ash Priors	1640	DD/SP/1640/20	
740	John BISHOP of Cutcombe	1670	DD/SP/1670/31	
741	John BISHOP of Wootton Courtenay	1720	DD/SP/1720/19	
742	John BISHOP of Wootton Courtenay	1720	DD/SP/442/70	Ad.ac.
743	William BISHOP, Husbandman of Donyatt	1737	DD/SP/1737/39	
BISHOP see HOLLAND				
744	Andrew BISHOPP of Cannington	1641	DD/SP/1641/16	See *T.C.W.*

745	Daniel BISHOPP, Innholder of Hinton St. George	1686	DD/SP/1686/5	
746	Robert BISHOPP, Husbandman of West Bagborough	1684	DD/SP/1684/75	
747	Gilbert BISSE, Yeoman of Frome Selwood	1674	T.N.A., PROB 4/10493	Will. ex. 1674
748	James BISSE, Gentleman of Wells	1623	D/D/cta/B5	Ad.ac.
749	James BISSE, Gentleman of Shepton Mallet	1690	T.N.A., PROB 4/1279	Will 1689
750	Katherine BISSE of Pensford St. Thomas, Publow	1623	D/D/cta/B11	Ad.ac.
751	William BITFORD, Yeoman of Stogursey	1607	DD/SAS/HV/42	
752	Elizabeth BLACKALLER, Widow of Chard	1800	T.N.A., PROB 31/1800/702	
753	John BLACKBOROWGH of Axbridge	1633	D/D/cta/B63	Ad.ac.
754	James BLACKER of Midsomer Norton	1707	D/D/cta/B62	Ad.ac.
755	Alexander BLACKFORD of Luccombe	1680	DD/SP/1680/15	
756	Richard BLACKFORD, Master Extraordinary in H.M. Court of Chancery of Dunster	1689	T.N.A., PROB 4/19563	Will also extant
BLACKFORD see STODDEN				
757	John BLACKMAN, Yeoman of Litton	1680	T.N.A., PROB 4/19796	Will also extant
758	Richard BLACKMARE of Heathfield	1637	DD/SP/1637/11	
759	Thomas BLACKMARE of Porlock	1642	DD/SP/1642/16	See *T.C.W.*
760	Edward BLACKMOORE, Sergemaker of West Buckland	1678	T.N.A., PROB 4/8300	Admon. ex. 1679
761	Agnis BLACKMORE of Porlock	1642	DD/SP/1642/15	
762	John BLACKMORE of Wootton Courtenay	1684	DD/SP/1684/41	
763	Hugh BLACKWILL, Husbandman of Dunster	1667	DD/SP/1667/50	
764	John BLACKWILL of Dunster	1646	DD/SP/1646/73	
765	Benedict BLAGDEN, Clerk of Hardington Mandeville	1676	T.N.A., PROB 4/10456	Will also extant
766	Nicholas BLAGDON of Clevedon	1584	D/D/cta/B53	Ad.ac.
767	Agnes BLAKE, Widow of Cutcombe	1639	DD/SP/1639/13	
768	Agnes BLAKE, Widow of Cutcombe	1645	DD/SP/1645/43	See *T.C.W.*
769	Agnes BLAKE of Halse	1646	DD/SP/1646/45	
770	Arthur BLAKE, Gentleman of Charlinch	1686	DD/SP/1686/22	
771	Barbarah BLAKE, Widow of Wembdon	1681	DD/SP/1681/115	
772	Edmond BLAKE, Husbandman of Durleigh	1680	DD/SP/1680/83	
773	Elizabeth BLAKE, Widow of Aisholt	1683	DD/SP/1683/83	
774	Elizabeth BLAKE, Widow of Alcombe, Dunster	1689	DD/SP/1689/12	
775	Francis BLAKE of Minehead	1720	DD/SP/1720/5	

776	George BLAKE of Selworthy	1744	DD/SP/1744/23	
777	John BLAKE of Minehead	1670	DD/SP/1670/61	
778	John BLAKE, Ironmonger of Langport Eastover, Langport	1677	T.N.A., PROB 4/6896	Will also extant
779	John BLAKE of Ash Priors	1731	DD/SP/1731/4	
780	Mary BLAKE, Spinster of Withycombe	1677	DD/SP/1677/27	
781	Nicholas BLAKE of Dunster	1646	DD/SP/1646/77	
782	Robert BLAKE of Cannington	1679	DD/SP/1679/40	
783	Robert BLAKE of Pitminster	1711	DD/CT/18	
784	Robert BLAKE of Pitminster	1711	DD/CT/63	
785	Robert BLAKE, Clothier of Minehead	1722	T.N.A., PROB 3/21/65	
786	Thomas BLAKE of Trull	1712	DD/CT/63	
787	William BLAKE, Yeoman of Spaxton	1664	DD/SP/1664/32	
788	William BLAKE of Cannington	1680	DD/SP/1680/91	
789	Elianore BLAKE alias DOLLINGE of Bridgwater	1680	DD/SP/1680/103	
790	William BLANCHARD of Batheaston	1678	DD/X/KEN/5	
791	William BLANCHARD, Esquire of Katherine Court, St. Catherine	1686	T.N.A., PROB 4/20229	Will. ex. 1687
792	Charles BLANCHFLOWER, Gentleman of Goathurst	1692	DD/SP/1692/29	
793	Thomas BLANCHFLOWER, Clerk of Goathurst	1664	DD/SP/1664/40	
794	John BLANDON of Chewton Mendip	1594	D/D/cta/B91	Ad.ac.
795	Julian BLANNING, Widow of Stoke St. Michael	1664	D/D/cta/B45	Ad.ac.
796	Mathias BLANNING of Compton Martin	1741	D/D/Cti 6	
797	[missing] BLECHLIE of Bath ?	n.d.	D/D/cta/B29	Ad.ac.
798	Thomas BLENMAN senior of Croscombe	1690	T.N.A., PROB 4/3839	Will 1691. ex. 1692
799	William BLEWET, Gentleman of Thorne St. Margaret	1582	DD/SF/11/1/19	Formerly DD/SF/1049
800	Mary BLEWETT, Widow of Thorne St. Margaret	1593	DD/SF/11/1/23	Formerly DD/SF/1052
801	Tristram BLEWIT of Stoke Pero	1675	DD/SP/1675/24	
802	William BLIASETT of Curry Rivel	1684	DD/SP/1684/140	
803	Ames BLINMAN, Gentleman of Wilton	1688	DD/SP/1688/54	
804	Ames BLINMAN of Wilton	1689	T.N.A., PROB 4/19647	Will 1688
805	Amos BLINMAN the elder, Gentleman of Wilton	1688	T.N.A., PROB 4/8526	
	Note: Will 1688. ex. 1689, goods left unadministered by Amos BLINMAN the younger, his son and executor also deceased			
806	Nathaniel BLINMAN, Doctor of Physic of Bridgwater	1684	DD/SP/1684/100	

807	Samuel BLINMAN of Whalley, Chew Stoke	1693	DD/OB/93	
808	Sarah BLINMAN of Durleigh	1702	DD/SP/442/43	Ad.ac.
809	Sarah BLINMAN of Durleigh	1702	DD/SP/442/45	Ad.ac.
810	Walter BLINMAN of Chew Stoke	1639	D/D/ct/1/B/100	
811	George BLYNMAN of Williton, St. Decumans	1666	DD/L/2/35/2	
812	[Female] BOBBETT of Pawlett	1694	DD/SP/1694/6	Part missing, mention of debts at Pawlett
813	Edmund BOBBETT, Merchant of Creech St. Michael	1693	T.N.A., PROB 4/15881	Will also extant
814	John BOBBETT of Creech St. Michael	1684	T.N.A., PROB 4/22086	Admon. ex. 1686
815	John BOBBETT, Shoemaker of North Newton, North Petherton	1688	DD/SP/1688/31	
816	Margaret BOBBETT, Widow of North Petherton	1716	DD/SP/1716/55	
817	Mathew BOBBETT of Dunwear, Bridgwater	1638	DD/SP/1638/51	
818	Alexander BODMAN, Skinner of Minehead	1713	DD/SP/1713/35	
819	John BODMAN of Weston-super-Mare	1584	D/D/cta/B94	Ad.ac.
820	Edith BODY of Glastonbury	1641	D/D/cta/B51	Ad.ac.
821	Annie BOND, Widow of Chedzoy	1645	DD/SP/1645/23	
822	Edith BOND, Widow of Chard	1680	T.N.A., PROB 4/10449	Admon. ex. 1681
823	Frances BOND, Widow of Pitminster	1693	T.N.A., PROB 4/9622	Will also extant
824	George BOND, Tanner of Dunster	1683	DD/SP/1683/80	
825	James BOND, Silk Thrower of Charlton, Shepton Mallet	1837	T.N.A., PROB 31/1837/212	
826	Jane BOND of Taunton St. Mary Magdalene	1697	DD/SP/1697/8	
827	Joel BOND of East Brent	1635	D/D/cta/B28	Ad.ac.
828	John BOND of Heathfield	1736	DD/SP/1736/30	
829	Martha BOND of East Brent	1625	D/D/cta/B13	Ad.ac.
830	Robert BOND of [no place]	1692	DD/SP/1692/5	
831	Robert BOND of North Petherton	1695	DD/SP/1695/21	
832	Sarah BOND, Widow of Taunton	1813	T.N.A., PROB 31/1813/145	
833	Thomas BOND of Taunton St. Mary Magdalene	1684	DD/SP/1684/55	
834	Thomas BOND of Chedzoy	1690	DD/SP/1690/9	
835	Nicholas BONFEILD of Combe St. Nicholas	1671	T.N.A., PROB 4/17515	Admon
836	Richard BONFIELD, Yeoman of Hardington Mandeville	1686	T.N.A., PROB 4/8000	Will also extant
837	Thomasine BONING (BONNING), Widow of Little Puckington, Barrington	1680	DD/SP/1680/62	

838	William BONNER of Wayford	1635	D/D/cta/B17	Ad.ac.
839	George BONNING of Barrington	1687	DD/SP/1687/57	
840	Thomas BONNING, Weaver of Little Puckington, Barrington	1696	DD/SP/1696/24	
841	Thomas BONNING, Cordwainer of Stocklinch Ottersey	1696	DD/SP/1696/8	With ages and names of his children
842	Robert BOOBIER, Husbandman of Brompton Ralph	1672	DD/SP/1672/16	
843	John BOOBY of Hillfarrance	1697	DD/SP/1697/39	
844	David BOODE, Husbandman of Brompton Regis	1646	DD/SP/1646/8	
845	Benjamin BOONE, Glover of Yeovil	1718	T.N.A., PROB 3/17/81	
846	Edward BOONE, Glover of Yeovil	1674	T.N.A., PROB 4/6947	Will also extant
847	John BOONE the elder, Fellmonger of North Petherton	1676	T.N.A., PROB 4/12969	Will also extant
848	Richard BOONE, Feltmaker of South Petherton	1677	DD/SP/1677/18	
849	Richard BOONE of North Petherton	1680	DD/SP/1680/7	
850	Robert BORNE, Husbandman of Langford Budville	1664	DD/SP/1664/16	
851	Thomas BORROWE of Curry Rivel	1836, 1839	DD/SW/Box 2	
852	Robert BOTELER of Old Cleeve	1605	DD/WO/56/3	
853	Edward BOUCHER of Wiveliscombe	1774	T.N.A., PROB 31/1774/486	
854	Edward BOUCHER, Yeoman of Whitefield, Wiveliscombe	1790	T.N.A., PROB 31/1790/507	
855	William BOUCHER of East Harptree	1624	D/D/cta/B6	Ad.ac.
856	John BOULTING, Yeoman of East Theale, Wedmore	1683	T.N.A., PROB 4/20190	Will also extant
857	Joseph BOUN, Sailor of Bridgwater	1730	DD/SP/1730/9	
858	James BOURCHIER of Milverton	1730	DD/SP/1730/8	
859	John BOURNE, Rector of Charlinch	1681	DD/SP/1681/1	
860	Roger BOURNE of North Petherton	1670	DD/SP/1670/20	Son of Gilbert, Gentleman
861	John BOVETT of Hatch Beauchamp	1684	DD/SP/1684/122	
862	Phillipp BOVETT of Taunton St. Mary Magdalene	1683	DD/SP/1683/40	
863	John BOWBEARE of Buckland St. Mary	1636	DD/SP/1636/54	See *T.C.W.*
864	George BOWDEN of Stogumber	1640	DD/SP/1640/45	
865	Judith BOWDEN, Spinster of Exton	1640	DD/SP/1640/67	
866	William BOWDEN, Fuller of Minehead	1725	DD/SP/1725/23	
867	Robert BOWDIDGE, Husbandman of Misterton	1640	DD/SP/1640/27	
868	Henry BOWDON of Luccombe	1693	DD/SP/1693/40	
869	John BOWEMAN of Lympsham	1611	D/D/cta/B34	Ad.ac.

870	Adrian BOWER, Gentleman of Wraxall	1685	*S.D.N.Q.* vol.26 p.232	
871	Adrian BOWER of Chapel Allerton	1685	T.N.A., PROB 4/25593	Admon. ex. 1686?
872	Griffis BOWER of North Petherton	1684	DD/SP/1684/15	
873	Nicholas BOWER of Ansford	1632	D/D/cta/B32	Ad.ac.
874	William BOWER of Steart, Babcary	1724	T.N.A., PROB 3/23/157	
875	Robert BOWERING of Upton	1667	T.N.A., PROB 4/6843	Will also extant
876	Alexander BOWLES, Grocer of Bridgwater	1690	T.N.A., PROB 4/19974	Will 1690
877	John BOWLTING of Easton, Wells	1660	DD/SAS/FA/161/23	
878	William BOWRIDGE of Chard	1640	D/D/cta/B26	Ad.ac.
879	John BOWRINGE, Husbandman of Trull	1667	DD/SP/1667/25	
880	William BOWRINGE of Tolland	1732	DD/SP/1732/3	
881	John BOWYER, Gentleman of Idstock, Cannington	1669	DD/SP/1669/66	
882	Sarah BOWYER of Idstock, Chilton Trinity	1671	DD/SP/1671/27	Wife of Edmund, Esquire
883	Joyce BOYCE of Staple Fitzpaine	1645	DD/SP/1645/48	
884	William BOYCE of Stawell	1611	D/D/cta/B76	Ad.ac.
885	Abraham BOYER of Glastonbury St. John	1666	D/D/cta/B47	Ad.ac.
886	William BOYS of [Blank] and New Inn, Middlesex	1666	T.N.A., PROB 4/13725	Will 1666
887	Robert BOYSE, Gentleman of Staple Fitzpaine	1645	DD/SP/1645/68	
888	Robert BOYSE, Gentleman of Staple Fitzpaine	1669	DD/SP/1669/102	
889	Robert BOYSE, Gentleman of Staple Fitzpaine	1669	DD/SP/1669/87	
890	William BRABHAN of North Petherton	1588	D/D/cta/B78	Ad.ac.
891	Agnes BRADFORD, Widow of Winsford	1665	DD/SP/1665/5	
892	Edward BRADFORD of Winsford	1673	DD/SP/1673/11	
893	John BRADFORD of Clevedon	1595	D/D/cta/B89	Ad.ac.
894	John BRADFORD of Clevedon	1663	D/D/cta/B44	Ad.ac.
895	William BRADFORD of Winsford	1683	DD/SP/1683/67	
896	John BRADSHAWE of Marston Bigot	1611	D/D/cta/B80	Ad.ac.
897	Margaret BRAGG of Seaborough	1674	T.N.A., PROB 4/9826	Will also extant
898	Roger BRAGG of Chillington	1669	DD/SP/1669/14	
899	Walter BRAGG of Uphill	1593	D/D/cta/B92	Ad.ac.
900	Walter BRAGG of Hewish, Crewkerne	1680	DD/SP/1680/50	
901	John BRAINE of Hinton St. George	1681	DD/SP/1681/11	
902	Arthur BRAMLEY of Minehead	1686	DD/SP/1686/18	

903	Bartholomew BRANCE, Husbandman of Stogursey	1635	DD/SP/1635/37	
904	John BRANGWELL, Clothier of North Petherton	1681	T.N.A., PROB 4/13061	Will also extant
905	John BRAYLEY, Tailor of Brushford	1700	DD/SP/1700/1	
906	Thomas BRAYLEY, Tailor of Brushford	1728	DD/SP/1728/39	
907	William BRAYME, Yeoman of Furland, Crewkerne	1637	DD/SP/1637/9	
908	Richard BRAYNE, Clerk of Seaborough	1677	T.N.A., PROB 4/10547	Will. ex. 1678
909	Bartholomew BREMBLE of Wells St. Cuthbert	1619	D/D/cta/B104	Ad.ac.
910	Sir Alexander BRETT of Somerset	1611	D.H.C., 1148MaDD/24/1	
911	Joseph BRETT of Milborne Port	1756	DD/YB/89	
912	Richard BRETT, Bachelor of Whitestaunton died at Ipswich, Suffolk	1673	T.N.A., PROB 4/12519	Admon
BRETT see BURT				
913	Anne BREWER, Widow of Lyng	1685	DD/SP/1685/75	
914	Edward BREWER, Yeoman of Kingston	1645	DD/SP/1645/5	See *T.C.W.*
915	Elizabeth BREWER of Skilgate	1646	DD/SP/1646/85	
916	James BREWER of Hawkridge	1635	DD/SP/1635/115	
917	Johane BREWER, Widow of Clatworthy	1634	DD/SP/1634/12	
918	John BREWER, Yeoman of Brompton Ralph	1685	DD/SP/1685/82	
919	Thomas BREWER of Bedminster	1644	D/D/cta/B39	Ad.ac.
920	William BREWER of Stogursey	1729	DD/SP/1729/57	
921	Robert BREWER alias BRIFFORD of Langford Budville	1678	DD/SP/1678/11	
922	Edward BRIANT of Minehead	1637	DD/SP/1637/13	
923	Edward BRIANT, King's Service of Bridgwater	1697	DD/SP/1697/29	
924	Elizabeth BRIANT, Widow of Dunster	1676	DD/SP/1676/50	
925	Francis BRIANT of Staplegrove	1691	DD/SP/1691/62	
926	William BRIANT of Enmore	1612	D/D/cta/B35	Ad.ac.
BRIANT see BRYANT				
927	George BRICE, Rector of Clutton	1692	T.N.A., PROB 4/15613	Will 1697
928	Judith BRICE, Widow of Bradford	1686	DD/SP/1686/48	
929	Margaret BRICE, Widow of Cannington	1640	DD/SP/1640/32	See *T.C.W.*
930	Susanna BRICE, Widow of West Lydford	1669	T.N.A., PROB 4/12283	Will also extant
931	Thomas BRICE of Stogursey	1674	DD/SP/1674/25	
932	Thomas BRICE of Baltonsborough	1739	D/D/Cti 7	

933	Thomas BRICE, Clerk of Duffryn, Aberdare, Glamorgan died at Bath	1790	T.N.A., PROB 31/1790/841	
934	Worthington BRICE of Dinnington	1723	DD/SP/1723/56	
935	Robert BRICKTHOUGHT of Taunton	1677	DD/SP/1677/12	
936	John BRIDELL of Crewkerne	1675	DD/SP/1675/40	
937	George BRIDGE of Creech St. Michael	1669	DD/SP/1669/71	
938	Joane BRIDGE, Widow of Chedzoy	1635	DD/SP/1635/32	
939	William BRIDGE of Creech St. Michael	1677	DD/SP/1677/78	
940	Anstice BRIDGEMAN, Widow of Wellington	1670	T.N.A., PROB 4/473	Will 1670
941	[missing] BRIDGES of [no place]	1696	DD/SP/1696/18	Mentions shop contents, cloth etc.
942	Ann BRIDGES, Widow of Chilton (*sic*)	1684	DD/SP/1684/2	
943	Lady Elizabeth BRIDGES, Widow of Keynsham	1627	D/D/cta/B4	Ad.ac.
944	Gregory BRIDGES of Rode	1588	D/D/cta/B77	Ad.ac.
945	Harry BRIDGES, Esquire of Keynsham	1729	T.N.A., PROB 3/28/105	
946	Harry BRIDGES, Esquire of Keynsham	1729	T.N.A., PROB 31/1729/445	
947	Jane BRIDGES of Leigh on Mendip	1695	T.N.A., PROB 4/16577	Will. ex. 1695
BRIFFORD see BREWER, BRISHFFORD				
948	John BRIGHT, Tanner of Enmore	1683	DD/SP/1683/1	
949	William BRIGHT of Broadway	1667	DD/SP/1667/90	
950	Edmond BRIMPTON, Clothier of Minehead	1679	T.N.A., PROB 4/6886	Will also extant
951	Johane BRIMSMEADE, Widow of Taunton	1641	DD/SP/1641/75	See *T.C.W.*
952	William BRISCOE of Bathford	1775	DD/BR/cc/2	
953	Robert BRISHFFORD alias HODGE, Sergeweaver of Moorland, North Petherton	1670	DD/SP/1670/26	
954	John BRISTOW of Weston [near Bath] Note: Ad.ac.; buried at Weston (near Bath) in 1625	1626	D/D/cta/B16	
955	Joseph BRISTTOW of Winsford	1664	DD/SP/1664/11	
956	Nicholas BRITTEN of North Stoke	1599	D/D/cta/B41	Ad.ac.
957	Joan BROAD of Cannington	1671	DD/SP/1671/33	
958	John BROAD of Bathampton	1619	D/D/cta/B102	Ad.ac.
959	John BROAD of Compton Dando	1724	T.N.A., PROB 3/23/73	
960	Samuel BROAD of Compton Dando	*c*.1729	D/D/cta/B88	Ad.ac.
961	James BROCK of North Petherton	1700	DD/SP/1700/19	

962	Thomas BROCK, Mason of West Monkton	1697	DD/SP/1697/37	
963	Samuel BRODERIP of Wyke Champflower, Bruton died in Ireland	1708	DD/SE/83	
964	William BRODRIPPE of Berrow	1612	D/D/cta/B36	Ad.ac.
965	Walter BROKE, Miller of Minehead	1671	DD/SP/1671/14	
966	Richard BROKEMAN, Yeoman of Stanton Prior, Marksbury	1630	D/D/ct/1/B/149	
967	Ann BROME of Abbots Leigh	1704	B.A., 1704/7	
968	John BROME, Yeoman of Isle Abbotts	1696	DD/SP/1696/26	
969	Philip BROME of Isle Abbotts	1731	DD/SP/1731/20	
970	Robert BROME, Husbandman of Curry Mallet	1593	D/D/cta/B87	Ad.ac.
BROME see BROOME				
971	Thomas BROOK of Ilton	1538	T.N.A., PROB 2/210	
972	William BROOK alias HODGES of Wells	1726	D/D/cta/B65	Ad.ac.
973	George BROOKE, Yeoman of Sampford Arundel	1636	DD/SP/1636/32	
974	Henry BROOKE of Minehead	1665	DD/SP/1665/35	
975	John BROOKE of Bishops Hull	1668	DD/SP/1668/15	
976	John BROOKE of Minehead	1670	DD/SP/1670/37	
977	Mary BROOKE of Bridgwater	1669	DD/SP/1669/1	
978	Thomas BROOKE of Barrington	1687	DD/SP/1687/24	
979	Charles BROOKEMAN of Kingston Seymour	1623	D/D/cta/B7	Ad.ac.
980	Edward BROOKES, Yeoman of West Weston alias Weston-super-Mare	1688	T.N.A., PROB 4/6460	Will 1688. ex. 1689
981	Henry BROOME of Lovington	1634	D/D/cta/B19	Ad.ac.
982	Hugh BROOME, Seaman of Broadway	1684	DD/SP/1684/108	
983	Richard BROOME, Shipwright of Abbots Leigh	1669	B.A., 1659/1	
984	Agnes BROUNSET of Heathfield	1636	DD/SP/1636/55	
985	William BROUSFORD of Bradford	1638	DD/SP/1638/56	
986	Benjamin F.T. BROWN of Norwood, Staplegrove	1924	DD/X/SAL/8	
987	Charles Collett BROWN, Merchant of Bristol	1835	DD/BR/hk/9	
988	Hannah BROWN, Spinster of West Lydford	1826	T.N.A., PROB 31/1826/1018	
989	Josslin BROWN of Wellington	1772	T.N.A., PROB 31/1772/95	
990	Richard BROWN, Cordwainer of Compton Dando	1735	D/D/Cti 8	
991	Samuel BROWN of Taunton	1762	T.N.A., PROB 31/1762/342	With ad.ac.

992	William BROWN, Yeoman of Wedmore	1679	T.N.A., PROB 4/10935	Will also extant
993	Daniel BROWNE of [no place]	1678	DD/SP/1678/37	
994	Elizabeth BROWNE, Spinster of Taunton St. James	1679	DD/SP/1679/50	
995	George BROWNE, Esquire of Wilton	1679	DD/SP/1679/48	
996	Grace BROWNE of Wrington	1697	D/D/cta/B68	Ad.ac.
997	James BROWNE, Yeoman of Meare	1683	T.N.A., PROB 4/8171	Will also extant
998	Joane BROWNE of Barrington	1635	DD/SP/1635/23	
999	Joane BROWNE, Widow of Borrow, Lyng	1670	DD/SP/1670/87	
1000	John BROWNE of Wellington	1623	D/D/cta/B8	Ad.ac.
1001	John BROWNE of Whatley	1705	D/D/cta/B67	Ad.ac.
1002	John BROWNE, Bachelor and Bastard of Shepton Mallet	1831	T.N.A., PROB 31/1831/1787	
1003	Katherine BROWNE of Charlton Mackrell	1712	D/D/cta/B66	Ad.ac.
1004	Mary BROWNE of Hinton St. George	1679	DD/SP/1679/32	
1005	Richard BROWNE of [no place]	1645	DD/SP/1645/17	
1006	Robert BROWNE of West Camel	1707/8	D/D/cta/R19	Ad.ac.
1007	Simon BROWNE of Shepton Mallet	1682	D/D/cta/B69	Ad.ac.
1008	Thomas BROWNE junior of Milverton	1681	DD/SP/1681/77	
1009	William BROWNE of Wells St. Cuthbert	1600	D/D/cta/B100	Ad.ac.
1010	Richard BROWNING, Vicar of Isle Abbotts	1686	DD/SP/1686/38	
1011	Thomas BROWNING of Alford	1594	D/D/cta/B90	Ad.ac.
1012	Peter BROWNINGE of East Quantoxhead	1667	DD/SP/1667/91	
1013	Thomas BROWNSELL, Husbandman of Barrington	1688	DD/SP/1688/8	
1014	Robert BROWNSEY, Weaver of Whitestaunton	1668	DD/SP/1668/33	
1015	Christopher BROWNSFORD of Bradford	1667	DD/SP/1667/37	
1016	George BROWNSFORD of Brompton Regis	1671	DD/SP/1671/43	
1017	Roger BROWNSWELL of Stocklinch Magdalene	1590	D/D/cta/B85	Ad.ac.
1018	Joseph BROWS of Minehead	1692	DD/SP/1692/21	
1019	Nicholas BROWSE, Clerk of Minehead	1635	DD/SP/1635/97	
1020	Gabriell BRUAR of West Quantoxhead	1640	DD/SP/1640/68	
1021	John BRUAR of [no place]	1645	D/D/cta/B	Ad.ac.
BRUAR see BREWER				
1022	William BRUER, Yeoman of Stoke St. Gregory	1649	DD/SP/1649/81	
BRUER see BREWER				

1023	Jeremiah BRUFORD of Cheddon Fitzpaine	1731	DD/SP/1731/18	
1024	Joan BRUFORD of Halse	1698	DD/SP/1698/19	Legacies left to the CORNISH family
1025	John BRUFORD of Bradford on Tone	1732	DD/SP/1732/13	
1026	Robert BRUFORD of Halse	1685	DD/SP/1685/57	
1027	Mary BRUGES, Singlewoman of Lydford	1718	T.N.A., PROB 3/17/113	
1028	Daniel BRUMAN of Stogumber	1693	DD/SP/1693/33	
1029	Robert BRUMHAM, Husbandman of Withypool	1641	DD/SP/1641/26	
1030	Anstice BRYANT, Widow of Dulverton	1678	DD/SP/1678/60	
1031	Anstice BRYANT of Minehead	1689	DD/SP/1689/28	
1032	Cristian BRYANT, Widow of Minehead	1648	DD/SP/1648/49	
1033	Emanuell BRYANT of Norton Fitzwarren	1684	DD/SP/1684/147	
1034	Francis BRYANT of Thurlbear	1696	DD/SP/1696/5	
1035	Gregory BRYANT of Huish Champflower	1728	DD/SP/1728/37	
1036	Henry BRYANT of Durston	1693	DD/SP/1693/4	
1037	Hugh BRYANT of Taunton St. Mary Magdalene	1676	T.N.A., PROB 4/15382	Will also extant
1038	James BRYANT, Husbandman of Treborough	1668	DD/SP/1668/63	
1039	Jane BRYANT, Widow of Wootton Courtenay	1688	DD/SP/1688/53	
1040	John BRYANT, Yeoman of Pitminster	1645	DD/SP/1645/57	
1041	John BRYANT, Husbandman of Brompton Ralph	1665	DD/SP/1665/57	Son of Mary
1042	John BRYANT of Pitminster	1684	DD/SP/1684/116	
1043	John BRYANT, Clerk of Timsbury	1688	T.N.A., PROB 4/17610	Admon
1044	John BRYANT, Husbandman of Chipstable	1713	DD/SP/1713/5	
1045	Lawrence BRYANT, Butcher of Bridgwater	1737	DD/SP/1737/41	
1046	Mary BRYANT of Halse	1675	DD/SP/1675/55	
1047	Robert BRYANT of Thurlbear	1674	DD/SP/1674/68	
1048	Robert BRYANT of Bicknoller	1685	DD/SP/1685/89	
	Note: Mentions his widow Margaret; appraisers Symon HYDON and George SULLY of Bicknoller			
1049	Robert Jeane BRYANT, Esquire of Dunster	1805	T.N.A., PROB 31/1805/747	
1050	Thomas BRYANT, Husbandman of Heathfield	1636	DD/SP/1636/50	See *T.C.W.*
1051	Thomas BRYANT of Minehead	1681	DD/SP/1681/71	
1052	Walter BRYANT of Withypool	1723	DD/SP/442/77	Ad.ac.
1053	William BRYANT of Bridgwater	1737	DD/SP/1737/38	
1054	Wilmot BRYANT of Timberscombe	1683	T.N.A., PROB 4/10540	Will. ex. 1683

1055	James BRYENT of Stogursey	1670	DD/SP/1670/48	
1056	James BRYNE, Paymaster H.M. 17th Regiment of Light Dragoons of Bath, died at Montivedeo, Uruguay	1808	T.N.A., PROB 31/1808/384	
1057	John BRYNE, Yeoman of Crewkerne	1674	DD/SP/1674/61	
1058	John BUCHER, Husbandman of Brompton Regis	1691	DD/SP/1691/45	
1059	Elizabeth BUCK, Widow of Abbots Leigh	1628	B.A., 1628/15	Will also extant
1060	Edward BUCKE, Husbandman of Cannington	1634	DD/SP/1634/6	
1061	John BUCKE of Compton Martin	1587	D/D/cta/B105	Ad.ac.
1062	Thomas BUCKERELL of Dowlish Wake	1664	DD/SP/1664/35	
1063	Francis BUCKERIDGE of Marlborough, Wiltshire died at Temple Combe	1760	T.N.A., PROB 3/59/12	
BUCKINGE see DOUDENY				
1064	Charles BUCKLAND, Gentleman of West Harptree	1699	T.N.A., PROB 4/16177	Will also extant
1065	Francis BUCKLAND of Merriott	1720	DD/SP/1720/22	
1066	William BUCKLE, Poulterer of Bath	1733	T.N.A., PROB 31/1733/748	With commissioner's account
1067	Jane BUCKLER, Widow of Great Chew, Chew Magna	1733	T.N.A., PROB 3/32/154	
1068	Robert BUCKMAN of East Brent	1608	D/D/cta/B96	Ad.ac.
1069	[missing] BUCKNALL of Bath formerly of Walcot	1806	D.H.C., 282M/test 9	
1070	[missing] BUCKNOLE of East Chard, Chard	1774	T.N.A., PROB 31/1774/279	
1071	William BUCKNOLE, Widower of South Chard, Chard	1774	T.N.A., PROB 31/1774/188	
1072	John BUCKRELL, Yeoman of Seavington St. Michael	1640	DD/SP/1640/138	
1073	Thomas BUCKRELL, Husbandman of Compton Durville, South Petherton	1646	DD/SP/1646/17	
1074	John BUDD, Carpenter of Dulverton	1721	DD/SP/1721/12	
1075	[missing] BUDGE of [no place]	1646	DD/SP/1646/31	Proved by William BUDG, natural son
1076	Thomas BUDGIN of Barwick	1638	D/D/cta/B18	Ad.ac.
1077	Ellinor BULFORD, Widow of Curland, Curry Mallet	1635	DD/SP/1635/127	
1078	John BULGIN of East Brent	1606	D/D/cta/B101	Ad.ac.
1079	Ann BULL of Cossington	n.d.	D/P/coss/13/10/1	
1080	Clement BULL, Cardmaker of Frome Selwood	1693	T.N.A., PROB 4/6913	Will also extant
1081	Henry BULL of Wells?	1692	DD/SG/4	
1082	Joanna BULL of Shapwick Note: See T.N.A., PROB 11/581 for inv. and declaration	1721	T.N.A., PROB 5/3297	

1083	John BULL of Trull	1577	D/D/cta/B56	Ad.ac.
1084	John BULL of Coombe, Crewkerne	1705	T.N.A., PROB 4/22511	Will also extant
1085	Robert BULL, Blacksmith of Taunton St. Mary Magdalene	1670	DD/SP/1670/36	
BULL see MEVERICK				
1086	Andrew BULLER, Cordwainer of Stogumber	1699	DD/SP/1699/11	
1087	Richard BULLER, Yeoman of Nettlecombe	1721	DD/SP/1721/30	
1088	George BULLIN of Bishops Hull	1664	DD/SP/1664/24	
1089	William BULLIN of Isle Abbotts	1691	DD/SP/1691/38	
1090	John BULLOCK, Esquire of Clevedon	1738	T.N.A., PROB 3/37/29	Goods at Wraxall, Kingston Seymour
1091	Richard BULLOCK, Yeoman of Cleeve, Yatton	1669	T.N.A., PROB 4/6439	Will also extant
1092	Thomas BULLOCK of Faukland, Hemington	1805	T.N.A., PROB 31/1805/694	
1093	William BULLOCK, Gentleman of Backwell	1687	T.N.A., PROB 4/11890	Will 1687
1094	Henry BULPAN of North Petherton	1672	DD/SP/1672/27	Incomplete
1095	John BULPAN of Woolavington	1626	D/D/cta/B31	Ad.ac.
1096	William BULPAN, Husbandman of North Petherton	1678	DD/SP/1678/43	
1097	Alexander BULPIN of Huntworthy, North Petherton	1696	DD/SP/1696/42	
1098	Hannah BULT of West Monkton	1672	DD/SP/1672/20	
1099	James BULT of Kingston St. Mary	1672	T.N.A., PROB 5/5032–3	
1100	James BULT of Kingston St. Mary	1672	T.N.A., PROB 5/5683	
1101	James BULT of Kingston	1675	T.N.A., PROB 4/11875	Will also extant
1102	John BULT of Trull	1698	DD/SP/1698/17	
1103	Thomas BULT of Kingston	1666	DD/SP/1666/46	
1104	Thomas BULT of Nailsborne, Kingston St. Mary	1690	DD/SP/1690/59	
1105	Robert BULTE of Taunton St. Mary Magdalene	1641	DD/SP/1641/1	
1106	Robert BULTE of Kingston	1672	DD/SP/1672/25	
1107	John BUNCKOMBE of Goathurst died at St. Andrews, Holborn	1681	T.N.A., PROB 4/8535	Will also extant
1108	John BUNCOMBE of West Monkton	1698	DD/SP/1698/7	
1109	Richard BUNCOMBE of Bishops Hull	1683	DD/SP/1683/84	Mentions Sarah his widow
1110	Richard BUNCOMBE of Bishops Hull	*c.*1684	D/P/b.hl/13/2/10	Inv. and ad.ac.
1111	William BUNCOMBE, Yeoman of West Monkton	1674	DD/SP/1674/18	
1112	William BUNCOMBE of Trull	1684	DD/SP/1684/135	
1113	Robert BUNKOM of Creech St. Michael	1671	DD/SP/1671/44	
1114	Leonard BUNLER of Cheddon Fitzpaine	1728	DD/SP/1728/40	

1115	Reverend Abel BUNNING, Rector of Aller of Aller	1720	T.N.A., PROB 3/19/41	
1116	Walter BURCHER of Brompton Ralph	1664	DD/SP/1664/27	
1117	William BURCHOLL of Chelvey	1599	D/D/cta/W67	Ad.ac.
1118	Richard BURCOMBE junior of Cannington	1667	DD/SP/1667/49	
1119	Barnard BURD of West Monkton	1666	DD/SP/1666/42	
1120	Cateryne BURD, Widow of Milverton	1640	DD/SP/1640/112	
1121	Edith BURD of Kittisford	1642	DD/SP/1642/33	
1122	Henry BURD of West Quantoxhead	1680	D/D/cta/B70	Ad.ac.
1123	John BURD, Yeoman of Milverton	1713	DD/SP/1713/23	
1124	Marjery BURD of Milverton	1696	DD/SP/1696/4	
1125	Mary BURD, Widow of Milverton	1729	DD/SP/1729/46	
1126	Richard BURD of Milverton	1680	DD/SP/1680/61	
1127	Richard BURD of Milverton	1680	DD/SP/1680/68	
1128	Richard BURD of Milverton	1721	DD/SP/1721/5	
1129	Richard BURD of Milverton	1729	DD/SP/1729/47	
1130	Robert BURD of Cheddon Fitzpaine	1682	DD/SP/1682/24	
1131	John BURDE of Halse	1639	DD/SP/1639/30	
1132	Joanne BURDGE of Chedzoy	1645	DD/SP/1645/24	
1133	Manaseth BURFORD of Seavington St. Mary	1730	DD/SP/1730/31	
1134	Elizabeth BURGE, Widow of Heathfield	1692	DD/SP/1692/23	
1135	George BURGE of Ston Easton	1689	D/D/cta/B71	Ad.ac.
1136	Henry BURGE of Brompton Ralph	1718	DD/SP/442/26	Ad.ac.
1137	Humphrey BURGE of Hillfarrance	1716	DD/SP/1716/15	
1138	John BURGE of Heathfield	1677	DD/SP/1677/59	
1139	Nathaniel BURGE of Adber, Marston Magna	1720	DD/SF/15/2/35	Formerly DD/SF/3888
1140	Nicholas BURGE of Kittisford	1635	DD/SP/1635/10	
1141	Richard BURGE of Clatworthy	1646	DD/SP/1646/78	
1142	Richard BURGE, Yeoman of Milverton	1647	DD/SP/1647/9	
1143	Robert BURGE of Fivehead	1678	DD/SP/1678/63	
1144	Thomas BURGE of Tolland	1688	DD/SP/1688/4	
1145	Thomas BURGE of Lyng	1713	DD/SP/1713/28	
1146	William BURGE, Husbandman of Chedzoy	1676	DD/SP/1676/17	
1147	William BURGE, Weaver of Clatworthy	1686	DD/SP/1686/6	

BURGE see CROSSE				
1148	James BURGES, Dyer of Kingstone	1669	DD/SP/1669/82	
1149	Peter BURGES of Taunton St. Mary Magdalene	1684	DD/SP/1684/13	
1150	Peter BURGES of Hawkridge	1688	DD/SP/1688/13	
1151	Thomas BURGES of Creech St. Michael	1687	DD/SP/1687/51	
1152	William BURGESS of Weacombe, Stogumber formerly of Demarary, British Guiana	1823	T.N.A., PROB 31/1823/714	
1153	[missing] BURGH of Staple Fitzpaine	1669	DD/SP/1669/11	Incomplete
1154	Samuel BURLAND, Tailor of Stogursey	1693	DD/SP/1693/32	
1155	John BURMAN of Uphill	1677	D/D/cta/B72	Ad.ac.
1156	Richard BURNALL of Cutcombe	1699	DD/SP/1699/14	
1157	Richard BURNALL, Carpenter of Kilve	1732	DD/SP/1732/6	
1158	Emanuell BURNARD of North Petherton	1668	DD/SP/1668/54	
1159	Joane BURNARD, Widow of Langford Budville	1684	DD/SP/1684/24	
1160	John BURNARD, Merchant of [no place]	1667	T.N.A., PROB 4/20360	Will 1668. ex. 1668
1161	John BURNARD of Minehead?	1668	T.N.A., PROB 4/19971	Will also extant
1162	Margery BURNARD, Widow of Fivehead	1664	DD/SP/1664/56	
1163	Walter BURNARD, Sergeweaver of Langford Budville	1696	DD/SP/1696/30	
1164	Jane BURNELL of Kilton	1703	DD/SP/442/47	Ad.ac.
1165	John BURNELL of Cutcombe	1694	DD/SP/1694/36	
1166	Michael BURNELL of Luccombe	1696	DD/SP/1696/14	
1167	Roger BURNELL of Cutcombe	1673	DD/SP/1673/6	
1168	James BURNETT of Minehead	1690	DD/SP/1690/42	
1169	John BURNETT of Baltonsborough	1729	D/D/cta/B73	Ad.ac.
1170	Roger BURNETT of Dunster	1691	DD/SP/1691/16	
1171	Elesebeth BURNOLE of Spaxton	1667	DD/SP/1667/71	
1172	Margaret BURNOLE, Widow of Kilve	1642	DD/SP/1642/34	
1173	Jane BURNOLL of Kilton	1696	DD/SP/1696/46	See DD/SP 442/47
1174	John BURNOLL, Husbandman of Stogursey	1675	DD/SP/1675/46	
1175	John BURNOLL of Cutcombe	1684	DD/SP/1684/10	
1176	Roger BURNOLL of Cutcombe	1684	DD/SP/1684/31	
1177	Thomas BURNOLL of Cutcombe	1670	DD/SP/1670/2	
1178	William BURNOLL, Yeoman of Stogursey	1731	DD/SP/1731/32	

1179	Mary BURNOLL alias DOWDING of Stogursey	1696	DD/SP/1696/47	
1180	Thomas BURRIDGE, Clothier of Taunton St. James	1679	T.N.A., PROB 4/6912	Will also extant
1181	Robert BURROUGH of Stawell	1699	DD/SP/1699/4	
1182	Joane BURROW, Widow of North Petherton	1635	DD/SP/1635/77	
1183	John BURROW of Biddisham	1621	D/D/cta/B33	Ad.ac.
1184	John BURROW of Curry Rivel	1637	DD/SP/1637/24	See *T.C.W.*
1185	Joane BURROWE of [no place]	1677	D/D/cta/B12	Ad.ac.
1186	John BURROWE of Barrow Gurney	1596	D/D/cta/B2	Ad.ac.
1187	Samuel BURROWES of Taunton St. Mary Magdalene	1685	DD/SP/1685/23	
1188	Thomas BURROWES of Creech St. Michael	1697	DD/SP/1697/62	
1189	Dorothy BURROWS of Minehead	1714	DD/SP/1714/5	
1190	Thomas BURROWS of Curry Rivel	1739	DD/SW/2/5	
1191	Jeffery BURSELL of Taunton St. James	1679	DD/SP/1679/57	
1192	Hugh BURSSELL, Husbandman of Hatch Beauchamp	1674	DD/SP/1674/45	
1193	Charles BURSTON, Yeoman of Brompton Regis	1704	T.N.A., PROB 4/22707	Will n.d.
1194	Richard BURSTON, Yeoman of Crowcombe	1733	DD/TB/18/19	Will
1195	Charles BURT, Victualler of Nunney	1789	T.N.A., PROB 31/1789/66	Account in 1789/759
1196	Elizabeth BURT of Curry Mallet	1738	DD/SP/1738/43	
1197	James BURT of Lyng	1682	DD/SP/1682/42	
1198	Jane BURT of Fivehead	1669	DD/SP/1669/68	
1199	John BURT senior of Dunster	1685	DD/SP/1685/32	
1200	Nicholas BURT of Milverton	1646	DD/SP/1646/12	
1201	Oadds BURT alias BRETT, Yeoman of Bradford	1672	DD/SF/11/1/71	Formerly DD/SF/103
1202	Robert BURTON, Yeoman of Wambrook	1717	W.S.H.C., P14/125	Inv. and will
1203	William BURTON of Broadway	1684	DD/SP/1684/151	
1204	Anna BUSH of Milborne Port	1850	T.N.A., PROB 37/1498	
1205	Elizabeth BUSH, Widow of Charlton, Creech St. Michael	1719	T.N.A., PROB 3/18/83	See also DD/CTV/311
1206	John BUSH of Keynsham	1695	D/D/cta/B74	Ad.ac.
1207	Samuel BUSHELL, Gentleman of Bath	1696	T.N.A., PROB 4/587	Will 1696
1208	Roger BUSHEN of Porlock	1694	DD/SP/1694/15	
1209	Benjamin BUSSELL of Pitminster	1740	DD/SP/1740/4	
1210	John BUSSELL, Husbandman of Stoughton, Wedmore	1693	DD/OB/90	
1211	John BUSSELL of Pitminster	1718	DD/SP/1718/6	

1212	George BUTCHER, Grocer (widower) of Bath	1835	T.N.A., PROB 31/1835/1675H	
1213	Henry BUTCHER, Clerk of Clapton	1625	B.A., 1625a and 1625/b	
	Note: Two documents, includes a list of some household goods with values			
1214	John BUTCHER, Victualler of Misterton	1681	DD/SP/1681/45	
1215	Thomas BUTCHER, Sergemaker of Milverton	1668	DD/SP/1668/22	
BUTCHER see SYMONS				
1216	John BUTCOMB of Ashbrittle	1641	DD/SP/1641/10	
1217	Andrew BUTLER, Husbandman of Stockland Bristol	1674	DD/SP/1674/59	
1218	Caradock BUTLER, Yeoman of Over Stowey	1713	DD/SP/1713/29	
1219	Nathaniel BUTLER of Mells	1708	D/D/cta/B75	Ad.ac.
1220	Robert BUTSON, Husbandman of Creech St. Michael	1682	DD/SP/1682/13	
1221	Elianor BUTT of Isle Brewers	1639	DD/SP/1639/18	
1222	George BUTT of Isle Brewers	1691	DD/SP/1691/78	
1223	John BUTT, Rough Mason of South Cheriton, Horsington	1700	DD/DNL/70	
1224	Thomas BUTT, Sergemaker of Rapps, Broadway	1690	T.N.A., PROB 4/6341	Will. ex. 1691
1225	Martin BUTTON, Gentleman of [no place]	1668	DD/WHb/48	
1226	Richard BUXTON of Wick, Wells St. Cuthbert	1678	T.N.A., PROB 4/8617	Will. ex. 1679
1227	Edith BYAM, Widow of Clatworthy	1668	DD/SP/1668/40	
1228	Thomas BYSHOPP of Weston Bampfylde	1625	D/D/cta/B14	Ad.ac.
1229	James CABBELL of Somerton	1735	D/D/Cti 11	
1230	Florence CABLE, Widow of Hinton St. George	1635	DD/SP/1635/16	
1231	John CABLE, Miller of Hinton St. George	1694	DD/SP/1694/34	
1232	Bridget CADE of Ashbrittle	1634	DD/SP/1634/29	
1233	Joan CADE of Pitminster	1677	DD/SP/1677/53	
1234	Katherine CADE, Spinster of Bradford	1670	DD/SP/1670/58	
1235	Symon CADE, Yeoman of Wilton	1661	DD/SP/1661/19	
CADE see PROWSE				
1236	Joan CALLOW of Baltonsborough	n.d.	D/D/cta/C46	Ad.ac.
1237	John CALLOW of Shapwick	1740	D/D/Cti 9	
1238	Thomas CALLOW of Broomfield	1668	T.N.A., PROB 4/18974	Admon
1239	Robert CALWAY, Dyer of Stogumber	1682	DD/SP/1682/27	
1240	Robert CALWAY of Taunton St. Mary Magdalene	1723	DD/SP/1723/42	
1241	Bartholomew CAME, Yeoman of Pitminster	1679	T.N.A., PROB 4/4700	Will also extant

1242	Henry CAME, Yeoman of Staplegrove	1640	DD/SP/1640/21	
1243	John CAME of North Petherton	1639	DD/SP/1639/58	
1244	Robert CAME of Huntspill	1611	D/D/cta/C19	Ad.ac.
1245	Samuel CAME of Stogursey	1667	DD/SP/1667/81	
1246	Thomas CAME of Weston-super-Mare	1612	D/D/cta/C51	Ad.ac.
1247	William CAME of Wembdon	1670	DD/SP/1670/27	
1248	William CAME of Thurloxton	1684	DD/SP/1684/56	
1249	John CAMELL of Glastonbury	1487	T.N.A., PROB 2/451	Will T.N.A., PROB 11/8/100
1250	Alexander CAMPBELL of Bath	1770	T.N.A., PROB 31/1770/515	With ad.ac.
1251	Mary CAMPBELL, Widow of Bath City	1773	T.N.A., PROB 31/1773/700	
1252	Phillis CAMPBELL, Widow of Bath	1808	T.N.A., PROB 31/1808/757	
1253	Charles CAMPIN, Mariner of Pill, Easton in Gordano	1731	B.A., 1731/14	Will also extant
1254	James CAMPLIN of [no place]	1738	D/D/cta/C80	Ad.ac.
1255	Thomas CANINGTON of Wells	1682	T.N.A., PROB 4/5346	Will. ex. 1683
1256	Sir William CANN, Widower, Baronet of Brislington	1726	T.N.A., PROB 3/25/116	
1257	Sir William CANN, Baronet of Brislington	1726	T.N.A., PROB 31/1726/335 and 1726/336	
1258	Edmund CANNICOTT, Carpenter of Thurlbear	1698	DD/SP/1698/44	
1259	Emanuel CANNICOTT of Donyatt	1681	DD/SP/1681/55	
1260	George CANNICOTT, Husbandman of Hambridge, Curry Rivel	1691	DD/SP/1691/48	
1261	John CANNICOTT of Stoke St. Mary	1786	T.N.A., PROB 31/1786/15 and 1786/919	
1262	Robert CANNICOTT of Staple Fitzpaine	1672	DD/SP/1672/23	
1263	William CANNICOTT of [no place]	1712	DD/SP/442/6	Ad.ac.
1264	Robert CANNON, Gentleman of Fitzhead	1690	T.N.A., PROB 4/8359	Admon. ex. 1691
1265	John CANTERBURY of Odcombe	1791	DD/SAS/C909/9	
1266	Elizabeth CAPON of [no place]	1591	D/D/cta/C24	Ad.ac.
1267	William CAPPELL of Milverton	1674	DD/SP/1674/2	
CAPPELL see CHAPEL				
1268	Edmond CARD, Merchant of Dunster	1684	T.N.A., PROB 4/9120	Will 1684. ex. 1685
1269	George CARD, Husbandman of Rodney Stoke	1670	T.N.A., PROB 4/10212	Admon
1270	George CARDE senior of Rodney Stoke	1670	T.N.A., PROB 5/2007	
1271	George CARDE the elder of Draycott, Cheddar	1689	DD/BRC/27	

1272	Dorothy CAREW, Widow of Camerton	1687	T.N.A., PROB 4/2771	Will 1687
1273	John CAREW, Esquire of Crowcombe	1684	T.N.A., PROB 4/12223	Admon
1274	Edward CARIE of Foddington, Babcary	1642	D/D/cta/C53	Ad.ac.
1275	Francis CARPENTER of Publow	1729	D/D/Cti 10	
1276	Philip CARPENTER of Berkley	1611	D/D/cta/C50	Ad.ac.
1277	Robert CARRE, Clothier of Thornfalcon	1669	DD/SP/1669/95	
1278	James CARRIER, Blacksmith of Stoke sub Hamdon	1714	A/CTP/11/8	
1279	Arthur CARSE of Dulverton	1632	DD/SP/1632/28	*T.C.W.*
1280	[missing] CARSWELL of [no place]	1670	DD/SP/1670/59	
1281	Katheryne CARSWELL of Thorne St. Margaret	1644	DD/SP/1644/68	
1282	John CARTER of Dunster and/or Monksilver	1646	DD/SP/1646/76	
	Note: Proved by Margerie CARTER alias LOXHAM, Widow			
1283	John CARTER of Langford Budville	1685	DD/SP/1685/111	
1284	John CARTER of Meare	1737	D/D/cta/C81	Ad.ac. and inv.
1285	Joseph CARTER, Husbandman of Crowcombe	1640	DD/SP/1640/75	
1286	Mary CARTER of Beckington	1676	T.N.A., PROB 4/11477	Will 1676. Relict of William CARTER
1287	Richard CARTER of Isle Abbotts	1648	DD/SP/1648/26	
1288	Thomas CARTER of Cannington	1664	DD/SP/1664/7	
1289	Thomas CARTER, Clothier of Beckington	1675	T.N.A., PROB 4/10494	Will 1675
1290	Thomas CARTER, Tailor of Ilminster	1689	T.N.A., PROB 4/5562	Will. ex. 1690
1291	Valentine CARTER, Yeoman of Trull	1679	T.N.A., PROB 4/17314	Will also extant
1292	Elizabeth CARTER formerly TONGE of Long Ashton	1789	T.N.A., PROB 31/1789/727	Wife of John CARTER
CARTER see ROUNSEVALL				
1293	Thomas CARTWRIGHT, Apothecary of Bridgwater	1664	DD/SP/1664/79	
1294	William CARTWRIGHT of Stogumber	1667	DD/SP/1667/92	
1295	Robert CARVEN of Taunton St. Mary Magdalene	1681	DD/SP/1681/106	
1296	Thomas CARVER, Husbandman of Winsham	1688	T.N.A., PROB 4/8429	Admon
1297	John CARVIN, Innholder of Taunton St. Mary Magdalene	1678	DD/SP/1678/57	
1298	John CARY of Bridgwater	1635	DD/SP/1635/47	
1299	Robert CARY, Esquire of Bath City	1735	T.N.A., PROB 3/34/1	
1300	William CARY of Stogursey	1681	DD/SP/1681/113	
1301	Stephen CARYE of Doulting	1592	D/D/cta/C75	Ad.ac.

1302	John CASE of Corton Denham	1622	D/D/cta/C3	Ad.ac.
1303	John CASE, Husbandman of Cutcombe	1697	DD/SP/1697/30	
1304	Lawrence CASE of Huish Champflower	1684	DD/SP/1684/5	
1305	Nicholas CASE, Mercer of Dulverton	1684	DD/SP/1684/86	
1306	Thomas CASE, Clerk, late Rector of Orchard Portman	1678	DD/SP/1678/86	
1307	Thomas CASE of Luxborough	1684	DD/SP/1684/106	
1308	William CASELY of [no place]	1715	D/D/cta/C17	Ad.ac.
1309	Jane CASLEY, Widow of Lydeard St. Lawrence	1665	DD/SP/1665/62	
1310	John CATFORD, Gentleman of Boomer, North Petherton	1685	T.N.A., PROB 4/3854	Will 1686. ex. 1687
1311	Katherine CATFORD of Enmore	1679	T.N.A., PROB 4/6958	Admon
1312	William CATFORD of West Melcombe alias Boomer, North Petherton	1644	DD/SL/4	
1313	William CATFORD of Dulverton	1720	DD/SP/1720/3	
1314	Hugh CATHCART, Esquire of Bath	1819	T.N.A., PROB 31/1819/679	
1315	Robert CATKOT, Gardener of Goathurst	1721	DD/SP/1721/21	
1316	[missing] CATTLE of Othery or Middlezoy ?	n.d.	D/D/cta/C7	Ad.ac.
1317	Dorothy CATTLE of Drayton	1713	DD/SP/1713/39	
1318	John CATTLE of Swell	1669	DD/SP/1669/49	
1319	John CEELIE of [no place]	n.d.	D/D/cta/C25	Ad.ac.
1320	Edward CEELY, Esquire of Charlton, Creech St. Michael	1677	DD/SP/1677/7	
1321	Mary CEELY, Widow of Chard Borough	1694	T.N.A., PROB 4/10387	Will 1694
1322	Maurice CEELY, Esquire of Bridgwater	1679	T.N.A., PROB 5/5318	
1323	William CEELY, Esquire of Charlton, Creech St. Michael	1724	T.N.A., PROB 3/23/40	
1324	Henry CHAFE of Taunton St. Mary Magdalene	1693	DD/BR/wr/3	
1325	Joseph CHAFFEY, Tanner of Whitelackington	1730	DD/SP/1730/21	
1326	Judith CHAFFEY, Widow of Galhampton, North Cadbury	1699	T.N.A., PROB 4/19281	Will also extant
1327	Thomas CHAFFEY of Hardington Mandeville	1774	D/PC/hard.m/6/3/10	
1328	Mary CHAFFIE, Widow of Merriott	1669	DD/SP/1669/52	
1329	John CHAINEY, Yeoman of Long Ashton	1680	T.N.A., PROB 4/8541	Will 1680. ex. 1681
1330	Arthur CHALLENDER, Whitebaker of Taunton St. Mary Magdalene	1697	DD/SP/1697/46	
1331	William CHALLICE of Bradford	1670	DD/SP/1670/60	

CHALLICE see SHALLISH

1332	Thomas CHAMBERLAIN, Yeoman of Evercreech	1831	T.N.A., PROB 31/1831/172	With ad.ac.
1333	John CHAMBERLAINE, Gentleman of North Petherton	1692	DD/SP/1692/17	
1334	John CHAMBERS of Bath	1620	D/D/cta/C48	Ad.ac.
1335	John CHAMBERS of Batcombe	1742	D/D/cta/C82	Ad.ac. and inv.
1336	Frances CHAMPION, Widow of Shapwick	1667	D/D/cta/C65	Ad.ac.
1337	Humphrey CHAMPION of Bleadon	1668	T.N.A., PROB 4/10465	Will 1668
1338	William CHAMPION of Portbury	1641	D/D/cta/C72	Ad.ac.
1339	William CHAMPION of Meare	1679	D/D/cta/C83	Ad.ac.
1340	John CHAMPNEYS the elder, Esquire of Orchardleigh	1678	T.N.A., PROB 4/3847	Will also extant
1341	Jonathon CHANDLER of Cossington	1738	D/D/Cti 12	
1342	Robert CHANE of Taunton St. Mary Magdalene	1675	DD/SP/1675/52	
1343	Laurence CHANING, Yeoman of Barrington	1647	DD/SP/1647/10	
1344	Thomas CHANNING, Husbandman of Barrington	1684	DD/SP/1684/128	
1345	John CHANNON of Wellington	1722	T.N.A., PROB 3/21/219	
1346	John CHANNON, Yeoman of Barrington	1731	DD/SP/1731/5	
1347	Robert CHANNON, Clothier of Combe St. Nicholas	1693	T.N.A., PROB 4/6959	Will also extant
1348	William CHANNON of Donyatt	1689	DD/SP/1689/8	
1349	Robert CHANT, Yeoman of Glastonbury and Chilthorne Domer	1735	D/D/cta/C84	Ad.ac. and inv.
1350	William CHANT of Taunton St. Mary Magdalene	1680	DD/SP/1680/56	
1351	John CHANTER of Selworthy	1635	DD/SP/1635/107	
1352	David CHAPL of Creech St. Michael	1640	DD/SP/1640/106	
1353	Jane CHAPLE, Widow of Kingston	1635	DD/SP/1635/17	
1354	John CHAPLE, Husbandman of North Petherton	1672	DD/SP/1672/30	
1355	Philip CHAPLE, Widow of North Petherton	1674	DD/SP/1674/64	
1356	Samuel CHAPLE of Swell	1672	DD/SP/1672/63	
1357	Joane CHAPLIN, Singlewoman of Crowcombe	1685	DD/SP/1685/62	
1358	William CHAPLIN of Taunton St. James	1667	DD/SP/1667/67	
1359	William CHAPLIN of Taunton St. Mary Magdalene	1683	DD/SP/1683/100	
1360	William CHAPLIN, Innholder of Taunton St. Mary Magdalene	1684	DD/SP/1684/148	
CHAPLIN see PORTER				
1361	Ebenezer CHAPLINE of Ashcott	1735	D/D/cta/C85	Ad.ac. and inv.
1362	Richard CHAPLYN, Clothier of Williton, St. Decumans	1677	T.N.A., PROB 4/10452	Will also extant

1363	Roger CHAPLYN, Gentleman of Taunton St. James	1628	DD/SAS/C112/17/1	
1364	Elizabeth CHAPMAN of Upton	1639	DD/SP/1639/52	
1365	Henry CHAPMAN of Chedzoy	1681	DD/SP/1681/23	
1366	Joan CHAPMAN, Widow of Wootton Courtenay	1675	DD/SP/1675/57	
1367	John CHAPMAN, Yeoman of Moorland, Bridgwater	1713	DD/SP/1713/26	
1368	John CHAPMAN senior, Yeoman of Cutcombe	1734	DD/SP/1734/23	
1369	Nicholas CHAPMAN of Hillfarrance	1680	DD/SP/1680/65	
1370	Roger CHAPMAN of Milverton	1667	DD/SP/1667/84	
1371	Symon CHAPMAN, Captain of Bath City	1675	T.N.A., PROB 4/7442	Will 1675
1372	Thomas CHAPMAN, Woolen Dyer of Stalls Parish, Bath	1604	B.C.R.O., Furman bdl 3/1	Admin 1604 with will 1604
1373	Thomas CHAPMAN of Upton	1636	DD/SP/1636/48	
1374	Walter CHAPMAN, Gentleman of Bath	1683	T.N.A., PROB 5/2006	Will T.N.A., PROB 11/374 and Sentence
1375	Walter CHAPMAN, Gentleman of Bath City	1684	T.N.A., PROB 4/9331	Will 1684
1376	Richard CHAPPEL of Norton Fitzwarren	1733	D/D/Cti 19	
1377	William CHAPPEL the elder of Crowcombe	1679	T.N.A., PROB 4/16156	Will also extant
1378	John CHAPPELL of Muchelney	1587	D/D/cta/C29	Ad.ac.
1379	John CHAPPELL of Chewton Mendip	1605	D/D/cta/C43	Ad.ac.
1380	John CHAPPELL of Chewton Mendip	1605	D/D/cta/C44	Ad.ac.
1381	John CHAPPELL of Kingstone	1716	DD/SP/1716/48	
1382	Jonathan CHAPPELL, Yeoman of Crowcombe	1692	DD/SP/1692/9	
1383	Peter CHAPPELL of Milverton	1721	DD/SP/1721/24	
CHAPPELL see CHAPLE, FERMER				
1384	Richard CHAPPINGTON of Wembdon	1635	DD/SP/1635/72	
1385	George CHAPPLE senior of Kingstone	1674	DD/SP/1674/40	
1386	Joan CHAPPLE, Widow of Creech St. Michael	1695	DD/SP/1695/33	
1387	John CHAPPLE of Hillfarrance	1732	DD/SP/1732/9	
1388	Mary CHAPPLE, Spinster of Drayton	1669	DD/SP/1669/38	
1389	Robert CHAPPLE of Hinton St. George	1668	T.N.A., PROB 4/8288	Will. ex. 1669
1390	Samuel CHAPPLE of Allowenshay, Kingstone	1672	DD/SP/1672/44	
1391	George CHAPPLE alias HUTCHINS, Yeoman of Ludney, Kingstone	1674	DD/SP/1674/39	
CHAPPLE see CHAPLE				

1392	Isaac CHARD, Yeoman of Taunton St. Mary Magdalene formerly of Corfe	1827	T.N.A., PROB 31/1827/819	
1393	Nathaniel CHARLTON, Clerk of Bishops Hull	1682	DD/SP/1682/29	
1394	Abigail CHASE of Chard	1725	T.N.A., PROB 5/91	Will T.N.A., PROB 11/606
1395	Margaret CHASE, Widow of Wambrook	1691	W.S.H.C., P14/77	Admon. bond, com., inv.
1396	William CHASE, Mercer of Taunton St. Mary Magdalene	1676	DD/SP/1676/12	
1397	William CHAUNT of Abbas and Temple Combe	1669	T.N.A., PROB 4/8292	Admon
1398	John CHAVE, Husbandman of West Bagborough	1665	DD/SP/1665/52	
1399	Henry CHEAD of Creech St. Michael	1739	DD/SP/1739/50	
1400	John CHEAD, Coal Carrier of Creech St. Michael	1670	DD/SP/1670/49	
1401	Marian CHEAD of Isle Abbotts	1665	DD/SP/1665/55	
1402	Mary CHEAD of Durston	1664	DD/SP/1664/50	
1403	Mary CHEAD, Spinster of Creech St. Michael	1678	DD/SP/1678/53	
1404	Michael CHEAD, Carpenter of Creech St. Michael	1671	DD/SP/1671/28	
CHEBETT see KITNOR				
1405	Agnes CHEEK, Widow of North Petherton	1618	DD/PH/243	
1406	George CHEEK, minor of Wootton Courtenay	1687	T.N.A., PROB 5/5267	
1407	Simon CHEEK, Widow of North Petherton	1638	DD/PH/243	
1408	Martin CHEEKE senior, Husbandman of North Petherton	1691	DD/SP/1691/81	
1409	Rebecca CHEEKE alias MUNDAY of Milverton	1682	DD/SP/1682/7	Wife of William CHEEKE
1410	Edmund CHELTENHAM of Ansford	1611	D/D/cta/C34	Ad.ac.
1411	Martin CHENEY of Kingston	167–[?]	T.N.A., PROB 4/12080	Admon. ex. 1677
1412	John CHEPMAN of Wells St. Cuthbert	1633	D/D/cta/C10	Ad.ac.
1413	John CHESTER of East Quantoxhead	1644	DD/SP/1644/69	
1414	John CHESTER, Fuller of Dunster	1671	DD/SP/1671/13	
1415	George CHESTERDON, Husbandman of Stogumber	1699	DD/SP/1699/8	
1416	Joan CHIBBITT of Porlock	1739	DD/SP/1739/53	
1417	Thomas CHICK of Chillington	1783	T.N.A., PROB 31/1783/178	
1418	Joane CHICKE, Widow of Barrington	1637	DD/SP/1637/25	
1419	Joane CHICKE of Milverton	1678	DD/SP/1678/18	
1420	Joane CHICKE, Widow of North Petherton	1696	DD/SP/1696/33	
1421	Joanne CHICKE, Widow of Isle Brewers	1648	DD/SP/1648/62	
1422	Margery CHICKE, Widow of Barrington	1651	DD/SP/1651/5	
1423	Richard CHICKE, Husbandman of Barrington	1647	DD/SP/1647/22	

1424	Richard CHICKE of North Petherton	1693	DD/SP/1693/46	
1425	Robert CHICKE of Isle Abbotts	1677	DD/SP/1677/66	
1426	William CHICKE of North Petherton	1691	DD/SP/1691/97	
1427	[Blank] CHILCOTT senior of Fiddington	1669	DD/SP/1669/79	
1428	[missing] CHILCOTT of [no place]	1646	DD/SP/1646/71	Proved by Elizabeth CHILCOTT, Widow
1429	[missing] CHILCOTT of [no place]	n.d.	DD/SP/17th Century/1	
1430	Edward CHILCOTT of Spaxton	1743	DD/SP/1743/20	
1431	Elizabeth CHILCOTT, Widow of Luccombe	1688	DD/SP/1688/14	
1432	Elizabeth CHILCOTT of Brompton Ralph	1727	DD/SP/442/82	Ad.ac.
1433	George CHILCOTT of Stogumber	1637	DD/SP/1637/53	
1434	George CHILCOTT of Stogumber	1667	DD/SP/1667/85	
1435	John CHILCOTT of Dulverton	1672	DD/SP/1672/3	
1436	John CHILCOTT, Yeoman of Dulverton	1681	DD/SP/1681/102	
1437	John CHILCOTT of Milverton	1684	DD/SP/1684/160	
1438	John CHILCOTT of Monksilver	1685	T.N.A., PROB 4/8848	Will. ex. 1686
1439	John CHILCOTT, Bachelor of Dulverton	1689	DD/SP/1689/42	
1440	Richard CHILCOTT of Dulverton	1667	DD/SP/1667/1	
1441	Robert CHILCOTT of Brushford	1640	DD/SP/1640/3	
1442	William CHILCOTT of Ash, Thornfalcon	1730	DD/SP/1730/17	
1443	William CHILCOTT, Innholder of Bridgwater	1730	DD/SP/1730/3	
1444	William CHILCOTT the elder, Yeoman of Monksilver	1605	D/D/ct/1/C/52	
1445	Lydia CHISWELL, Widow of Chew Magna	1743	DD/SH/79/10/30 c/2480	
1446	Richard CHORLEY of Bathealton	1645	DD/SP/1645/19	
1447	Richard CHORLEY, Coal Merchant of Taunton St. James	1744	DD/SP/1744/24	
1448	William CHORLEY of Exton	1857	DD/CCH Box 2/11	
1449	Elizabeth CHUBB, Widow of Crewkerne	1687	DD/SP/1687/43	
1450	John CHUBB, Alehouse Keeper of Crewkerne	1674	DD/SP/1674/56	
1451	John CHUBB, Tobacconist of Crewkerne	1686	DD/SP/1686/14	
1452	William CHUBB, Haberdasher of Crewkerne	1686	T.N.A., PROB 4/10397	Admon
CHUBBERYE see HILL				
1453	Henry CHURCHELL, Cooper of Pitminster	1684	DD/SP/1684/1	
1454	John CLAPP, Yeoman of Combe Sydenham, Stogumber died at Wilton	1764	T.N.A., PROB 31/1764/695	

1455	Grace CLARE, Widow of Porlock	1746	DD/SP/1746/28	
1456	Ann CLARKE of South Petherton	1690	DD/SP/1690/40	
1457	Clement CLARKE of Woolmerson, Crewkerne	1679	DD/SP/1679/42	
1458	Edward CLARKE senior of Chipley, Nynehead	1679	DD/SF/11/1/82	Formerly DD/SF/283
1459	George CLARKE, Husbandman of Woolminstone, Crewkerne	1679	DD/SP/1679/35	
1460	George CLARKE of Dunster	1699	DD/SP/1699/12	See DD/SP 44258
1461	George CLARKE of Dunster	1707	DD/SP/442/58	
	Note: Ad.ac. of Jane CROSSE the 'Aunt Tutrix and Guardian at law lawfully Assigned to and for Anne CLARKE the naturall and lawfull daughter and administratrix'			
1462	James CLARKE of Lyon's Inn, Middlesex died at Sandford, Westbury	1681	T.N.A., PROB 4/15324	Admon
1463	Jo-- CLARKE of [no place]	1675	DD/SP/1675/9	
1464	Joan CLARKE of South Petherton	1675	T.N.A., PROB 5/5660	
1465	John CLARKE of Wells	1675	T.N.A., PROB 4/6844	Admon
1466	John CLARKE of Wells St. Cuthbert	1690	T.N.A., PROB 5/5669	
1467	John CLARKE of Wells	1742	D/D/Cti 13	
1468	Martin CLARKE of Taunton St. Mary Magdalene formerly of Bishops Lydeard	1691	DD/SP/1691/56	
1469	Mary CLARKE of Taunton St. James	1716	DD/SP/1716/31	
1470	Matthew CLARKE, Yeoman of Bedminster	1675	T.N.A., PROB 4/535	Admon
1471	Moses CLARKE of Walcot	1807	T.N.A., PROB 31/1807/263	
1472	Richard CLARKE of Greinton	1711	D/D/cta/C33	Ad.ac.
1473	Richard CLARKE, Gentleman of Combe St. Nicholas	1728	T.N.A., PROB 3/27/110	
1474	Richard CLARKE, Gentleman of Combe St. Nicholas	1728	T.N.A., PROB 31/1728/371	
1475	Robert CLARKE, Esquire of Sandford, Wembdon	1661	DD/SP/1661/21	See *T.C.W.*
1476	Roger CLARKE of Brompton Ralph	1671	DD/SP/1671/20	
1477	Thomas CLARKE, Brazier of Taunton St. Mary Magdalene	1689	DD/SP/1689/37	
1478	William CLARKE, Yeoman of Wrington	1678	T.N.A., PROB 4/8916	Will also extant
1479	William CLARKE, Husbandman of Chedzoy	1688	DD/SP/1688/34	
1480	William CLARKE senior, Gentleman of Witham Friary	1690	T.N.A., PROB 4/18390	Will also extant
1481	John CLASE of High Ham	n.d.	D/D/cta/C47	Ad.ac.
1482	Elinor CLATWORTHY of Luccombe	1685	DD/SP/1685/33	
1483	Margaret CLATWORTHY, Widow of North Newton, North Petherton	1689	DD/SP/1689/27	

1484	Richard CLATWORTHY, Husbandman of North Newton, North Petherton	1669	DD/SP/1669/20	
1485	Walter CLATWORTHY of Langford Budville	1688	D.H.C., 49/9/1/680	
1486	George CLAVELSHAIE, Miller of Donyatt	1698	DD/SP/1698/41	
1487	Charles CLAVEY of Frome	1785	T.N.A., PROB 31/1785/860	
1488	John CLAVEY the elder, Brickmaker of Bridgwater	1831	T.N.A., PROB 31/1831/1475	
1489	Samuel CLEALE, Blacksmith of Misterton	1690	DD/SP/1690/70	
1490	John CLEARKE of Lydeard St. Lawrence	1636	DD/SP/1636/9	
1491	Richard CLEEVE of Ashbrittle	1685	DD/SP/1685/91	
1492	John CLEEVELAND of Upton Noble	1641	D/D/cta/C70	Ad.ac.
1493	John CLEMENS of [no place]	n.d.	D/D/cta/C5	Ad.ac.
1494	Ann CLEMENT, Widow of Bath and Box, Wiltshire	1792	W.S.H.C., P3/C/1115	Admon. bond, com., inv.
1495	Elizabeth CLEMENT, Widow of Durston	1687	DD/SP/1687/16	
1496	Hugh CLEMENT of Taunton St. Mary Magdalene	1639	DD/SP/1639/41	
1497	Leonard CLEMENT, Husbandman of Huntworth, Bridgwater	1670	DD/SP/1670/102	
1498	Thomas CLEMENT of Kingstone	1684	DD/SP/1684/87	
1499	Thomas CLEMENT (CLEAMANT) of North Petherton	1670	DD/SP/1670/24	
1500	John CLEMENTS, Glover of Bridgwater	1716	DD/SP/1716/25	Lists goods
1501	Mary CLEMENTS of Dunster	1697	DD/SP/1697/66	
1502	William CLEMSON?, Clerk of Monksilver	1675	T.N.A., PROB 4/19848	Will also extant
1503	John CLENCH of South Petherton	1648	DD/SP/1648/28	See also D/P/pet.s. 2/1/1
1504	Thomas CLENCH of Ilchester	1685	T.N.A., PROB 4/15374	Admon
1505	Charles CLEVENGER of West Buckland	1638	DD/SF/2/58/2	Formerly DD/SF/3150
1506	Thomas CLEY of Muchelney	1599	D/D/cta/T41	Ad.ac.
1507	Richard CLIFFORD of Yeovilton	1594	D/D/cta/C74	Ad.ac.
CLIFFORD see CLYFFORD				
1508	John CLIPSON of [no place]	1666	DD/SG/58	
1509	Thomas CLIST senior of Ashbrittle	1690	DD/SP/1690/34	
1510	Anne CLOTHIER, Widow of Shepton Beauchamp	1705	T.N.A., PROB 4/25266	Will. ex. 1704
1511	John CLOTHIER of Coxley, Wells St. Cuthbert	1670	T.N.A., PROB 4/9467	Will also extant
1512	John CLOTHIER of Charlton Horethorne	1730	D/D/Cti 22b	
1513	Robert CLOTHYER of Chard	1704	T.N.A., PROB 4/22557	Will also extant
1514	Lawrence CLOTWORTHIE of West Monkton	1612	D/D/cta/C32	Ad.ac.

1515	Walter CLOTWORTHY, Sergemaker of Langford Budville	1688	T.N.A., PROB 4/6496	Will. ex. 1689
1516	Thomas CLOWTERR of Lyng	1689	DD/SP/1689/14	
1517	Peter CLUTTERBUCK of [no place]	1597	D/D/cta/C18	Ad.ac.
1518	Thomas CLUTTLER, Clerk of Stoke St. Gregory	1633	D/D/cta/C9	Ad.ac. for a clergyman
1519	Thomas CLYFFORD of West Monkton	1667	DD/SP/1667/97	
1520	Alice CLYNTON, Widow of Glastonbury	1601	D/D/cta/C41	Ad.ac.
1521	Richard COALE of Chew Stoke	1705	D/D/Cti 18	
COALE see COLE				
1522	Richard COALES of Lilstock	1637	DD/SP/1637/46	
COALES see COLE				
1523	Roger COAPE, Mariner of Bridgwater	1665	DD/SP/1665/34	
1524	Agnes COATE, Widow of Burton, Drayton	1674	DD/SP/1674/10	
1525	Christopher COATE of Drayton	1636	DD/SP/1636/43	See *T.C.W.*
1526	John COATE of Curry Rivel	1714	DD/SP/1714/12	
1527	Marmaduke COATE of Curry Rivel	1664	D/D/cta/C61	Ad.ac.
1528	Richard COATE of Moorland, North Petherton	1669	DD/SP/1669/5	
1529	John COATES, Husbandman of Selworthy	1667	DD/SP/1667/51	
1530	Hester COBBE of Claverham, Yatton	1729	T.N.A., PROB 3/30/104	
1531	Hester COBBE of Claverham, Yatton	1729	T.N.A., PROB 31/1729/646	
1532	George COCK of Taunton St. Mary Magdalene	1677	DD/SP/1677/46	
1533	Richard COCK, Carpenter of Batheaston	1688	T.N.A., PROB 4/19728	Will 1688
1534	James COCKERMAN of Dulverton	1669	DD/SP/1669/24	
1535	Christopher COCKING of Frome Selwood	1803	T.N.A., PROB 31/1803/655	
1536	Elizabeth COCRUM, Widow of Dulverton	1635	DD/SP/1635/86	
1537	Ann CODD, Widow of Milverton	1685	DD/SP/1685/19	
1538	Richard CODINGE (or CORDINGE*) of Exton	1637	DD/SP/1637/14	See *T.C.W.*
1539	[Female] COFFIN of [no place]	1694	DD/SP/1694/37	Part missing
1540	Alice COFFIN, Widow of Selworthy	1637	DD/SP/1637/15	
1541	William COFFIN, Fuller of Dunster	1669	DD/SP/1669/2	
1542	Anthony COGAN of Montacute	1598	D/D/cta/C56	Ad.ac.
1543	Benjamin COGAN of Crewkerne	1678	DD/SP/1678/28	
1544	Elizabeth COGDEN of Bower, Bridgwater	1720	DD/SP/1720/2	
1545	Mrs Elizabeth COGGAN, Widow of Trull	1732	DD/SP/1732/2	

1546	Elizabeth COGGAN of Stocklinch Magdalene	1743	DD/SP/1743/22	
1547	John COKE, Rector of Stocklinch Magdalene	1639	DD/SP/1639/53	
1548	John COLBERD of Over Stratton, South Petherton	1674	DD/SP/1674/54	
1549	John COLBERD of Over Stratton, South Petherton	1677	DD/SP/1677/81	
1550	Thomas COLBERD, Yeoman of Hinton St. George	1684	DD/SP/1684/181	
1551	Andrew COLBERT of Lopen	1630s	DD/SP/1632/29	Undated; mentions a debt owed by Elias RAWLINS
1552	Katherine COLBERTT, Widow of Over Stratton, South Petherton	1640	DD/SP/1640/28	
1553	John COLBORNE, Innholder of Wellington	1670	T.N.A., PROB 4/19412	Will also extant
1554	John COLBORNE, Innholder of Wellington	1672	T.N.A., PROB 5/3008	
1555	Martin COLBORNE, Yeoman of North Petherton	1688	DD/SP/1688/20	
1556	Christian COLE, Widow of Spaxton	1634	DD/SP/1634/39	
1557	Daniel COLE of Wellington	1686	T.N.A., PROB 4/8950	Admon
1558	Edward COLE of Stogursey	1721	DD/SP/1721/27	
1559	George COLE of Moorland, North Petherton	1671	DD/SP/1671/3	
1560	George COLE, Wheelwright of Sherston, North Petherton	1672	DD/SP/1672/14	
1561	George COLE the elder, Husbandman of North Petherton	1662	DD/SP/1662/28	
1562	James COLE, Clerk (Vicar) of Bradford	1635	DD/SP/1635/131	See *T.C.W.*
1563	Joane COLE, Widow of Chewton Mendip	1685	T.N.A., PROB 4/8294	Will also extant
1564	Mary COLE, Widow of Spaxton	1640	DD/SP/1640/52	
1565	Robert COLE, Yeoman of Kingston	1684	DD/SP/1684/125	
1566	William COLE of North Petherton	1640	DD/SP/1640/94	
1567	John COLEBERT, Feltmaker of South Petherton	1646	DD/SP/1646/7	
1568	John COLEFORD of Enmore	1685	DD/SP/1685/111a	
1569	Elizabeth COLEMAN of Thurlbear	1678	DD/SP/1678/47	
1570	Reuben COLEMAN of Norton Fitzwarren	1723	DD/SP/1723/53	
1571	Abraham COLES of Bridgwater	1677	DD/SP/1677/8	
1572	Edward COLES of Bridgwater	1675	DD/SP/1675/44	
1573	Elizabeth COLES of Lilstock	1693	DD/SP/1693/57	
1574	Florence COLES, Widow of Kingston	1763	T.N.A., PROB 31/1763/976	With ad.ac.
1575	Joane COLES, Widow of Curry Mallet	1684	DD/SP/1684/4	
1576	John COLES the elder of Nether Stowey	1684	T.N.A., PROB 4/17809	Will also extant

1577	Ruth COLES of Bishops Lydeard	1795	DD/FS/7/4	
1578	Tacey COLES of Cannington	1714	DD/SP/1714/11	
1579	Thomas COLES, Yeoman of Cannington	1689	DD/SP/1689/24	
1580	William COLES, Currier of Taunton St. Mary Magdalene	1723	DD/SP/1723/36	
COLES see COLE				
1581	Abell COLESWORTHY of Pitminster	1687	DD/SP/1687/50a	
1582	Edward COLFORD, Tanner of Enmore	1691	DD/DP/50/5	
1583	Joane COLFORD, Widow of Spaxton	1691	DD/SP/1691/26	
1584	John COLFORD of Enmore	1685	DD/SP/1685/73	
1585	Mary COLFORD of Bridgwater	1691	DD/SP/1691/72	
1586	Nicholas COLFORD, Gentleman of Charlinch	1667	T.N.A., PROB 4/16076	Admon
1587	Thomas COLFORD, Gentleman of Spaxton	1690	DD/SP/1690/26	
1588	Agnes COLFOX, Widow of Bridgwater	1640	DD/SP/1640/82	
1589	Alexander COLLARD of Wilton	1679	DD/SP/1679/12	
1590	Edward COLLARD of Lydeard St. Lawrence	1639	DD/SP/1639/5	
1591	Edward COLLARD, Yeoman of Trull	1671	DD/SP/1671/7	
1592	John COLLARD of Nettlecombe	1669	DD/SP/1669/56	
1593	John COLLARD, Gentleman of Spaxton	1679	T.N.A., PROB 4/16760	Will. ex. 1680
1594	John COLLARD of Over Stowey	1714	DD/SP/1714/26	
1595	Peter Carthew COLLARD, Hatter of Taunton	1830	T.N.A., PROB 31/1830/1073	With ad.ac.
1596	Samuel COLLARD, Yeoman of Norton Fitzwarren	1739	DD/SP/1739/51	
1597	Thomas COLLARD, Cordwainer of Dulverton	1684	DD/SP/1684/73	
1598	William COLLARD of Norton Fitzwarren	1677	DD/SP/1677/39	
1599	William COLLARD, Gentleman of Pludd, Kilton	1692	T.N.A., PROB 4/20552	Admon. ex. 1693
1600	Robert COLLECKE of [no place]	1664	DD/SP/1664/52	
1601	John COLLENS the elder of Creech St. Michael	1641	DD/SP/1641/2	
1602	Lawrence COLLENS of North Curry	1661	DD/TBL/1	
1603	Thomas COLLENS of [no place]	1588	D/D/cta/C20	Ad.ac.
1604	William COLLETT alias COLLETT MOORE of Thurloxton	1787	T.N.A., PROB 31/1787/844	
1605	Thomas COLLETT or COLLAT, Yeoman of Bedminster	1680	T.N.A., PROB 5/4703	
1606	Joan COLLEY, Widow of Weston Bampfylde	1701	T.N.A., PROB 4/22582	Will 1701
1607	Thomas COLLICK, Tobacconist of [no place]	1671	DD/SP/1671/34	
1608	Robert COLLICK alias AMBROSE, Yeoman of North Petherton	1684	DD/SP/1684/78	

1609	Henry COLLIER of Winford	1666	D/D/cta/C63	Ad.ac.
1610	Josiah COLLIER of Huntspill	n.d.	A/AEH/18/2	*c.*1740
1611	Richard COLLIER of Curry Mallet	1685	DD/SP/1685/85	
1612	Edward COLLINGS of White Lyon, Bridgwater	1733/4	D/B/bw 2131	
1613	Edward COLLINS, Butcher of Brewham	1599	D/D/cta/C59	Ad.ac.
1614	Edward COLLINS, Victualler of Barwick	1675	T.N.A., PROB 4/8516	Admon
1615	Edward COLLINS of Bishops Hull	1685	DD/SP/1685/56	
1616	Henry COLLINS, Yeoman of Stoke St. Gregory	1697	T.N.A., PROB 4/3762	Admon
1617	James COLLINS, Farmer of Farrington Gurney	1741	D/D/cta/C88	Ad.ac. and inv.
1618	John COLLINS, Mercer of Ilminster	1688	T.N.A., PROB 4/8598	Will. ex. 1689
1619	Mary COLLINS, Widow of Crewkerne	1686	T.N.A., PROB 4/5581	Admon
1620	Philip COLLINS of Wells St. Cuthbert	1666	D/D/cta/C64	Ad.ac.
1621	Philippa COLLINS of Bath	1691	D/D/cta/C89	Ad.ac.
1622	Robert COLLINS, Mercer of Somerton	1673	T.N.A., PROB 4/6957	Will. ex. 1674
1623	Robert COLLINS, Yeoman of Long Ashton	1683	T.N.A., PROB 4/10564	Admon
1624	Robert COLLINS, Clothier of Horton, Ilminster	1730	T.N.A., PROB 3/29/17	
1625	Robert COLLINS of Chard	1764	T.N.A., PROB 31/1764/648	
1626	William COLLINS of Winscombe	1639	D/D/cta/C15	Ad.ac.
1627	William COLLINS of Ilminster	1687	T.N.A., PROB 4/2612	Will also extant
1628	George COLLWELL of Otterhampton	1640	DD/SP/1640/23	
1629	Humphrey COLMER, Baker of Butleigh	1732	D/D/Cti 20	
1630	William COLMER of [no place]	1631	D/D/cta/C86	Ad.ac.
1631	Edward COLTHURST, Gentleman of North Newton, North Petherton	1713	DD/SP/1713/11	
1632	[missing] COLYNS of Temple Cloud, Cameley	1573	DD/HI/286	
1633	Giles COMBE, Esquire of Otterford	1678	T.N.A., PROB 4/8773	Admon
1634	John COMBE of Taunton St. Mary Magdalene	1648	DD/SP/1648/31	
1635	John COMBE of Taunton St. Mary Magdalene	1684	DD/SP/1684/94	
1636	John COMBE of Otterford	1687	DD/SP/1687/19a	
1637	John COMBE of Otterford	1687	DD/SP/1687/50	
1638	John COMBE, Yeoman of Wambrook	1700	W.S.H.C., P14/91	Inv. and will
1639	Mary COMBE of Pitminster	1672	DD/SP/1672/56	
1640	John COMBSTOCK of Curry Rivel	1645	DD/SP/1645/55	

1641	Robert COMBSTOCKE of Curry Rivel	1635	DD/SP/1635/18	
1642	Christopher COMER, Husbandman of Hillfarrance	1664	DD/SP/1664/68	
1643	George COMER, Yeoman of Huish Champflower	1678	DD/SP/1678/49	
1644	Grace COMER of Crowcombe	1761/2	DD/TB/18/13	
1645	Henry COMER of Luxborough	1690	DD/SP/1690/56	
1646	John COMER, Yeoman of Brompton Ralph	1668	DD/SP/1668/1	
1647	John COMER of Stogumber	1682	DD/SP/1682/40	
1648	John COMER senior of Crowcombe	1728	DD/SP/1728/34	
1649	Mary COMER, Spinster of North Petherton	1688	DD/SP/1688/25	
1650	Thomas COMER, Bachelor of Halse	1665	DD/SP/1665/30	
1651	Thomas COMER of Luxborough	1689	T.N.A., PROB 4/19300	Admon
1652	Mary CONENT, Widow of Shepton Beauchamp	1645	DD/SP/1645/45	CONNIETT (*T.C.W.*)
CONIBER see CONNIBERE				
1653	Alexander CONNIBERE of Monksilver	1710	DD/SP/442/51	Ad.ac.
1654	John CONNIBERE of West Quantoxhead	1640	DD/SP/1640/69	See *T.C.W.*
1655	Michael CONNIBERE (or CONIBER) of West Quantoxhead	1640	DD/SP/1640/46	
CONNIETT see CONENT				
1656	Joseph CONWAY, Sergemaker of East Quantoxhead	1678	DD/SP/1678/69	
1657	Mary CONWAY, Widow of Crewkerne	1666	DD/SP/1666/12	
1658	Thomas CONWAY of Kilton	1683	DD/SP/1683/36	
1659	Charles COODE of Stawley	1710	DD/SP/442/2	Ad.ac.
1660	Abraham COOK, Shipwright of Abbots Leigh	1721	B.A., 1721/8	
1661	Isaac COOK of Shepton Mallet	1690	T.N.A., PROB 4/10257	Admon. Illegible
1662	Isaac COOK of Shepton Mallet	n.d.	T.N.A., PROB 5/4919	
1663	John COOK of Baltonsborough	n.d.	D/D/cta/C35	Ad.ac.
1664	John Lamb COOK of West Camel	1795	T.N.A., PROB 31/1795/667	
1665	Roger COOK ? of Brockley	1587	D/D/cta/C76	Ad.ac.
1666	Abraham COOKE of Evercreech	1674	T.N.A., PROB 4/12177	Will, died 14 Nov. 1674
1667	Adryan COOKE of Isle Brewers	1687	DD/SP/1687/66	
1668	Adryan and Joan (his wife) COOKE of Isle Brewers	1688	DD/SP/1688/18a	
1669	Agnes COOKE, Widow of Brislington	1809	T.N.A., PROB 31/1809/403	With account and com.
1670	Elizabeth COOKE, Widow of Churchill	1677	T.N.A., PROB 4/435	Will also extant
1671	Elizabeth COOKE, Widow of Chew Magna	1714	D/P/che.m/23/1	

1672	George COOKE, Yeoman of [no place]	1646	DD/SP/1646/46	
1673	Hercules and Alice (his wife) COOKE of Milverton	1667	DD/SP/1667/73	
1674	John COOKE, Husbandman of Shapwick	1592	D/D/cta/C38	Ad.ac.
1675	John COOKE of Exford	1640	DD/SP/1640/91	
1676	John COOKE of Taunton St. Mary Magdalene	1668	DD/SP/1668/14	
1677	John COOKE of Hurcot, Somerton	1678	T.N.A., PROB 4/22192	Will also extant
1678	John COOKE junior of Creech St. Michael	1680	DD/SP/1680/60	
1679	Richard COOKE, Cardmaker of Buckland Dinham	1674	T.N.A., PROB 4/10412	Will 1675. ex. 1675
1680	Richard COOKE of Baltonsborough	1743	D/D/cta/C87	Ad.ac. and inv.
1681	Roger COOKE of Brockley	1587	D/D/cta/C27	Ad.ac.
1682	Samuel COOKE, Fuller of Frome Selwood	1678	T.N.A., PROB 4/2779	Will 1676
1683	Thomas COOKE, Gentleman of Shepton Mallet	1681	T.N.A., PROB 4/6943	Will. ex. 1682
1684	Thomas COOKE, Gentleman of Shepton Mallet	1690	T.N.A., PROB 4/25633	Will 1691. ex. 1690
1685	William COOKE the elder of [no place]	1646	DD/SP/1646/67	
1686	Hugh COOKSLEY, Husbandman of Brompton Regis	1687	DD/SP/1687/28	
1687	James COOKSLEY of Otterhampton	1691	DD/SP/1691/55	
1688	John COOKSLEY of Upton	1681	DD/SP/1681/80	
1689	Mary COOKSLEY of Chipstable	1680	DD/SP/1680/26	
1690	Prudence COOKSLEY of Upton	1681	DD/SP/1681/79	
1691	Richard COOKSLEY of Dunster	1680	DD/SP/1680/30	
1692	Robert COOKSLEY, Innholder of Taunton St. James	1723	DD/SP/1723/54	
1693	Humphry COOMBE of Milverton	1635	DD/SP/1635/63	See *T.C.W.*
1694	John COOMBE of Glastonbury	1678	D/D/cta/C77	Ad.ac.
1695	Thomas COOMBE of [no place]	1705	D/D/cta/C90	Ad.ac.
1696	James COOMBES of Mells	1712	D/D/cta/C91	Ad.ac.
1697	Stephen COOMBS, Haberdasher of Frome Selwood	1720	DD/SF/15/2/35	Formerly DD/SF/3888
1698	Harriet COOMBSTOCK, Spinster and Bastard of Taunton	1825	T.N.A., PROB 31/1825/435	
1699	Elizabeth COOMER, Widow of East Brent	1727	D/D/cta/C92	Ad.ac.
1700	George COOPER of Glastonbury St. John	1612	D/D/cta/C52	Ad.ac.
1701	John COOPER, Gentleman of Bishops Hull	1670	DD/SP/1670/38	
1702	John COOPER of Hudesham, East Pennard	1707	T.N.A., PROB 5/1964	
1703	Thomas COOPER of Bishops Hull	1698	DD/SP/1698/10	
1704	William COOPER of Glastonbury	1685	T.N.A., PROB 4/17417	Admon

1705	William COOPER of Glastonbury	1687	T.N.A., PROB 5/5134	
1706	Edward COPNER of Ash Priors	1634	DD/SP/1634/33	
COPP see WHELLER				
1707	Alexander CORAM of Milverton	1637	DD/SP/1632/30	Undated (Reg.)
1708	Alexander CORAM, Yeoman of Milverton	1637	DD/SP/1637/35	
1709	Jane CORAM, Widow of Milverton	1696	DD/SP/1696/32	
1710	Marmaduke CORAM of Taunton	1664	DD/SP/1664/30	
1711	Nicholas CORAM of Bradford	1695	DD/SP/1695/27	
1712	Robert CORAM of Bradford	1664	DD/SP/1664/71	
1713	Roger CORAM of Capland, Broadway	1635	DD/SP/1635/124	
1714	William CORAM of Milverton	1636	DD/SP/1636/33	
1715	John CORDING of Brompton Regis	1738	DD/SP/1738/46	
1716	Mary CORDING of Brompton Ralph	1684	DD/SP/1684/176	
CORDINGE see CODINGE				
1717	Edward CORDWENT, Husbandman of Oake	1670	DD/SP/1670/97	
1718	George CORDWENT of Kilton	1641	DD/SP/1641/27	
1719	Humphrey CORDWENT, Gentleman of Wells	1681	T.N.A., PROB 5/5154	
1720	John CORDWENT of Dodington	1662	DD/SP/1662/27	
1721	William CORFEELD of Winscombe	1626	D/D/cta/C8	Ad.ac.
1722	John CORFIELD, Esquire of Kempsey, Worcestershire formerly of St. Peter le Poor, London afterwards of St. Marylebone, Middlesex later of Taunton	1825	T.N.A., PROB 31/1825/817	
1723	Peter CORNELIUS of Croft, Hinton St. George	1691	DD/SP/1691/20	
1724	Peter CORNELIUS of Hinton St. George	1691	DD/SP/1691/5	
1725	Alice CORNISH of Taunton St. James	1679	DD/SP/1679/26	
1726	Ann CORNISH of Kingstone	1681	DD/SP/1681/97	
1727	Bartholomew CORNISH of Ash Priors	1679	DD/SP/1679/19	
1728	Benjamin CORNISH of Newton St. Loe	1735	D/D/Cti 17	
1729	Eleaner CORNISH, Spinster of Exton	1698	DD/SP/1698/25	
1730	George CORNISH, Yeoman of Kingston	1669	DD/SP/1669/77	
1731	Henry CORNISH of Kingston St. Mary	1729	DD/SP/1729/52	
1732	Hugh CORNISH senior, Yeoman of Dinnington	1693	DD/SP/1693/21	
1733	Joan CORNISH, Widow of Staplegrove	1690	DD/SP/1690/62	

1734	John CORNISH, Innholder of Taunton St. Mary Magdalene	1666	DD/SP/1666/43	Reference to inns called Maidenhead and Half Moon
1735	John CORNISH of Taunton St. James	1686	DD/SP/1686/45	
1736	John CORNISH of Cutcombe	1697	DD/SP/1697/58	
1737	John CORNISH of Cutcombe	1698	DD/SP/1698/34	
1738	Philip CORNISH of Taunton St. Mary Magdalene	1687	DD/SP/1687/26	
1739	Philip CORNISH senior, Tailor of Taunton St. Mary Magdalene	1682	DD/SP/1682/60	
1740	Thomas CORNISH of [no place]	1640	DD/SP/1640/105	Proved by Joan CORNISH, Widow
1741	Thomas CORNISH, Yeoman of Kingston	1643	DD/SP/1643/46	
1742	Thomas CORNISH of Withiel Florey	1682	DD/SP/1682/62	
1743	Thomas CORNISH of Taunton St. Mary Magdalene	1714	DD/SP/1714/27	
1744	William CORNISH, Yeoman of Ditcheat	1640	D/D/cta/C69	Ad.ac.
1745	William CORNISH of Minehead	1677	DD/SP/1677/1	
CORNISH see BRUFORD				
1746	James CORPE of Edington	1611	D/D/cta/C49	Ad.ac.
1747	John CORUM of Hewish, Crewkerne	1690	DD/SP/1690/13	
1748	Thomas CORY, Butcher of Yeovil	1646	D/D/cta/C54	Ad.ac.
1749	William COSBY of Taunton St. Mary Magdalene	1682	D/D/cta/C97	Ad.ac.
1750	Roger COSSINS of Crewkerne	1705	T.N.A., PROB 4/22770	Will. ex. 170–?
1751	William COTTEN of [no place]	1602	D/D/cta/C21	Ad.ac.
1752	Richard COTTLE of Combhay	1678	T.N.A., PROB 4/22145	Admon. ex. 1679
1753	Richard COTTLE of Barrow Gurney	1733	D/D/Cti 22	
1754	Samuel COTTLE of Batheaston	1730	T.N.A., PROB 3/29/200	
1755	Richard COTTON, Chapman of Shepton Mallet	1609	D/D/cta/C40	Ad.ac.
1756	Samuel COTTRELL, Blacksmith of Bedminster	1679	T.N.A., PROB 4/6916	Will 1679
1757	Hugh COUCH of Wootton Courtenay	1666	DD/SP/1666/39	
1758	Marmaduke COUCH of Stockland Bristol	1666	DD/SP/1666/5	
1759	William COUCH, Yeoman of Williton, St. Decumans	1670	T.N.A., PROB 4/12936	Admon
1760	Thomas COUCH alias ELLIOTT of Aisholt	1646	DD/SP/1646/47	
1761	Richard COULLEN, Carpenter of Charlinch	1669	DD/SP/1669/61	
1762	[male] COUNSELL of East Brent ?	*c*.1700	D/D/cta/C6	
	Note: Ad.ac.; mentions a daughter Ann who married Daniel BURROW at East Brent in 1695, plus three unmarried children			
1763	John COUNSELL of Congresbury	1667	D/D/cta/C67	Ad.ac.

1764	Henry COURT of Marksbury	1734	D/D/Cti 16	
1765	John COURT of Exford	1669	DD/SP/1669/69	
1766	Robert COURT of Wootton Courtenay	1724	DD/SP/1724/59	
1767	Ann COURTE, Widow of Dulverton	1731	DD/SP/1731/27	
1768	John COURTE of Skilgate	1646	DD/SP/1646/40	
1769	John COURTE, Gentleman of North Curry	1701	T.N.A., PROB 5/3172	
1770	John COURTNEY, Thatcher of Huish Champflower	1666	DD/SP/1666/20	
1771	John COURTNEY, Yeoman of Taunton St. Mary Magdalene	1682	DD/SP/1682/15	
1772	John and Jane COURTNEY of Huish Champflower	1694	DD/SP/1694/22	
1773	Grace COURTT of Exford	1691	DD/SP/1691/91	
1774	Thomas COUSINS of Fivehead	1731	DD/SP/1731/33	
1775	Anthony COUSONS of Staple Fitzpaine	1647	DD/SP/1647/20	
COUSONS see COZEN				
1776	John COVANT, Gentleman of Portbury	1727	T.N.A., PROB 3/26/60	
1777	James COWARD of Beckington, died abroad	1724	T.N.A., PROB 31/1724/344	
1778	John COWARD of West Pennard	1662	D/D/cta/C60	Ad.ac.
1779	Richard COWARD, Yeoman of West Pennard	1678	DD/JC/2	
1780	Richard COWLING of Minehead	1677	DD/SP/1677/68	
1781	Humphrey COWPER, Blacksmith of Banwell	1683	T.N.A., PROB 4/6838	Will 1685. ex. 1685
1782	[missing] COX of West Bagborough	1686	DD/SP/1686/9	
1783	Alice COX, Widow of Chelwood	1640	D/D/cta/C16	Ad.ac.
1784	Ann COX of Wells	1690	DD/FS/27/2/3	
1785	Christian COX, Gentleman of Crewkerne	1690	DD/SP/1690/69	
1786	Christopher COX of Thurlbear	1640	DD/SP/1640/76	
1787	Cuthbert COX the elder of Frome Selwood	1639	D/D/cta/C13	Ad.ac.
1788	Edward COX, Gentleman of Corston	1647	D/D/cta/C55	Ad.ac.
1789	Edward COX, Surgeon and Apothecary of Crewkerne	1764	T.N.A., PROB 31/1764/420	With ad.ac.
1790	Edward COX the elder of Brewham	1739	T.N.A., PROB 3/38/81	
1791	Henry COX of Blagdon	1634	D/D/cta/C12	Ad.ac.
1792	Henry COX, Yeoman of Pensford St. Thomas, Publow	1734	D/D/cta/C93	Ad.ac. and inv.
1793	Jane COX of Curry Rivel	1678	DD/SP/1678/36	
1794	Jeremiah COX, Gentleman of Langford, Burrington	1674	T.N.A., PROB 4/13228	Will also extant
1795	John COX of West Bagborough	1684	DD/SP/1684/138	

1796	John COX, Yeoman of Bratton Seymour	1758	DD/HN/2/6/9	
1797	Katherine COX, Widow of Crewkerne	1687	DD/SP/1687/1	
1798	Richard COX, Husbandman of Shepton Beauchamp	1676	T.N.A., PROB 4/25562	Will also extant
1799	Richard COX, Gentleman of Merriott	1687	T.N.A., PROB 4/18359	Will also extant
1800	Robert COX of Puckington	1684	DD/SP/1684/92	
1801	Robert COX of Corston	1744	T.N.A., PROB 31/1744/451 and 1744/452	
1802	Samuel COX, Farmer, widower of West Harptree	1737	T.N.A., PROB 3/36/51	
1803	Samuel COX, Widower of West Harptree	1737	T.N.A., PROB 31/1737/176	
1804	Simon COX of Taunton St. Mary Magdalene	1585	D/D/cta/C37	Ad.ac.
1805	Thomas COX of Congresbury	1595	D/D/cta/C73	Ad.ac.
1806	William COX, Gentleman of Fayland, Wraxall	1681	T.N.A., PROB 4/5331	Will also extant
1807	Elias COXE, Blacksmith of Taunton St. Mary Magdalene	1676	DD/SP/1676/10	
1808	George COXE, Yeoman of St. Michaelchurch	1630s	DD/SP/1632/32	
	Note: Undated; appraised by John BATT, Henry YEATS and Richard LEWIS			
1809	John Hippisley COXE of Ston Easton	1769	DD/HI/A/328	
1810	Robert COXE of Taunton St. Mary Magdalene	n.d.	DD/SP/17th Century/2	Fragment
1811	Roger COXE of Curry Rivel	1670	DD/SP/1670/85	
1812	William COXE, Husbandman of Barrington	1647	DD/SP/1647/11	
1813	John COZEN of Bickenhall	1664	DD/SP/1664/66	
1814	Silvester COZEN of Minehead	1639	DD/SP/1639/60	See *T.C.W.*
1815	Richard COZENER of [no place]	1640	D/D/cta/C71	Ad.ac.
1816	Joseph CRABB? of Lullington	1687	T.N.A., PROB 4/10458	Admon
1817	William CRAFT of Curry Rivel	1694	DD/SP/1694/26	
1818	Archibald Cummings CRAIG of Philadelphia, North America died at Bedminster, Somerset	1802	T.N.A., PROB 31/1802/1014	
1819	John CRAMER of Bath St. James	1745	T.N.A., PROB 31/1745/363 and 1745/369 and 1745/376	
1820	John CRANDON of Wambrook	1675	W.S.H.C., P14/34	Inv.
1821	John CRANDON, Yeoman of Bridgwater	1690	DD/SP/1690/24	
1822	Agnes CRANE of Chedzoy	1591	D/D/cta/C22	Ad.ac.
1823	Francis CRANE, Yeoman of Somerton Erleigh (Somerton Early), Somerton	1676	T.N.A., PROB 4/6853	Will also extant

1824	John CRANE of Somerton	1603	D/D/cta/C42	Ad.ac.
1825	John CRANE, Pewterer of Minehead	1685	DD/SP/1685/35	
1826	Christopher CRANG of Exford	1667	DD/SP/1667/14	
1827	John CRANN of Hardington Mandeville	1666	D/D/cta/C66	Ad.ac.
1828	Christopher CRAPP, Mercer of Bridgwater	1687	T.N.A., PROB 4/8505	Will 1686. ex. 1680 (*sic*)
1829	John CRAY, Husbandman of Locking	1587	D/D/cta/C98	Ad.ac.
1830	Francies CREDLAND of West Monkton	1634	DD/SP/1634/34	
1831	Elizabeth CREEB, Spinster of Creech St. Michael	1679	DD/SP/1679/4	
1832	John CREECH, Yeoman of Porlock	1685	T.N.A., PROB 4/2264	Will also extant
1833	John CREECH the elder, Tipler of Porlock	1640	DD/SP/1640/97	
CREECH see BICKHAM				
1834	Jonathon CREED, Baker of Bruton	1733	D/D/Cti 21	
1835	Henry CREIDLE of Milverton	1637	DD/SP/1637/30	
1836	William CRIBB, Husbandman of Stapleton, Martock	1588	D/D/cta/C31	Ad.ac.
1837	Frances CRIDLAND, Yeoman of Trull	1648	DD/SP/1648/39	
1838	Joane CRIDLAND, Widow of Lydeard St. Lawrence	1635	DD/SP/1635/98	See *T.C.W.*
1839	Richard CRIDLAND of West Monkton	1620	D/D/cta/C1	Ad.ac.
1840	Richard CRIDLAND of West Monkton	1697	DD/SAS/C432/21	
1841	Richard CRIDLAND, Yeoman of West Monkton	1697	DD/SP/1697/71	
1842	Robert CRIDLAND of Wembdon	1646	DD/SP/1646/48	See *T.C.W.*
1843	Thomas CRIDLAND of Cannington	1669	DD/SP/1669/39	
1844	William CRIDLAND of West Monkton	1678	DD/SAS/C432/21	
CRIDLAND see CREDLAND				
1845	John CRIDLE, Yeoman of Over Stowey	1696	DD/SP/1696/22	
1846	Henry CRIPPS of Dunster	1635	DD/SP/1635/65	See *T.C.W.*
1847	John CRIPPS of Huntspill	1581	D/D/cta/C39	Ad.ac.
1848	Ames CROCKER of Norton Fitzwarren	1691	DD/SP/1691/79	
1849	Henry CROCKER of Stoke St. Gregory	1642	DD/SAS/FA/161/8	
1850	Henry CROCKER the younger of Stoke St. Gregory	1644	DD/SAS/FA/161/31	
1851	Hugh CROCKER of Bishops Hull	1671	DD/SP/1671/38	
1852	John CROCKER of Bishops Hull	1675	DD/SP/1675/73	Legacy to Henry BINDON deceased
1853	John CROCKER of Milverton	1686	DD/SP/1686/21	
1854	John CROCKER, Carpenter of Swell	1687	DD/SP/1687/29	

1855	Humphrey CROCKER alias GRAVE of Spaxton	1678	DD/SP/1678/23	
1856	Robert CROCKER alias GRAVE, Yeoman of Spaxton	1678	DD/SP/1678/52	Reference to a grist mill
CROCKER see GRAVE				
1857	John CROCKFORD, Yeoman of Old Cleeve	1687	DD/X/RMN/8	
1858	Mary CROCKFORD, Widow of Carhampton	1678	T.N.A., PROB 4/10577	Will 1678
1859	George CROFT of Glastonbury St. John	1684	D/D/cta/C94	Ad.ac.
1860	Hugh CROFTMAN, Tailor of Stogumber	1678	DD/SP/1678/21	
1861	Thomas CROOKE of Chipstable	1714	DD/SP/1714/30	See DD/SP 442(17)
1862	Thomas CROOKE of Chipstable	1715/6	DD/SP/442/17	Ad.ac.
CROOKE see BAKER				
1863	Dioness CROOM, Widow of Kelston	1726	D/D/cta/C36	Ad.ac.
1864	Joseph CROOM of Kelston	1727	D/D/cta/C95	Ad.ac.
1865	John CROOPE of Wambrook	1613	W.S.H.C., P5/1613/14	Inv., will
1866	Thomas CROSMAN of Kingston Seymour	1622	D/D/cta/C2	Ad.ac.
1867	Francis CROSS, Widow of Abbots Leigh	1662	B.A., 1662/15	Will also extant
1868	George CROSS of North Petherton	1697	DD/SP/1697/40	
1869	Joel CROSS, Yeoman of Thurlbear	1714	DD/SP/1714/33	
1870	John CROSS, Leather cutter of Taunton St. Mary Magdalene	1742	T.N.A., PROB 3/41/65	
1871	Robert CROSS of Creech St. Michael	1640	DD/SP/1640/140	
1872	William CROSS the elder of Cannington	1668	DD/SP/1668/68	
1873	Bartholomew CROSSE of Curry Rivel	1684	DD/SP/1684/103	
1874	Charles CROSSE the elder, Gentleman of Aisholt	1684	DD/SP/1684/43	
1875	Clement CROSSE of East Bower, Bridgwater	1676	DD/SP/1676/15a+b	
1876	John CROSSE of [no place]	1642	DD/SP/1642/6	
1877	John CROSSE of Langaller, Creech St. Michael	1679	DD/SP/1679/7	
1878	John CROSSE of Taunton St. Mary Magdalene	1682	DD/SP/1682/39	
1879	Mary CROSSE of Taunton St. James	1645	DD/SP/1645/9	
1880	Mary CROSSE of Taunton St. Mary Magdalene	1683	DD/SP/1683/30	
1881	Richard CROSSE of West Monkton	1640	DD/SP/1640/102	
1882	Robert CROSSE, Yeoman of Taunton	1732	DD/SP/1732/11	
1883	Thomas CROSSE, Clothier of Taunton St. Mary Magdalene	1676	DD/SP/1676/48	
1884	Thomas CROSSE alias BURGE, Husbandman of North Petherton	1649	DD/SP/1649/74	

1885	Simon CROSTMAN of Bridgwater	1672	DD/SP/1672/6	
1886	John CROUCH of Bath City	1739	T.N.A., PROB 31/1739/98	With ad.ac.
1887	Roger CROW of High Ham	1665	D/D/cta/C62	Ad.ac.
1888	Edward CROYDON of Westonzoyland	1599	D/D/cta/C58	Ad.ac.
1889	George CROYDON of Westonzoyland	1639	D/D/cta/C14	Ad.ac.
1890	Richard CRUDGE of Brushford	1702	DD/SP/442/46	Ad.ac.
1891	Alce CRUSE, Widow of Brushford	1674	DD/SP/1674/22	
1892	John CRUSE of Upton	1677	DD/SP/1677/67	
1893	William CRUSE of Dulverton	1698	DD/SP/1698/40	
1894	Robert CUDBELL of Curry Mallet	1682	DD/SP/1682/22	
1895	John CUFF of Wells St. Cuthbert	n.d.	D/D/cta/C57	Ad.ac.
1896	Nicholas CUFFE of Martock	1592	D/D/cta/C78	Ad.ac.
1897	Robert CUFFE of Creech St. Michael	1662	DD/SF/11/2/25	Formerly DD/SF/3929
1898	Thomas CUFFE of Martock	1591	D/D/cta/C79	Ad.ac.
1899	William CUFFE, Yeoman of Curry Rivel	1683	DD/SP/1683/77	
1900	William CULIVORD of Kingsbury Episcopi	1587	D/D/cta/C26	Ad.ac.
1901	Gertrude CULLIFORD, Widow of Hambridge, Curry Rivel	1680	DD/SP/1680/81	
1902	Thomas CULPEPER, Gentleman of Porlock	1714	DD/SP/1714/21	
1903	Abraham CULVERWELL of Stogursey	1683	DD/SP/1683/87	
1904	Anthony CULVERWELL of Ruishton	1716	DD/SP/1716/17	
1905	Humphry CULVERWELL of North Curry	1698	T.N.A., PROB 4/16594	Admon
1906	Mary CULVERWELL, Widow of Spaxton	1638	DD/SP/1638/64	
1907	Thomas CULVERWELL, Husbandman of Wootton Courtenay	1640	DD/SP/1640/70	
1908	Thomas CULVERWELL of Stogursey	1681	DD/SP/1681/26	
1909	William CULVERWELL, Tanner of North Petherton	1642	DD/SP/1642/12	
1910	Stephen CUNDICT, Maltster of Dunkerton	1749	T.N.A., PROB 31/1749/864	With ad.ac.
1911	John CUNDIT, Gentleman of Kilve	1690	DD/SP/1690/63	
1912	William CURNOCK of Freshford	1588	D/D/cta/C30	Ad.ac.
1913	Francis CURRANT of North Petherton	1687	T.N.A., PROB 4/9027	Admon. ex. 1688
1914	Joan CURREY, Widow of West Monkton	1697	DD/SP/1697/67	
1915	[missing] CURRY of [no place]	1673	DD/SP/1673/17	Incomplete entry
1916	Francis CURRY of Milverton	1682	DD/SP/1682/8	
1917	Robert CURRY of Spaxton	1738	D/D/Cti 14	

1918	John CURSE, Bachelor of Wells died in H.M.S. *Royal James*	1672	T.N.A., PROB 4/5582	Admon
1919	Robert CURTIS of Milborne Port	1737	D/D/Cti 15	
1920	Samuel CURTIS of Chewton Mendip	1738	D/D/cta/C96	Ad.ac.
1921	George CUTHBERT, Yeoman of Stoke St. Mary	1698	DD/SP/1698/13	
1922	Stephen CUTLER, Husbandman of Thornfalcon	1698	DD/SP/1698/22	
1923	William CUTLER, Clerk of Thornfalcon	1646	DD/SP/1646/18	
1924	Thomas CUTLY of Winsford	1637	DD/SP/1637/2	
1925	Zacharias CUTTLY of Winsford	1670	DD/SP/1670/93	
1926	Robert DABB of Dodington	1636	DD/SP/1636/10	See *T.C.W.*
1927	James DABBS, Blacksmith of Bedminster	1695	T.N.A., PROB 4/5383	Admon
1928	Henry DABINOTT, Weaver of Barrington	1677	DD/SP/1677/15	
1929	John DABINOTT of Donyatt	1639	DD/SP/1639/12	
1930	Margaret DABINOTT, Widow of Barrington	1678	DD/SP/1678/38	
1931	John DADSCOMBE of Huish Champflower	1677	DD/SP/1677/76	
1932	Thomas DADSCOMBE alias HILL of Brompton Regis	1670	DD/SP/1670/111	
1933	Margery DALE, Widow of Loxton	n.d.	D/D/cta/D23	Pre 1634 ad.ac. and inv.
1934	Richard DALE of Taunton St. Mary Magdalene	1664	DD/SP/1664/70	
1935	Edward DALLY of Edington	1619	D/D/cta/D18	Ad.ac.
1936	Robert DALTON of Moorlinch	1642	D/D/cta/D20	Ad.ac.
1937	William DAMPIER of Blackford	1718	DD/SAS/C238/59	
1938	Avis and Anne DANDO of Paulton	1600	D/D/cta/D45	Ad.ac.
1939	Benjamin DANER of Ilminster	1675	T.N.A., PROB 4/6857	Admon
1940	Marmaduke DANIEL, Clothier of Frome Selwood	1734	T.N.A., PROB 3/33/125	
1941	Elinor DANIELL of Chedzoy	1639	DD/SP/1639/44	
1942	James DANIELL of East Bower, Bridgwater	1663	D/D/cta/D26	Ad.ac.
1943	James DANIELL, Yeoman of Abbots Leigh	1681	B.A., 1681/19	Appraised 1671
1944	Mary DANIELL, Widow of Abbots Leigh	1711	B.A., 1711/15	Will also extant
1945	William DANIELL, Yeoman of Abbots Leigh	1676	B.A., 1676/11	Will also extant
1946	William DANIELL, Butcher of Crowcombe	1680	DD/SP/1680/88	
1947	William DANIELL of Stogursey	1681	DD/SP/1681/35	
1948	William DANIELL, Widower of Yeovil	1779	T.N.A., PROB 31/1779/379	
1949	George DANTER, Merchant of Minehead	1683	DD/SP/1683/94	
1950	Henry DARBY, Yeoman of South Petherton	1716	DD/SP/1716/38	

1951	Humphry DARBY of Dinnington	1684	DD/SP/1684/132	
1952	Thomas DARBY of Dinnington	1683	DD/SP/1683/86	
1953	Thomas DARBY of Dinnington	1730	DD/SP/1730/1	
1954	James DARCH, Mason of Selworthy	1686	DD/SP/1686/17	
1955	John DARCH senior, Husbandman of Lyng	1640	DD/SP/1640/98	
1956	Sarah DARCH, Widow of Bridgwater	1769	T.N.A., PROB 31/1769/68	
1957	Thomas DARCH, Esquire of Pinehill, Kentucky, North America formerly of Taunton	1801	T.N.A., PROB 31/1801/447	
1958	William DARE, Butcher of Taunton St. Mary Magdalene	1679	DD/SP/1679/1	Reference to Shuttern and East Street
1959	William DARE, Butcher of Trull	1749	DD/SP/1749/34	
1960	Elianor DASHWOOD, Widow of Rowdon, Stogumber	1678	T.N.A., PROB 4/6956	Will. ex. 1679
1961	George DASHWOOD of Bicknoller	1697	DD/SP/1697/18	
1962	John DASHWOOD, Yeoman of Stogumber	1669	T.N.A., PROB 4/18870	Admon
1963	Richard DASHWOOD of Clatworthy	1681	DD/SP/1681/69	
1964	Robert DASHWOOD of Stogumber	n.d.	DD/SP/17th Century/3	Fragments
1965	Anne DATE, Spinster of Catsfield, Sussex formerly of Bridgwater then of Plymouth, Devon	1825	T.N.A., PROB 31/1825/334	
1966	Elizabeth DATE of Tolland	1677	DD/SP/1677/41	
1967	Phillippe DATSCOMBE alias HILL of Dulverton	1674	DD/SP/1674/46	
1968	Lewes DATTESCOMBE, Yeoman of Brushford	1674	T.N.A., PROB 4/9603	Will 1675. ex. 1675
1969	Elizabeth DAUCKINGS of Selworthy	1673	DD/SP/1673/36	
1970	Morgan DAVEY of Bishops Hull	1682	DD/SP/1682/30	
1971	Thomas DAVEY of Hamp, Bridgwater	1675	DD/SP/1675/14	
1972	Elizabeth DAVIDGE, Widow of Charlinch	1687	DD/SP/1687/14	
1973	Joan DAVIDGE, Widow of Stoke St. Gregory	1674	T.N.A., PROB 4/6864	Will also extant
1974	Joane DAVIDGE, Widow of Taunton St. James	1679	DD/SP/1679/2	
1975	Mary DAVIDGE, Widow of Spaxton	1669	T.N.A., PROB 4/10453	Will 1669. ex. 1670
1976	Agnes DAVIE of [no place]	1637	DD/SP/1637/45	
1977	Arthur DAVIE, Weaver of Creech St. Michael	1665	DD/SP/1665/8	
1978	Mary DAVIE, Widow of Minehead	1690	DD/SP/1690/44	
1979	Nicholas DAVIE, Doctor of Physic of Wiveliscombe	1729	DD/SP/1729/53	
1980	Richard DAVIE of Minehead	1634	DD/SP/1634/4	
1981	Richard DAVIE of Minehead	1641	DD/SP/1641/35	

1982	Walter DAVIE of Minehead	1637	DD/SP/1637/49	
1983	Andrew DAVIES of Broadway	1683	DD/SP/1683/32	
1984	George DAVIES of Luccombe	1673	DD/SP/1673/33	
1985	Howell DAVIES of Carhampton	1670	DD/SP/1670/62	
1986	John DAVIES of Minehead	1690	DD/SP/1690/12	
1987	Nathaniel DAVIES, Cordwainer of Taunton	1644	DD/SP/1644/65	
1988	James DAVIS, Cordwainer of Monksilver	1727	DD/SP/1727/30	
1989	John DAVIS of Creech St. Michael	1667	DD/SP/1667/29	
1990	John DAVIS, Mariner of Bridgwater	1689	DD/SP/1689/39	
1991	Julian DAVIS of Taunton St. Mary Magdalene	1637	DD/SP/442/32	Ad.ac.
1992	Nicholas DAVIS of Ditcheat	1666	D/D/cta/D29	Ad.ac.
1993	Robert DAVIS of Easton in Gordano	1675	T.N.A., PROB 4/669	Will 1675
1994	Thomas DAVIS of Enmore	1692	DD/SP/1692/27	Absent of this 'Kingdome six yeares past'
1995	William DAVIS of Taunton St. James	1674	DD/SP/1674/13	
1996	John DAVISON of Freshford	1708	T.N.A., PROB 5/3271	
1997	Richard DAVISSE of Taunton St. Mary Magdalene	1688	DD/SP/1688/19	
1998	Arthur DAVY of Creech St. Michael	1682	DD/SP/1682/3	
1999	Bartholomew DAVY senior, Husbandman of Milverton	1684	DD/SP/1684/38	
2000	Dorothy DAVY, Widow of Creech St. Michael	1675	DD/SP/1675/6	
2001	Griffith DAVY of Minehead	1683	DD/SP/1683/20	
2002	John DAVY of Minehead	1679	DD/SP/1679/58	
2003	John DAVY of Hawkridge	1681	DD/SP/1681/4	
2004	Thomas DAVY of West Monkton	1670	DD/SP/1670/78	
2005	John DAVYE of Milverton	1645	DD/SP/1645/20	
2006	John DAVYES of Wanstrow	1619	D/D/cta/D44	Ad.ac.
2007	Isaac DAVYS, Mariner of Minehead	1683	DD/SP/1683/21	
2008	[missing] DAW, Widow of Crowcombe	1676	DD/SP/1676/26	
2009	Aldred DAW, Yeoman of Brompton Regis	1642	DD/SP/1642/24	
2010	Ambros DAW, Husbandman of Brompton Regis	1645	DD/SP/1645/3	
2011	John DAW of North Petherton	1675	DD/SP/1675/22	
2012	Elizabeth DAWBENEY of Wayford	1640	DD/HI/B/453	
2013	[missing] DAWBENY of Wayford	1674	DD/SP/1674/27	

2014	Elizabeth DAWBENY, Widow of Wayford	1640	DD/SP/1640/86	
2015	Giles DAWBENY, Clothier of Misterton	1735	D/D/Cti 23	
2016	Alice DAWE, Widow of Crowcombe	1635	DD/SP/1635/94	
2017	Francis DAWE, Yeoman of Merriott	1670	DD/SP/1670/104	
2018	Joane DAWE, Widow of Clatworthy	1646	DD/SP/1646/2	
2019	John DAWE, Yeoman of Wootton Courtenay	1640	DD/SP/1640/118	
2020	William DAWE, Tanner of Crowcombe	1685	DD/SP/1685/22	
2021	Anastacia DAWES, Widow of Bridgwater	1694	DD/SP/1694/4	
2022	Edmund DAWES of Bridgwater	1689	DD/SP/1689/35	
2023	George DAWES of West Monkton	1635	DD/SP/1635/116	
2024	George DAWES of Bridgwater	1691	DD/SP/1691/49	Late of the ship *Blessing*
2025	Joan DAWES, Spinster of Bridgwater	1685	DD/SP/1685/47	
2026	Elizabeth DAY of Stogursey	1686	DD/SP/1686/15	
2027	Gertrude DAY of Woolavington	1686	D/D/cta/D34	Ad.ac.
2028	Henry DAY of Spaxton	1664	DD/SP/1664/43	
2029	Hugh DAY of South Barrow	1634	D/D/cta/D6	Ad.ac.
2030	John DAY of Kingston Seymour	1640	D/D/cta/D31	Ad.ac.
2031	John DAY the elder of Worle	1604	D/D/cta/D16	Ad.ac.
2032	Robert DAY of Stogursey	1678	DD/SP/1678/71	
2033	Samuel DAY, Rector of Wootton Courtenay	1689	T.N.A., PROB 4/8524	Will also extant
2034	William DAY of Seaborough	1636	DD/SP/1636/19	
2035	William DAY, Gentleman of Discove, Bruton	1679	T.N.A., PROB 4/20221	Will also extant
2036	William DAY, Gentleman of Wincanton	1705	T.N.A., PROB 4/22491	Admon
2037	William DAY, Yeoman of North Petherton	1736	DD/SP/1736/28	
2038	William DAY of North Petherton	1737	DD/SP/442/84	Ad.ac.
2039	Richard DAYE of Yarlington	1622	D/D/cta/D3	Ad.ac.
2040	Thomas DAYE of Kewstoke	1625	D/D/cta/D10	Ad.ac.
2041	William DAYE of [no place]	1626	DD/SP/1626/11	
2042	Thomas DAYES of Otterhampton	1675	DD/SP/1675/21	
2043	Bauldwen DEACON of Kingston	1635	DD/SP/1635/136	
2044	Thomas DEACON of Somerton	1640	D/D/cta/D32	Ad.ac.
2045	Robert DEAKE of Minehead	1635	DD/SP/1635/66	
2046	Robert DEAKE of East Quantoxhead	1677	DD/SP/1677/55	

2047	William DEAMONT, Husbandman of Merriott	1637	DD/SP/1637/42	
2048	Edmund DEANE of Bleadon	1588	D/D/cta/D43	Ad.ac.
2049	Elizabeth DEANE of Kingsbury Episcopi	1667	DD/HLM Box 2	
2050	George DEANE, Woolen Draper of Ilminster	1678	T.N.A., PROB 4/2445	Will also extant
2051	John DEANE of East Brent	1588	D/D/cta/D12	Ad.ac.
2052	Richard DEANE, Clothworker of Crewkerne	1687	DD/SP/1687/44	
2053	Samuel DEANE of Chard	1747	T.N.A., PROB 3/46/43	
2054	Samuel DEANE of Chard	1747	T.N.A., PROB 31/1747/523	
2055	Reverend Bartholomew DEEKESMITH, Clerk of Timsbury	1828	T.N.A., PROB 31/1828/1341	
2056	George DEEPE, Barber of Axbridge	1622	D/D/cta/D4	Ad.ac.
2057	William DELBRIDGE, Husbandman of Withypool	1689	DD/SP/1689/16	
2058	Samuel DELL, Goldsmith of Taunton	1698	DD/SP/1698/18	
2059	Philip DELLBRIDGE of Withypool	1699	DD/SP/1699/13	
2060	Thomas DENHAM of East Quantoxhead	1640	DD/SP/1640/64	
2061	James DENISH, Helliar of Bridgwater	1687	DD/SP/1687/67	
2062	Allen DENMAN of Stratton, South Petherton	1640	DD/SP/1640/36	
2063	Thomas DENMAN of Donyatt	1720	DD/SP/1720/15	
2064	Adam DENMEAD of South Petherton	1646	DD/SP/1646/19	
2065	William DENNER, Yeoman of Kingston	1825	T.N.A., PROB 31/1825/1078	
2066	Thomas DENNING of Wellington	1626	D/D/cta/P8a	Ad.ac.
DENNIS see HANNCE				
2067	David DENOONE, Doctor of [no place]	1708	DD/TD Box 16	Pvd. 1711
2068	George DERBY, Gentleman of Chard	1686	T.N.A., PROB 4/8195	Admon
2069	John DERRETT of .....ford	1678	T.N.A., PROB 4/6950	Admon. ex. 1679
2070	Charles DEVERELL of Twerton	1822	T.N.A., PROB 31/1822/93 and PROB/1822/362	
2071	Charles DEVERELL of Twerton	1825	T.N.A., PROB 31/1825/334	
2072	Robert DEVONSHIRE of Minehead	1684	DD/SP/1684/173	
2073	Richard DEWNELL of Crewkerne	1636	DD/SP/1636/3	
2074	William DEY of Stogumber	1671	DD/SP/1671/37	
2075	John DIBBIN the elder of Orchard Portman	1702	DD/SP/442/44	Ad.ac.
2076	[missing] DIBBLE of [no place]	1684	DD/SP/1684/47	Incomplete
2077	Andrew DIBBLE, Yeoman of Crowcombe	1678	DD/SP/1678/14	

2078	Catherin DIBBLE, Widow of Crowcombe	1685	DD/SP/1685/3	
2079	Henry DIBBLE, Weaver of Holford	1684	DD/SP/1684/48	
2080	Joan DIBBLE, Widow of Middlezoy	1629	D/D/ct/1/D/39	
2081	John DIBBLE of Thurloxton	1668	DD/SP/1668/25	
2082	Richard DIBBLE of West Bagborough	1639	DD/SP/1639/68	
2083	Richard DIBBLE, Yeoman of Moorland, Lyng	1675	DD/SP/1675/20	
2084	Robert DIBBLE of Thurloxton	1683	DD/SP/1683/96	
2085	Thomas DIBBLE of Taunton St. James	1669	DD/SP/1669/50	
2086	John DICER of Bruton	1588	D/D/cta/D33	Ad.ac.
2087	William DICKES, Clerk of Elworthy	1635	DD/SP/1635/92	
2088	Henry DIER of Tolland	1636	DD/SP/1636/16	
2089	Robert DIER, Husbandman of Bleadon	1612	D/D/cta/D19	Ad.ac.
2090	[missing] DIER alias LAWRENCE ? of [no place]	1638	DD/SP/1638/37	
	Note: Mentions the natural father Roger DIER alias LAWRENCE; damaged			
DIER see LAWRENCE				
2091	Elizabeth DIGHT, Widow of Ilminster	1789	T.N.A., PROB 31/1789/693	
2092	Elizabeth DIGHT, Widow of Ilminster	1793	T.N.A., PROB 31/1793/288	
2093	John DIGHT, Husbandman of Donyatt	1684	DD/SP/1684/111	
2094	John DIGHT of Halse	1684	DD/SP/1684/44	
2095	Anne DIGHTON, Widow of Bath	1810	T.N.A., PROB 31/1810/49	
2096	Thomas DIKE of Street	1611	D/D/cta/D15	Ad.ac.
2097	Lewes DINGHURST of [no place]	n.d.	D/D/cta/D8	Ad.ac.
2098	John DINGIE of Corfe	1700	DD/SP/1700/23	
2099	John DINHAM of Ilminster	1679	T.N.A., PROB 5/5517	
2100	John DINHAM of Staple Fitzpaine	1697	DD/SP/1697/21	
2101	John DINHAM, Gentleman of Ilminster	1675, 1678	T.N.A., PROB 4/8702	Will 1675
2102	William DIRROCK of Winford	1605	D/D/cta/D42	Ad.ac.
2103	George DISH of Kittisford	1696	DD/SP/1696/9	
2104	Margaret DITCHER, Widow of Bath	1666	D/D/cta/D28	Ad.ac.
2105	John DITTIE of Wincanton	1662	D/D/cta/D25	Ad.ac.
2106	John DIX the younger of Glastonbury St. John	1640	D/D/cta/D30	Ad.ac.
2107	James DOBIN of North Petherton	1735	DD/SP/1735/25	

2108	Simon DOBIN of Ashcott	1686	D/D/cta/D35	Ad.ac.
2109	Simon DOBIN of Ashcott	1702	D/D/cta/D36	Ad.ac.
2110	Alce DOBLE of Crowcombe	1640	DD/SP/1640/33	
2111	Edward DOBLE of Otterhampton	1684	DD/SP/1684/145	
2112	Elizabeth DOBLE of Crowcombe	1722	DD/SP/442/75	Ad.ac.
2113	John DOBLE of Crowcombe	1712	DD/SP/442/4	Ad.ac.
2114	Robert DOBLE, Mariner of Minehead	1713	DD/SP/1713/18	
2115	Thomas DOBLE of Kingsbury Episcopi	1661	DD/SAS/FA/161/5	
2116	William DOBLE, Gentleman of Freethy, Bishops Hull	1691	DD/SP/1691/17	
2117	John DOD, Yeoman of Burnham on Sea	1682	T.N.A., PROB 4/5605	Will 1682
2117a	John DOD, Carrier of Compton Bishop	1750	W.S.H.C., 161/133	Will
2118	John DODDINGTON, Mercer of Bishops Hull	1691	DD/SP/1691/32	
2119	Mary DODDINGTON, Widow of Bishops Hull	1674	DD/SP/1674/28	
2120	John DODDRIDGE of North Petherton	1722	DD/SP/442/73	Ad.ac.
DODESCOMBE see HILL				
2121	John DODINGTON of [no place]	1608	A/CZA/2/2	Ad.ac.
2122	John DODINGTON, Esquire of Dodington, died in London	1674	T.N.A., PROB 5/364	Admon 1674
2123	John DODRIDGE, Yeoman of North Petherton	1721	DD/SP/1721/22	
2124	George DODSWORTHY, Gentleman of Stoford, Barwick	1694	T.N.A., PROB 4/11520	Will 1694
2125	Thomas DOGGERELL, Linen Weaver of South Petherton	1646	DD/SP/1646/20	See *T.C.W.*
2126	[male] DOGGETT of Croscombe ?	1640	D/D/cta/D1	
	Note: Ad.ac.; Elizabeth DOGGETT, administratrix, was buried at Croscombe in 1642			
2127	George DOLEMAN, Borier of Capland, Broadway	1681	DD/SP/1681/64	
2128	Francis DOLLAMAN of Goathurst	1694	DD/SP/1694/39	
DOLLEN see DOLLING				
2129	Nicholas DOLLING, Yeoman of Trull	1635	DD/SP/1635/129	
2130	Thomas DOLLING, Yeoman of Trull	1635	DD/SP/1635/130	
2131	Richard DOLLING alias DOLLEN of Taunton St. Mary Magdalene	1672	T.N.A., PROB 5/5159	
DOLLINGE see BLAKE				
2132	Agnis DOLPHEN of Taunton St. James	1642	DD/SP/1642/26	
2133	George DOMINIE of Ditcheat	1662	D/D/cta/D24	Ad.ac.
2134	Edward DOMMETT of Angersleigh	1640	DD/SP/1640/22	

2135	[missing] DONN of [no place]	1692	DD/SP/1692/32	Incomplete, wife Rachel
2136	Benjamin DONNE of South Petherton	1753	DD/MR/67	
2137	James DONNE of Buckland St. Mary	1692	DD/SP/1692/15	
2138	John DONNE of Langford Budville	1669	DD/SP/1669/28	
2139	John DONNE of Seavington St. Mary	1673	DD/SP/1673/19	
2140	Joseph DONNE of Hinton St. George	1677	T.N.A., PROB 4/8497	Will. ex. 1678
2141	Susanna DONNE of Crewkerne	1762	DD/MR/66	
2142	John DORRANT alias QUICKE of Kittisford	1634	DD/SP/1634/35	
2143	John DORSETT of Wells	n.d.	D/D/cta/D13	Ad.ac.
2144	Arthur DORVILL of Ansford	1665	D/D/cta/D27	Ad.ac.
2145	John DORY of Ston Easton	1690	DD/FS/35/17/2	
2146	Thomas DORY of Cameley	1673	D/D/cta/D37	Ad.ac.
2147	Agnes DOSSE, Widow of Chedzoy	1641	DD/SP/1641/48	
2148	John DOSSE, Husbandman of Chedzoy	1669	DD/SP/1669/73	
2149	Phillipp DOSSE, Widow of Chedzoy	1637	DD/SP/1637/19	
2150	Thomas DOSSE of Chedzoy	1640	DD/SP/1640/133	
2151	John DOTHERED of Crowcombe	1696	DD/SP/1696/6	
2152	John DOTHERIDGE of Crowcombe	1701	DD/SP/442/40	Ad.ac.
2153	Samuel DOUDENY alias BUCKINGE, Husbandman of North Petherton	1662	DD/SP/1662/24	
DOUDING see DOWDING				
2154	John DOWDENY, Husbandman of Otterhampton	1726	DD/SP/1726/26	
2155	Thomas DOWDING (or DOUDING) of Stogursey	1665	DD/SP/1665/33	
DOWDING see BURNOLL				
2156	William DOWDNEY of Ashbrittle	1681	DD/SP/1681/43	
2157	Richard DOWLING of High Littleton	1735/6	D/D/Cti 24	
2158	William DOWLING, Victualler of Chewton Mendip	1705	DD/PINC/9/2	See the burial register for 1700/1
2159	Mary DOWN, Widow of Shepton Mallet	1810	T.N.A., PROB 31/1810/95	With ac. and com.
2160	Nicholas DOWNAHAM, Husbandman of Chillington	1646	DD/SP/1646/32	
2161	John DRAKE, Husbandman of Crewkerne	1682	DD/SP/1682/32	
2162	Jonathan DRAKE, Yeoman of Otterford	1668	DD/SP/1668/66	
2163	Richard DRAKE of Puckington	1638	DD/SP/1638/19	
2164	Richard DRAKE of Stogumber	1697	DD/SP/1697/26	

2165	William DRAKE of Wellington	1744	T.N.A., PROB 3/43/31	
2166	William DRAKE of Wellington	1744	T.N.A., PROB 31/1744/423	
2167	Hugh DRAPER, Yeoman of Drayton and South Petherton	1677	DD/SP/1677/3	
2168	Margaret DRAPER, Spinster of North Perrott	1730	D/D/cta/D38	Ad.ac.
2169	John DRAPPER, Husbandman of South Petherton	1674	DD/SP/1674/47	
2170	Mary DRAYTON, Spinster of Little Puckington, Barrington	1696	DD/SP/1696/36	
2171	Mary DRAYTON of Drayton	1697	DD/SP/1697/59	
2172	Thomas DRAYTON of Barrington	1675	DD/SP/1675/69	
2173	John DREW the younger of Curry Rivel	1644	DD/SP/1644/59	
2174	Robert DREW of Dunster	1693	DD/SP/1693/12	
2175	Richard DREWSSE, Husbandman of Merriott	1645	DD/SP/1645/33	
2176	John DRIALL of Chewton Mendip	1607	D/D/cta/D22	Ad.ac.
2177	Catherine DRINKWATER, Widow of Isle Abbotts	1674	DD/SP/1674/5	
2178	William DRINKWATER of Isle Abbotts	1668	DD/SP/1668/17	
2179	Richard DRUCE, Baker of Bath	1676	T.N.A., PROB 4/6902	Will 1676
2180	Richard DRUER of Seavington St. Michael	1667	DD/SP/1667/65	
2181	William DRUER otherwise TOOGOOD of Frome Selwood	1621	D/D/cta/D5	Ad.ac.
2182	Edith DRYER of Winsham died at Tiverton, Devon	1708	T.N.A., PROB 5/3209	See T.N.A., PROB 5/3270
2183	Edith DRYER of Winsham died at Tiverton, Devon	1708	T.N.A., PROB 5/3270	See T.N.A., PROB 5/3209
2184	Robert DUCKE, Sergemaker of Fiddington	1714	DD/SP/1714/23	
2185	William DUCKWORTH of Orchardleigh	1876	DD/DU/148	
2186	Mary and Edith DUDDYNG of [no place]	n.d.	D/D/cta/D9	Ad.ac.
2187	James DUKES, Husbandman of Stogursey	1693	DD/SP/1693/22	
2188	John DULING of Axbridge	1639	D/D/cta/D7	Ad.ac.
2189	John DUMETT of Swell	1684	DD/SP/1684/3	
2190	Edward DUN of Barwick	1620	D/D/cta/D14	Ad.ac.
2191	Reverend John DUNCAN, Rector (D.D.) of Bath	1809	T.N.A., PROB 31/1809/100	Rector of South Wanborough, Southampton
2192	Edward DUNGEY, Soapboiler of West Monkton	1684	DD/SP/1684/110	
2193	Christopher DUNHAM, Yeoman of Hinton St. George	1634	DD/SP/1634/3	
2194	Joane DUNHAM, Widow of Hinton St. George	1639	DD/SP/1639/9	
2195	John DUNMAN of West Monkton	1688	DD/SP/1688/18	
2196	Edward DUNN of Barwick	1620	D/D/cta/D2	Ad.ac.

2197	Henry DUNN of Wootton Courtenay	1675	DD/SP/1675/95	
2198	John DUNN of Hillfarrance	1668	DD/SP/1668/2	
2199	William DUNN of Brent Knoll	1644	D/D/cta/D21	Ad.ac.
2200	William DUNN, Carpenter of Pitminster	1691	DD/SP/1691/37	
2201	John DUNNING, Innholder of Taunton St. Mary Magdalene	1699	DD/SP/1699/15	
2202	John DUNSCOMBE, Yeoman of Exton	1648	DD/SP/1648/42	
2203	John DUNSCOMBE, Yeoman of Exton	1683	DD/SP/1683/52	
2204	Robert DUNSCOMBE of Winsford	1680	DD/SP/1680/14	An indigent person
2205	Arthur DUNSTER, Husbandman of Buckland St. Mary	1696	DD/SP/1696/11	
2206	Henry DUNSTER, Yeoman of Ruishton	1664	DD/SP/1664/1	
2207	Henry DUNSTER of Seavington St. Michael	1668	DD/SP/1668/62	
2208	Mercy DUNSTER of Chaffcombe	1802	DD/WL/31	
2209	Thomas DUNSTER, Yeoman of Ilminster	1675	T.N.A., PROB 4/10523	Admon. ex. 1676
2210	Thomas DUNSTER of Seavington St. Michael	1678	DD/SP/1678/41	
2211	John DUNSTONE of Bridgwater	1692	DD/SP/1692/28	
2212	Richard DURBAN the elder, Yeoman of Cheddar	1681	T.N.A., PROB 4/10651	Will. ex. 1682
2213	Richard DURBAN the elder, Yeoman of Cheddar	1684	T.N.A., PROB 4/9594	Wills 1684 and 1684
2214	[male] DURBER of [missing]	1632	D/D/cta/D39	
	Note: Ad.ac. by his sister Grace PLUSH; his children are listed with their ages			
2215	John DURLINGE the elder of [no place]	1635	DD/SP/1635/7	
2216	Thomas DURMAN the elder, Cordwainer of Crewkerne	1684	DD/SP/1684/22	
2217	William DURMAN, Clerk of Stratton on the Fosse	1691	D/D/cta/D40	Ad.ac. for a clergyman
2218	Edith DURNELL of Camerton	1604	D/D/cta/D17	Ad.ac.
2219	Giles DURSTON of Catcott	1673	T.N.A., PROB 5/5505	
2220	John DURSTON, Yeoman of Pitminster	1678	T.N.A., PROB 4/2781	Admon
2221	John DURSTON, Yeoman of Dunwear, Bridgwater	1683	T.N.A., PROB 4/6908	Will. ex. 1684
2222	John DURSTON of Chard	1690	T.N.A., PROB 4/668	Will 1690
2223	Robert DURSTON senior of South Petherton	1693	DD/SP/1693/30	
2224	Thomas DURSTON of Catcott	1686	DD/X/GRT/1	
2225	Alice DYER, Widow of Minehead	1678	DD/SP/1678/61	
2226	Francis DYER, Yeoman of Curry Rivel	1713	DD/SP/1713/45	
2227	Henry DYER of Lydeard St. Lawrence	1667	DD/SP/1667/82	
2228	John DYER of Milton Falconbridge, Martock	1641	D/D/cta/D11	Ad.ac.

2229	John DYER of Monksilver	1675	DD/SP/1675/74	
2230	John DYER of Cutcombe	1684	DD/SP/1684/42	
2231	John DYER, Husbandman of East Quantoxhead	1730	DD/SP/1730/20	
2232	John DYER, Yeoman of St. Catherine	1738	D/D/cta/D41	Ad.ac. and inv.
2233	Robert DYER of Lydeard St. Lawrence	1690	DD/SP/1690/36	
2234	Robert DYER, Weaver of Lydeard St. Lawrence	1690	DD/SP/1690/7	
2235	Robert DYER of Combe St. Nicholas	1738	T.N.A., PROB 31/1738/186	With ad.ac.
2236	William DYER, Yeoman of Bathealton	1677	DD/SP/1677/26	
2237	William DYER of Catherine	1760	T.N.A., PROB 31/1760/80	
2238	John DYER alias LARRENCE, Clothworker of Cannington	1716	DD/SP/1716/23	
DYER see DIER				
2239	Edward DYMOND of Taunton St. Mary Magdalene	1680	T.N.A., PROB 4/4744	Will also extant
2240	John EADES of Hutton	1668	T.N.A., PROB 4/21034	Admin
2241	George EAME of Luccombe	1696	DD/SP/1696/45	
2242	[missing] EAMES of [no place]	1673	DD/SP/1673/15	Joane EAMES relict; damaged
2243	Christabel EAMES of Greinton	1685	D/D/cta/E14	Ad.ac.
2244	Elizabeth EAMES, Widow of Torweston, Sampford Brett	1668	T.N.A., PROB 4/6862	Will also extant
2245	Phillip EAMES, Fuller of Minehead	1678	DD/SP/1678/79	
2246	Stephen EAMES of Stogursey	1670	DD/SP/1670/81	
2247	John EARLE, Clerk of Shipham	1674	D/D/cta/E15	Ad.ac. of a clergyman
2248	Richard EARLE, Clerk of Hemington	1678	T.N.A., PROB 4/4576	Will 1678. ex. 1679
2249	Richard EARLE, Clerk of Hemington Note: PROB 5/453, Sentence, Vicar of Hemington 1628–78	1699	T.N.A., PROB 5/2010	
2250	Janet EARLUM, Widow of Cheddon Fitzpaine	1716	DD/SP/1716/32	
2251	John EASCOTT, Fuller of Taunton St. Mary Magdalene	1685	DD/SP/1685/44	
2252	Elizabeth EASON of Lopen	1731	DD/SP/1731/19	
2253	John EASTCOURT of Over Stowey	1706	T.N.A., PROB 5/5288	
2254	John EASTMOND, Gentleman of Barrington	1675	T.N.A., PROB 4/19890	Will 1675
2255	Thomasin EASTMOND, Widow of Barrington	1686	T.N.A., PROB 4/17186	Admon. ex. 1687
2256	Reuben EASTMUND of Haselbury Plucknett	1681	T.N.A., PROB 4/6865	Will T.N.A. PROB 11/366/83
2257	Thomas EASTON, Carpenter of Beercrocombe	1731	DD/SP/1731/11	
2258	William EASTON of East Pennard	1594	D/D/cta/E13	Ad.ac.
2259	Reverend Charles Steuart (*sic*) ECCLES, Clerk of Bath St. Peter and St. Paul	1778	T.N.A., PROB 31/1778/617	With ad.ac.

2260	Joane EDBROOKE, Widow of Cutcombe	1634	DD/SP/1634/5	
2261	John EDBROOKE of Exford	1697	DD/SP/1697/11	
2262	John EDBROOKE, Husbandman of Cutcombe	1720	DD/SP/1720/20	
2263	William EDBROOKE of Exford	1680	DD/SP/1680/40	
2264	James EDCOX of Congresbury	1596	D/D/cta/E12	Ad.ac.
2265	John EDGAR, Rector of Donyatt	1697	DD/SP/1697/49	
2266	George EDGELL of Norton St. Philip	1666	D/D/cta/E11	Ad.ac.
2267	John EDGHILL, Chandler of Wells	1725	D/D/cta/E16	Ad.ac.
2268	William EDMONDES of South Petherton	1667	DD/SP/1667/13	
2269	Joan EDMONDS, Widow of South Petherton	1677	DD/SP/1677/19	
2270	John EDMONDS, Esquire of Bath	1844	T.N.A., PROB 37/1314	Com.
2271	Mathew EDMONDS of South Petherton	1636	DD/SP/1636/44	
2272	Samuel EDMONDS of South Petherton	1667	DD/SP/1667/43	
2273	William EDMONDS senior of Moorhasocke, South Petherton	1675	DD/SP/1675/38	
2274	Mary EDMUND, Widow of Dunster	1675	DD/SP/1675/39	
2275	John EDMUNDS, Cordwainer of Shepton Beauchamp	1691	DD/SP/1691/28	
2276	Cisseli EDNEY, Widow of Mells	1629	D/D/ct/1/E/6	
2277	Lawrence EDNEY of Cannington	1725	DD/SP/1725/16	
2278	Margaret EDNEY, Widow of Heathfield	1686	DD/SP/1686/47	
2279	William EDSON of Backwell	1619	D/D/cta/E10	Ad.ac.
2280	Andrew EDWARDS of Chilton (*sic*)	1664	DD/SP/1664/78	
2281	George EDWARDS, Maltster of Sherston, North Petherton	1666	DD/SP/1666/8	
2282	Henry EDWARDS of Chard	1751	DD/CN/33/4	
2283	Jane EDWARDS, Widow of Trull	1703	DD/SP/442/48	Ad.ac.
2284	Jane or Joanne EDWARDS of Mudgeley, Wedmore	1680	T.N.A., PROB 5/3265	
2285	Jane EDWARDS senior, Widow of Durleigh	1677	DD/SP/1677/63	
2286	John EDWARDS of Stoke St. Michael	1681	T.N.A., PROB 4/17227	Admon
2287	John EDWARDS of Wilton	1689	DD/SP/1689/21	
2288	Thomas EDWARDS of Walcot	1825	T.N.A., PROB 31/1825/759	
2289	William EDWARDS of D......	1634	DD/SP/1634/24	
2290	William EDWARDS of Saltford	1688	T.N.A., PROB 4/17668	Admon
2291	Robert EDWARDS ? of Durston ?	1636	DD/SP/1636/63	
	Note: Appraised by Francis STARKEY, mentions a lease for the lives of Robert, William and Alice EDWARDS (Reg.)			

EDWARDS see STRANGE				
2292	John EEDES the elder of Crewkerne	1636	DD/SP/1636/61	
2293	[missing] EGBY of [no place]	1633	D/D/cta/E17	Ad.ac.
2294	Elesabeth ELERY, Widow of Chedzoy	1667	DD/SP/1667/26	
2295	Amos ELFORD, Clerk of Martock	1625	D/D/cta/E2	Ad.ac. of a clergyman
2296	Anne ELLIOT, Widow of Bridgwater	1728	D/D/cta/E18	Ad.ac.
2297	Andrew ELLIOTT of Stratton, South Petherton	1670	DD/SP/1670/6	Buried at South Petherton
2298	Andrew ELLIOTT senior, Husbandman of South Petherton	1671	DD/SP/1671/5	
2299	Anthony ELLIOTT, Yeoman of South Petherton	1675	DD/SP/1675/93	
2300	Henry ELLIOTT, Girth-web Weaver of Wayford	1637	DD/SP/1637/43	
2301	Henry ELLIOTT of Bridgwater	1716	DD/SP/442/18	Ad.ac.
2302	James ELLIOTT senior of South Harp, South Petherton	1716	DD/SP/1716/58	
2303	John ELLIOTT of Glastonbury St. John	1588	D/D/cta/E7	Ad.ac.
2304	John ELLIOTT of Yeovil	1690	T.N.A., PROB 4/16869	Will 1690
2305	John ELLIOTT of Ruishton	1695	DD/SP/1695/17	
2306	John ELLIOTT the elder, Husbandman of Orchard Portman	1680	DD/SP/1680/79	
2307	Lawrence ELLIOTT of Ruishton	1680	DD/SP/1680/67	
2308	Philip ELLIOTT of Wells St. Cuthbert	1607	D/D/cta/E8	Ad.ac.
2309	Robert ELLIOTT of Bridgwater	1682	DD/SP/1682/9	
2310	Thomas ELLIOTT of Cannington	1734	DD/SP/1734/21	
2311	William ELLIOTT, Husbandman of Barrington	1647	DD/SP/1647/12	
2312	William ELLIOTT, Yeoman of South Petherton	1683	DD/SP/1683/15	
ELLIOTT see COUCH				
2313	Alexander ELLIS of Stogursey	1684	DD/SP/1684/34	
2314	Alse ELLIS of Monksilver	1635	DD/SP/1635/57	See *T.C.W.*
2315	Hugh ELLIS of Chipstable	1694	DD/SP/1694/14	
2316	John ELLIS of Hornblotton	1635	D/D/cta/E5	Ad.ac.
2317	John ELLIS, Soapboiler of Minehead	1667	DD/SP/1667/52	
2318	Osmond ELLIS of Edgarley, Glastonbury	1678	DD/EV/23	
ELLIS see HOLCOMBE				
2319	Elizabeth ELLYS of Bath	1724	T.N.A., PROB 3/23/247	
	Note: Wife of Richard ELLYS, also of Doddington, Lincolnshire			
2320	Katherine ELMES, Widow of Nunney	1678	T.N.A., PROB 4/19109	Admon

2321	Samuel ELMS of Timsbury	1730	D/D/Cti 26	
2322	James ELSON of Chipstable	1721	DD/SP/1721/18	
2323	William ELSTONE alias HOOPER of Selworthy	1684	DD/SP/1684/12	
2324	Arthur ELSWORTHY of Withycombe	1670	DD/SP/1670/63	
2325	Edmund ELSWORTHY of Cutcombe	1698	DD/SP/1698/28	
2326	[missing] ELSWORTHY ? of Dunster or Minehead ?	1694	DD/SP/1694/33	
	Note: Thomas ELSWORTHY father, appraised by Richard START, Edmund SPURRIER, Henry CLEMENT and Robert PEARCE senior; damaged (Reg.)			
2327	John ELSWORTHY alias STRETTINGER of Dunster	1665	DD/SP/1665/37	
2328	Ann ELVARD of Wookey	n.d.	DD/SAS/C795/SE/125/1	
2329	Peter otherwise Elvin WRENCH ELWIN of Cape of Good Hope, South Africa formerly of Bath	1782	T.N.A., PROB 31/1782/493	With ad.ac.
2330	Peter otherwise Elvin WRENCH ELWIN, Esquire of Cape of Good Hope, South Africa formerly of Bath	1810	T.N.A., PROB 31/1810/897	
2331	Edmund ELWORTHY, Husbandman of Cutcombe	1698	DD/SP/1698/20	
2332	Richard ELWORTHY, Yeoman of Withiel Florey	1680	DD/SP/1680/37	
2333	William EMBLEN of Frome	1733	D/D/Cti 25	
2334	Thomas EMERY of Ashwick	1623	D/D/cta/E4	Ad.ac.
2335	John ENGLAND of West Monkton	1645	DD/SP/1645/40	
2336	John ENGLAND of North Petherton	1668	DD/SP/1668/52	
2337	John ENGLAND, Yeoman of Creech St. Michael	1745	DD/SP/1745/27	
2338	John ENGLAND junior, Husbandman of Durston	1685	DD/SP/1685/28	
2339	Robert ENGLAND of Trull	1685	DD/SP/1685/74	
2340	Thomas ENGLAND senior, Weaver of Shepton Beauchamp	1677	DD/SP/1677/20	
2341	John ENGLISH senior of North Petherton	1691	DD/SP/1691/69	
2342	John ENGRAM of Stogursey	1672	DD/SP/1672/8	
ENGRAM see INGRAM				
2343	Robert ERLUM of Taunton St. Mary Magdalene	1698	DD/SP/1698/33	
2344	George ESCOTT, Mariner of Minehead	1664	DD/SP/1664/19	
2345	James ESCOTT, Yeoman of Treborough	1716	DD/SP/1716/8	
2346	Lawrence ESCOTT of Dunster	1607	D/D/cta/E9	Ad.ac.
2347	Thomas ESCOTT, Gentleman of Sandhill, Withycombe	1765	DD/L/2/35/1–2 Box 138	
2348	John ESTCOURT, Gentleman of Over Stowey	1704	T.N.A., PROB 5/5790	

2349	Agnes EVANS, Widow of East Quantoxhead	1691	DD/SP/1691/67	
2350	Anne EVANS, Widow of Portbury?	1685	T.N.A., PROB 4/16883	Admon
2650a	Gawin EVANS of East Quantoxhead	1683	D/D/cta/E19	
	Note: Ad.ac. by Agnes his relict; damaged			
2351	Joane EVANS, Widow of Winsford	1665	DD/SP/1665/26	
2352	John EVANS of Winsford	1666	DD/SP/1666/65	
2353	John EVANS, Clerk of West Harptree	1680	T.N.A., PROB 4/6909	Will also extant
2354	John EVANS, Gentleman of Burcott, Wells St. Cuthbert	1690	T.N.A., PROB 4/10522	Admon. ex. 1691. Intestate
2355	Lewis EVANS of Bridgwater	1647	DD/SP/1647/21	
2356	Philip EVANS of Cutcombe	1690	DD/SP/1690/5	
2357	Thomas EVANS of Wilton	1680	DD/SP/1680/3	
2358	Thomas EVANS, Whittawer of Bedminster	1698	T.N.A., PROB 4/9832	Admon
2359	William EVANS the elder of West Quantoxhead	1678	DD/SP/1678/76	
2360	James EVATT of Luxborough	1627	DD/SP/1627/12	
EVATT see EVETT				
2361	Johane EVENS, Widow of Minehead	1635	DD/SP/1635/99	
2362	John EVENS, Poor Labourer of Winsford	1665	DD/SP/1665/9	
2363	Robert EVENS of Dunster	1684	DD/SP/1684/18	
2364	John EVERAD of Bradford	1609	DD/X/PLY/6	
2365	Frances EVERARD, Widow of Stockland Bristol	1691	DD/SP/1691/61	Widow of William
2366	George EVERARD of Aller, Carhampton	1617	DD/S/GLY/19	Wife Christian
2367	John EVERARD of Spaxton	1696	DD/TRANS/3/36	
2368	Lewis EVERARD of Aller, Carhampton	1680	DD/S/GLY/19	Wife Florence
2369	Mary EVERARD of Otterhampton	1672	DD/SP/1672/42	
2370	Nicholas EVERATT of Bruton	1799	T.N.A., PROB 31/1799/922 and 1799/926	
2371	Nicholas EVERATT of Bruton	1800	T.N.A., PROB 31/1800/43	
2372	Elizabeth EVERED, Widow of Stockland Bristol	1636	DD/SAS/C795/HV/56	
2373	Nicholas EVERETT of Kilve	1712	DD/SP/442/5	Ad.ac.
2374	William EVERGLADE of Creech St. Michael	1645	DD/SP/442/30	Ad.ac.
2375	[missing] EVERIE ? of Hatch Beauchamp	n.d.	D/D/cta/E3	
	Note: Ad.ac.; see D/D/cta/E6 for the other part of this document			
2376	[missing] EVERIE ? of Hatch Beauchamp	n.d.	D/D/cta/E6	

	Note: Ad.ac.; see D/D/cta/E3 for the other part of this document			
2377	Amy EVERY of Creech St. Michael	1676	DD/SP/1676/41	
2378	John EVERY of Hatch Beauchamp	1668	DD/SP/1668/32	
2379	John EVERY of Pitminster	1675	DD/SP/1675/56	
2380	Thomas EVERY of Donyatt	1669	DD/SP/1669/100	
2381	Valentine EVERY, Tailor of Creech St. Michael	1665	DD/SP/1665/31	
2382	William EVERY of Cothay, Kittisford	1652	DD/SF/9/3/5	Formerly DD/SF/3128
2383	John EVETT of Dunster	1669	DD/SP/1669/8	
2384	John EVETT, Husbandman of Torweston, Sampford Brett	1675	DD/SP/1675/17	
2385	Margaret EVETT of Dunster	1665	DD/SP/1665/44	
2386	John EVILL senior of Keinton Mandeville	1696	DD/FS Box 8	
2387	Rebecca Mason EVILL formerly COYDE of Bath	1826	T.N.A., PROB 31/1826/817	Wife of Luke EVILL
2388	Bethell EWENS, Cordwainer of Dunster	1689	DD/SP/1689/13	
2389	Emmanuel EWENS, Gentleman of Witham Friary	1683	DD/SAS/C151/18	
2390	John EWENS of Dunster	1691	DD/SP/1691/15	
2391	Thomas EWENS of Porlock	1640	DD/SP/1640/122	Inv. shows YEVEN
2392	Thomas EWENS, Gentleman of Penselwood	1685	DD/X/AR/5/5	
2393	Richard EWINS of Stogumber	1639	DD/SP/1639/6	
2394	Dorothy EXON, Woolcomber of Taunton	1689	DD/SP/1689/19	
2395	Ellen EXTON, Widow of Milverton	1682	DD/SP/1682/28	
2396	John EYERS of Stocklinch Ottersey	1646	DD/SP/1646/49	
2397	Thomas EYRE, Yeoman of Carhampton	1702	T.N.A., PROB 4/22722	Will also extant
2398	Benjamin FACKRELL of Haygrove, Bridgwater	1721	DD/SP/1721/32	
2399	Robert FACY of Cannington	1635	DD/SP/1635/61	
2400	Stephen FANING of Moorlinch	1675	D/D/cta/F28	Ad.ac.
2401	Thomas FAREWELL, Esquire of Holbrook, Charlton Musgrove	1680	T.N.A., PROB 4/13131	Will also extant
2402	Thomas FAREWELL, Esquire of Holbrook, Charlton Musgrove	1688	T.N.A., PROB 4/19803	Will 1689
2403	Anthony FARLEY of East Coker	1757	T.N.A., PROB 3/56/32	
2404	Anthony FARLEY of East Coker	1757	T.N.A., PROB 31/1757/510	
2405	John FARLEY of Yeovil	1752	DD/PR/28	
2406	William FARMER of Over Stowey	1671	DD/SP/1671/22	
FARMER see FERMER				
2407	Thomas FARNHAM, Blacksmith of Wambrook	1636	W.S.H.C., P30/67	Inv. and will

2408	John FARNUM, Thatcher of Orchard Portman	1698	DD/SP/1698/4	
2409	Samuel FARR, Baker of Bath	1736	D/D/cta/F29	Ad.ac. and inv.
2410	Simon FARRE, Woolcomber of Frome Selwood	1724	T.N.A., PROB 3/23/89	
2411	Alice FARRINGTON, Widow of Cannington	1667	DD/SP/1667/10	
2412	John FARROW, Mariner and Seaman of Somerton formerly of H.M.S. *Yarmouth* and H.M.S. *Royal George*	1783	T.N.A., PROB 31/1783/323	
2413	Bartholomew FARTHING, Gentleman of Stogursey	1685	DD/SP/1685/11	
2414	Elizabeth FARTHING, Widow of Dulverton	1680	DD/SP/1680/34	
2415	Elizabeth FARTHING of Stawell, Moorlinch	1699	D/D/cta/F30	Ad.ac.
2416	Joane FARTHING, Widow of Monksilver	1680	DD/SP/1680/9	
2417	John FARTHING, Yeoman of Milverton	1665	DD/SP/1665/12	
2418	John FARTHING of Kingston	1665	DD/SP/1665/61	
2419	Mary FARTHING, Widow of Stogumber	1684	DD/SP/1684/84	
2420	Robert FARTHING of Taunton St. James	1640	DD/SP/1640/119	See *T.C.W.*
2421	Thomas FARTHING of Bishops Lydeard	n.d.	DD/SP/17th Century/5	
2422	William FARTHING of Oake	1731	DD/SP/1731/24	
FARTHING see FURTHINGE				
2423	George FATHERS, Tanner of Kingston	1681	DD/SP/1681/94	
2424	Benjamin FAWKES, Papermaker of Saltford	1738	T.N.A., PROB 3/37/100	
2425	Benjamin FAWKS, Papermaker of Saltford	1738	T.N.A., PROB 31/1738/507	
2426	John FAWSITT, Tobacconist and grocer of Bridgwater	1745	T.N.A., PROB 3/44/18	Mentions tobacco and grocery
2427	James FEARE, Clothweaver of North Petherton	1686	DD/SP/1686/36	
2428	John FEARE, Sergeweaver of North Petherton	1684	DD/SP/1684/150	
2429	John FEERE of Chew Magna	1674	T.N.A., PROB 4/8689	Admon. ex. 1675
2430	Frances FENNER of Westonzoyland	1600	D/D/cta/F17	Ad.ac.
2431	John and Agnes FENNER of Westonzoyland	1588	D/D/cta/F24	Ad.ac.
2432	John and Agnes FENNER of Westonzoyland	1588	D/D/cta/F25	Ad.ac.
2433	Thomas FENNER, Husbandman of Enmore	1681	DD/SP/1681/33	
2434	Richard FENNER (FINNER) of Fiddington	1639	DD/SP/1639/62	See *T.C.W.*
2435	Roger FERMER alias CHAPPELL, Blacksmith of Milverton	1668	DD/SP/1668/6	
2436	Francis FERRIS senior of Milverton	1680	DD/SP/1680/38	
2437	Joan FERRIS of Cannington	1698	DD/SP/1698/27	
2438	John FERRIS, Miller of Minehead	1665	DD/SP/1665/17	

FESSHER see FYSHER				
2439	Elizabeth FIDOE, Widow of Curry Rivel	1714	DD/SP/1714/32	
2440	William FIELD, Gentleman of Shepton Montague	1735	D/D/Cti 29	
2441	Samuel FILOR of East Harptree	1663	D/D/cta/F1	Ad.ac.
2442	Agnes FINNER, Widow of Chedzoy	1640	DD/SP/1640/10	
FINNER see FENNER				
2443	Ambrose FISHE of Ashbrittle	1636	DD/SP/1636/45	
2444	Agnes FISHER of Othery	1615	D/D/ct/1/F/9	
2445	Alice FISHER, Widow of Chedzoy	1635	DD/SP/1635/33	
2446	Amos FISHER of Bridgwater	1670	DD/SP/1670/68	
2447	David FISHER, Yeoman of Spaxton	1635	DD/SP/1635/73	
2448	Edward FISHER the elder of Spaxton	1641	DD/SP/1641/3	
2449	James FISHER of Spaxton	1668	DD/SP/1668/48	
2450	John FISHER of Taunton St. James	1641	DD/SP/1641/43	
2451	John FISHER the younger of Spaxton	1640	DD/SP/1640/55	
2452	Samuel FISHER of Glastonbury St. Benedict	1707	D/D/cta/F31	Ad.ac.
2453	Thomazine FISHER, Widow of Crewkerne	1648	DD/SP/1648/38	
2454	Sarah FITCHETT of Haselbury Plucknett	1695	DD/BD/42	
2455	Thomas FITCHETT of Crewkerne	1705	DD/BD/42	
2456	Michael FLAY, Gentleman of Monksilver	1689	T.N.A., PROB 4/2775	Will also extant
2457	Humphry FLEMMAN of Minehead	1681	DD/SP/1681/67	
FLEWELLING see LLWELLYN				
2458	Christian FLOWELL (FLOWER) of Milverton	1648	DD/SP/1648/65	See *T.C.W.*
2459	Ann FLOWER, Widow of Beckington	1783	T.N.A., PROB 31/1783/160	
FLOWER see FLOWELL				
2460	John FLOYD of Taunton St. Mary Magdalene	1669	DD/SP/1669/78	
2461	John FLOYD of Taunton St. Mary Magdalene	1686	DD/SP/1686/3	
2462	Thomas FLOYD of Bridgwater	1716	DD/SP/1716/24	
2463	John FLUD of Nether Stowey	1646	DD/SP/1646/82	See *T.C.W.*
2464	Henry FOANE, Miller of Haselbury Plucknett	1724	T.N.A., PROB 3/23/208	
2465	Samuel FOARTT of Goathurst	1677	DD/SP/1677/45	
FOARTT see FORTE				
2466	Robert FOLLETT of Sandford Orcas	1686	D/D/cta/F32	Ad.ac.

2467	Richard FOLLWELL, Clothier of Beckington	1678	T.N.A., PROB 4/10364	Will 1679. ex. 1680
2468	John FOOKE of Lyng	1668	DD/SP/1668/19	
2469	William FOOKE of Thurloxton	1666	DD/SP/1666/6	
2470	Edward FOORD of Witham Friary	1808	T.N.A., PROB 31/1808/308	
2471	Mary FOORD, Spinster of Mangotsfield, Gloucestershire formerly of Jamaica latter of Farrington Gurney	1804	T.N.A., PROB 31/1804/769	
FOORT(E) see FORTE				
2472	Edith FOORTE, Spinster of South Petherton	1686	DD/SP/1686/2	
2473	John FOORTE of Compton Durville, South Petherton	1646	DD/SP/1646/50	
2474	Roger FOORTE senior, Yeoman of South Petherton	1681	DD/SP/1681/40	
FOOTE see ALLEN				
2475	[missing] FORD of [no place]	n.d.	D/D/cta/F2	
	Note: Ad.ac.; mentions sisters named Agnes FORD, Rebecca FORD and Marie FORD alias STEVENS			
2476	Alexander FORD of Ilchester	1624	D/D/cta/F6	Ad.ac.
2477	Alexander FORD of Crewkerne	1634	DD/SP/1634/46	See *T.C.W.*
2478	Alexander FORD of Crewkerne	1635	DD/SP/1635/19	See *T.C.W.*
2479	Giles FORD of [no place]	n.d.	DD/SP/442/29	Ad.ac.
2480	John FORD, Yeoman of Crewkerne	1690	DD/SP/1690/14	
2481	John FORD, Yeoman of Trent	1730	T.N.A., PROB 3/29/205	
2482	Sarah FORD of Taunton	1665	DD/SP/1665/18	Wife of a Grocer
2483	Susanna FORD of Nettlecombe	1687	DD/SP/1687/62	
2484	Thomas FORD of Compton Martin	1612	D/D/cta/F20	Ad.ac.
2485	Thomas FORD of Frome Selwood	1622	D/D/cta/F5	Ad.ac.
2486	Thomas FORD, Gentleman of Farrington Gurney	1627	D/D/cta/F7	Ad.ac.
2487	Thomas and Mellany (wife) FORD of Taunton	1671	DD/SP/1671/1	
2488	Tristram FORD of Whitestaunton	1667	DD/SP/1667/15	
2489	Henrietta FORDYCE, Widow of Bath	1826	T.N.A., PROB 31/1826/1184	
2490	Henry FORREST, Innholder of Minehead	1677	DD/SP/1677/80	
2491	Andrew FORT of Over Stowey	1645	DD/SP/1645/32	
2492	Joane FORT, Widow of South Petherton	1684	DD/SP/1684/90	
2493	Marmaduke FORT of Drayton	1682	DD/SP/1682/37	
2494	James FORTE of Stocklinch Ottersey	1667	DD/SP/1667/17	
2495	James FORTE of Stocklinch Ottersey	1667	DD/SP/1667/76	

2496	Phillip FORTE, Widow of South Petherton	1641	DD/SP/1641/33	
2497	Robert FORTE of Taunton St. James	1587	D/D/cta/F26	Ad.ac.
2498	Robert FORTE of Taunton St. James	1588	D/D/cta/F16	Ad.ac.
2499	Thomas FORTE, Yeoman of Compton Durville, South Petherton	1661	DD/SP/1661/22	
2500	Jane FORWARD, Widow of Pitminster	1663	DD/SP/1663/33	
2501	William FORWARD, Clothier of Sampford Arundel	1691	T.N.A., PROB 4/6941	Will also extant
FORWARD see FORWOOD				
2502	Dorothy FORWOOD of Pitminster	1690	DD/SP/1690/80	
FORWOOD see FORWARD				
2503	Charlotte FOSKETT of Bath	1855	D.H.C., 58/9 box 57/13	
2504	Elizabeth FOSTER, Widow of Somerton	1778	T.N.A., PROB 31/1778/321	
2505	Ferdinando Bacon FOSTER, Esquire of Pontefract, Yorkshire died at St. Peter and Paul, Bath	1758	T.N.A., PROB 31/1758/76	With ad.ac.
2506	John FOSTER of Bridgwater	1691	DD/SP/1691/39	
2507	Samuel FOSTER, Esquire of St. Elizabeth, Jamaica late of Somerton	1778	T.N.A., PROB 31/1778/322	
2508	Thomas FOSTER of Wells	1691	D/D/cta/F10	Ad.ac.
2509	Thomas FOSTER of North Petherton	1713	DD/SP/1713/32	
2510	Edward FOURACRE of Hillfarrance	1696	DD/SP/1696/2	
2511	John FOURACRE of Hillfarrance	1696	DD/SP/1696/23	
2512	Reginald FOWDEN the elder, Esquire of Bath formerly of Cheadle, Cheshire	1819	T.N.A., PROB 31/1819/849	
2513	Chris FOWERACRE of Bradford on Tone	1676	DD/SP/1676/24	See also D/P/bra. t 2/1/2
2514	Christopher FOWERACRE of Hillfarrance	1667	DD/SP/1667/23	
2515	George FOWERACRE of Milverton	1678	DD/SP/1678/55	
2516	Johane FOWERACRE of Bradford	1637	DD/SP/1637/4	
2517	Hugh FOWERAKOR of Staplegrove	1646	DD/SP/1646/41	
2518	John FOWLE, Blacksmith of Frome Selwood	1678	T.N.A., PROB 4/6890	Will also extant
2519	[missing] FOWLER, Weaver ? of [no place]	1640	DD/SP/1640/126	Proved by Margaret Fowler widow; damaged
2520	George FOWLER of Othery	1584	D/D/cta/F3	Ad.ac. and inv.; part only
2521	Henry FOWLER, Cordwainer of Milverton	1670	DD/SP/1670/82	

2522	Richard FOWLER of Swell	1692	D/D/cta/F11	Ad.ac.
2523	William FOWLER of Swell	1698	DD/SP/1698/48	Minor, son of Richard
2524	William FOWLER of Yeovil	1736	D/D/Cti 30	
2525	Edward FOWLES, Yeoman of Durston	1679	DD/SP/1679/3	
2526	Andrew FOX of Porlock	1729	DD/SP/1729/55	
2527	Charles FOX, Peruke Maker (Peinke-maker) of Taunton St. Mary Magdalene	1737	DD/SP/1737/42	
2528	Robert FOX of Stogumber	1694	T.N.A., PROB 4/15894	Admon
2529	Stephen FOX, Clothier of Dunster	1688	DD/SP/1688/36	
2530	Francis FOXWELL of Aisholt	1685	DD/SP/1685/53	
2531	Philip FOXWORTHY of Cricket St. Thomas	1660	DD/HI/B/443	
2532	Agnes FOY, Widow of Porlock	1675	DD/SP/1675/76	
2533	Theofiloe (Theophila) FOYE of Buckland St. Mary	1646	DD/SP/1646/90	See *T.C.W.*
2534	Isabel FRANCES, Widow of Clutton	1666	D/D/cta/F23	Ad.ac.
2535	Peter FRANCIS, Thatcher of Crewkerne	1685	DD/SP/1685/70	
2536	Thomas FRANCIS of Muchelney	1591	D/D/cta/F27	Ad.ac.
FRANCK see YORCK				
2537	Agnes FRANCKE of Porlock	1638	DD/SP/1638/23	
2538	Henry FRANCKE of Porlock	1674	DD/SP/1674/42	
2539	Mary FRANCKE of Porlock	1680	DD/SP/1680/13	
2540	Robert FRANCKE of Porlock	1677	DD/SP/1677/56	
2541	John FRANK of Minehead	1714	DD/SP/1714/6	
2542	Walter FRANK of Porlock	1670	DD/SP/1670/9	
2543	John FRANKE of Porlock	1679	DD/SP/1679/54	
2544	Mary FRANKE of Porlock	1684	DD/SP/1684/169	
2545	Paul FRANKESH of Bath and Wells died at St. Martin-in-the-Fields, Middlesex	1675	T.N.A., PROB 4/10954	Will 1675
2546	Hannah FRANKLIN of Bridgwater	1689	DD/SP/1689/10	Wife of John
2547	Mary Ann FRANKLIN of Hammet Street, Taunton	1846	DD/DP/112/2	
2548	William FRANKLIN, Husbandman of Hatch Beauchamp	1688	DD/SP/1688/52	
2549	Daniel FRANKLING of Chedzoy	1716	DD/SP/1716/22	
2550	Richard FRANKPITT of Ashbrittle	1684	DD/SP/1684/157	
2551	Edith FREAKE, Widow of Chilthorne Domer	1619	D/D/cta/F19	Ad.ac.

2552	John FREEKE of Corton Denham	1720	DD/SF/15/2/35	Formerly DD/SF/3888
2553	Thomas FREEMAN of Hinton Charterhouse	1588	D/D/cta/F15	Ad.ac.
2554	Robert FREKE of Ilton	1729	T.N.A., PROB 31/1729/429	With ad.ac.
2555	George FRENCH, Woolcomber of Taunton St. Mary Magdalene	1700	DD/SP/1700/31	
2556	Gregory FRENCH, Innholder of Cannington	1667	DD/SP/1667/63	
2557	Joan FRENCH of [no place]	1755	DD/HKE/2/1	
2558	William FRENCH, Husbandman of Chipstable	1679	DD/SP/1679/23	
FRENCH see W—				
2559	Elizabeth Louisa FRIDAY, Spinster and Bastard of Shepton Mallet	1831	T.N.A., PROB 31/1831/962	
2560	Henry FRIE of Martock	1620	D/D/cta/F4	Ad.ac.
2561	William FRIE of West Pennard	1637	D/D/cta/F8	
	Note: Ad.ac.; buried at West Pennard in 1637			
2562	William FRIERIE, Husbandman of Milverton	1669	DD/SP/1669/10	
2563	Edward FRITH of Wincanton	1685	T.N.A., PROB 4/8239	Admon
2564	William FROOMAN of Goathurst	1683	DD/SP/1683/62	
2565	Andrew FROST the elder, Yeoman of Dulverton	1670	DD/SP/1670/64	
2566	John FROST, Yeoman of Shepton Beauchamp	1723	DD/SP/1723/40	
2567	Ann FRY, Widow of Axbridge	1677	T.N.A., PROB 4/468	Will 1677
2568	Bernard FRY of Oathill, Crewkerne	1665	DD/SP/1665/11	
2569	Christopher FRY of Dulverton	1680	DD/SP/1680/72	
2570	Edward FRY, Thatcher of Creech St. Michael	1698	DD/SP/1698/5	
2571	Elizabeth FRY of Axbridge	1845	DD/OB/58	
2572	Francis FRY, Victualler of East Harptree	1675	T.N.A., PROB 4/8372	Admon
2573	Hugh FRY of Chedzoy	1694	DD/SP/1694/19	
2574	James FRY of Lyncombe and Widcombe	1774	T.N.A., PROB 31/1774/827	With ad.ac.
2575	Joan FRY, Widow of Berrow	1664	D/D/cta/F21	Ad.ac.
2576	John FRY of Minehead	1691	DD/SP/1691/60	
2577	John FRY of Martock	1694	DD/DN/3/6/3	
2578	John FRY of Langport Westover, Curry Rivel	1731	DD/SP/1731/17	
2579	Richard FRY of [no place]	1662	DD/SP/1662/29	
2580	Robert FRY, Mariner of Minehead	1697	DD/SP/1697/51	
2581	Robert FRY of Bruton	1724	T.N.A., PROB 3/23/180	Died at St. Mary Woolnoth, London

2582	Thomas FRY of Broadway	1673	DD/SP/1673/45	Incomplete
2583	Thomas FRY, Clothier of Broadway	1675	DD/SP/1675/25	
2584	William FRY of Winscombe	1739	D/D/Cti 27–28	
FRY see URCHE				
2585	John FRYE of Badgworth	1631	D/D/cta/F14	Ad.ac.
2586	John FRYER the elder of Wells St. Cuthbert	1664	D/D/cta/F22	Ad.ac.
2587	James FUGARS of Minehead	1637	DD/SP/1637/54	
2588	Tristram FULJAMES of Pawlett	1631	D/D/cta/F9	Ad.ac. by Susan HOW
2589	William FULLER of Cheddar	1589	D/D/ct/1/F/2	
2590	John FURNELL of Freshford	1675	D/D/cta/F12	Ad.ac.
2591	William FURNELL, Yeoman of Horsington	1668	DD/DNL/151	Printed in *S.D.N.Q.* vol.28 p.51
2592	Margaret FURSE of Lyng	1673	DD/SP/1673/8	
2593	Thomas FURSE, Yeoman of Stogumber	1677	DD/SP/1677/79	
2594	Ellen FURTHINGE of Kingston	1635	DD/SP/1635/100	
2595	Joan FURZE, Spinster of Cothelstone	1680	DD/SP/1680/2	
2596	Robert FURZE of Broomfield	1674	T.N.A., PROB 4/343	Will 1674
2597	Thomas FURZE of Wiveliscombe	1773	T.N.A., PROB 31/1773/811	
2598	William FUSSELL of West Bradley	1718	D/D/cta/F13	Ad.ac.
2599	John FYSHER alias FESSHER of Portbury	1539	D/D/ct/1/F/7	
2600	Emmanuel GADD, Bachelor of Cheddon Fitzpaine	1772	T.N.A., PROB 31/1772/126	
2601	Emmanuel GADD, Bachelor of Cheddon Fitzpaine	1774	T.N.A., PROB 31/1774/593/602	
2602	John GADD of Taunton St. Mary Magdalene	1685	DD/SP/1685/16	
2603	John GADD of North Petherton	1685	DD/SP/1685/4	
2604	John GADD, Bachelor of West Monkton	1691	DD/SP/1691/7	
2605	John GADD of Creech St. Michael	1693	DD/SP/1693/52	
2606	Margaret GADD of North Petherton	1691	DD/SP/1691/29	Wife of Robert
2607	Philip GADD, Mercer of Taunton	1679	T.N.A., PROB 4/4111	Will 1679. ex. 1680
2608	Robert GADD of Trull	1716	DD/SP/1716/9	
GADD see REED				
2609	Conand GAGE, Yeoman of Nettlecombe	1669	DD/SP/1669/57	
2610	William GAGE of Publow	1723	T.N.A., PROB 3/22/189	
2611	John GAIGE of Enmore	1690	DD/SP/1690/74	

2612	[Female] GALE, Widow of West Monkton	1684	DD/SP/1684/162	
2613	Elianor GALE of West Monkton	1685	DD/CR/1	
2614	John GALE of Huish Champflower	1666	DD/SP/1666/9	
2615	Peter GALE of West Monkton	1635	DD/SP/1635/76	
2616	Peter GALE of West Monkton	1684	DD/CR/1	
2617	Peter GALE, Weaver of Taunton St. Mary Magdalene	1693	DD/SP/1693/59	
2618	Philipe GALE of Taunton	1646	DD/SP/1646/91	
2619	Robert GALE, Clerk of Angersleigh	1673	DD/SP/1673/7	Mentions 'Lexicon Heptaglotton'
2620	Robert GALE the elder of Taunton St. Mary Magdalene	1668	DD/SP/1668/46	
2621	Roger GALE of West Monkton	1684	DD/CR/1	
2622	Roger GALE junior of West Monkton	1684	DD/SP/1684/161	Minor, approx. 6 months
2623	Walter GALE of Staplegrove	1647	DD/SP/1647/5	Son of Peter
2624	Francis GALHAMPTON, Gentleman of West Newton, North Petherton	1648	DD/SP/1648/32	
2625	Nicholas GALHAMPTON of North Petherton	1668	DD/SP/1668/50	
2626	John GALL of Hillfarrance	1638	DD/SP/1638/62	
2627	Thomas GALLER of Broadway	1684	DD/SP/1684/127	
2628	Thomas GALLER, Purser and Bachelor of Minehead	1835	T.N.A., PROB 31/1835/245	On half pay in H.M. Navy
2629	Mary GALLINGTON, Widow of Wells	1682	T.N.A., PROB 4/17968	Will also extant
2630	Hubert GALTON, Yeoman of Kingston, Dorset, formerly of Hinton St. George	1677	W.S.H.C., P5/1677/22	Inv. and will
2631	John GAME of Yeovil	1698	T.N.A., PROB 5/5317	Books inventoried
2632	John GAME, Apothecary of Yeovil	1699	T.N.A., PROB 4/8755	Will 1694
2633	Joane GAMLEN of West Quantoxhead	1663	DD/SP/1663/32	
2634	John GAMLIN of Ruishton	1688	DD/SP/1688/33	
2635	William GAMLIN of [no place]	n.d.	D/D/cta/G33	Ad.ac.
2636	William GAMLYN, Husbandman of Aller	1619	D/D/cta/G18	Ad.ac.
2637	William GAMLYN of Aller	1636	D/D/cta/C11	Ad.ac.
2638	Francis GANDYE of Chillington	1688	DD/SP/1688/55	
2639	James GANE, Bachelor of Croscombe	1812	T.N.A., PROB 31/1812/697	
2640	Thomas GANE of Frome Selwood	1674	T.N.A., PROB 4/8356	Will. ex. 1675
2641	Thomas GANE, Cardmaker of Frome Selwood Note: Will T.N.A., PROB 11/347, sentence T.N.A., PROB 11/349	1674	T.N.A., PROB 5/503	

2642	Lawrence GANE ? of Shepton Mallet	1630	D/D/cta/G34	Ad.ac.
GANE see HOOKE				
2643	Abraham GAPPER, Yeoman of Sutton Mallett, Moorlinch	1685	T.N.A., PROB 4/8754	Admon
2644	Abraham GAPPER, Gentleman of Wincanton	1692	T.N.A., PROB 4/15083	Will also extant
2645	Abraham GAPPER, Gentleman of [no place]	1701	T.N.A., PROB 4/22731	Will 1701
2646	Mary GAPPER, Widow of Chedzoy	1641	DD/SP/1641/28	
2647	Thomas GAPPER of Crewkerne	1635	DD/SP/1635/79	
2648	John GARD, Clerk of Swell	1716	DD/SP/1716/13	
2649	Edward GARDINER, Clerk of [no place]	1644	DD/SP/1644/70	
2650	Joel GARDINER of Cheddar	1683	T.N.A., PROB 4/10369	Will. ex. 1684
2651	Annis GARDNER, Widow of Cheddar	1684	T.N.A., PROB 4/753	Admon
2652	Dorothy GARDNER, Widow of Taunton St. James	1641	DD/SP/1641/13	See *T.C.W.*
2653	Edward GARDNER of Somerton	1681	T.N.A., PROB 4/22024	Will also extant
2654	John GARDNER of Cheddar	1634	D/D/cta/G10	Ad.ac.
2655	John GARDNER, Yeoman of Chelwood	1672	DD/SAS/H70/10	With probate
2656	John GARDNER of Bicknoller	1681	DD/SP/1681/49	
2657	Tristram GARDNER of Taunton St. James	1670	DD/SP/1670/79	
2658	Tristram GARDNER of Taunton St. James	1676	DD/SP/1676/9	
2659	Valentine GARDNER of Fiddington	1670	DD/SP/1670/46	
2660	William GARDNER, Yeoman of Cheddar	1678	T.N.A., PROB 4/11936	Admon
2661	John GARLIFORD of Dulverton	1636	DD/SP/1636/4	
2662	Baldwine GARNSHAY of Langford Budville	1637	DD/SP/1637/5	
2663	Henry GARRETT, Husbandman of Curry Rivel	1680	DD/SP/1680/58	
2664	Virtue GARRETT, Yeoman of Yenston, Henstridge	1687	T.N.A., PROB 5/3006	
2665	Virtue GARRETT, Yeoman of Yenston, Henstridge	1688	T.N.A., PROB 4/8473	Will also extant
2666	Robert GASPEY of Taunton	1645	DD/SP/1645/35	
2667	Alexander GASSE of Crewkerne	1686	DD/SP/1686/33	
2668	John GATCHELL of Bridgwater	1687	DD/SP/1687/5	
2669	Richard GATCHELL, Tanner of Crowcombe	1690	DD/SP/1690/84	
2670	Christian GATCOMBE of Taunton	1666	DD/SP/1666/57	
2671	Edward GATCOMBE of Chedzoy	1624	DD/D/ST/19/2	
2672	Francis GATCOMBE, Yeoman of North Petherton	1729	DD/SP/1729/60	
2673	Henry GATCOMBE of Durleigh	1691	DD/SP/1691/96	

2674	John GATCOMBE, Carpenter of Dunwear, Bridgwater	1675	DD/SP/1675/32	
2675	John GATCOMBE of North Petherton	1698	DD/SP/1698/26	
2676	William GATCOMBE of Taunton St. Mary Magdalene	1675	DD/SP/1675/30	
2677	William GATCOMBE of Bridgwater	1691	DD/SP/1691/73	
2678	William GATCOMBE of Huntworth, Bridgwater	1716	DD/SP/1716/42	
2679	John GATEN of Milverton	1718	DD/SP/442/66	Ad.ac.
2680	Henry GAULER, Fuller of Broadway	1727	DD/SP/1727/29	
GAULER see GAWLER				
2681	Roger GAVE of [no place]	1633	D/D/cta/G35	Ad.ac.
2683	John and Joan GAWLER, Husbandman of Butleigh	1591	D/D/cta/G32	Ad.ac.
2684	Mary GAWLER, Spinster of Lower Stratton, South Petherton	1668	DD/SP/1668/23	
2685	Samuel GAWLER, Yeoman of Lower Stratton, South Petherton	1688	DD/SP/1688/30	
2686	Katherine GAWLER alias SILVESTER of South Harp, South Petherton	1672	DD/SP/1672/61	Wife of John
2687	John GAY, Gentleman of Englishcombe	1730	T.N.A., PROB 3/29/56	
2688	Robert GAY of St. Christopher in the Stocks, London died at Nettlecombe	1673	T.N.A., PROB 4/21376	Admon
GAYER see GYARE				
2689	Edmond GAYLARD, Tanner of Trull	1684	DD/SP/1684/52	
2690	Elizabeth GAYLARD of Drayton	1679	DD/SP/1679/53	
2691	John GAYLARD, Husbandman of Barrington	1672	DD/SP/1672/52	
2692	Edmond GAYLERD of Pitminster	1663	DD/SP/1662/31	
2693	Susanne GAYLERD alias MARTYN of Pitminster	1666	DD/SP/1666/70	
2694	Thomas GEARS, Innkeeper [?] of Kings Head Inn, Merriott	1815	D.H.C., 1044B/M/E37	
2695	Iset GEENS of Stoke Pero	1640	DD/SP/1640/71	
2696	Thomas GENT of Bishops Hull	1679	DD/SP/1679/28	
GENTLE see WEAVER				
2697	John GENYNS of Temple Cloud, Cameley	1573	DD/HI/286	
2698	[missing] GEORGE, Saddler of West Monkton	1684	DD/SP/1684/63	
2699	David GEORGE, Husbandman of Abbots Leigh	1666	B.A., 1666/21	
2700	Thomas GEORGE, Clothier of Croscombe	1692	T.N.A., PROB 4/7996	Will. ex. 1693
2701	Mary GERISH, Widow of Rode	1793	T.N.A., PROB 31/1793/580	

2702	Henry GERVIS, Bachelor of Physic of Taunton St. Mary Magdalene	1686	T.N.A., PROB 4/8341	Will 1687. ex. 1688
2703	Charles GERVISE of Beckington	1706	D/D/cta/G36	Ad.ac.
2704	John GESSE of Bridgwater	1666	D/D/cta/G25	Ad.ac.
2705	Thomas GIBBES of Wick St. Lawrence	1599	D/D/cta/G22	
	Note: Ad.ac.; see burial register for 26 April 1630			
2706	Mary GIBBONS of Taunton St. Mary Magdalene	1640	D/D/cta/G28	Ad.ac.
2707	Thomas GIBBONS, Glassmaker of Bedminster	1698	T.N.A., PROB 5/3859	
2708	Benedict GIBBS of Chedzoy	1675	DD/SP/1675/89	
2709	Catherine GIBBS, Widow of Thornfalcon	1637	DD/SP/1637/26	
2710	George GIBBS, Physician of Crewkerne	1702	T.N.A., PROB 4/22367	Admon. ex. 1701
2711	John GIBBS, Clerk of Chipstable	1669	DD/SP/1669/85	
2712	Thomas GIBBS of Publow	1637	D/D/cta/G6	Ad.ac.
2713	Thomas GIBBS of Chelwood	1736	D/D/Cti 31	
2714	William GIBBS, Clothier of Taunton St. Mary Magdalene	1637	DD/SP/1637/31	
2715	William GIBBS, Sergemaker of Taunton St. Mary Magdalene	1679	DD/SP/1679/55	
2716	William GIBBS of Barrington	1716	DD/SP/1716/63	
2717	William GIBBS of Combe Florey	1802	DD/X/WON/7	
2718	Joan GIBLETT, Widow of Meare	1611	D/D/cta/G15	Ad.ac.
2719	Thomas GIBLETT of Meare	1663	D/D/cta/G24	Ad.ac.
2720	John GIBSON of Stogumber	1693	DD/SP/1693/29	
2721	Thomas GIFFORD of Wellington	n.d.	D/D/cta/G5	Ad.ac.
2722	Susan GIFFORD alias HOLWAY, Widow of Crewkerne	1668	DD/SP/1668/29	
2723	Elizabeth GILBERT of West Camel and Caundle Marsh, Dorset	1633	W.S.H.C., P5/1633/22	Inv. and will
2724	William GILBERT of Prestleigh, Doulting	1662	D/D/cta/G23	Ad.ac.
2725	David GILES, Tailor of Selworthy	1725	DD/SP/1725/13	
2726	John GILES of Creech St. Michael	1647	DD/SP/1647/16	
2727	John GILES of Porlock	1664	DD/SP/1664/73	
2728	John GILES, Gentleman of East Coker	1672	T.N.A., PROB 5/5162	
2729	John GILES of Minehead	1688	DD/SP/1688/40	
2730	John GILES of Ilminster	1696	T.N.A., PROB 5/5102	
2731	John GILES of Ilminster	1697	T.N.A., PROB 4/21703	Will also extant
2732	Robert GILES of Freshford	1719	T.N.A., PROB 3/18/48	

2733	Robert GILES junior of Ellicombe, Dunster	1697	DD/SP/1697/10	
2734	Thomas GILES the elder of Minehead	1645	DD/SP/1645/58	
2735	William GILES, Yeoman of Minehead	1664	DD/SP/1664/37	
2736	Agnes GILL of Stogursey	1636	DD/SP/1636/28	
2737	Andrew GILL of St. Decumans	1677	T.N.A., PROB 4/25677	Will also extant
2738	Elizabeth GILL of Bridgwater	1675	DD/SP/1675/54	
2739	Elizabeth GILL of Otterhampton	1688	DD/SP/1688/21	
2740	George GILL of Minehead	1684	DD/SP/1684/130	
2741	John GILL, Husbandman of Milverton	1667	DD/SP/1667/88	
2742	John GILL of Lyng	1684	DD/SP/1684/70	
2743	John GILL of Shutteroaks, Merriott	1730	DD/SP/1730/2	
2744	Nathan GILL junior of Cutcombe	1697	DD/SP/1697/63	
2745	Robert GILL of Creech St. Michael	1643	DD/SP/1643/45	See *T.C.W.*
2746	Valentine GILL of Trull	1635	DD/SP/1635/11	
2747	William GILL of Spaxton	1635	DD/SP/1635/12	
2748	William GILL, Yeoman of Trull	1684	DD/SP/1684/166	
2749	John GILLARD of Langford Budville	1687	DD/SP/1687/15	
2750	Nathan GILLARD of Bridgwater	1672	DD/SP/1672/4	
2751	Mary GILLET of Lopen	1635	DD/SP/1635/80	See *T.C.W.*
2752	Eleanor GILLETT, Widow of Buckland St. Mary	1713	DD/SP/1713/20	
2753	John GILLETT the elder of Glastonbury St. John	1622	D/D/cta/G2	Ad.ac.
2754	William GILLETT, Yeoman of Chillington	1737	D/D/Cti 33	
2755	William GILLETT, Yeoman of Wambrook	1740	W.S.H.C., P5/17	
	Note: Admon. bond, renunciation; inv. is of the goods of 'widdow Gillet Latly deseasd'			
2756	[Male] GILLING of [no place]	1692	DD/SP/1692/36	Wife Mary
2757	Samuel GILLING of Cheddar	1795	D/D/Pdc 4	
2758	John GILLINGAME, Husbandman of Charterhouse, Blagdon	1669	T.N.A., PROB 4/8669	Will also extant
2759	Edward GILLUM, Husbandman of Wootton Courtenay	1664	DD/SP/1664/20	
2760	Thomas GIMLETT of St. Decumans	1710	T.N.A., PROB 5/5319	
2761	Nicholas GIRRISHE of Laverton	1624	D/D/cta/G1	Ad.ac.
2762	Silvester GITTOE, Mariner of Minehead	1691	DD/SP/1691/86	
2763	John GLADE of Wambrook	1590	W.S.H.C., P5/1590/24	Admon. bond, inv., will
2764	Hester GLADWYN, Widow of Taunton St. Mary Magdalene	1716	DD/SP/1716/1	

2765	Dinah GLAS of Selworthy	1635	DD/SP/1635/49	
2766	Elizabeth GLASBROOKE, Widow of Swell	1682	DD/SP/1682/6	
2767	George GLASBROOKE, Physician of Taunton	1665	DD/SP/1665/3	
2768	John GLASS of Charlinch	1691	DD/SP/1691/59	
2769	Agnes GLASSE of Old Cleeve ?	n.d.	D/D/cta/Blank/9	Damaged ad.ac.
2770	Israell GLESON, Gentleman of Brislington	1689	T.N.A., PROB 4/8241	Will 1689
2771	James GLOVER of Moor Hassocke, South Petherton	1644	DD/SP/1644/62	
2772	John GLOVER of Frome Selwood	1755	T.N.A., PROB 31/1755/818	With ad.ac.
2773	Valentine GLOVER of South Petherton	1688	DD/SP/1688/6	
2774	Valentine GLOVER of Seavington St. Michael	1697	DD/SP/1697/16	
2775	William GLOVER of South Petherton	1644	DD/SP/1644/63	
2776	John GLOVER alias RAWLINGES of Combwich, Otterhampton	1674	DD/SP/1674/57	
GLOVER see RAWLINS				
2777	John GLOYEN of Wincanton	1699	T.N.A., PROB 4/16872	Will also extant
2778	Richard GOARE of Winsford	1695	DD/SP/1695/25	
2779	William GOAT of North Petherton	1700	DD/SP/1700/32	See North Petherton burials 14 August 1700
GOD see THOMAS				
2780	John GODD of Aisholt	1637	DD/SP/1637/50	
2781	John GODDARD of North Petherton	1685	DD/SP/1685/107	
2782	Mary GODDARD, Spinster of North Petherton	1700	DD/SP/1700/30	
2783	Thomas GODDARD of [no place]	1676	DD/SP/1676/2	
2784	Leonard GODDEN, Clothier of Chard	1696	T.N.A., PROB 4/8297	Will 1696. ex. 1697
2785	Francis GODEICH, Husbandman of Bridgwater	1693	DD/SP/1693/62	
2786	[Female] GODFREY, Widow of Chedzoy	1796	D/P/chedz/13/10/5,6	Widow of William
2787	John GODFREY, Weaver of Mells	1588	D/D/cta/G31	Ad.ac.
2788	John GODFREY of Haygrove, Bridgwater	1672	DD/SP/1672/49	
2789	John GODFREY, Yeoman of Wembdon	1691	DD/SP/1691/14	
2790	John GODFREY of Haygrove, Bridgwater	1691	DD/SP/1691/36	
2791	George GODFRY, Yeoman of North Petherton	1670	DD/SP/1670/88	Reference to land in East Saltmore
2792	Joane GODFRY, Widow of Bridgwater	1682	DD/SP/1682/50	
2793	Thomas GODFRY of Chedzoy	1725	DD/SP/1725/3	

2794	William GODFRY, Husbandman of North Petherton	1672	DD/SP/1672/7	
2795	Robert GODNING of Henlade, Ruishton	1695	DD/SP/1695/18	
2796	Hugh GODSALL senior of Bewley, Tintinhull	1723	T.N.A., PROB 3/22/5	
2797	John GODSALL, Clothier of Corfe	1635	DD/SP/1635/13	
2798	Margaret GODSALL, Widow of Staplegrove	1686	T.N.A., PROB 4/10196	Will. ex. 1687
2799	Thomas GODSALL of Staplegrove	1679	T.N.A., PROB 4/21896	Will also extant
2800	Thomas GODSALL, Gentleman of Taunton St. Mary Magdalene	1680	DD/SP/1680/8	
2801	Thomas GODSALL, Gentleman of Taunton St. Mary Magdalene	1680	T.N.A., PROB 4/10532	Will. ex. 1684
2802	John GODWIN of Street	1731	D/D/cta/G37	Ad.ac.
2803	Peter GODWIN the elder of Minehead	1720	DD/SP/1720/6	
2804	Peter GODWIN the elder of Minehead	1720	DD/SP/442/68	Ad.ac.
2805	Bishop Thomas GODWIN, Bishop of Bath and Wells of Wells and Wokingham, Berkshire	1591	W.S.H.C., P5/1590/26	
	Note: Account, admon. bond, bond to collect goods, inv.			
2806	Robert GODWYN, Gentleman of Wells	1677	T.N.A., PROB 4/10478	Will 1677. ex. 1678
2807	Francis GOFF of Meare	1710	D/D/cta/G38	Ad.ac.
2808	William GOFFE of Skilgate	1690	DD/SP/1690/73	
GOFFIN see COFFIN				
2809	Thomas GOLFREY, Husbandman of Chedzoy	1700	DD/SP/1700/27	
2810	John GOLLEDGE of Westbury ?	n.d.	D/D/cta/G13	
	Note: Ad.ac.; mentions several men of Westbury; temp Elizabeth			
2811	William GOLLEDGE of Pylle	1623	D/D/cta/G3	Ad.ac.
2812	Alce GOLLOPP of Buckland St. Mary	1642	DD/SP/1642/32	
2813	Robert GOMMER, Husbandman of South Petherton	1669	DD/SP/1669/18	
2814	[missing] GOOD of Durleigh, Bridgwater	1667	DD/SP/1667/89	
2815	John GOOD of Bridgwater	1690	DD/SP/1690/78	
2816	Thomas GOOD of [no place]	1699	DD/SP/1699/10	
2817	Joseph GOODIN of Chedzoy	1636	DD/SP/1636/56	
2818	Henry GOODING, Gentleman of Halse	1677	DD/SP/1677/52	
2819	John GOODING, Husbandman of Lyng	1678	DD/SP/1678/82	
2820	John GOODING of Halse	1691	DD/SP/1691/70	

2821	John GOODING of Nynehead	1725	DD/SP/1725/8	
2822	Nicholas GOODING, Clothier of Monksilver	1730	DD/SP/1730/22	
2823	Richard GOODING of Huntworth, Bridgwater	1681	DD/SP/1681/25	
2824	Robert GOODING of Enmore	1714	DD/SP/1714/4	
2825	John GOODLAND of Dowlish Wake	1686	DD/SP/1686/46	
2826	Thomas GOODLAND of Curry Rivel	1691	DD/SP/1691/92	
2827	William GOODLAND of North Petherton	1686	DD/SP/1686/35	
2828	John GOODMAN of Dulverton	1609	DD/SP/1609/2	
2829	Robert GOODMAN of Taunton St. Mary Magdalene	1686	DD/SP/1686/44	
GOODMAN see SPICER				
2830	Barbara GOODRIDGE of Bridgwater	1677	DD/SP/1677/69	
2831	William GOODRIDGE of Bridgwater	1690	DD/SP/1690/60	
2832	Ann GOODWYN of Bedminster	1698	T.N.A., PROB 4/16467	Will 1699
2833	William GOODWYN of [no place]	1732/3	DD/BD/105	
2834	Elizabeth GOOLD, Widow of Curry Rivel	1676	DD/SP/1676/31	
2835	Henry GOOLD alias GOULD of East Pennard	1729	T.N.A., PROB 3/28/54	
GOOLD see GOULD, WEAVER				
2836	John GOOLDE of Doulting	1611	D/D/cta/G14	Ad.ac.
2837	Anne GORDON, Widow of Abbots Leigh	1783	DD/WO/37/13	
2838	Edward GORE of Barrow Gurney	1731	T.N.A., PROB 31/1731/795	With ad.ac.
2839	John GORE of Stogumber	1636	DD/SP/1636/23	
2840	John GORE of Taunton St. James	1672	DD/SP/1672/33	
2841	John GORE senior and William, his son of Wiveliscombe	1731	DD/SP/1731/16	
2842	Joseph GORE, Clerk of West Quantoxhead	1685	DD/SP/1685/66	
2843	Sir Thomas GORE of Barrow Gurney	1675	DD/GB/114	
2844	William GORE, Esquire of Barrow Gurney	1662	T.N.A., PROB 4/9056	Will 1662. ex. 1664
GORE see GOARE				
2845	George GORTON of Hillfarrance	1645	DD/SP/1645/27	
2846	Richard GORTON of Lydeard St. Lawrence	1668	D/D/cta/G27	Ad.ac.
2847	Roger GORTON, Yeoman of Huish Champflower	1721	T.N.A., PROB 5/5711	
2848	John GORWAY of Chew Magna	n.d.	D/D/cta/G39	Ad.ac.
2849	Henry GOSS, Tailor of Dulverton	1690	DD/SP/1690/76	
2850	[missing] GOSSE of [no place]	1664	DD/SP/1664/74	Incomplete

2851	Edmund GOSSE, Yeoman of Shiplade, Bleadon	1677	T.N.A., PROB 4/663	Will 1677
2852	John GOSSE, Linen Draper of Axbridge	1669	T.N.A., PROB 5/2015	
2853	Thomas GOSSE, Cheesemonger? of Bleadon	1677	T.N.A., PROB 4/8982	
2854	George GOUGH, Woolen Draper of Merriott	1693	DD/SP/1693/55	
2855	Catherine GOULD of Stoke St. Mary	1641	DD/SP/1641/88	
2856	Charles GOULD of West Monkton	1674	DD/SP/1674/4	
GOULD see GOOLD				
2857	Christian GOVER of Tolland	1687	DD/SP/1687/33	
2858	William GOVER of Sparkford	1594	D/D/cta/G11	Ad.ac.
2859	William GOVER, Husbandman of Sparkford	1594	D/D/cta/G30	Ad.ac.
2860	Richard GOVETT, Husbandman of West Monkton	1691	DD/SP/1691/31	
2861	Robert GOVETT of Kilton	1663	D/D/cta/G40	Ad.ac.
2862	Amos GOVIER, Yeoman of Stawley	1693	DD/SP/1693/24	
2863	Covenant GOVIER, Husbandman of Tolland	1675	DD/SP/1675/36	
2864	John GOVIER, Carpenter of Milverton	1671	DD/SP/1671/35	
2865	John GOVIER of Ashbrittle	1677	DD/SP/1677/43	
2866	Richard GOVIER of Huish Champflower	1671	DD/SP/1671/18	
2867	Simon GOVIER of Hillfarrance	1684	DD/SP/1684/120	
2868	Thomas GOVIER of Tolland	1664	DD/SP/1664/36	
2869	Thomas GOVIER of Stawley	1679	DD/SP/1679/31	
2870	John GOYEN of Minehead	1684	DD/SP/1684/156	
2871	Andrew GRABHAM of Donyatt	1676	DD/SP/1676/16	
2872	Robert GRABHAM of Donyatt	1640	DD/SP/1640/35	
2873	Edmund GRADEN of Taunton	1626	D/D/cta/C4	Ad.ac.
2874	Richard GRADON of Taunton St. Mary Magdalene	1665	DD/SP/1665/32	
2875	John GRADY of Spaxton	1679	DD/SP/1679/29	
2876	Grace GRANDFEILD, Widow of Spaxton	1678	DD/SP/1678/83	
2877	Joane GRANDFEILD of Cheddon Fitzpaine	1677	DD/SP/1677/35	
2878	John GRANGER of Milverton	1667	DD/SP/1667/74	
2879	William GRANGER, Vicar of Milverton	1694	DD/SAS/HV/43/1,2	
2880	William GRANGER, Joiner of Minehead	1700	DD/SP/1700/10	
2881	John GRANNT the elder, Yeoman of Crowcombe	1637	DD/SP/1637/55	
2882	Francis GRANT of Spaxton	1695	DD/SP/1695/10	

2883	Jane GRANT of Batcombe	1823	T.N.A., PROB 31/1823/1130	Wife of James GRANT
2884	Richard GRANT, Innholder of Taunton St. Mary Magdalene	1677	DD/SP/1677/40	
2885	Edith GRAVE alias CROCKER of Milverton	1686	DD/SP/1686/43	
2886	William GRAVE alias CROCKER of Milverton	1674	DD/SP/1674/34	
GRAVE see CROCKER, HOOK				
2887	Hugh GRAY junior of Taunton St. Mary Magdalene	1670	DD/SP/1670/89	
2888	Jane Dorothea GREATHEED formerly STEPHENSON, Widow of Bishops Hull	1829	T.N.A., PROB 31/1829/983	
2889	William GREEN, Clothier of Taunton St. James	1685	DD/SP/1685/93	
2890	[missing] GREENE of [no place]	1665	DD/SP/1665/50	Incomplete
2891	Philip GREENE of Glastonbury St. John	1638	D/D/cta/G7	Ad.ac.
2892	Catherine GREENE alias SHALGROVE, Widow of Nynehead	1666	DD/SP/1666/31	
2893	William GREENFEILD, Husbandman of Cheddon Fitzpaine	1684	DD/SP/1684/54	
GREENFEILD see GREINFEILD and GRYNFIELD				
2894	Christopher GREENHAM, Husbandman of East Quantoxhead	1684	DD/SP/1684/33	
GREENHAM see GRINHAM				
2895	Benjamin GREENHILL of Holcombe	1817	DD/FS/35/11	
2896	Francis GREENSLADE, Yeoman of Treborough	1723	DD/SP/1723/55	
2897	James GREENSLADE of Nettlecombe	1669	DD/SP/1669/58	
2898	Margaret GREENSLADE of Winsford	1640	DD/SP/1640/124	
2899	Martin GREENSLADE of Exford	1684	DD/SP/1684/149	
2900	Phillip GREENSLADE of Brompton Regis	1665	DD/SP/1665/16	
2901	William GREENSLADE of Creech St. Michael	1645	DD/SP/1645/6	
2902	Bridget GREENWAY, Widow of Woolminstone, Crewkerne	1712	DD/PT/H452/23	
2903	John GREGORIE of Ditcheat	1612	D/D/cta/G20	Ad.ac.
2904	Mary GREGORIE of Nynehead	1641	DD/SP/1641/54	
2905	Elener GREGORY of Nynehead	1640	DD/SP/1640/107	
2906	Hester GREGORY of Exford	1690	DD/SP/1690/25	
2907	Hugh GREGORY of Wootton Courtenay	1690	DD/SP/1690/6	
2908	James GREGORY of Charlton Horethorne	1714	D/D/cta/G17	Ad.ac.
2909	John GREGORY, Grocer of Taunton St. Mary Magdalene	1716	T.N.A., PROB 5/2845	
2910	Robert GREGORY of Selworthy	1689	DD/SP/1689/46	
2911	Robert GREGORY the elder of Barton St. David	1641	D/D/cta/G29	Ad.ac.

2912	William GREGORY, Yeoman of Dulverton	1755	DD/SP/1755/35	
2913	William GREINFEILD, Innholder of Bridgwater	1698	DD/SP/1698/23	
GREINFEILD see GREENFEILD and GRYNFIELD				
2914	John GRIBBLE of Cheddon Fitzpaine	1713	DD/SP/1713/19	
2915	Richard GRIBBLE of Cheddon Fitzpaine	1691	DD/SP/1691/22	
2916	Charles GRIDLY of Bath	1831	T.N.A., PROB 31/1831/1263	
2917	David GRIFFETH of Minehead	1672	DD/SP/1672/21	
2918	John GRIFFIN, Yeoman of Old Cleeve	1738	D/D/Cti 32	
2919	Dennis GRIFFITHS, Widow of Minehead	1674	DD/SP/1674/35	
2920	Thomas GRIFTE of Glastonbury	1611	D/D/cta/G16	Ad.ac.
2921	Ann GRIGG, Spinster of Bath	1823	T.N.A., PROB 31/1823/666	
2922	John GRIGGS of Middlezoy	1626	D/D/cta/G4	Ad.ac.
2923	Francis GRIMES, Yeoman of Carhampton	1722	T.N.A., PROB 3/21/46	
2924	William GRIMES of Durleigh	1694	DD/SP/1694/40	
2925	Humphrey GRIMSTED, Yeoman of Baltonsborough	1694	T.N.A., PROB 4/12231	Will 1694
2926	Andrew GRIMSTEEDE of Baltonsborough	1641	D/D/cta/G21	Ad.ac.
2927	Agnes GRINHAM of East Quantoxhead	1639	DD/SP/1639/54	
2928	John GRINHAM the elder of East Quantoxhead	1684	DD/SP/1684/16	
GRINHAM see GREENHAM				
GRINSLADE see PALMER				
2929	John GRISE of West Pennard	1598	D/D/cta/G26	Ad.ac.
2930	William GRISSTOCKE of North Petherton	1667	DD/SP/1667/54	
2931	George GRISTOCKE, Blacksmith of Creech St. Michael	1680	DD/SP/1680/78	
2932	Amias ? GROOME of [no place]	n.d.	D/D/cta/G12	Ad.ac.; mentions a brother Giles
2933	George GROVE of Stockland Bristol	1731	DD/SP/1731/25	
2934	Thomas GROVE of Stogursey	1669	DD/SP/1669/62	
2935	Henry GROVES, Butcher of Ilminster	1734	T.N.A., PROB 3/33/34	
2936	Humphrey GRYNFIELD, Husbandman of Cheddon Fitzpaine	1676	DD/SP/1676/36	
GRYNFIELD see GREENFEILD and GREINFEILD				
2937	Robert GUBB, Miller of Dulverton	1666	DD/SP/1666/7	
2938	John GUBE of Chedzoy	1645	DD/SP/1645/38	Name occurs in parish
2939	John GUDDRIDGE, Whitebaker of Taunton St. Mary Magdalene	1719	DD/SP/1719/7	
2940	Elizabeth GULLEY of Isle Brewers	1679	DD/SP/1679/24	

2941	Mary GULLEY, Widow of Thornfalcon	1640	DD/SP/1640/77	
2942	Thomas GULLEY of Staple Fitzpaine	1646	DD/SP/1646/37	
2943	John GULLIFER of Wells St. Cuthbert	1612	D/D/cta/G19	Ad.ac.
2944	John GULLIFORD of Taunton St. Mary Magdalene	1716	DD/SP/1716/43	
2945	William GULLOCK of Middleny, Drayton	1672	DD/SP/1672/62	
2946	John GULLY of Isle Brewers	1672	DD/SP/1672/34	
2947	Katherine GULLY of Bishops Hull	1685	DD/SP/1685/43	
2948	Thomas GULLY of West Monkton	1681	DD/SP/1681/76	
2949	William GULLY of Stoke St. Mary	1697	DD/SP/1697/64	Wife Susanna
2950	John GULLYFORD of Curry Rivel	1668	DD/SP/1668/51	
2951	James GUNDERY of Exford	1634	DD/SP/1634/43	See *T.C.W.*
2952	Elizabeth GUNDIE of Staple Fitzpaine	1635	DD/SP/1635/38	
2953	Anthony GUNDREY, Gentleman of Trent	1704	T.N.A., PROB 4/22684	Will T.N.A., PROB 11/478/414
2954	John GUNDRIE of South Petherton	1634	D/D/cta/G8	Ad.ac.
2955	Arthur GUNDRY, Widower of Chard	1802	T.N.A., PROB 31/1802/1037	
2956	Joane GUNDRY, Widow of South Petherton	1636	DD/SP/1636/34	
2957	Joane GUNDRY, Widow of Street	1675	T.N.A., PROB 4/14988	
	Note: Admon. ex. 1685 relict of Arthur GUNDRY, yeoman			
2958	Nathaniel GUNDRY, Yeoman of South Petherton	1676	T.N.A., PROB 4/9740	Will also extant
GUNDRY see GUNDERY				
2959	Richard GUNING of Bicknoller	1684	DD/SP/1684/74	
2960	Robert GUNINGEHAM of Kilton	1634	DD/SP/1634/17	
2961	Mathew GUNNINGHAM of Winscombe	1606	D/D/cta/C45	Ad.ac.
2962	John GUNSTON, Sergemaker of Bishops Hull	1695	DD/SP/1695/3	
2963	Hugh GUNSTONE of Taunton St. Mary Magdalene	1696	DD/SP/1696/48	
2964	Robert GUNSTONE, Butcher of Staplegrove	1671	DD/SP/1671/32	
2965	Richard GUPPEY of Hardington Mandeville	1760	D/PC/hard.m/6/3/2	
2966	William GUPPY of Broadway	1723	DD/SP/1723/43	
2967	Henry GUTCH, Mercer of Glastonbury	1679	T.N.A., PROB 4/9340	Admon
2968	Hannah GUTTERIDGE of Dorset	1765	DD/TOR/298	
2969	Richard GUY, Apothecary of Wells	1694	T.N.A., PROB 4/22127	Will 1694
2970	Elizabeth GYARE, Widow of Bath	1689	T.N.A., PROB 4/660	Will 1689
2971	John GYLES, Mariner of Dunster	1706	B.A., 1706/15	

2972	Thomas GYLES, Mariner of Minehead	1697	DD/SP/1697/4	
2973	William GYLLET, Rector of Chaffcombe	1641	DD/SP/1641/12	Printed in *S.D.N.Q.* vol.17 p.121
2974	William GYLLET, Yeoman of Chaffcombe	1690	DD/SP/1690/31	
2975	Martin HABBERFEILD of North Petherton	1688	DD/SP/1688/17	
2976	William HABBERFEILD, Worsted Comber of North Petherton	1681	DD/SP/1681/85	
2977	Andrew HABERFEILD of Sherston, North Petherton	1639	DD/SP/1639/42	Names 3 sons
2978	Margery HACKER, Widow of Limington	1626	D/D/cta/H16	Ad.ac.
HADDEN see MICHELL				
2979	John HADDON of Dodington	1689	DD/SP/1689/31	
2980	William HADDON of [no place]	1667	DD/SP/1667/3	
2981	Thomas HADDON alias MYCHELL, Husbandman of Merriott	1581	D/D/ct/1/H3a	
2982	[missing] HADDRIDGE of [no place]	1699	DD/SP/1699/7	Illegible
2983	George HADDRIDGE of Stogursey	1684	DD/SP/1684/101	
2984	Hugh HADDRIDGE, Weaver of Stogursey	1686	DD/SP/1686/25	
2985	Edward HAGGARD of Sandford Orcas	1666	D/D/cta/H47	Ad.ac.
2986	Ralph HAGGER, Gentleman of Bedminster	1619	D/D/cta/H67	Ad.ac.
2987	[missing] HAGGETT of Crewkerne	1716	DD/SP/1716/26	
	Note: Exhibited at Crewkerne, Joan and John junior buried there 20 March 1715/6 (Reg.)			
2988	Edward HAGGOTT of Sandford Orcas	1666	D/D/cta/H47b	Ad.ac.
2989	Humphrey HAGLEY of West Monkton	1670	DD/SP/1670/76	
2990	Joan HAGLEY of West Monkton	1698	DD/SP/1698/15	
HAGLEY see SORRAGE				
2991	Adrian HAINE of Somerton	1686	DD/SAS/C96/20	
2992	John HAINE, Clerk of Stoke sub Hamdon	1687	T.N.A., PROB 4/4126	Admon
2993	John HAISE of Combe Florey	1634	DD/SP/1634/18	
2994	Thomas HAKE of Whitestaunton	1683	DD/SP/1683/69	
2995	Thomas HALES of Marston Magna	1619	D/D/cta/H70	Ad.ac.
2996	Flory HALL of Kilmersdon	1697	D/D/cta/H80	Ad.ac.
2997	Francis HALL of [no place]	1718	DD/SF/10/2/6	Formerly DD/SF/3865
2998	John HALL of Elworthy	1646	DD/SP/1646/92	See *T.C.W.*
2999	John HALL of Crewkerne	1697	DD/SP/1697/41	
3000	Jonathan HALL, Esquire of Croydon, Old Cleeve and of St. Georges, Southwark, Surrey	1766	T.N.A., PROB 3/61/14	

3001	Peter HALL of Porlock	1664	DD/SP/1664/5	
3002	Robert HALL of Monksilver	1684	DD/SP/1684/8	
3003	Susanna HALL, Widow of North Petherton	1693	DD/SP/1693/19	
3004	Thomas HALL, Husbandman of Durston	1691	DD/SP/1691/82	
3005	William HALL, Barber and perickmaker of Minehead	1730	DD/SP/1730/6	
3006	George HALL of [no place]	1632	D/D/cta/T23	Ad.ac.
3007	Robert HALLERD of Ash Priors	1685	DD/SP/1685/54	
3008	Walter HALLETT, Husbandman of Corfe	1634	DD/SP/1634/7	
HALLETT see MICHELL				
3009	Henry HALSWELL of Goathurst	1637	DD/S/WH/91	Rooms specified
3010	John HAM, Husbandman of Wootton, Butleigh	1669	D/D/ct/1/H10	
3011	John HAM of Dunwear, Bridgwater	1670	DD/SP/1670/16	
3012	Stephen HAM, Hosier of Croscombe	1680	T.N.A., PROB 4/4719	Will. ex. 1681
3013	Thomas HAMBLEN, Yeoman of Thurlbear	1684	DD/SP/1684/27	
3014	Albert HAMILTON of South Stoke	1876	DD/BR/sx/20	
3015	Right Honourable Ann HAMILTON, Esquire of Lyncombe and Widcombe	1751	T.N.A., PROB 31/1751/384	Commonly called Lord Ann Hamilton
3016	Thomas HAMILTON, Doctor? of Bishops Lydeard	1779	DD/FS/7/4	
3017	Simon HAMLEN, Tailor of Pitminster	1690	DD/SP/1690/30	
3018	Isabel HAMLYN of Bridgwater	n.d.	T.N.A., PROB 2/462	Pre 1501
3019	John HAMM of Butleigh	1638	D/D/cta/H22	Ad.ac.
3020	Jasper HAMME of Kingsdon	1640	D/D/cta/H52	Ad.ac.
3021	Elizabeth HAMMET, Widow of West Monkton	1786	T.N.A., PROB 31/1786/620	
3022	John HAMMET, Esquire of West Monkton	1786	T.N.A., PROB 31/1786/621	
3023	Christopher HANCOCK of Wiveliscombe	1626	D/D/cta/H15	Ad.ac.
3024	John HANCOCK the elder, Gentleman of Lyncombe and Widcombe	1798	T.N.A., PROB 31/1798/635	
3025	Abraham HANCOCKE of Halse	1685	DD/SP/1685/77	
3026	Agnes HANCOCKE, Widow of Halse	1691	DD/SP/1691/33	
3027	Alice HANCOCKE, Widow of Withiel Florey	1666	DD/SP/1666/75	
3028	James HANCOCKE of Withiel Florey	1684	DD/SP/1684/37	
3029	John HANCOCKE of Lydeard St. Lawrence	1636	DD/SP/1636/14	
3030	John HANCOCKE of Luxborough	1695	DD/SP/1695/15	

3031	Robert HANCOCKE of Upton	1676	DD/SP/1676/28	
3032	William HANCOCKE of Lydeard St. Lawrence	1646	DD/SP/1646/80	
3033	William HANCOCKE of Lyng	1664	DD/SP/1664/80	
3034	William HANCOCKE of Nettlecombe	1676	DD/SP/1676/44	
3035	Thomas HANCOKE of Spaxton	1620	D/D/ct/1/H17a	
3036	Thomas HANDOVER of Ilchester	17–	D/D/Cti 45	
3037	William HANKER the elder of Creech St. Michael	1640	DD/SP/1640/136	
3038	William HANKER the younger of Creech St. Michael	1640	DD/SP/1640/137	
HANKINE see ARMY				
3039	Aaron HANKOCK, Butcher of Oake	1710	DD/SP/442/1	Ad.ac.
3040	William HANKOCK of Lilstock	1667	DD/SP/1667/40	
3041	Charlotte HANKS, Spinster of St. George Hanover Square, Middlesex formerly of Keynsham	1799	T.N.A., PROB 31/1799/886	
3042	Henry HANNAM of Compton Pauncefoot	1641	D/D/cta/H57	Ad.ac.
3043	John HANNAM the elder of Littleton, Dundry	1635	D/D/cta/H19	Ad.ac.
3044	Sarah HANNAM, Widow of Wincanton	1678	DD/X/AR/4/3	
3045	Richard HANNCE of Dunster	1646	DD/SP/1646/60	
	Note: Proved by Agnes DENNIS alias HANNSE, Widow			
HANNSE see HANNCE				
3046	Richard HANNY of Pensford St. Thomas, Publow	1627/8	D/D/ct/1/H22	
3047	John HANS, Sub-dean of Wells of Wells	1509	T.N.A., PROB 2/189	
3048	William HANSON, Vicar of Twerton	1646	D/D/cta/H51	Ad.ac.
3049	Joane HARCOMBE, Widow of Kingston	1640	DD/SP/1640/47	
3050	Nicholas HARCOMBE of Lydeard St. Lawrence	1676	DD/SP/1676/37	
3051	Sydrach HARDICK of Shepton Mallet	1625	D/D/cta/H10	Ad.ac.
3052	William HARDIMAN of Crewkerne	1684	DD/SP/1684/19	
3053	Alexander HARDING of East Quantoxhead	1664	DD/SP/1664/76	
3054	Alexander HARDING of Luccombe	1730	DD/SP/1730/5	
3055	John HARDING, Clothier of Whatley	1679	T.N.A., PROB 4/20637	Will 1680. ex. 1681
3056	John HARDING, Husbandman of East Quantoxhead	1685	DD/SP/1685/90	
3057	John HARDING, Husbandman of East Quantoxhead	1685	DD/SP/442/64	Ad.ac.
3058	John HARDING of Bossington, Porlock	1731	DD/SP/1731/39	
3059	Nicholas HARDING of Luccombe	1679	DD/SP/1679/27	

3060	Samuel HARDING of North Stoke	1796	T.N.A., PROB 31/1796/234	With ac. com.
3061	Andrew HARDMAN of Staple Fitzpaine	1685	DD/SP/1685/101	
3062	Richard HARDMAN, Butcher of Pitminster	1666	DD/SP/1666/47	
3063	Roger HARDMAN of Taunton	1669	DD/SP/1669/3	
3064	John HARDWICK of [no place]	1592	D/D/cta/H5	Ad.ac.
3065	Robert HARDWITCH of Burnham on Sea	1611	D/D/cta/H72	Ad.ac.
3066	Agnes HARE, Widow of Lyng	1667	DD/SP/1667/93	
3067	Ambrose HARE of Curland, Curry Mallet	1671	T.N.A., PROB 4/17537	Will also extant
3068	Henry HARE of Bridgwater	1634	DD/SP/1634/40	
3069	Isott HARE of Taunton St. James	1690	DD/SP/1690/57	
3070	Jane HARE of Stoke St. Gregory	1636	DD/SP/1636/62	
3071	John HARE, Yeoman of Wiveliscombe	1683	T.N.A., PROB 4/11836	Will also extant
3072	John HARE the elder, Yeoman of West Monkton	1648	DD/SP/1648/58	
3073	Martha HARE of Taunton St. James	1690	DD/SP/1690/58	
3074	Richard HARE, Clerk of Hatch Beauchamp	1669	DD/SP/1669/86	
3075	Mary HARES, Widow of Withycombe	1635	DD/SP/1635/4	
3076	Reverend Robert HARKNESS of East Brent	1839	T/PH/had 1	
3077	Gregory HARKWORTHY, Clerk of Cannington	1735	DD/SP/1735/26	
3078	Edward HARLE of North Petherton	1640	DD/SP/1640/11	
3079	John HARNAM of Orchard Portman	1700	DD/SP/442/36	Ad.ac.
HARPER see HIX				
3080	William HARRES of Glastonbury St. John	1596	D/D/cta/H36	Ad.ac.
3081	John HARRIES, Tailor of Milverton	1650	DD/SP/1650/1	
3082	Aaron HARRINGTON of Hooksplace, Southfleet, Kent and Great Slade, Essex and Tooting, Surrey and London	1740	T.N.A., PROB 31/1740/61	Died at Bath
3083	[missing] HARRIS of [no place] Note: Ad.ac.; details his daughter's marriage settlement	1633	D/D/cta/H81	
3084	Anne HARRIS, Spinster of Midsomer Norton	1720	T.N.A., PROB 3/19/29	
3085	Dorothy HARRIS, Widow of Edington, Moorlinch	1677	T.N.A., PROB 4/18625	Will also extant
3086	H.F. HARRIS of Bath	1870	DD/BR/sx/21	
3087	James HARRIS, Husbandman of Oake	1637	DD/SP/1637/40	
3088	James HARRIS of Milverton	1670	DD/SP/1670/41	
3089	John HARRIS of East Coker	1624	D/D/cta/H28	Ad.ac.

3090	John HARRIS of Tickenham	1632	D/D/cta/H18	Ad.ac.
3091	John HARRIS of Spaxton	1693	DD/SP/1693/63	
3092	John HARRIS of Bridgwater	1731	DD/SP/1731/2	
3093	Leonard HARRIS of West Bagborough	1687	D/D/cta/H82	Ad.ac.
3094	Thomas HARRIS of Chew Stoke	1771	T.N.A., PROB 31/1771/386	
3095	Thomas HARRIS junior of Lydeard St. Lawrence	1664	DD/SP/1664/38	
3096	William HARRIS, Yeoman of Hedging, North Petherton	1731	DD/SP/1731/40	
3097	William HARRIS the elder of Stocklinch Ottersey	1670	DD/SP/1670/112	
3098	William HARRIS the elder of Stocklinch Ottersey	1670	DD/SP/1670/54	
HARRIS see MARTIN				
3099	Stephen HARRISE of Bridgwater	1710	DD/SP/1710/2	
3100	Agnes HARRISON of Luccombe	1597	D/D/cta/H34	Ad.ac.
3101	Alexander HARRISON, Gentleman of West Quantoxhead	1665	DD/SP/1665/45	
3102	John HARRISON, Innholder of Bridgwater	1747	DD/SP/1747/32	
3103	...... HARRYSON, Yeoman of Preston Plucknett	1642	D/D/ct/1/H42	
3104	Richard HARSE of Hutton	1689	D/D/cta/H83	Ad.ac.
3105	John HARSLEY, Esquire of Hinton Charterhouse	1766	T.N.A., PROB 31/1766/494	With ad.ac.
3106	Hugh HARSNETT, Gentleman of Yeovil	1703	T.N.A., PROB 5/2009	
3107	Edward HART, Innholder of Churchill	1678	T.N.A., PROB 4/11955	Admon
3108	Robert HART of Durston	1681	DD/SP/1681/36	
3109	Tobias HART of Nailsea	1707	D/D/cta/H92	Ad.ac.
3110	William HART of Drayton	1732	DD/SP/1732/4	
3111	George HARTE of [no place]	1677	T.N.A., PROB 4/6894	Admon
3112	Ferdinando HARTGILL, Esquire of Somerset	1737	T.N.A., PROB 3/36/26	
3113	John HARTON of Porlock	1640	DD/SP/1640/65	
3114	William HARTON senior of Porlock	1697	DD/SP/1697/13	
3115	John HARVARD of Isle Abbotts	1714	D/D/cta/H68	Ad.ac.
3116	John HARVARD senior of Isle Abbotts	1683	DD/SP/1683/33	
3117	Joseph HARVARD of Isle Abbotts	1714	DD/SP/442/16	Ad.ac.
3118	Arthur HARVEY of North Petherton	1672	DD/SP/1672/10	
3119	Richard HARVEY of Crewkerne	1676	DD/SP/1676/47	
3120	Richard HARVEY of Crewkerne	1677	DD/SP/1677/16	
3121	Thomas HARVEY, Silkweaver of Bath	1676	T.N.A., PROB 4/10405	Admon

3122	John HARVIE, Weaver of Whitestaunton	1629	D/D/ct/1/H43a-g	
3123	John HARVORD of Aller	1665	D/D/cta/H77	Ad.ac.
3124	Simon HARVORD of Portbury	1613	B.A., 1613/28	
3125	George HARWOOD, Yeoman of [no place]	1681	T.N.A., PROB 4/15252	Admon. ex. 1682
3126	John HARWOOD of Withypool	1670	DD/SP/1670/83	
3127	Thomas HARWOOD of Curland, Curry Mallet	1667	DD/SP/1667/38	
HARWOOD see HORWOOD				
3128	Samuel HASELBER, Woolen Draper of Crewkerne	1694	T.N.A., PROB 4/19899	Will also extant
3129	Elias HASKETT of Henstridge	1697	T.N.A., PROB 5/5686	
3130	Elizabeth HASSELL, Spinster of Cannington	1678	DD/SP/1678/44	
3131	James HASSELL of Bridgwater	1684	DD/SP/1684/50	
3132	William HATHERLYE, Mariner of Minehead	1675	DD/SP/1675/15	
3133	Edward HATTON of Lympsham	1640	D/D/cta/H2	Ad.ac.
3134	Joane HAUCKWELL, Widow of Cutcombe	1666	DD/SP/1666/17	
3135	Robert HAUCKWELL of Withypool	1669	DD/SP/1669/29	
HAUCKWELL see HAWKWELL				
3136	John HAULL of Crewkerne	1684	DD/SP/1684/88	
3137	Charles HAUTEN of Winsford	1695	DD/SP/1695/26	
3138	Anstis HAVILAND, Widow of Charlinch	1669	DD/SAS/HV/58/9	
3139	Robert HAVILAND of Bridgwater	1666	DD/SP/1666/1	
3140	Matthew HAVYLAND of Langford Budville	1717	DD/SP/442/24	Ad.ac.
3141	Jane HAWKENS, Widow of Cheddar	1662	DD/SAS/FA/161/4	
3142	John HAWKENS, Husbandman of Trull	1637	DD/SP/1637/28	
3143	Robert HAWKENS, Yeoman of Combe Florey	1721	DD/SP/1721/13	
3144	[missing] HAWKENS ?, Husbandman of [no place]	1670	DD/SP/1670/86	
	Note: Appraised by John MILES senior, Thomas HAWKENS and Robert HAWKENS; damaged			
3145	Charles HAWKER, Esquire of Thorne Coffin	1740	DD/SF/11/2/59	Formerly DD/SF/3148
3146	Ellen HAWKER, Widow of Chillington	1636	DD/SP/1636/40	
3147	Florence HAWKER, Widow of Curry Mallet	1682	DD/SP/1682/23	
3148	Henry HAWKER, Husbandman of Hambridge, Curry Rivel	1675	DD/SP/1675/84	
3149	John HAWKER of West Monkton	1686	DD/SP/1686/34	
3150	Margery HAWKER, Widow of Chaffcombe	1680	DD/SP/1680/5	
3151	Miss HAWKER of Poundisford Lodge, Pitminster	1858	DD/HLM Box 9	

3152	Robert HAWKER of Taunton St. Mary Magdalene	1663	DD/SP/1663/34	
3153	Thomas HAWKER, Esquire of Vagg, Chilthorne Domer	1697	T.N.A., PROB 4/6897	Will also extant
3154	Lawrence HAWKINGS of Barrington	1672	DD/SP/1672/64	
3155	Ben HAWKINS of Stogumber	1714	DD/SP/1714/20	
3156	Grace HAWKINS, Widow of Wiveliscombe	1662	DD/SAS/FA/161/27	
3157	John HAWKINS of Stogumber	1761	T.N.A., PROB 31/1761/757	
3158	John HAWKINS of Cheddar	1813	DD/FS/42/9	
3159	Lawrence and Ann (his wife) HAWKINS of Barrington	1681	DD/SP/1681/7	
3160	Lewis HAWKINS, Miller of Hillfarrance	1691	DD/SP/1691/8	
3161	Mary HAWKINS, Widow of Puckington	1639	DD/SP/1639/57	
3162	Sarah HAWKINS, Widow of Dowlish Wake	1716	DD/SP/1716/10	
3163	Sarah HAWKINS, Spinster of Yeovil formerly of East Brent, Somerset died at Halstock, Dorset	1829	T.N.A., PROB 31/1829/1660	
3164	Thomas HAWKINS of Minehead	1691	DD/SP/1691/87	
3165	William HAWKINS the elder, Yeoman of Dowlish Wake	1684	DD/SP/1684/104	
3166	Thomas HAWKINS alias TARR of Bishops Lydeard	1679	T.N.A., PROB 4/4556	Will 1679
HAWKINS see ARMY				
3167	Grace HAWKWELL of Cannington	1667	DD/SP/1667/33	
3168	William HAWKWELL of Exford	1667	DD/SP/1667/7	
HAWKWELL see HAUCKWELL				
3169	Giles HAWLEY of [no place]	1678	T.N.A., PROB 4/15987	Admon
3170	James HAWTEN of Winsford	1670	DD/SP/1670/92	
3171	Jane HAWTEN, Widow of Chipstable	1696	DD/SP/1696/19	
3172	Joan HAWTEN, Widow of Winsford	1679	DD/SP/1679/56	
3173	William HAWTEN of Chipstable	1696	DD/SP/1696/20	
3174	William HAYBALL, Clothworker of Donyatt	1691	DD/SP/1691/3	
3175	Simon HAYDON, Husbandman of Wambrook	1622	W.S.H.C., P5/1622/35	Com., inv. and will
3176	Thomas HAYDON of Uphill	1662	D/D/cta/H96	Ad.ac.
3177	William HAYDON ? of Pensford St. Thomas, Publow	n.d.	D/D/cta/Blank/11	Damaged; ad.ac.
3178	David HAYE of Yarlington	1616	D/D/cta/H69	Ad.ac.
3179	Alice HAYES, Widow of Moorland, North Petherton	1639	DD/SP/1639/45	
3180	George HAYES of North Petherton	1681	DD/SP/1681/75	
3181	Jemima? HAYES, Spinster of Broadway	1770	T.N.A., PROB 31/1770/359	

3182	Ralph HAYES, Cordwainer of Bridgwater	1720	DD/SP/1720/18	
3183	Richard HAYES of Orchard Portman	1664	DD/SP/1664/59	
3184	Robert HAYES, Hosier of Evercreech	1676	T.N.A., PROB 4/9024	Will also extant
3185	Robert HAYES, Husbandman of Brompton Regis	1693	DD/SP/1693/11	
3186	Joane HAYES alias HOWE of Cutcombe	1666	DD/SP/1666/18	
3187	Simon HAYMAN, Merchant of Minehead	1675	T.N.A., PROB 4/8211	Admon
3188	John HAYME of Banwell	1752	T.N.A., PROB 3/51/37	
3189	John HAYMES, Shoemaker of Glastonbury St. John	1606	D/D/cta/H76	Ad.ac.
3190	Henry HAYNE of Ruishton	1641	DD/SP/1641/62	See *T.C.W.*
3191	Joan HAYNE, Spinster of Ruishton	1690	DD/SP/1690/48	
3192	Robert HAYNES, Innholder of Wells	1726	D/D/Cti 36	
3193	Mary HAYSAM, Widow of Frome Selwood	1677	T.N.A., PROB 4/10373	Will. ex. 1678
3194	Elizabeth HAYSE of [no place]	1723	D/D/cta/H84	Ad.ac.
3195	Ann HAYWARD, Widow of Bathwick	1831	T.N.A., PROB 31/1831/434	Relict of Joseph
3196	James HAYWARD of Woolavington	1734	T.N.A., PROB 3/33/56	
3197	James HAYWARD of Woolavington	1734	T.N.A., PROB 31/1734/264	
3198	Joan HAYWARD of Long Sutton	1590	D/D/cta/H38	Ad.ac.
3199	John HAYWARD of Porlock	1669	DD/SP/1669/84	
3200	John HAYWARD of Porlock	1694	DD/SP/1694/2	
3201	John HAYWARD of Huish Champflower	1698	DD/SP/1698/16	
3202	John HAYWARD, Toyman of Bath	1731	T.N.A., PROB 3/30/123	
3203	William HAYWARD of Porlock died at Poole	1670	T.N.A., PROB 4/4717	Will also extant
3204	William HAYWARD of Truddoxhill, Nunney	1788	T.N.A., PROB 31/1788/99	
3205	William HAYWARD alias POOLE of Porlock	1670	DD/SP/1670/108	
HAYWARD see POOLE				
3206	William HAYWOOD of Truddoxhill, Nunney	1784	T.N.A., PROB 31/1784/765 and 1784/850	
3207	[missing] HAYWOOD ? of Sanford ? Note: Damaged ad.ac.; mentions Sir Edward PECCAME	n.d.	D/D/cta/Blank/1	
3208	Samuel HAZELL, Husbandman of Cannington	1675	DD/SP/1675/27	
3209	Thomas HAZSARD of Staplegrove	1693	DD/SP/1693/7	
3210	Robert HEADFORD, Yeoman of Bridgwater	1732	D/D/Cti 54	
HEADFORD see HEDFORD				

3211	John HEADLAND of Pylle	1683	T.N.A., PROB 4/10365	Will; buried at Pilton, 1683
3212	William HEAL, Coalmine shareholder of Nailsea	1735	D/D/Cti 46	
HEALING see HOLLAND				
HEALLING see HOLLANE				
3213	Richard HEAREING of Pitminster	1635	DD/SP/1635/24	
3214	Thomas HEARLY, Husbandman of East Quantoxhead	1678	DD/SP/1678/12	
3215	Thomas HEARNE of Creech St. Michael	1684	DD/SP/1684/139	
3216	William HEARNE of Crewkerne	1700	DD/SP/1700/15	
3217	John HEARNS of Hardington Mandeville	1762	D/PC/hard.m/6/3/2	
3218	James HEATH of Bath	1826	T.N.A., PROB 31/1826/810	
3219	George HEATHFIELD of Langford Budville	1670	DD/SP/1670/21	
3220	John HEATHFIELD of Bridgwater	1648	DD/SP/1648/61	
HEATHFIELD see TORR				
3221	Henry the elder HEBDICHE of Sparkford	1634	D/D/cta/H21	Ad.ac.
3222	Henry HEBDITCH, Yeoman of Creech St. Michael	1690	DD/SP/1690/27	
3223	William HEBDITCH of Creech St. Michael	1683	DD/SP/1683/101	
HEBDITCH see HIBDITCH				
3224	Giles HEDFORD of Withycombe	1645	DD/SP/1645/54	
3225	Jane HEDFORD of Withycombe	1689	DD/SP/1689/15	
3226	Robert HEDFORD of Withycombe	1664	DD/SP/1664/65	
HEDFORD see HEADFORD				
3227	Jane HEDGE alias HEDGES, Widow of Clevedon	1734	T.N.A., PROB 3/33/121	
3228	Andrew HEDGES of Beckington ?	1633?	D/D/cta/H85	
	Note: Ad.ac.; mentions his children with their ages who were baptised at Beckington; damaged			
HEDGES see HEDGE				
HEERING see HERRING				
3229	Robert HELLARD of South Petherton	1678	DD/SP/1678/22	
3230	Walter HELLBART of Upton	1687	DD/SP/1687/13	
3231	John HELLIAR, Husbandman of Curry Mallet	1664	DD/SP/1664/72	
3232	John HELLIAR of Hinton St. George	1687	DD/SP/1687/42	
HELLIAR see HELLIOR, HILLIARS and HELLIER				
3233	George HELLIER, Widower of Limington	1681	T.N.A., PROB 4/4723	Admon
3234	George HELLIER of Burton, Drayton	1716	DD/SP/1716/39	

3235	James HELLIER of [no place]	1640	D/D/cta/H11	
	Note: Ad.ac. mentions his wife Mary and children Jasper, Simon and John			
3236	Robert HELLIER, Glover of Taunton St. Mary Magdalene	1683	DD/SP/1683/27	
3237	Thomas HELLIER of Taunton St. James	1715	DD/SP/1715/34	
HELLIER see HELLIOR, HILLIARS and HELLIAR				
3238	James HELLING of Milverton	1685	DD/SP/1685/72	
3239	Thomas HELLING of Milverton	1670	DD/SP/1670/65	
3240	John HELLIOR of Chipstable	1665	DD/SP/1665/43	
3241	William HELLIOR, Husbandman of Brompton Regis	1634	DD/SP/1634/44	
HELLIOR see HILLIARS, HELLIAR and HELLIER				
3242	Ann HELPS, Widow of Lyncombe and Widcombe	1822	T.N.A., PROB 31/1822/679	
3243	Henry HELYAR of East Coker	1634	DD/WHh/7	
3244	William HELYAR of East Coker	1723	DD/WHh/1106	
3245	William HELYAR of East Coker	1728	DD/WHh/27a	
3246	William HELYAR of East Coker	1820	DD/WHh/51, 52	
3247	John HEMBBROW, Husbandman of Combe Florey	1705	DD/SP/1705/38	
3248	John HEMBOROUGH of East Quantoxhead	1718	DD/SP/442/27	Ad.ac.
3249	Mary HEMBOROW alias SAVAGE, Widow of Combe Florey	1685	DD/SP/1685/97	
HEMBOROW see SAVAGE				
3250	Philip HEMBROUGH, Gentleman of Bishops Lydeard	1686?	T.N.A., PROB 4/26053	Admon. ex. 1685?
3251	Richard HEMBROUGH of Bridgwater	1666	DD/SP/1666/25	
3252	Martha HEMINGS, Widow of Lyng	1716	DD/SP/1716/62	
3253	Henry HEMMYNGS, Clothier of Keynsham	1672	T.N.A., PROB 5/2011	Will T.N.A., PROB 11/335
3254	John HENSLEIGH, Gentleman of Clatworthy	1685	DD/SP/1685/64	
3255	William HENSLEIGH, Gentleman of Sindercombe, Clatworthy	1672	DD/SP/1672/5	
3256	George HENSLY of Selworthy	1669	DD/SP/1669/30	
3257	Ralph HENVILL, Gentleman of Milverton	1675	T.N.A., PROB 5/5383	
3258	Thomas HERBERT of Bridgwater	1669	DD/SP/1669/65	
3259	William HERBERT of Lydeard St. Lawrence	1677	DD/SP/1677/60	
3260	John HERIN, Butcher of Dulverton	1726	DD/SP/1726/27	
HERIN see HERRING				
3261	William HERNIMAN, Yeoman of Hawkridge	1721	DD/SP/1721/11	
3262	Edward HERRING of Bishops Hull	1640	DD/SP/1640/37	Inv. shows HEERING

3263	Job HERRING of Pitminster	1731	DD/SP/1731/37	
3264	John HERRING of West Monkton	1683	DD/SP/1683/82	A minor
3265	John HERRING, Husbandman of Bradford	1683	DD/SP/1683/9	
3266	Richard HERRING of Isle Brewers	1681	T.N.A., PROB 4/10625	Admon
3267	Roger HERRING, Yeoman of Exton	1688	DD/SP/1688/2	
HERRING see HERIN				
3268	Henry HERSSE, Mariner of Abbots Leigh	1628	B.A., 1628/37	Will also extant
3269	Bartholomew HETHAR of Mudford	1693	D/D/cta/H86	Ad.ac.
3270	John HEWES, Cordwainer of Lydeard St. Lawrence	1700	DD/SP/1700/29	
3271	Mary HEWETT of Chesham, Buckinghamshire died at Bath	1831	T.N.A., PROB 31/1831/1272	With ad.ac.
3272	Pressell HEWETT of Broadway	1678	DD/SP/1678/27	
3273	Thomas HEWETT of Ruishton	1720	DD/SP/442/71	Ad.ac.
3274	Thomas HEWLETT, Shoemaker of Hardington Mandeville	1737	D/D/Cti 42	
3275	John HEWSEY, Curate of Trull	1675	DD/SP/1675/33	
3276	Sir Edward HEXT of Low Ham, High Ham	1635	DD/SOG/447	
3277	Bernard HEYDON, Husbandman of Wambrook	1631	W.S.H.C., P5/1631/51	Inv. and will
3278	Petronel HEYDON, Widow of Wambrook	1638	W.S.H.C., P5/1638/54	
	Note: Tuition bond relates to Bernard, Margaret and Thomasine HEYDON			
3279	Henry HEYSHAM, Yeoman of Frome Selwood	1604	D/D/cta/H75	Ad.ac.
3280	Mathew HIBDITCH of South Petherton	1677	DD/SP/1677/25	
3281	Simon HIBDITCH of South Petherton	1670	DD/SP/1670/4	
HIBDITCH see HEBDITCH				
3282	...... HICHINS of East Harptree	1644/5	D/D/ct/1/H84	
3283	Francis HICKES, Husbandman of Cannington	1697	DD/SP/1697/60	
3284	Jeffrey HICKES, Yeoman of Westbury	1696	T.N.A., PROB 5/3267	
3285	Matthew HICKES, Innholder of Taunton	1667	DD/SP/1667/4	
3286	Sarah HICKES, Widow of Stogumber	1668	DD/SP/1668/58	
3287	William HICKS, Yeoman of North Petherton	1695	DD/SP/1695/12	
3288	Elizabeth HICKS alias PLIMPTON of Wells	1685	T.N.A., PROB 4/9012	Admon
HIER see THOMAS				
3289	Juliana / Julyan HIGDON of Maperton	1629	D/D/ct/1/H89a	
3290	Thomas HIGDON of West Bradley	1667	D/D/cta/H49	Ad.ac.
3291	William HIGDON of Shapwick	n.d.	D/D/cta/H4	

Note: Ad.ac.; this could be two different accounts as it is annotated 'Clarke et Clarke' and mentions Edith relict of John TROWBRIDGE of Hutton

3292	James HIGGENS of Ditcheat	1685	T/PH/bbs/30	
3293	John HIGGENS of Yarlington	1664	D/D/cta/H48	Ad.ac.
3294	John HIGGINBOTTOME, Milliner of Bedminster	1681	T.N.A., PROB 4/3944	Admon. ex. 1682
3295	William HIGGINS, Carpenter of Baltonsborough	1738	D/D/Cti 34	
3296	William HIGGINS, Carpenter of Baltonsborough	1738	D/D/Cti 37	
3297	Thomas HIGHNAM of Cameley	1634	D/D/cta/H20	Ad.ac.
3298	...... HIKES of Chew Stoke	1562	D/D/ct/1/H93	
3299	Henry HILDIBRAND, Gentleman of Somerton	1703	T.N.A., PROB 4/22434	Admon
3300	John HILES the elder of Withycombe Hadley, Withycombe	1667	DD/SP/1667/20	
3301	Abraham HILL of Brompton Regis	1710	DD/SP/442/49	Ad.ac.
3302	Abraham HILL, Yeoman of Brompton Regis	1710	DD/SP/442/50	Ad.ac.
3303	Ann HILL, Widow of Paulton formerly of St. Mary Redcliffe, Bristol	1791	T.N.A., PROB 31/1791/768	
3304	Ann HILL, Widow of Taunton St. Mary Magdalene	1821	T.N.A., PROB 31/1821/397	
3305	Beatrice HILL, Widow of Crewkerne	1688	DD/SP/1688/37	Also her son John
3306	Charity HILL of Skilgate	1634	DD/SP/1634/30–31	
3307	Christopher HILL of Cutcombe	1646	DD/SP/1646/38	
3308	Christopher HILL, Husbandman of Chipstable	1697	DD/SP/1697/56	
3309	Daniel HILL, Husbandman of Weare	1680	D/D/ct/1/H94	
3310	Edith HILL of Creech St. Michael	1687	DD/SP/1687/60	
3311	Edmond HILL, Gentleman of Combe Florey	1690	DD/SP/1690/46	
3312	Edmond HILL, Gentleman of Combe Florey	1690	DD/SP/1690/50	
3313	Edward HILL, Esquire, Lieutenant Colonel in Royal Marines of Walcot	1835	T.N.A., PROB 31/1835/1161	
3314	Elizabeth HILL, Spinster of East Harptree	1627	D/D/ct/1/H96	
3315	Elizabeth HILL of Winsford	1672	DD/SP/1672/58	
3316	Elizabeth HILL, Widow of Stogursey	1714	DD/SP/1714/28	
3317	Francis HILL of Minehead	1672	DD/SP/1672/36	
3318	George HILL, Husbandman of Winsford	1671	DD/SP/1671/45	
3319	Henry HILL, Husbandman of Taunton St. James	1667	DD/SP/1667/55	
3320	Hugh HILL, Haberdasher of Taunton	1634	DD/SP/1634/20	

3321	James HILL of Taunton St. Mary Magdalene	1630s	DD/SP/1632/35	
	Note: Undated; mentions a lease of the Salutation in Taunton			
3322	Joan HILL of Bruton	1632	W.S.H.C., P2/H/446	Inv., letter, receipt
3323	John HILL, Gentleman of Chard	1620	D/D/cta/H26	Ad.ac.
3324	John HILL of Pitminster	1664	DD/SP/1664/46	
3325	John HILL of Chilton (*sic*)	1669	DD/SP/1669/72	
3326	John HILL, Tailor of Kilve	1676	DD/SP/1676/45	
3327	John HILL of Compton Dundon	1681	T.N.A., PROB 4/162	Will also extant
3328	John HILL of Bridgwater	1682	DD/SP/1682/21	
3329	John HILL of Withypool	1682	DD/X/ETH/1	
3330	John HILL, Clerk of Combe Florey	1687	T.N.A., PROB 4/21410	Will also extant
3331	John HILL, Weaver of Crewkerne	1688	DD/SP/1688/37	Son of Beatrice
3332	John HILL of Taunton St. Mary Magdalene	1728	DD/SP/1728/38	
3333	John HILL of Dulverton	1730	DD/SP/1730/7	
3334	Joseph HILL of Wrington	1736	D/D/cta/H87	Ad.ac. and inv.
3335	Joseph HILL of Wrington	1736	D/D/Cti 38	
3336	Judith HILL, Widow of Winford	1738	D/D/cta/H87a	Ad.ac.
3337	Lawrence HILL of Wells St. Cuthbert	1621	D/D/cta/H27	Ad.ac.
3338	Nathaniel HILL of Skilgate	1690	DD/SP/1690/65	
3339	Peter HILL of Withypool	1626	D/D/ct/1/H102a	
3340	Richard HILL of Winsford	1665	DD/SP/1665/1	
3341	Richard HILL of High Littleton	1687	DD/GL/131	
3342	Richard HILL of Simonsbath, Exmoor	1694	DD/SP/1694/9	
3343	Robert HILL of Taunton St. Mary Magdalene	1635	DD/SP/1635/132	
3344	Sybil HILL, Widow of Wembdon	1592	D/D/cta/H79	Ad.ac.
3345	Thomas HILL of [no place]	1648	DD/SP/1648/23	
3346	Thomas HILL of Brompton Regis	n.d.	D/D/cta/H63	Ad.ac.
3347	Timothy HILL of Cheddar	1819	DD/WM/6	
3348	William HILL, Gentleman of Taunton St. Mary Magdalene	1670	DD/SP/1670/80	
3349	William HILL, Clothier of Stogumber	1676	T.N.A., PROB 4/18626	Will also extant
3350	William HILL of Chipstable	1764	T.N.A., PROB 31/1764/269	
3351	William and John, his brother HILL of Cutcombe	1683	DD/SP/1683/88	
3352	[missing] HILL ? of Selworthy or Wootton Courtenay ?	1684	DD/SP/1684/170	

	Note: Mentions a lease of a 'Cole house', appraised by John SIDERFIN, Thomas TRILL; Charles HILL natural son and John TRULL son-in-law mentioned; damaged (*H.T.* and Reg.)			
3353	Christopher HILL alias CHUBBERYE of Withypool	1639	DD/SP/1639/22	
3354	Robert HILL alias DODESCOMBE of Brushford	1639	DD/SP/1639/25	
HILL see DADSCOMBE, DATSCOMBE, THRASHER				
3355	Christian HILLARD of Compton Durville, South Petherton	1646	DD/SP/1646/51	
3356	John HILLARD of Cote, Martock	1639	D/D/ct/1/H109	
3357	Mary HILLARD, Widow of Curry Rivel	1668	DD/SP/1668/39	
3358	Robert HILLARD, Yeoman of Curry Rivel	1636	DD/SP/1636/12	
HILLARD see SEELEY				
3359	Richard HILLARY of Winsham	1660	DD/X/RDN/1	Rooms specified
3360	William HILLE, Baker of Publow	1628/9	D/D/ct/1/H107	
3361	Elizabeth HILLERSON of [no place]	1584	DD/WO/55/5	
3362	Edmund HILLHOWSE, Yeoman of Congresbury	1619	D/D/cta/H66	Ad.ac.
3363	William HILLIARD of Ilminster	1668	*S.D.N.Q.* vol. 8 p. 3	
3364	Edward HILLIARS (HELLIARE) of Taunton St. Mary Magdalene	1639	DD/SP/1639/11	See *T.C.W.*
HILLIARS see HELLIOR, HELLIAR and HELLIER				
3365	John? HILLINGE of Milverton?	1635	DD/SP/1635/120	
	Note: Proved by Mary, on bahalf of Michael, natural son			
3366	Samuel HILLMAN, Yeoman of Wrington	1669	T.N.A., PROB 4/6874	Will also extant
3367	Thomas HILLYARD of Ilchester	1684	T.N.A., PROB 4/5696	Admon
3368	William HIMMINGS of Lyng	1684	DD/SP/1684/79	
3369	John HINAM of Dulverton	1741	DD/SP/1741/11	
3370	[missing] HINBOROW, Widow of [no place]	1651	DD/SP/1651/4	
3371	Emet HINDHAM of Winsford	1639	DD/SP/1639/14	
3372	William HINDHAM, Bachelor of Winsford	1637	DD/SP/1637/1	
3373	Zacharias HINDHAM of Hawkridge	1645	DD/SP/1645/41	
3374	[missing] HINDHAM ? of Dulverton ?	1638	DD/SP/1638/15	
	Note: Appraised by ..... COMER and Christopher HILL, proved on behalf of John HINDHAM a minor; damaged (Reg.)			
3375	Michell HINDOM of Winsford	1637	DD/SP/1637/6	
3376	Mary HINTON of Banwell	n.d.	D/P/ban/13/2/17	
3377	Richard HIPPESLEY of Wookey	1655	DD/SAS/FA/161/35	

3378	Richard HIPPESLEY, Gentleman of Wells	1697	T.N.A., PROB 4/8389	Admon
3379	Anne HIPPISLEY, Widow of Chewton Mendip	1677	T.N.A., PROB 4/8463	Admon
3380	Christopher HIPPISLEY, Gentleman of Cricket St. Thomas	1689	T.N.A., PROB 4/8753	Will also extant
3381	Pheobe HIPPISLEY, Spinster of Ston Easton	1729	T.N.A., PROB 31/1729/476	
3382	John HIPSLEY, Yeoman of Cocklake, Wedmore	1710	D/D/Pd/21	Possibly not proved
3383	John HISCE the younger of Mark	1582	D/D/cta/H7	Ad.ac.
3384	James HISCOX, Weaver of Bedminster	1674	T.N.A., PROB 4/8614	Admon
3385	Stephen HISCOX of Frome Selwood	1590	D/D/cta/H39	Ad.ac.
3386	Ellen HITCHCOCK, Widow of Wellington	1629	D/D/ct/1/H119a	
3387	Giles HITCHCOCK of Wayford	1669	DD/SP/1669/53	
3388	Nicholas HITCHCOCKE of Chaffcombe	1677	DD/SP/1677/2	
3389	William HITCHCOCKE of Wellington	1685	T.N.A., PROB 4/15633	Will also extant
3390	William HITCHFILD of North Petherton	1587	D/D/cta/H44	Ad.ac.
3391	Robert HITCHINGS, Merchant of Frome Selwood	1699	T.N.A., PROB 4/9439	Admon
3392	William HITE of Aisholt	1638	DD/SP/1638/71	
3393	William HITE of Goathurst	1688	DD/SP/1688/46	
3394	Elizabeth HIX, Spinster of Stogumber	1668	DD/SP/1668/7	
3395	Francis HIX of Stawell, Moorlinch	1680	D/D/ct/1/H121	
3396	John HIX of West Harptree	1601	D/D/cta/H74	Ad.ac.
3397	Mary HIX of Puriton	1732	DD/X/SPW/2	
3398	Margaret HIX alias HARPER, Widow of Saltford	1628/9	D/D/ct/1/H120a	
3399	Edmund HIXE, Husbandman of West Pennard	1625	D/D/cta/H12	Ad.ac.
3400	Roger HOARE, Esquire of Bridgwater	1700	T.N.A., PROB 5/2012	
3401	Roger HOARE, Gentleman of Bridgwater	1728	T.N.A., PROB 3/27/221	
3402	Henry HOBART of Intwood, Norfolk died at Bath	1802	T.N.A., PROB 31/1802/598	With ac. com.
3403	Alice HOBBS, Widow of Othery	1619	D/D/cta/H64	Ad.ac.
3404	James HOBBS, Woolcomber of Dulverton	1680	DD/SP/1680/84	
3405	James HOBBS of Cutcombe	1697	DD/SP/1697/31	
3406	John HOBBS of Timberscombe	1734	D/D/Ppb 91	
3407	Thomas HOBBS of Charlton Horethorne	1667	D/D/cta/H50	Ad.ac.
3408	Thomas HOBHOUSE of Watchett, St. Decumans	1676	T.N.A., PROB 4/18251	Admon. ex. 1676
3409	Tobey HOCKENEL of North Cadbury	1639	D/D/cta/H33	Ad.ac.
3410	Toby HOCKNELL of North Cadbury	1639	D/D/cta/H3	Ad.ac.

3411	John HODDEN of Stogursey	1700	DD/SP/1700/16	
3412	John HODDS of Portishead	1662	D/D/cta/H45	Ad.ac.
3413	John HODDY of South Brent	1738	D/D/Cti 39	
3414	Francis HODGE, Husbandman of West Monkton	1672	DD/SP/1672/57	
HODGE see BRISHFFORD				
3415	Bartholomew HODGES of Stogursey	1687	D/D/cta/H88	Ad.ac.
3416	Edward HODGES, Joiner of Curry Rivel	1729	DD/SP/1729/50	
3417	George HODGES of Wedmore	1634	DD/SH/79/9 c/2480	
3418	George HODGES, Esquire of High Littleton	1762	T.N.A., PROB 31/1762/670	
3419	Giles HODGES, Widower of Seavington St. Mary	1831	T.N.A., PROB 31/1831/445	
3420	John HODGES of Wedmore	1641	D/D/cta/H56	Ad.ac.
3421	John HODGES of Muchelney	1641	D/D/cta/H58	Ad.ac.
3422	John HODGES of Stockland Bristol	1713	DD/SP/1713/30	
3423	John HODGES of Bishops Sutton, Chew Magna	1733	D/D/Cti 44	
3424	Robert HODGES of Spaxton	1641	DD/SP/1641/67	
3425	Robert HODGES, Labourer of Knighton, Stogursey	1731	DD/SP/1731/6	
3426	Samuel HODGES of Spaxton	1667	DD/SP/1667/18	
3427	Thomas HODGES of Enmore	n.d.	D/D/cta/H32	Ad.ac.
3428	William HODGES, Gentleman of Speckington, Yeovilton	1647	D/D/cta/H60	Ad.ac.
3429	William HODGES of Crewkerne	1686	T.N.A., PROB 4/8858	Admon
3430	William HODGES, Gentleman of Locking	1687	T.N.A., PROB 4/4332	Will 1688
3431	William HODGES, Husbandman of Stogursey	1690	DD/SP/1690/22	
HODGES see BROOK				
3432	Joan HOITE, Widow of Hewish, Crewkerne	1674	DD/SP/1674/58	
3433	Nathaniel HOLBACHE, Esquire of Whitchurch	1645	D/D/ct/1/H134	
3434	John HOLBROOK of Winford	1737	D/D/Cti 40	
3435	Naboth HOLCOMBE of Hawkridge	1685	DD/SP/1685/30	
3436	Nicholas HOLCOMBE senior, Yeoman of Streame, St. Decumans	1679	T.N.A., PROB 4/9540	Will also extant
3437	[missing] HOLCOMBE alias ELLIS ?, Widow of Over Stowey	1669	DD/SP/1669/19	
	Note: Mentions her daughter Elizabeth HOLCOMBE alias ELLIS; damaged			
3438	Thomas HOLDER of Easton, Wells St. Cuthbert	1685	T.N.A., PROB 4/2247	Admon. ex. 1686
3439	Edward HOLDWAY, Cardmaker of Frome Selwood	1723	T.N.A., PROB 3/22/71	

3440	Edward HOLDWAY of Frome Selwood	1723	T.N.A., PROB 31/1723/267	
3445	[missing] HOLE of Luccombe	1689	DD/SP/1689/7	Mentions sons William, Thomas and George
3441	Abraham HOLE junior of Porlock	1693	DD/SP/1693/25	
3442	Alice HOLE of Winsford	1686	DD/SP/1686/40	
3443	Ames HOLE the elder of Winsford	1637	DD/SP/1637/58	
3444	Amos HOLE of Simonsbath, Exmoor	1772	T.N.A., PROB 31/1772/494	
3446	Edward HOLE of Castle Cary	1683	D/D/cta/H89	Ad.ac.
3447	Joan HOLE of Rushcombe, Wootton Courtenay	1677	DD/SP/1677/87	
3448	John HOLE of North Cadbury	1630	D/D/ct/1/H139	
3449	Richard HOLE, Yeoman of West Lydford	1697	T.N.A., PROB 4/15439	Will also extant
3450	Robert HOLE, Seamen of Porlock	1696	DD/SP/1696/31	
3451	Robert HOLE of Moorlinch	1733	D/D/Cti 35	
3452	Roger HOLE of Selworthy	1637	DD/SP/1637/51	
3453	William HOLE of Luccombe	1640	DD/SP/1640/72	
HOLE see HOLL				
3454	John HOLEBROKE of North Petherton	1696	DD/SP/1696/38	
3455	Michael HOLL of Selworthy	1635	DD/SP/1635/5	
3456	John HOLLAND, Clothier of Beckington	1618	W.S.H.C., P2/H/328	Inv. and will
3457	Thomas HOLLAND, Colonel of Artillery of Bath	1805	T.N.A., PROB 31/1805/388	
	Note: In the service of the London Company of Merchants of England trading to the East Indies on the Bengal Establishment			
3458	Sarah HOLLAND alias BISHOP, Servant, Spinster and Bastard of Westmore (*sic*), Middlesex formerly of Bath	1828	T.N.A., PROB 31/1828/254	Servant to Mrs. CALVERT
3459	John HOLLAND alias HEALING of Wiveliscombe	1723	T.N.A., PROB 5/2005	Will T.N.A., PROB 11/591
3460	John HOLLANE alias HEALLING of Wiveliscombe	1724	T.N.A., PROB 3/23/11	
HOLLIDAY see TYNDALE				
3461	Thomas HOLLISTER of Publow	1698	D/D/cta/H90	Ad.ac.
3462	Agnes HOLLWAY of Westonzoyland	1622	D/D/cta/H29	Ad.ac.
3463	John HOLLWAY of Goathurst	1707	DD/RN/27	
HOLLWAY see HOLLWELL				
3464	John HOLLWELL, Yeoman of Othery	1610	D/D/cta/H71	Ad.ac.
3465	William HOLLWELL alias HOLLWAY of Camerton	1620	D/D/cta/H25	Ad.ac.
3466	Ann HOLLWILL of Minehead	1734	DD/SP/1734/20	

3467	Richard HOLMAN, Yeoman of Butleigh	1737	D/D/Cti 41	
3468	William HOLMEAD, Husbandman of Brushford	1642	DD/SP/1642/40	
3469	John HOLMES of Ilminster	1690	T.N.A., PROB 4/15618	Admon
3470	Simon HOLMES of Glastonbury	1588	D/D/cta/H35	Ad.ac.
3471	Francis HOLWAY, Fuller of Crewkerne	1680	DD/SP/1680/25	
3472	John HOLWAY of Over Stowey	1675	DD/SP/1675/31	
HOLWAY see GIFFORD				
3473	Anne HOLWELL, Widow of Westonzoyland	1622	D/D/cta/H31	Ad.ac.
3474	George HOLWELL, Tanner of Chaffcombe	1676	DD/SP/1676/46	
3475	Elnathan HOLWEY of Frome Selwood	1769	T.N.A., PROB 31/1769/692	
3476	John HOMET alias PRELAT of Wootton Courtenay	1636	DD/SP/1636/5	
3477	Hugh HONIBONE of Donyatt	1694	DD/SP/1694/24	
3478	Robert HOOK of Spaxton	1730	DD/SP/1730/14	
3479	Stephen HOOK alias GRAVE, Yeoman of Spaxton	1674	DD/SP/1674/7	
3480	Robert HOOKE alias GANE of Cannington	1676	DD/SP/1676/40	
3481	[missing] HOOPER of [no place]	1694	DD/SP/1694/30	
3482	Alexander HOOPER, Chandler of Witham Friary	1685	T.N.A., PROB 4/8613	Will also extant
3483	Ann HOOPER of Hatch Beauchamp	1732	DD/SP/1732/5	
3484	George HOOPER, Gentleman of Dunster	1670	DD/SP/1670/94	
3485	George HOOPER, Carpenter of Creech St. Michael	1734	DD/SP/1734/19	
3486	George HOOPER the elder of Taunton St. James	1634	DD/SP/1634/13	
3487	Henry HOOPER of Broadway	1725	DD/SP/1725/15	
3488	Isable HOOPER of Othery	1628/9	D/D/ct/1/H145a-c	
3489	Joane HOOPER of Watchet, St. Decumans	1699	T.N.A., PROB 4/12004	Will also extant
3490	Mary HOOPER, Widow of Taunton St. James	1684	DD/SP/1684/121	
3491	Richard HOOPER, Husbandman of Bickenhall	1686	DD/SP/1686/29	
3492	Robert HOOPER of Watchet, St. Decumans	1691	T.N.A., PROB 4/22020	Will 1691
3493	Zacheus HOOPER of Bridgwater	1694	T.N.A., PROB 4/17657	Will 1694
HOOPER see ELSTONE, SMALLE				
3494	Paule HOOPPER, Miller of Dulverton	1640	DD/SP/1640/38	
3495	Mary HOPKINS of Nynehead	1677	DD/SP/1677/47	
3496	Thomas HOPKINS of Drayton	1678	DD/SP/1678/67	
3497	Thomas HOPKINS, Innholder of Taunton St. Mary Magdalene	1721	DD/SP/1721/29	

3498	John HORLER, Mercer of Beckington	1675	T.N.A., PROB 4/8371	Will 1676. ex. 1676
3499	John HORLER, Mercer of Beckington	1687	T.N.A., PROB 4/20814	Will 1687
3500	John HORLER, Merchant of Beckington	1687	T.N.A., PROB 5/348	Will T.N.A., PROB 11/387
3501	Richard HORLOCK of Bridgwater	1640	DD/SP/1640/12	
3502	Henry HORNE of Selworthy	1640	DD/SP/1640/131	
3503	Phillipp HORNE of Porlock	1638	DD/SP/1638/10	
3504	Richard HORNE of Wellow	1587	D/D/cta/H41	Ad.ac.
3505	Elizabeth HORNER, Spinster of Barwick	1686	T.N.A., PROB 4/18965	Admon. ex. 1686
3506	Elizabeth HORNER, Lunatic, Spinster of Barwick	1686	T.N.A., PROB 4/3421	Admon
3507	John HORSEY, Husbandman of North Petherton	1697	DD/SP/1697/53	
3508	John HORSEY of Somerton	1735	D/D/Cti 43	
3509	Joseph HORSEY of Taunton St. Mary Magdalene	1682	DD/SP/1682/53	
3510	William HORSEY, Yeoman of Somerton	1676	T.N.A., PROB 4/19177	Will also extant
3511	William HORSEY of Bedminster	1722	D/D/cta/H91	Ad.ac.
3512	John HORSFORD, Esquire of Antigua, West Indies died at Bath	1796	T.N.A., PROB 31/1796/84	
3513	William HORSINGTON of Compton Dando	1593	D/D/cta/H37	Ad.ac.
3514	Robert HORT of Winscombe	1646	D/D/cta/H61	Ad.ac.
3515	William HORT of Compton Dando	1642	D/D/cta/H54	Ad.ac.
3516	John HORTE of [no place]	1600	D/D/ct/1/H160	
3517	Thomas HORTE of Goathurst	1692	DD/SP/1692/33	
3518	Anne HORTON of Pensford St. Thomas, Publow	1709	D/D/cta/H93	Ad.ac.
3519	Honourable Dame Henrietta HORTON, Widow of Walcot	1831	T.N.A., PROB 31/1831/982	
3520	John HORWOOD of Winford	1629	D/D/ct/1/H67	
3521	Robert HORWOOD, Husbandman of Barrington	1681	DD/SP/1681/5	
HORWOOD see HARWOOD				
3522	Thomas HOSGOOD of Brompton Regis	1665	DD/SP/1665/59	
HOSIER see WALTER				
3523	Joane HOSKINS, Widow of Cheddon Fitzpaine	1688	DD/SP/1688/43	
3524	John HOSKINS, Yeoman of Chewton Mendip	1619	D/D/cta/H65	Ad.ac.
3525	John HOSKINS of Chelvey	1619	D/D/cta/H78	Ad.ac.
3526	William HOSKINS of Westbury, Wiltshire formerly of Rode, Somerset died at Westchester, North America	1808	T.N.A., PROB 31/1808/224	
3527	William HOSKINS the younger of Puckington	1666	DD/SP/1666/58	

3528	Thomas HOSSOM of Taunton St. Mary Magdalene	1672	DD/SP/1672/47	
3529	William HOUSE of West Monkton	1680	DD/SP/1680/27	
3530	John HOW junior of Lydeard St. Lawrence	1684	DD/SP/1684/95	
3531	Robert HOW, Gentleman of Taunton St. Mary Magdalene	1684	DD/SP/1684/30	
3532	Robert HOW of Withypool	1687	DD/SP/1687/4	
3533	William HOW of Curland	1720	DD/SP/1720/4	
3534	Edward HOWE, Worsted Comber of Fitzhead	1674	DD/SP/1674/66	
3535	John HOWE of Luxborough	1636	DD/SP/1636/35	
3536	Robert HOWE, Yeoman of Stogumber	1664	DD/SP/1664/21	
3537	William HOWE, Weaver of Otterhampton	1629	D/D/ct/1/H173a	
HOWE see HAYES				
3538	George HOWELL of North Petherton	1727	DD/SP/1727/33	
3539	Henry HOWELL of Taunton St. Mary Magdalene	1721	DD/SP/1721/28	
3540	John HOWELL of Bridgwater	1693	DD/SP/1693/64	
3541	Katherine HOWELL, Widow of Taunton	1672	DD/SP/1672/60	
3542	Richard HOWELL of Withypool	1689	DD/SP/1689/4	
3543	William HOWELL of Carlingcott, Camerton	1664	D/D/cta/H46	Ad.ac.
3544	Joane HOWLET of Meare	1595/6	D/D/ct/1/H174	
3545	Hugh HOWSE of Curry Mallet	1682	DD/SP/1682/44	
3546	Richard HOWSE of Dundry	1638	D/D/cta/H1	Ad.ac.
3547	Richard HOWSE, Yeoman of Curry Mallet	1716	DD/SP/1716/44	
3548	Robert HOWSE of Curry Mallet	1666	DD/SP/1666/50	
3549	Robert HOWSE of Curry Mallet	1667	DD/SP/1667/79	
3550	Charles HOWSEN of Wellington	1625	D/D/cta/H13	Ad.ac.
3551	Charles HOWSEN of Wellington	1625	D/D/cta/H14	Ad.ac.
3552	Charles HOWSEN of Wellington	1624/5	D/D/ct/1/H177a	
3553	Mary HOWSEN, Widow of Wellington	1682	T.N.A., PROB 4/13257	Will also extant
3554	Henry HUCKER of Ruishton	1678	DD/SP/1678/31	
3555	John HUCKER of Taunton St. Mary Magdalene	1684	DD/SP/1684/58	
3556	Philip HUCKER, Joiner of Broadway	1680	DD/SP/1680/24	
3557	William HUCKER, Husbandman of Durston	1683	DD/SP/1683/75	
3558	Alice HUCKINGES, Widow of Hinton St. George	1639	DD/SP/1639/63	
HUCKINGES see HUTCHINGS				

3559	Henry HUCKINGS of Bradford	1726	D/P/b.hl/23/1	
3560	George HUCKLEBRIDGE of Middlezoy	1697	D/D/cta/H95	Ad.ac.
3561	Nicholas HUDDY of Beercrocombe	1723	DD/SP/1723/37	
3562	Nicholas HUDDY of Beercrocombe	1723	DD/SP/442/74	Ad.ac.
3563	Mrs [missing] HUDSON of Hot Wells, Bristol	1779	DD/WO/37/13	
3564	Ann HUDSON, Widow of Tetton House, Taunton	1821	T.N.A., PROB 37/494	With ad.ac.
3565	Henry HUGHES, Yeoman of North Wootton	1678	T.N.A., PROB 4/8551	Will also extant
3566	John HUGHES of Abbots Leigh	1692	B.A., 1692/20	
HUGHES see HEWES				
3567	John HUISH, Husbandman of Nettlecombe	1691	DD/SP/1691/54	
3568	Mary HUISH, Widow of Taunton St. James	*c*.1663	DD/SF/11/1/51	Formerly DD/SF/1041
3569	Robert HUISH, Yeoman of Taunton St. James	1635	DD/SP/1635/128	
3570	Robert HUISH, Yeoman of Corfe	1665	DD/SP/1665/4	
3571	Robert HUISH of Cannington	1674	DD/SP/1674/21	
3572	Wynyfred HUISH, Spinster of Taunton St. James	1645	DD/SP/1645/8	
3573	John HUISHE, Gentleman of Old Cleeve	1625	D/D/cta/H23	Ad.ac.
3574	Margaret HULAT, Widow of Dulcote, Wells St. Cuthbert	1669	T.N.A., PROB 4/2238	Admon. ex. 1670
3575	Mary HULBERT, Widow of Wincanton	1749	T.N.A., PROB 3/48/51	
3576	George HULET of Lyng	1648	DD/SP/1648/63	
3577	[missing] HULETT, Husbandman of [no place]	1692	DD/SP/1692/35	
3578	Thomas HULL of Crewkerne	1636	DD/SP/1636/60	See *T.C.W.*
3579	William HULL of Stogumber	1641	DD/SP/1641/20	Proved by Robert, natural Son
3580	Ursula HULLOCK of Stogursey	1639	D/D/ct/1/H182a	
3581	Dorothie HUMFRIE, Widow of Shepton Beauchamp	1634	DD/SP/1634/9	
3582	John HUMPHREY, Currier of Bridgwater	1691	DD/SP/1691/40	
3583	Samuel HUMPHREY of Drayton	1691	DD/SP/1691/19	
3584	William HUMPHREY, Whitebaker of Crewkerne	1671	DD/SP/1671/9	
3585	Larnech [Male] HUMPHRYS of Stogumber	1698	DD/SP/1698/47	
3586	Joan HUNGERFORD, Widow of Wellow	1680	T.N.A., PROB 4/5683	Will also extant
3587	[missing] HUNT of [no place]	1640	D/D/cta/H6	
	Note: Ad.ac.; mentions Thomas and William HUNT minors			
3588	Edmund HUNT of Bristol City died at Compton Pauncefoot	1731	T.N.A., PROB 3/30/75	
3589	Edmund HUNT, Bachelor of Bristol died at Compton Pauncefoot	1731	T.N.A., PROB 31/1731/365	

3590	Edward HUNT junior of Stogumber	1686	DD/SP/1686/23	
3591	Francis HUNT of Wellington	1708	T.N.A., PROB 5/5772	
3592	John HUNT of Bittescombe, Upton	1610	DD/SP/1610/5	
3593	John HUNT of Thurloxton	1682	DD/SP/1682/52	
3594	John HUNT of West Monkton	1683	DD/SP/1683/72	
3595	John HUNT of Creech St. Michael	1693	DD/SP/1693/17	
3596	John HUNT, Butcher of Broadway	1725	DD/SP/1725/2	
3597	Richard HUNT, Yeoman of Horsington	1668	DD/DNL/10	
3598	Thomas HUNT of Dundry	1640	D/D/cta/H55	Ad.ac.
3599	Vertue HUNT of Wells	1634	D/D/cta/H17	Ad.ac.
3600	William HUNT of Barrow Gurney	1622	D/D/cta/H24	Ad.ac.
3601	William HUNT of Taunton	n.d.	DD/SP/17th Century/6	Fragments
3602	John HUNTE of Long Ashton	1590	D/D/cta/H40	Ad.ac.
3603	George HUNTER of Bedminster	1644	D/D/cta/H59	Ad.ac.
3604	James HUNTER of Taunton St. Mary Magdalene	1684	DD/SP/1684/146	
3605	Jane HUNTLEY, Widow of Pilton	1772	T.N.A., PROB 31/1772/831	
3606	John HUNTLEY of Bleadon	1496	T.N.A., PROB 2/114	Will T.N.A., PROB 11/10/31
3607	Philip HUNTLEY of Wells	1611	D/D/cta/H53	Ad.ac.
3608	Thomas HUNTT, Yeoman of North Petherton	1682	DD/SP/1682/59	
3609	[missing] HURD, Widow of Sowey (*sic*)	1692	D/D/cta/H94	
	Note: Ad.ac. mentions a son John HURD of Ashcott and a Thomas HURD			
3610	[missing] HURFORD of Huntspill ?	n.d.	D/D/cta/H8	Ad.ac.
3611	David HURFORD, Husbandman of Luxborough	1680	DD/SP/1680/11	
3612	Edward HURFORD of Clatworthy	1678	DD/SP/1678/70	
3613	John HURFORD of Luxborough	1642	DD/SP/1642/27	
3614	John HURFORD, Yeoman of Charlinch	1694	A/CTP/11/5	
3615	John HURFORD, Butcher of Carhampton	1704	T.N.A., PROB 4/22437	Admon. ex. 1703
3616	Robert HURFORD of Milverton	1636	DD/SP/1636/51	
3617	Robert HURFORD of Kingstone	1687	DD/SP/1687/8	
3618	William HURFORD of Chedzoy	1636	DD/SP/1636/29	
3619	William HURFORD, Husbandman of Luccombe	1680	DD/SP/1680/17	
3620	Michael HURL, Husbandman of Selworthy	1637	DD/SP/1637/65	
3621	Michael HURLE of Selworthy	1637	DD/SP/1637/66	

3622	William HURLE of Broomfield	1679	T.N.A., PROB 5/5322	
3623	John HURLEY of Crowcombe	1636	DD/SP/1636/36	
3624	Robert HURLEY of Milverton	1723	DD/SP/1723/44	
3625	Robert HURLEY, Gentleman of Wellington	1727	T.N.A., PROB 3/26/157	
3626	Thomas HURLEY of London	1677	T.N.A., PROB 4/17949	Will. Died at Taunton
3627	William HURLEY of Taunton St. Mary Magdalene	1684	DD/SP/1684/7	
3628	Henry HURLY, Yeoman of Crowcombe	1673	DD/SP/1673/3	
3629	Richard HURLY of West Bagborough	1677	DD/SP/1677/64	
3630	Richard HURLY of West Bagborough	1677	DD/SP/1677/84	
HURLY see TARR				
3631	Joan HURNE, Widow of Abbots Leigh	1628	B.A., 1628/39	Will also extant
3632	William HURSTON, Tanner of West Monkton	1723	DD/SP/1723/41	
3633	Joane HURT of Otterhampton	1635	DD/SP/1635/48	
3634	Joseph HURT, Husbandman of Charlinch	1693	DD/SP/1693/42	
3635	Susan HURT, Widow of West Bower, Bridgwater	1685	DD/SP/1685/2	
3636	Thomas HURT of West Bower, Bridgwater	1646	DD/SP/1646/24	
3637	John HURTNELL of North Petherton	1672	DD/SP/1672/43	
3638	John HURTNOLL of Bradford	1686	DD/SP/1686/19	
3639	William HURTNOLL, Husbandman of Bradford	1670	DD/SP/1670/50	
3640	Ralph HUSEN of Horsington	1623	D/D/cta/H30	Ad.ac.
3641	Joan HUSSEY, Spinster of Wambrook	1694	W.S.H.C., P14/83	Inv. and will
3642	John HUTCHENS of Crewkerne	1682	DD/SP/1682/12	
3643	John HUTCHENS, Servant of Hinton St. George	1737	DD/SP/1737/35	
3644	James HUTCHESON of Martock	1677	T.N.A., PROB 4/17394	Will, 'a Scotsman', died at Martock
3645	Ambrose HUTCHINGS the elder, Joiner of Crewkerne	1685	DD/SP/1685/24	
3646	Giles HUTCHINGS, Yeoman of Seavington St. Mary	1716	DD/SP/1716/16	
3647	Nicholas HUTCHINGS of Allowenshay, Kingstone	1734	T.N.A., PROB 31/1734/281	
3648	Roger HUTCHINGS of Hinton St. George	1641	DD/SP/1641/86	
3649	William HUTCHINGS, Husbandman of Hinton St. George	1640	DD/SP/1640/99	
3650	Christopher HUTCHINS of Glastonbury St. John	1588	D/D/cta/H42	Ad.ac.
3651	Christopher HUTCHINS of Glastonbury St. John	1588	D/D/cta/H43	Ad.ac.
3652	Nathaniel HUTCHINS, Clothier of Wilton	1682	T.N.A., PROB 4/13151	Admon
HUTCHINS see CHAPPLE, LAX				

3653	Philip HUXTABLE of Churchill	1826	T.N.A., PROB 31/1826/1189	
	Note: With ad.ac.; buried at Bridgwater, Sion Chapel in Tuam Street			
3654	Catherine HYDON of Charlinch	1670	DD/SP/1670/47	
3655	Joan HYDON, Widow of Thurloxton	1732	DD/SP/1732/14	
3656	John HYDON, Yeoman of North Petherton	1725	DD/SP/1725/19	
3657	Thomas HYDON of Brompton Regis	1685	DD/SP/1685/20	
3658	William HYER alias THOMAS of North Petherton	1640	DD/SP/1640/39	See *T.C.W.*
3659	Richard HYLHOUSE of Burrington	1611	D/D/cta/H73	Ad.ac.
3660	George HYLL, Cordwainer of North Petherton	1713	DD/SP/1713/8	
3661	Ralfe HYLL, Milliner of Dunster	1667	DD/SP/1667/30	
3662	Christian HYND, Widow of Bishops Hull	1625	DD/SP/1625/8	
3663	Thomas HYTE, Bachelor of Staplegrove	1635	DD/SP/1635/117	
3664	John ILET of Isle Abbotts	1669	DD/SP/1669/83	
3665	John ILLARIE of Closworth	1588	D/D/cta/I4	Ad.ac.
3666	William ILLE of [no place]	1600	D/D/cta/I1	Ad.ac.
3667	John INDOE of Ash, Martock	1738	D/D/Cti 50	
3668	William INGEPEN of North Petherton	1680	DD/SP/1680/45	
3669	[missing] INGRAM, Weaver of Milverton	1646	DD/SP/1646/26	Proved by Catherine INGRAM, Widow
3670	Elizabeth INGRAM, Spinster of Brompton Regis	1684	DD/SP/1684/174	
3671	Elizabeth INGRAM of Goathurst	1713	DD/SP/1713/40	
3672	John INGRAM of Spaxton	1639	DD/SP/1639/34	
3673	John INGRAM, Tailor of Dunster	1666	DD/SP/1666/34	
3674	John INGRAM of Spaxton	1677	DD/SP/1677/48	
3675	John INGRAM, Yeoman of North Petherton	1684	DD/SP/1684/80	
3676	Mary INGRAM, Widow of Milverton	1639	DD/SP/1639/61	Inv. shows ENGRAM
3677	Thomas INGRAM of Stogumber	1692	DD/SP/1692/13	
3678	William INGRAM the elder of Stogumber	1641	DD/SP/1641/44	
INGRAM see ENGRAM				
3679	Humphry INGRAMS, Husbandman of North Petherton	1639	DD/SP/1639/26	
3680	John INGRAMS of Bicknoller	1677	DD/SP/1677/50	
3681	John INMAN, Yeoman of Burrington	1708	D/D/Cti 47	
3682	Martha INMAN, Widow of Puxton	1680	T.N.A., PROB 4/12016	Will. ex. 1682
3683	Elizabeth INNALL of Lyng	1720	DD/SP/1720/26	

3684	Elizabeth INNALL of Lyng	1726	DD/SP/442/80	Ad.ac.
3685	William IRELAND, Carrier of Frome	1735	T.N.A., PROB 31/1735/362	
3686	John IRISH, Gentleman of Congresbury	1682	T.N.A., PROB 4/8064	Will also extant
3687	William IRWIN of Taunton St. Mary Magdalene	1741	T.N.A., PROB 3/40/129	
3688	William IRWIN of Taunton St. Mary Magdalene	1741	T.N.A., PROB 31/1741/804	
3689	William IRWIN of Taunton	1742	T.N.A., PROB 3/41/1	
3690	William IRWIN, Mercer of Taunton	1742	T.N.A., PROB 31/1742/95	
3691	Charles ISAAC, Pilot of Abbots Leigh	1737	B.A., 1737/3	
3692	Jane ISAAC of Dulverton	1679	DD/SP/1679/21	
3693	Richard ISAACK of Otterhampton	1667	DD/SP/1667/12	
3694	Andrew ISACKE of Huntspill	1662	D/D/cta/I5	Ad.ac.
3695	Hercules ISGAR, Husbandman of East Brent	1604	D/D/ct/1/I9	
3696	John ISGAR of [no place]	n.d.	D/D/cta/I2	Ad.ac.
3697	Robert ISGAR of East Brent	1639	D/D/cta/I3	Ad.ac.
3698	Hannah ISGER of Abbots Leigh	1667	B.A., 1667/42	
3699	John ISHAM, Gentleman of Langport Eastover, Langport	1676	T.N.A., PROB 4/6960	Will also extant
3700	William ISHAM, Sergeweaver of Isle Brewers	1666	DD/SP/1666/66	
3701	Thomas ITHILL of Brislington	1662	DD/SX/10/3,4	
3702	Thomas IVERY of Donyatt	1674	DD/SP/1674/26	
3703	James IVEY, Gentleman of Ilminster	1682	T.N.A., PROB 4/10447	Admon. ex. 1688
3704	Gregory JA.... of Bradford	1681	DD/SP/1681/114	Susanna relict; damaged
3705	Elizabeth JACKSON, Widow of Bristol formerly of Combhay	1686	B.A., 1686/40B	Will also extant; see also 1684/24 and 1684/CP
3706	John JACKSON of [no place]	1689	T.N.A., PROB 4/17052	Admon
3707	Tobias JACKSON, Gentleman of Bath	1644	D/D/cta/J1	Ad.ac.
3708	John JACOB the elder of North Cheriton	1632	D/D/cta/J8	Ad.ac.
3709	Thomas JACOB of Stoke Trister	1665/6	DD/DNL/151	
3710	William JACOB of Alhampton, Ditcheat	1638	D/D/cta/J4	Ad.ac.
3711	William JACOB, Yeoman of Minehead	1691	DD/SP/1691/18	
3712	Margaret JACOB alias SNOW of Luccombe	1637	DD/SP/1637/36	
3713	Thomas JACOBB of Cucklington	1598	D/D/cta/J9	Ad.ac.
3714	Christopher JAMES of Wincanton	1663	D/D/cta/J3	Ad.ac.
3715	Gilbert JAMES, Yeoman of Stowell	1679	T.N.A., PROB 4/16175	Will also extant

3716	John JAMES, Yeoman of Shepton Mallet	1606	D/D/cta/J10	Ad.ac.
3717	John JAMES, Husbandman of Oake	1612	D/D/ct/1/J2	
3718	John JAMES, Apothecary of Crewkerne	1677	DD/SP/1677/31	
3719	Mary JAMES, Widow of Dunster	1691	DD/SP/1691/84	
3720	Richard JAMES of Staplegrove	1664	DD/SP/1664/10	
3721	Robert JAMES of Dunster	1687	DD/SP/1687/46	
3722	Walter JAMES of Dowlish Wake	1640	DD/SP/1640/29	
3723	Walter JAMES of West Bagborough	1693	DD/SP/1693/71	
3724	William JAMES of Ruishton	1680	DD/SP/1680/77	
3725	William JAMES of Pitminster	1739	DD/SP/1739/48	
3726	Thomazine JARMAN of Hillfarrance	1679	DD/SP/1679/36	
3727	William JEAMES of Martock	1679	D/D/cta/J15	Ad.ac.
3728	John JEANE, Gentleman of Wiveliscombe	1732	T.N.A., PROB 31/1732/516	With account com.
3729	Philippa JEANE, Widow of West Monkton	1682	DD/SP/1682/31	
3730	Christopher JEANES, Sailcloth Weaver of East Chinnock	1734	D/D/Cti 48	
3731	Edmund JEANES of Middlezoy	1739	D/D/cta/J16	Ad.ac. and inv.
3732	Gregory JEANES of Bradford	1684	DD/SP/1684/49	
3733	Richard JEANES of Bridgwater	1714	DD/SP/442/13	Ad.ac.
3734	Robert JEANES of Moorlinch	1592	D/D/cta/J13	Ad.ac.
3735	Mr Thomas JEANES of Hatch Beauchamp	1739	DD/SP/1739/52	
3736	William JEANES of Taunton St. James	1668	DD/SP/1668/45	
3737	William, youngman JEANES of West Monkton	1635	DD/SP/1635/39	
JEANES see GEENS				
3738	Christopher JEANS of East Chinnock	1735	D/D/cta/J14	Ad.ac.
3739	William JEFFERIE of Stocklinch Ottersey	1668	DD/SP/1668/30	
3740	Mary JEFFERIES of Kilmington	1616	D/D/cta/J11	Ad.ac.
3741	Philip JEFFERIES of Taunton St. Mary Magdalene	1684	DD/SP/1684/64	
3742	Thomas JEFFERIES of Taunton St. Mary Magdalene	1684	DD/SP/1684/113	
3743	Anthony JEFFERIS of Chew Magna	1682	G.A., D2071/E57	
3744	Francis JEFFERY, Gentleman of Huntspill	1797	DD/X/AJ/1	
3745	John JEFFERY of Stocklinch Ottersey	1678	DD/SP/1678/40	
3746	John JEFFERY, Plomber of Chard	1680	T.N.A., PROB 4/4653	Will 1680
3747	John JEFFERY, Yeoman of Beercrocombe	1740	DD/SP/1740/2	

3748	Nicholas JEFFERY of Stocklinch Ottersey	1685	DD/SP/1685/17	
3749	Robert JEFFERY of Huntspill	1676	D/D/cta/J17	Ad.ac.
3750	Robert JEFFERY, Merchant of Bridgwater	1717	DD/SP/1717/5	
3751	Robert JEFFERY of Swan Inn, Wells	1770	DD/TD Box 1	
3752	James JEFFERYE, Gentleman of Axbridge	1682	T.N.A., PROB 4/5780	Will 1682. ex. 1683
3753	John JEFFORD of Stogumber	1683	DD/SP/1683/70	
	Note: A minor and legatory named in the will of William SULLY, late of Stogumber			
3754	Richard JEFFRES of Yatton	1641	D/D/ct/1/J7	
3755	William JEFFREY of Creech St. Michael	1691	DD/SP/1691/43	
3756	Robert JEFFRY of North Petherton	1713	DD/SP/1713/12	
3757	John JELLY, Clothier of Frome Selwood	1725	T.N.A., PROB 3/24/42	
3758	John JELLYE, Husbandman of Pitcombe	1629	D/D/ct/1/J10	
3759	Richard JENISON of Durborough, Stogursey	1668	DD/SP/1668/44	
3760	Margaret JENKENS of Bridgwater	1693	DD/SP/1693/28	
3761	Arthur JENKINGS, Yeoman of Spaxton	1670	DD/SP/1670/51	
3762	Mary JENKINGS of Spaxton	1683	T.N.A., PROB 4/1067	Will. ex. 1684
3763	Alexander JENKINS of [no place]	1604	D/D/ct/1/J19	
3764	Amos JENKINS of Frome Selwood	1789	DD/SAS/S416/7	
3765	John JENKINS of Charlinch	1680	DD/SP/1680/19	
3766	John JENKINS senior, Yeoman of Broomfield	1674	T.N.A., PROB 4/6661	Will 1674
3767	Richard JENKINS, Dyer of Spaxton	1679	T.N.A., PROB 4/21051	Will. ex. 1680
3768	Richard JENKINS of Fiddington	1690	DD/SP/1690/11	
3769	Thomas JENKINS of Nailsea	1695	D/D/cta/J18	Ad.ac.
3770	William JENKINS, Husbandman of Dunster	1687	DD/SP/1687/11	
3771	John JENNES of Taunton St. Mary Magdalene	1693	DD/SP/1693/65	
3772	Robert JENNES of Bridgwater	1693	DD/SP/1693/39	
3773	Robert JENNINGES of Curry Rivel	1672	DD/SP/1672/24	
3774	Christopher JENNINGS, Husbandman of Thurlbear	1688	DD/SP/1688/32	
3775	John JENNINGS of Wedmore	1625	D/D/cta/J6	Ad.ac.
3776	John JENNINGS of Milverton	1670	DD/SP/1670/75	
3777	John JENNINGS the elder, Husbandman of Thurlbear	1683	DD/SP/1683/64	
3778	Marmaduke JENNINGS, Esquire of Curry Rivel	1658	T.N.A., PROB 2/721	Will T.N.A., PROB 11/277/157
3779	Marmaduke JENNINGS of Isle Abbotts	1687	DD/SP/1687/35	

3780	Mary JENNINGS of Curry Rivel	1611	D/P/cur.r/24/5	
3781	Robert JENNINGS of Milverton	1667	DD/SP/1667/64	
3782	Robert JENNINGS, Gentleman of Curry Rivel	1670	DD/SP/1670/96	
3783	Thomas JENNINGS, Esquire of Burton, Curry Rivel	1680	T.N.A., PROB 4/19749	Will 1680
3784	Walter JENNINGS, Husbandman of Hillfarrance	1688	DD/SP/1688/44	
3785	Robert JENNINGS alias APPLEDORE of Milverton	1680	DD/SP/1680/23	
3786	[missing] JENT of Lyng	1671	DD/SP/1671/26	
3787	Elizabeth JEPP of Sutton Court, Chew Magna	1662	DD/SF/2/1/29	Formerly DD/SF/2129
3788	Edward JERMAN of Fivehead	1675	DD/SP/1675/8	
3789	John JERMAN, Clothier of Bishops Hull	1666	DD/SP/1666/53	
3790	John JERMAN of Fivehead	1678	DD/SP/1678/24	
3791	Maurice JERVICE of Doulting	1679	T.N.A., PROB 4/6942	Will 1678
3792	Elizabeth JERVIS, Widow of Corfe	1684	DD/SP/1684/14	
3793	John JERVIS of Huntspill	1703	D/D/cta/J19	Ad.ac.
3794	William JERVIS of Huntspill	1679	T.N.A., PROB 5/3230	
3795	Christopher JESSE, Yeoman of Thurlbear	1683	DD/SP/1683/59	
3796	Heline JESSE, Widow of Stoke St. Mary	1593	D/D/ct/1/J17	
3797	John JESSE, Yeoman of Thurlbear	1688	DD/SP/1688/24	
3798	John JESSER, Mercer of Frome Selwood	1676	T.N.A., PROB 4/12837	Will also extant
3799	Thomas JESSER, Clothier of Marston Bigot	1695	T.N.A., PROB 4/18885	Will 1694
3800	Abel JESSOP of Mark	1673	T.N.A., PROB 5/4434	
3801	Alice JEWELL of Stockland Bristol	1691	DD/SP/1691/27	
3802	Thomas JEWELL the elder, Husbandman of Langford Budville	1678	DD/SP/1678/20	
3803	William JEY of Thornfalcon	1670	DD/SP/1670/84	
3804	Katherine JOANES of Selworthy	1670	DD/SP/1670/32	
3805	Magdalene JOANES of [no place]	1635	DD/SP/1635/1	
3806	Richard JOANES, Clerk of Norton Fitzwarren	1649	DD/SP/1649/77	
3807	Samuel JOBBINS of Backwell	1683	T.N.A., PROB 4/8013	Will 1683
3808	Robert JOCE of Milverton	1635	DD/SP/1635/90	
JOCE see JOYCE				
3809	Ann JOHNSON of Bath formerly of Hammersmith, Middlesex	1821	T.N.A., PROB 31/1821/712	
3810	John JOHNSON, Esquire, Bachelor of Richmond, Surrey, late of Bath	1745	T.N.A., PROB 31/1745/419 with account 1745/823	

3811	Ralph JOHNSON, Tailor of Barrington	1675	DD/SP/1675/75	
3812	Gilbert JOLLVORD of Meare	1623	D/D/cta/J7	Ad.ac.
3813	Reverend Charles JONES of Nettlecombe	1724	DD/SP/1724/61	
3814	David JONES of [no place]	1696	DD/SP/1696/29	
3815	Elizabeth JONES, Widow of Wells	1668	D/D/cta/J12	Ad.ac.
3816	Elizabeth JONES, Spinster of Llandaff, Glamorgan formerly of Walcot, Somerset and Llancarfan, Glamorgan	1775	T.N.A., PROB 31/1775/634 and 1775/856	
3817	Elizabeth JONES, Widow of Bath	1805	T.N.A., PROB 31/1805/725	With ad.ac.
3818	Evan JONES of Stogursey	1678	DD/SP/1678/74	
3819	Henry JONES, Husbandman of Misterton	1645	DD/SP/1645/59	
3820	Hugh JONES, Mariner of Minehead	1678	T.N.A., PROB 4/12412	Admon
3821	John JONES, Mariner of Minehead	1680	DD/SP/1680/102	
3822	John JONES of Crewkerne	1695	DD/SP/1695/22	
3823	John JONES, Cordwainer of Bridgwater	1714	DD/SP/1714/31	
3824	John ? JONES of [no place]	1688	T.N.A., PROB 4/19488	Admon
3825	Meredith JONES of Merriott	1693	DD/SP/1693/18	
3826	Reece JONES of Bridgwater	1686	DD/SP/1686/37	
3827	Richard JONES of Congresbury	1627	D/D/cta/J5	Ad.ac.
3828	Richard JONES, Innholder of Bridgwater	1698	DD/SP/1698/38	
3829	Samuel JONES of Cossington	1736	D/D/Cti 49	
3830	Sarah JONES, Widow of Bridgwater	1699	DD/SP/1699/5	
3831	Reverend Thomas JONES, Clerk of High Ham	1740	T.N.A., PROB 31/1740/355	
3832	William JONES of Lydeard St. Lawrence	1682	DD/SP/1682/5	
3833	William JONES, Esquire of Sheerness, Kent died at Bath	1738	T.N.A., PROB 31/1738/487	
JONES see JOANES				
3834	Edward JORDAN of [no place]	n.d.	D/D/cta/J20	Ad.ac.
3835	Robert JORDAN of Minehead	1667	DD/SP/1667/34	
3836	Alice JORDANE, Widow of East Chinnock	1621	D/D/cta/J22	Ad.ac.
3837	Agnes JORDEN of Bradford	1646	DD/SP/1646/83	
3838	Agnis JOYCE, Widow of Milverton	1636	DD/SP/1636/52	
3839	John JOYCE, Yeoman of Brompton Regis	1646	DD/SP/1646/66	
3840	John JOYCE junior, Gentleman of Brompton Regis	1695	DD/SP/1695/13	
3841	Robert JOYCE, Sergeweaver of Pitminster	1667	DD/SP/1667/35	

3842	William JOYCE of Brompton Regis	1698	DD/SP/1698/11	
3843	Richard JOYE of Huntspill	1600	D/D/cta/C23	Ad.ac.
3844	William JOYNER ? of Burnham on Sea	1630	D/D/cta/J21	Ad.ac.
3845	William JUDD of Bruton	1683	T.N.A., PROB 4/16249	Admon
3846	Agnes JURDEN, Spinster of Martock	1669	D/D/cta/J2	Ad.ac.
3847	Mrs JUTSOM of Calway House, West Buckland	1801	DD/RC Box 2	
3848	Nicholas KATE, Yeoman of Witham Friary	1685	T.N.A., PROB 4/8245	Will also extant
3849	William KEARLE of Bickenhall	1740	DD/SP/1740/5	
3850	Michael KEBBY, Clerk of Staplegrove	1741	DD/SP/1741/12	
3851	William KEBBY of Kilve	1672	DD/SP/1672/41	
3852	John KEEDWELL of Flax Bourton	1820	T.N.A., PROB 31/1820/249	
3853	Thomas KEEDWELL of Dundry	1731	D/D/Cti 52	
3854	...... KEELE of [no place]	1629	D/D/ct/1/K4	
3855	William KEELE, Yeoman of [no place]	1629	D/D/ct/1/K6	
3856	Alice KEEMPE, Widow of Chedzoy	1649	DD/SP/1649/80	
3857	Edmund KEEN, Esquire of Bath	1724	T.N.A., PROB 31/1724/160	
3858	Lucies KEEN, Widow of Trull	n.d.	DD/SP/17th Century/7	Fragment
3859	Susannah KEEN of Bleadon	1711	D/D/cta/K9	Ad.ac.
3860	Andrew KEENE of Westonzoyland	1681	D/D/cta/K11	Ad.ac.
3861	John KEENE, Yeoman of Bleadon?	1678	T.N.A., PROB 4/4749	Admon
3862	John KEENE of Tolland	1679	DD/SP/1679/18	
3863	John KEENE of Wincanton	1690	T.N.A., PROB 4/1090	Will. ex. 1691
3864	John KEENE, Printer of Bath	1800	T.N.A., PROB 31/1800/644	
3865	Thomas KEENE of Kingston Seymour	1623	D/D/cta/K3	Ad.ac.
3866	William KEETCH, Yeoman of Burton, Curry Rivel	1721	DD/SP/1721/14	
KEETCH see KITCH				
3867	John and Margaret KELLOND of [no place]	*c.*1698	DD/L/2/35/1 Box 138	
3868	George KELSON the elder, Gentleman of Farmborough	1812	T.N.A., PROB 31/1812/239	
3869	John KELSON of Camerton	1621	D/D/cta/K1	Ad.ac.
3870	Nicholas KELSON, Gentleman of Huntspill	1680	DD/ALN Box 1	
3871	Elner KELWAY of Butleigh	1675	DD/AH Box 47/7	
3872	Agnes KEMPE, Widow of Brompton Regis	1639	DD/SP/1639/35	
3873	Marie KEMPE, Widow of West Quantoxhead	1666	DD/SP/1666/19	

3874	Symone KEMPE of Chedzoy	1649	DD/SP/1649/73	
3875	Christian KENT of Luccombe	1638	DD/SP/1638/11	
3876	John KENT of Luccombe	1641	DD/SP/1641/85	
3877	John KENT, Headmaster of Bishops Hull	1690	DD/SP/1690/32	Clerk and Headmaster of Taunton Grammar School
3878	William KENT of Exton	1641	DD/SP/1641/82	
3879	William KENT, Miller of Porlock	1671	DD/SAS/H202/11	
3880	William KENT, Tanner of Porlock	1729	DD/SP/1729/44	
KENT see REED				
3881	Elizabeth KENTE, Widow of St. Catherine	1580	T.N.A., PROB 2/735	
3882	John KERLE of Lyng	1680	DD/SP/1680/80	
3883	John KERSLAKE, Gentleman of Wellington	1732	T.N.A., PROB 3/31/62	
3884	William KERSLAKE, Miller of Nynehead	1666	DD/SP/1666/22	
3885	Michael KETTENER, Husbandman of Wootton Courtenay	1693	DD/SP/1693/16	
3886	John KETTINGALE, Shoemaker of Congresbury	1733	D/D/Cti 51	
3887	John KEW of Winscombe	1681	T.N.A., PROB 4/21108	Admon
3888	John KEWAR, Fuller of Taunton St. James	1679	DD/SP/1679/16	
3889	Roger KEWAR of Hatch Beauchamp	1640	DD/SP/1640/24	
3890	Joan KEWER of Hatch Beauchamp	1694	DD/SP/1694/13	
KEWER see QUEAR				
3891	John KEYFORD of Yeovilton	1638	D/D/ct/1/K12	
3892	Absolom KIDDILL of Bayford, Stoke Trister	1681	D/D/ct/1/K13	
3893	Samuel KIDDLE of High Ham	1729	T.N.A., PROB 3/28/44	
3894	William KIDLEY, Bachelor of Queen Camel	1739	T.N.A., PROB 3/38/101	
3895	Joan KIDNER of [no place]	1690	DD/SP/1690/86	Part only
3896	Richard KIDNER of Aisholt and London	1635	DD/SP/1635/135	See *T.C.W.*
3897	Richard KIDNER of London	1636	DD/SP/1636/24	
3898	William KIDNOR of Nynehead	1687	DD/SP/1687/49	
3899	Joseph KIMBLE, Husbandman of Hinton St. George	1720	DD/SP/1720/13	
3900	William KIMP, Innholder of Bridgwater	1743	DD/SP/1743/18	
3901	John KIMPLAND of West Monkton	1655	DD/DP/80/4	
3902	Richard KIMPLAND, Grocer of Taunton	1680	DD/DP/74/5	
3903	Daniel and John KING of Bridgwater	1685	DD/SP/1685/45	

3904	Edward KING of Bruton	1754	T.N.A., PROB 31/1754/210	With ad.ac.
3905	George KING, Gentleman of Felton, Winford	1693	T.N.A., PROB 5/5152	
3906	John KING of Badgworth	1608	D/D/ct/1/K16	
3907	John KING, Yeoman of Winford	1680	DD/HI/A/142	
3908	John KING of Chedzoy	1727	DD/SP/1727/32	
3909	Nicholas KING of Tolland	1727	DD/SP/1727/31	
3910	Richard KING of Chedzoy	1677	DD/SP/1677/13	
3911	Samuel KING of Kingston Seymour	1642	D/D/cta/K8	Ad.ac.
3912	Thomas KING of Chilton, Bridgwater	1648	DD/SP/1648/53	
3913	Thomas KING of Fivehead	1681	DD/SP/1681/6	
3914	Thomas KING of Frome Selwood	1695	T.N.A., PROB 4/523	Will also extant
3915	William KING of Dundry	1641	D/D/cta/K7	Ad.ac.
3916	William KING of Pitcombe died in London	1692	T.N.A., PROB 5/5233	
3917	William KING of Pitcombe died in London	1692	T.N.A., PROB 5/5234	
3918	William KING senior of Wilton	1686	T.N.A., PROB 4/16060	Will 1686. ex. 1687
3919	Mellor KINGE of Chipstable	1664	DD/SP/1664/51	
3920	Richard KINGSBURY the elder of Taunton St. James	1664	DD/SP/1664/62	
3921	William KIPPING, Yeoman of Rode	1667	T.N.A., PROB 4/10653	Will. ex. 1668
3922	James KIRKPATRICK of Taunton	1681	DD/SP/1681/88	
3923	James KIRKPATRICK, Esquire of Taunton	1770	T.N.A., PROB 31/1770/249	
3924	John KIRKPATRICK of Taunton St. Mary Magdalene	1681	DD/SP/1681/44	
3925	Edward KITCH of North Petherton	1716	DD/SP/1716/5	
3926	Thomas KITCH of Creech St. Michael	1720	DD/SP/1720/10	
3927	William KITCH, Yeoman of North Petherton	1721	DD/SP/1721/9	
KITCH see KEETCH				
3928	William KITNOR alias CHEBETT of Luccombe	1665	DD/SP/1665/36	
3929	Ludwell and Elizabeth KITTE of Nunney	1590	D/D/cta/K6	Ad.ac.
3930	Richard KITTERMASTER, Widower of Yeovil	1764	T.N.A., PROB 31/1764/1005	
3931	Joan KNAPP of Curry Rivel	1736	DD/SP/1736/32	
3932	John KNAPP, Mason of North Petherton	1675	DD/SP/1675/78	
3933	Marmaduke KNAPP of Langport Westover, Curry Rivel	1681	DD/SP/1681/84	
3934	Robert KNAPP of Curry Rivel	1730	DD/SP/1730/11	
3935	Stephen KNAPP, Husbandman of Curry Rivel	1716	DD/SP/1716/29	

3936	William KNAPP of Curry Rivel	1672	DD/SP/1672/48	
3937	William KNAPP, Clerk of Brockley	1686	T.N.A., PROB 4/9541	Will 1686
3938	Edward KNEWSTUBB of Bruton or Nunney	1622	D/D/cta/K2	Ad.ac.
3939	Abraham KNIGHT of Elworthy	1675	DD/SP/1675/67	
3940	Anne KNIGHT, Widow of Taunton St. Mary Magdalene	1672	DD/SP/1672/54	
3941	Baldwin KNIGHT of Kingston	1610	DD/SP/1610/4	
3942	Edmund KNIGHT of Kewstoke	1638	D/D/ct/1/K31	
3943	Elizabeth KNIGHT, Widow of Middleny, Drayton	1636	DD/SP/1636/20	
3944	Elizabeth KNIGHT, Widow of Drayton	1641	DD/SP/1641/89	
3945	Elizabeth KNIGHT, Spinster of West Monkton	1680	DD/SP/1680/98	
3946	Francis KNIGHT of Radlett, Spaxton	1678	DD/SP/1678/64	
3947	George KNIGHT of Taunton St. Mary Magdalene	1672	DD/SP/1672/53	
3948	George KNIGHT of Kingstone	1681	DD/SP/1681/61	
3949	Giles KNIGHT of Stoke sub Hamdon	1638	D/D/cta/K4	Ad.ac.
3950	Hugh KNIGHT of Bridgwater	1609	DD/SP/1609/3	
3951	James KNIGHT, Yeoman of Broomfield	1681	T.N.A., PROB 4/7491	Will 1682. ex. 1682
3952	James KNIGHT, Clerk of Brompton Regis	1701	DD/SP/1701/33	
3953	Joan KNIGHT of Crewkerne	1714	DD/MR/113	
3954	John KNIGHT of Congresbury	1587	D/D/cta/K5	Ad.ac.
3955	John KNIGHT of Bradford	1667	DD/SP/1667/32	
3956	John KNIGHT of Elworthy	1690	DD/SP/1690/51	
3957	John KNIGHT, Bachelor of Cromhall, Gloucestershire formerly of Wick St. Lawrence, Somerset	1817	T.N.A., PROB 31/1817/942	
3958	Joseph KNIGHT of Cucklington	1759	DD/X/FN/6	
3959	Mark KNIGHT, Innkeeper of Taunton	1625/6	DD/SF/11/1/34	Formerly DD/SF 1080
3960	Martha KNIGHT of Crewkerne	1688	T.N.A., PROB 4/17434	Admon, wife of Richard
3961	Mary KNIGHT, Widow of Brompton Ralph	1683	DD/SP/1683/60	Widow of Richard
3962	Matthew KNIGHT of Bridgwater	1667	DD/SP/1667/47	
3963	Nicholas KNIGHT of Taunton St. Mary Magdalene	1683	DD/SP/1683/49	
3964	Richard KNIGHT of Pitminster	1728	DD/SP/1728/35	
3965	Richard KNIGHT the elder of Cheddon Fitzpaine	1683	DD/SP/1683/8	
3966	Robert KNIGHT of Kingston	1634	DD/SP/1634/45	
3967	Robert KNIGHT of Kingston	1682	T.N.A., PROB 4/8938	Will. ex. 1683

3968	Robert KNIGHT of Taunton St. James	1683	DD/SP/1683/43	
3969	Robert KNIGHT, Clothier of Cucklington	1701	T.N.A., PROB 4/22632	Admon
3970	Robert KNIGHT junior of Kingston	1680	DD/SP/1680/42	
3971	Thomas KNIGHT, Yeoman of Portbury	1678	T.N.A., PROB 4/995	Will also extant
3972	Thomas KNIGHT, Yeoman of Abbots Leigh	1725	B.A., 1725/9	Will also extant
3973	Thomasina KNIGHT of Kingston	1680	DD/SP/1680/43	
3974	William KNIGHT of Cucklington	1641	DD/X/FN/5	
3975	Emanuell KNIGHT alias MACY of Bridgwater	1646	DD/SP/1646/86	
3976	Richard KNIGHT alias WHITE of North Petherton	1648	DD/SP/1648/37	
3977	Charles KNOLLES of Minehead	1731	T.N.A., PROB 3/30/128	
3978	Charles KNOLLES of Minehead	1731	T.N.A., PROB 31/1731/590	
3979	Thomas KNOYLE, Esquire of Sandford Orcas	1684	T.N.A., PROB 4/210	Will 1684
3980	Richard KNUBLEY of Bath	1827	T.N.A., PROB 31/1827/847	
3981	Richard KNUBLEY of Bath	1828	T.N.A., PROB 31/1828/344	
3982	George KNYFTON of Uphill	1740	A/AEH/11/1	
3983	William KYPYNG of Buckland Dinham	1539	T.N.A., PROB 2/238	
3984	Silvester LABY of [no place]	1677	T.N.A., PROB 4/21772	Admon
3985	John LACIE, Husbandman of Blagdon	1606	D/D/cta/L18	Ad.ac.
3987	William LACY of Hamp, Bridgwater	1694	DD/SP/1694/38	
3988	John LAGGETT, Yeoman of Drayton	1700	DD/SP/442/37	Ad.ac.
3989	Jonathan LAGHTON of Horton, Ilminster	1677	T.N.A., PROB 4/13203	Admon
3990	John LAKE of Taunton	1666	DD/SP/1666/72	
3991	Edmund LAMBE of Kingstone	1669	DD/SP/1669/16	
3992	John LAMBE of Frome Selwood	1637	D/D/cta/L15	Ad.ac.
3993	William LAMBE, Minister of Broadway	1666	DD/SP/1666/35	
3994	Blazie LAMBERT, Husbandman of Pawlett	1635	D/D/ct/1/L2a	
3995	Joane LAMBERT, Spinster of Wembdon	1669	DD/SP/1669/46	
3996	John LAMPARD of Glastonbury St. John	1731	D/D/Cti 55	
3997	Katherine LAMPREY, Widow of Isle Abbotts	1679	DD/SP/1679/22	
3998	Thomas LAMPRIERE, Commander of H.M.S. *Centaur*, Esquire, formerly of H.M.S. *Canterbury* died at Bath	1765	T.N.A., PROB 31/1765/150	
3999	John LANCASTER of Milverton	1687	T.N.A., PROB 4/15253	Will also extant
4000	John LANCASTER, Gentleman of Milverton	1687	T.N.A., PROB 5/5690	

4001	John LANCASTER of Milverton?	1688	T.N.A., PROB 4/19475	Will 1687
4002	[missing] LANE of Wrington	1630	D/D/cta/L19	
	Note: Ad.ac.; '– Lane, Wrington, 1630' is written on the outside but there is no evidence for this on the face of the document, only metions of Portishead and Portbury			
4003	John LANE, Husbandman of Worle	1635	D/D/ct/1/L5a	
4004	John LANE, Yeoman of Milborne Port	1680	T.N.A., PROB 4/8549	Will also extant
4005	John LANE of Taunton St. Mary Magdalene	1700	DD/SP/1700/3	
4006	John LANE of Hot Wells, Bristol formerly of Bath	1809	T.N.A., PROB 31/1809/409	With ac. and com.
4007	Mary LANE, Widow of Crewkerne	1664	DD/SP/1664/14	
4008	Richard LANE, Gentleman of [no place]	1611	D/D/cta/L17	Ad.ac.
4009	Robert LANE of Curry Rivel	1691	DD/SP/1691/93	
4010	Thomas LANE, Tailor of Curry Rivel	1682	DD/SP/1682/57	
4011	William LANE, Blacksmith of Westover, Curry Rivel	1671	DD/SP/1671/4	
4012	William LANE of Rodney Stoke	1703	D/D/cta/L20	Ad.ac.
4013	William LANE, Husbandman of Curry Rivel	1729	DD/SP/1729/62	
4014	Aquilla LANGBRIDGE, Widow of Puckington	1691	DD/SP/1691/94	
4015	George LANGBRIDGE of Puckington	1689	DD/SP/1689/18	Reference to Brick
4016	John LANGBRIDGE of Crewkerne	1592	D/D/cta/L32	Ad.ac.
4017	Joseph LANGBRIDGE of Hewish, Crewkerne	1628	DD/MR/70	Buried at Crewkerne
4018	William LANGCASTELL of Wedmore	1634/5	D/D/ct/1/L7a	
4019	Edward LANGDON, Yeoman of Merriott	1664	DD/SP/1664/57	
4020	Elinor LANGDON of Merriott	1635	DD/SP/1635/87	
4021	John LANGDON, Husbandman of Exton	1698	DD/SP/1698/35	
4022	John LANGDON of Brompton Regis	1716	DD/SP/1716/7	
4023	Simon LANGDON, Apothecary of Taunton St. Mary Magdalene	1683	DD/SP/1683/41	
4024	Thomas LANGDON of West Camel	1620	D/D/cta/L6	Ad.ac.
4025	William LANGDON, Yeoman of Merriott	1673	DD/SP/1673/34	
4026	William LANGDON, Saddler of Taunton St. Mary Magdalene	1725	DD/SP/1725/22	
4027	William LANGE, Husbandman of Upton	1682	DD/SP/1682/63	
4028	Roger LANGFORD of Staple Fitzpaine	1684	DD/SP/1684/25	
4029	William LANGFORD, Husbandman of Lyng	1640	DD/SP/1640/25	
4030	Alice LANGHAM of Toobridge, West Monkton	1640	DD/SP/1640/139	See *T.C.W.*

4031	Hugh LANGHAM, Sergemaker of Milverton	1700	DD/SP/1700/13	
4032	Thomas and Sarah LANGHAM of Taunton St. Mary Magdalene	1675	DD/SP/1675/59	
4033	George LANGHELL of Exford	1681	DD/SP/1681/101	
4034	William LANGLIE alias BATT, Blacksmith of Winford	1629	D/D/ct/1/L8a	
4035	William LANGMAN of East Quantoxhead	1680	DD/SP/1680/52	
4036	John LANSDON of Cloford	1611	D/D/cta/L7	Ad.ac.
4037	Thomas LANSDON of Camerton	1672	D/D/cta/L21	Ad.ac.
4038	John LANSDOWNE, Worsted Comber of Taunton St. Mary Magdalene	1676	DD/SP/1676/13	
4039	John LANTEROE of Wembdon	1669	DD/SP/1669/63	
4040	David LANTROW, Yeoman of Cannington	1684	DD/SP/1684/29	
4041	Edward LANTROW of Enmore	1699	DD/SP/1699/16	
4042	William LARCOMBE of Cannington	1681	DD/SP/1681/91	
4043	Richard LARCOME of Wembdon	1671	DD/SP/1671/31	
4044	William LARCOME of Wembdon	1669	DD/SP/1669/80	
4045	Richard LARDER of Hutton	1640	D/D/cta/L33	Ad.ac.
LARRANCE see DYER				
4046	Richard LARWAY of Brompton Ralph	1687	DD/SP/1687/32	
4047	Obadiah LATHAM, Tailor of Keynsham	1694	T.N.A., PROB 4/22050	Will also extant
4048	Samuel LATHBURY of Keynsham	1674	D/D/cta/L23	Ad.ac.
4049	Joane LATY, Widow of Lopen	1590	D/D/ct/1/L12	
4050	Robert LATY of Merriott	1665	DD/SP/1665/27	
4051	Alice LAUGHALL, Widow of Minehead	1668	DD/SP/1668/35	
4052	Edward LAUGHWELL of Minehead	1644	DD/SP/1644/64	
4053	Joane LAUGHWELL of Exford	1682	DD/SP/1682/34	
4054	Robert LAUGHWELL of Luxborough	1678	T.N.A., PROB 4/20799	Will also extant
4055	John LAVER of Drayton	1697	DD/SP/1697/44	
4056	John LAVER, Sergemaker of Broadway	1723	T.N.A., PROB 3/22/218	
4057	Robert LAVER, Yeoman of Stoke St. Mary	1671	DD/SP/1671/29	
4058	Samuel LAVER of South Petherton	1692	DD/SP/1692/7	
4059	Alice LAVOR of Martock	1625	D/D/cta/L12	Ad.ac.
4060	Dorothy LAVOR, Widow of Drayton	1674	DD/SP/1674/20	

4061	Edward LAVOR of Long Load	1622	D/D/cta/L10	Ad.ac.
4062	Thomas LAVOR of Hambridge, Curry Rivel	1723	DD/SP/1723/57	
4063	Amy LAW of Puckington	1731	DD/SP/1731/22	
4064	William LAWFILLS of Porlock	1728	DD/SP/1728/41	
4065	Thomas LAWRANCE, Yeoman of Nether Stowey	1676	T.N.A., PROB 4/25965	Will. ex. 1676
4066	Agnes LAWRENCE, Widow of Stogumber	1640	DD/SP/1640/144	
4067	Edward LAWRENCE, Weaver of North Petherton	1680	D/D/cta/L24	Ad.ac.
4068	Edward LAWRENCE, Husbandman of Merriott	1683	DD/SP/1683/12	
4069	Henry LAWRENCE of Kingston Seymour	1595	D/D/cta/L31	Ad.ac.
4070	John LAWRENCE of North Petherton	1641	DD/SP/1641/87	
4071	John LAWRENCE of North Petherton	1642	DD/SP/1642/18	
4072	John LAWRENCE of Merriott	1673	DD/SP/1673/28–29	
4073	John LAWRENCE of Broadway	1676	DD/SP/1676/19	
4074	John LAWRENCE of Barrington	1683	DD/SP/1683/66	
4075	John LAWRENCE of North Petherton	1695	DD/SP/1695/32	
4076	John LAWRENCE the elder, Yeoman of Merriott	1670	DD/SP/1670/55	
4077	Joyce LAWRENCE of [no place]	1619	DD/WO/55/8	
4078	Richard LAWRENCE of Pepperhill, Over Stowey	1640	DD/SP/1640/128	
4079	Richard LAWRENCE of North Petherton	1683	DD/SP/1683/28	
4080	Robert LAWRENCE, Gentleman of West Bagborough	1683	DD/SP/1683/5	
4081	Roger LAWRENCE of Crewkerne	1668	DD/SP/1668/31	
4082	Thomas LAWRENCE, Husbandman of Merriott	1637	DD/SP/1637/22	
4083	Thomas LAWRENCE, Husbandman of Merriott	1685	DD/SP/1685/55	
4084	Thomas LAWRENCE of North Petherton	1696	DD/SP/1696/27	
4085	Thomas LAWRENCE, Apothecary of Wiveliscombe	1733	DD/SP/1733/17	
4086	Joan LAWRENCE alias DIER of Fiddington	1636	DD/SP/1636/41	
4087	Philip LAWRENCE alias DYER of Over Stowey	1689	DD/SP/1689/29	
LAWRENCE see DIER				
4088	John LAX, Husbandman of Ditcheat	1693	A/CMA/10/22/12	
4089	John LAX alias HUTCHINS of East Wells, Wells	1693	A/CMA/10/22/12	
4090	Jane LAY, Widow of Bath	1764	T.N.A., PROB 31/1764/75	
4091	Jane LAY, Widow of Bath City	1765	T.N.A., PROB 3/60/37	
4092	Elizabeth LEA, Widow of Whitestaunton	1649	DD/SP/1649/71	

4093	William LEA of Whitestaunton	1682	DD/SP/1682/61	
4094	...... LEACH of Ash, Martock	1639	D/D/ct/1/L18	
4095	Henry LEACH of Taunton St. Mary Magdalene	1698	T.N.A., PROB 4/18888	Admon
4096	John LEACH of Kingston St. Mary	1691	DD/SP/1691/23	
4097	Richard LEACH of Chard	1619	D/D/cta/L4	Ad.ac.
4098	Ann LEADON, Widow of Dunster	1666	DD/SP/1666/62	
4099	Susan LEAKEY, Widow of Minehead	1634	DD/SP/1634/41	
4100	Thomas LEAKEY, Flaxdresser of Bridgwater	1736	DD/SP/1736/29	
4101	Thomas LEAST of South Brent	1647	D/D/ct/1/L19	
4102	Margaret LEAVE of Cannington	1668	DD/SP/1668/49	
4103	Roger LEAWORTHY of Oare	1687	DD/SP/1687/9	
4104	Samuel LEDGINGHAM, Gentleman of Taunton St. Mary Magdalene	1684	DD/SP/1684/28	
4105	Humphrey LEE, Blacksmith of Cheddon Fitzpaine	1684	DD/SP/1684/99	
4106	John Lee LEE of Dillington, Ilminster	1874	DD/CA/146	
4107	Vaughan Hanning LEE of Dillington, Ilminster	1882	DD/CA/146	
4108	William LEE of Thurloxton	1683	DD/SP/1683/92	
LEE see BALE				
4109	Robert LEEMING of Stogursey	1665	DD/SP/1665/60	
4110	James LEES of Norton Fitzwarren	1687	DD/SP/1687/63	
4111	Humphry LEGG junior of Wellington	1729	T.N.A., PROB 31/1729/47	
4112	Mary LEGG, Widow of Goathurst	1677	DD/SP/1677/82	
4113	Thomas LEGG of Chard	1686	T.N.A., PROB 4/16288	Will 1686
4114	John LEGGAT of Drayton	1699	DD/SP/1699/6	
4115	John LEGGAT of Drayton	1700	DD/SP/1700/7	
4116	William LEGGAT of Drayton	1648	DD/SP/1648/66	
4117	Thomas LEGGATT of Muchelney	1640	D/D/cta/L1	Ad.ac.
4118	Humphrey LEGGE junior of Wellington	1729	T.N.A., PROB 3/28/6	
4119	Alce LEIGH of Wootton Courtenay	1641	DD/SP/1641/76	
4120	John LEIGH of Bicknoller	1675	DD/SP/1675/86	
4121	John LEIGH of Withycombe	1683	DD/SP/1683/22	
4122	Reverend John LEIGH of St. John's, Newfoundland, late of Wiveliscombe	1823	A/CYW/1/3/4	

4123	William LEIGH of Pitminster	1697	DD/SP/1697/17	
4124	Ellen LEIKER, Widow of Bishops Lydeard	1677	T.N.A., PROB 4/6876	Will 1677
4125	Joan LEMMON of North Petherton	1730	DD/SP/1730/30	
4126	Robert LENERD of Taunton	1583	T.N.A., PROB 2/740	Exhibited 1583
4127	Joan LESTER of Salisbury, Wiltshire, formerly of Wells	1637	W.S.H.C., P4/1636/8	Admon. bond, inv., will
4128	Edith LEVASHER of Otterhampton	1640	DD/SP/1640/60	Inv. shows LEVASHOWE
LEVASHOWE see LEVASHER				
4129	Walter LEVERSEDGE of Compton Dando	1674	D/D/cta/L26	Ad.ac.
4130	Charles LEWDON of Winscombe	1723	D/D/cta/L27	Ad.ac.
4131	Ann LEWES of Stogumber	1638	DD/SP/1638/54	See *T.C.W.*
4132	Joseph LEWES of Staplegrove	1690	DD/SP/1690/77	
4133	Richard LEWES, Yeoman of Churchill	1688	T.N.A., PROB 4/5839	Will. ex. 1689
4134	Robert LEWES, Glover of Dunster	1635	DD/SP/1635/40	
4135	Thomas LEWES of Elborough, Hutton	1685	T.N.A., PROB 4/4435	Will also extant
4136	William LEWES of Winscombe	1635	D/D/cta/L13	Ad.ac.
4137	William LEWES of Charlinch	1667	DD/SP/1667/78	
4138	William LEWES of Taunton St. James	1676	DD/SP/1676/14	Mentions spices
4139	William LEWES, Clerk of Pitminster	1682	DD/SP/1682/20	
LEWES see TYDDER				
4140	William LEWESE of Portishead	1676	D/D/ct/1/L29	
4141	James LEWIS of Wincanton	1669	T.N.A., PROB 4/17360	Will also extant
4142	John LEWIS of Sidcot, Winscombe	1677	T.N.A., PROB 4/9984	Will also extant
4143	John LEWIS of Dulverton	1681	DD/SP/1681/83	
4144	John LEWIS, Husbandman of Combe Florey	1686	DD/SP/1686/8	
4145	Richard LEWIS, Gentleman of Yatton	1692	T.N.A., PROB 4/9146	Will also extant
4146	Susannah LEWIS, Widow of Bath	1805	T.N.A., PROB 31/1805/867	
4147	Walter LEWIS of St. Michaelchurch	1639	DD/SP/1639/20	Inv. shows LOWESES
4148	Morgan LEWIS alias APRISE of Bicknoller	1644	DD/SP/1644/66	
4149	John LEWORTHY of Porlock	1723	DD/SP/1723/52	
4150	Alexander LIDDEN of Dunster	1666	DD/SP/1666/2	
4151	Thomas LIDNER, Yeoman of Dunwear, Bridgwater	1716	DD/SP/1716/14	
4152	Nicholas LIGHT of East Brent	1733/4	D/D/Cti 53	
4153	Stephen LIGHT of Ruishton	1692	DD/SP/1692/34	

4154	Stephen LIGHT senior of Ruishton	1638	DD/SP/1638/42	
4155	Elizabeth LIGHTFOOTE, Widow of North Petherton	1661	DD/SP/1661/16	
4156	Elizabeth LIGHTFOOTE, Widow of Ruishton	1698	DD/SP/1698/31	
4157	John LIGHTFOOTE alias QUALE of Cheddon Fitzpaine	1679	DD/SP/1679/43	
4158	William LIKER of Spaxton	1668	DD/SP/1668/41	
4159	Elizabeth LILLY, Spinster of Kingston	1684	DD/SP/1684/97	
4160	William LIMBERY of Curry Mallet	1676	DD/SP/1676/42	
4161	William LIMBRIE, Tailor of Curry Mallet	1646	DD/SP/1646/52	See *T.C.W.*
4162	William LINE of Abbots Leigh	1723	B.A., 1723/15	
4163	Marmaduke LING, Yeoman of North Petherton	1682	DD/SP/1682/19	
4164	Richard LING of North Petherton	1682	DD/SP/1682/18	
4165	Elizabeth LINLEY of Bridgwater	167–[?]	T.N.A., PROB 4/18837	Admon ?
4166	Philip LISSANT senior, Mercer of Taunton	1688	T.N.A., PROB 4/4454	Will 'not exhibited'
LISSANT see ROSSITER				
4167	Robert LITTELL of Upton	1677	DD/SP/1677/34	
4168	Nicholas LITTLEJOHN of Langford Budville	1635	DD/SP/1635/64	
3986	William LLEWELLIN of Portbury	1630	D/D/cta/L22	Ad.ac.
4169	Elizabeth LLOYD, Widow of Bedminster	1691	T.N.A., PROB 4/10435	Will 1692. ex. 1692
4170	Mary LLOYD, Widow of Kewstoke	1754	T.N.A., PROB 31/1754/728	
4171	William LLOYD, Merchant of Bedminster	1690	T.N.A., PROB 4/5807	Admon. ex. 1691
4172	William LLOYD of Westonzoyland	1810	T.N.A., PROB 31/1810/1056	
4173	Mary LLWELLYN (FLEWELLING) of Bridgwater	1692	DD/SP/1692/16	
4174	Abraham LOADEN of Kingstone	1678	DD/SP/1678/7	
4175	Joseph LOADER, Miller of Combe Florey	1721	DD/SP/1721/3	
4176	Christian LOB, Widow of Winsford	1640	DD/SP/1640/78	
4177	Alce LOBB of Luccombe	1667	DD/SP/1667/19	
4178	James LOBB of Winsford	1635	DD/SP/1635/67	
4179	John LOBB, Mariner of Minehead	1671	DD/SP/1671/15	
4180	Henry LOCK of Winsford formerly of North Molton, Devon	1701	DD/SP/1701/35	
4181	Robert LOCK of Long Sutton	1662	DD/SAS/FA/161/11a+b	
4182	William LOCK of Minehead	1684	DD/SP/1684/159	
4183	William LOCK, Yeoman of Cutcombe	1697	DD/SP/1697/9	
4184	John LOCKE of Tolland	1716	DD/SP/1716/11	

4185	James LOCKIER of Goathurst	1713	DD/SP/1713/34	
4186	John LOCKIER, Innholder of Taunton St. Mary Magdalene	1693	DD/SP/1693/10	
4187	John LOCKYER of Ilchester	1686	T.N.A., PROB 4/7726	Will also extant
4188	John LOCKYER of Bath	1806	T.N.A., PROB 31/1806/434	
4189	Thomas LOCKYER, Yeoman of Limington	1677	T.N.A., PROB 4/10376	Admon
4190	James LODGE of Wells	1621	D/D/cta/L9	Ad.ac.
4191	Daniel LODON of Cannington	n.d.	D/D/cta/L3	Ad.ac.
4192	Laurence LODON of Moorlinch	1641	D/D/cta/L2	Ad.ac.
4193	Francis LOKER of Dunwear, Bridgwater	1680	DD/SP/1680/53	
4194	Andrew LOKIER of Moorlinch	1629	D/D/ct/1/L42a-c	
4195	Elizabeth LOKIER, Widow of Milverton	1636	DD/SP/1636/46	
4196	Robert LOKYER of Yeovilton	1621	D/D/cta/L8	Ad.ac.
4197	[missing] LONG of [no place]	1670	DD/SP/1670/56	Incomplete
4198	Hercules LONG, Yeoman of West Monkton	1726	DD/SP/1726/28	
4199	John LONG of Abbas and Temple Combe	1598	D/D/cta/L29	Ad.ac.
4200	John LONG, Husbandman of Crowcombe	1673	DD/SP/1673/2	
4201	John LONG of Taunton	1733	T.N.A., PROB 31/1733/303	With com.
4202	John LONG senior of West Monkton	1709	DD/SP/1709/41	
4203	Joseph LONG, Yeoman of Chillington	1685	DD/SP/1685/26	
4204	Simon LONG, Joiner of Woolstone, Bicknoller	1675	DD/SP/1675/87	
4205	Thomas LONG of Bridgwater	1678	DD/SP/1678/56	
4206	Thomas LONG of Wootton Courtenay	1693	DD/SP/1693/58	
4207	Thomas LONG of Luccombe	1721	DD/SP/1721/16	
4208	John LOOCKE of Tolland	1639	DD/SP/1639/19	See *T.C.W.*
4209	Arthur LORWELL of Bridgwater	1696	DD/SP/1696/10	
4210	Augustine LOVELL of Allum, Batcombe	1619	D/D/cta/L25	Ad.ac.
4211	John LOVELL of Langford, Burrington	1700	T.N.A., PROB 4/18752	
	Note: Admon, buried at Burrington in 1699 described as being of the parish of Churchill			
4212	Mrs Margaret LOVELL of Axbridge	1731	W.S.H.C., 161/1	
4213	Christian LOVERING, Widow of Martock	n.d.	D/D/cta/L16	Ad.ac.
4214	Thomas LOVERING of [no place]	1623	D/D/cta/L11	Ad.ac.
4215	Joane LOWDALL, Widow of Taunton St. Mary Magdalene	1684	DD/SP/1684/6	
4216	Thomas LOWDALL of Taunton St. Mary Magdalene	1678	DD/SP/1678/30	

LOWESES see LEWIS
LOXHAM see CARTER

4217	Timothy LOYD of Glastonbury St. John	1738/9	D/D/Cti 56	
4218	John LUCAS of Kingston, Yeovil	1622	D/D/ct/1/L56	
4219	Attewell LUCKIS of St. Decumans	1670	T.N.A., PROB 4/18412	Admon
4220	William LUCKIS, Husbandman of Milverton	1681	DD/SP/1681/52	
4221	William LUCKIS of Oake	1731	DD/SP/1731/23	
4222	James LUCKWELL of Cutcombe	1685	DD/SP/1685/10	
4223	Julian LUDLOW of Taunton St. James	1716	DD/SP/1716/41	
4224	Robert LUDWELL, Mercer of Bruton	1679	T.N.A., PROB 4/8411	Will 1679
4225	Thomas LUDWELL of Wincanton	1587/8	D/D/ct/1/L59	
4226	John LUFF of Isle Brewers	1632/3	DD/SP/1632/26	
4227	Fraunces LUFFE, Spinster of Isle Brewers	1632	DD/SP/1632/22	
4228	Fraunces LUFFE, Spinster of Isle Brewers	1632	DD/SP/1632/23	
4229	John? LUFFE, Saddler? of Bridgwater	1672	DD/SP/1672/22	
4230	Matthew LUFFE of Bridgwater	1727	DD/SP/442/83	Ad.ac.
4231	John LUKIN? of Bishops Hull	1692	T.N.A., PROB 4/19687	Admon 1692
4232	John LUMBARD of Chaffcombe	1635	DD/SP/1635/20	
4233	John LUMBARD, Yeoman of Isle Abbotts	1732	DD/SP/1732/12	
4234	Robert LUMBARD senior of Wayford	1670	DD/SP/1670/100	
4235	Thomas LUMBARD, Widower of Creech St. Michael	1687	DD/SP/1687/48	
4236	Elizabeth LUNDY, Widow of North Petherton	1673	DD/SP/1673/35	
4237	Robert LUSH of Bridgwater	1681	DD/SP/364	
4238	Christopher LUTLEY of Hillfarrance	1645	DD/SP/1645/21	
4239	Edward LUTTERELL, Gentleman of Charlinch	1678	DD/SP/1678/26	
4240	Elizabeth LUTTRELL, Widow of Honibere, Lilstock	1637	DD/SP/1637/71	
4241	Francis LUTTRELL, Esquire of Dunster Castle, Dunster	1691	T.N.A., PROB 4/3594	Will ex. 1693; see S.H.C., T/PH/pro/5 for a copy
4242	Francis LUTTRELL, Esquire of Dunster Castle, Dunster	1693	T.N.A., PROB 4/1827	Will. See S.H.C., T/PH/pro/5 for a copy
4243	Henry LUTTRELL of [no place]	1781	DD/L/2/35/1–2 Box 138	
4244	John Fownes LUTTRELL, Esquire of Dunster Castle, Dunster	1824	T.N.A., PROB 31/1824/1026	Account in 1824/1027
4245	Richard LUX, Vicar of Stogumber	1736	DD/SP/1736/31	
4246	Joane LYDDON, Spinster of Brompton Regis	1642	DD/SP/1642/1	

4247	Nicholas LYDDON of Kilve	1596	D/D/cta/L30	Ad.ac.
4248	Thomas LYDDON, Yeoman of Brompton Regis	1685	DD/SP/1685/63	
4249	William LYDDON, Yeoman of Brompton Regis	1680	DD/SP/1680/36	
4250	John LYDE of Walton	1629	D/D/ct/1/L66a	
4251	John LYDE of Wembdon	1667	DD/SP/1667/11	
4252	William LYDE of Stanton Drew	1644	D/D/cta/L28	Ad.ac.
4253	William LYDE the younger, Gentleman of Knighton Sutton, Chew Magna	1706	T.N.A., PROB 4/22700	Admon
4254	Elizabeth LYE of Hinton St. George	1640	DD/SP/1640/116	
4255	Elizabeth LYE of Hinton St. George	1641	DD/SP/1641/5	
4256	John LYE, Fuller of [no place]	1645	DD/SP/1645/25	
4257	Margaret LYE, Widow of Middle Lambrook, Kingsbury Episcopi	1599	D/D/ct/1/L68	
4258	Henry LYNDON of Milverton	1674	DD/SP/1674/14	
4259	Matthew LYNDON of Creech St. Michael	1713	DD/SP/1713/17	
4260	Richard LYNDON of North Curry	1590	D/D/ct/1/L36a	
4261	Joseph LYNNIS, Husbandman of Churchill	1679	T.N.A., PROB 4/5848	Will. ex. 1680
4262	John LYNTON, Mariner of Bridgwater	1684	DD/SP/1684/98	
4263	John LYON of Burnham on Sea	1620	D/D/cta/L5	Ad.ac.
4264	William LYONS of Compton Dando	1635	D/D/cta/L14	Ad.ac.
4265	Mary MABBARD of Chedzoy	1686	DD/SP/1686/1	
4266	James MABY of Ditcheat	1692	T.N.A., PROB 4/9721	Will. ex. 1693
4267	Robert MACEY of Shepton Mallet	1716	D/D/cta/M14	Ad.ac.
MACEY see READE				
4268	John MACKGLASHAN of Bath	1830	T.N.A., PROB 31/1830/2024	
4269	Roger MACKNES of Dunster	1666	DD/SP/1666/3	
MACY see KNIGHT				
4270	John MADDOX, Gentleman of Kilmington?	1676	T.N.A., PROB 4/6869	Admon. ex. 1677
4271	Richard MADDOX of Ditcheat	1694	T.N.A., PROB 4/7966	Admon. ex. 1695
4272	Henry MAGER of Milverton	1676	DD/SP/1676/3	
MAGER see MAJOR				
4273	Agnes MAGGES of Chew Magna	1588	D/D/cta/M41	Ad.ac.
4274	Thomas MAGGES of North Cadbury	1662	D/D/cta/M25	Ad.ac.

4275	Thomas MAIDE of Shipham	1623	D/D/cta/M6	Ad.ac.
4276	Giles MAINE of Whitelackington	1699	DD/SP/1699/3	
4277	William MAINE the younger of West Harptree	1743	T.N.A., PROB 31/1743/292	With ad.ac.
4278	John MAISTES ? of [no place]	1638	DD/SP/1638/5	Damaged
4279	John MAJOR of Bradford	1680	DD/SP/1680/59	
4280	Richard MAJOR of [no place]	1645	DD/SP/1645/34	
4281	Thomas MAJOR of Milverton	1688	DD/SP/1688/41	
MAJOR see MAGER				
4282	Katherine MALEN of North Petherton	1645	DD/SP/1645/61	
4283	Joan MALLACK, Widow of Taunton St. Mary Magdalene	1687	T.N.A., PROB 4/7697	Will 1686
4284	Joan MALLET, Widow of Abbots Leigh	1641	B.A., 1641/33	Will also extant
4285	Stephen MAN, Clerk of Curry Rivel	1686	T.N.A., PROB 4/4557	Will also extant
4286	William MANDER, Soapboiler of Hillfarrance	1700	T.N.A., PROB 4/25290	Will also extant
4287	Agnes MANINGE, Widow of Shepton Beauchamp	1681	DD/SP/1681/87	
4288	Henry MANLEY of Ashbrittle	1681	DD/SP/1681/99	
4289	Joan MANN, Widow of Curry Rivel	1690	DD/SP/1690/35	
4290	Edward MANNEN of Dinnington	1731	DD/SP/1731/14	
4291	John MANNING of Nettlecombe died at South Molton, Devon	1663	T.N.A., PROB 4/10519	Admon
4292	John MANNING of Milverton	1725	DD/SP/1725/6	
4293	Mary MANNING of South Petherton	1672	DD/SP/1672/12	
4294	Stephen MANNING, Husbandman of Barrington	1697	DD/SP/1697/34	
4295	William MANNING, Clerk of Bedminster	1702	B.A., 1702/18	
	Note: Vicar of Bedminster, including St. Thomas and St. Mary, Redcliffe			
4296	John MANNINGE, Tailor of Shepton Beauchamp	1669	DD/SP/1669/70	
4297	Samuel MANSHIPP of Locking	1664	D/D/cta/M48	Ad.ac.
4298	Mary MANTLE, Widow of Cheddon Fitzpaine	1683	DD/SP/1683/29	
4299	Christopher MARCHANT of Winsford	1686	DD/SP/1686/27	
4300	John MARCHANT of Lydeard St. Lawrence	n.d.	DD/SP/17th Century/8	Fragment, mentions Maria, relict
4301	John MARCHE of Cucklington	1624	D/D/cta/M7	Ad.ac.
4302	Alexander MARCHH, Clothier of Taunton St. James	1681	T.N.A., PROB 4/8035	Will 1681. ex. 1683?
4303	Samuel MARCHH, Sergemaker of Taunton St. James	1683	T.N.A., PROB 4/15717	Will also extant
4304	John MARDY, Husbandman of Swell	1620	D/D/ct/1/M13a	
4305	Edward MARE, Husbandman of Bradford	1668	DD/SP/1668/26	

4306	Hugh MARGERY of Kingston St. Mary	1676	DD/SP/1676/7	
4307	John MARIE of Weston (near Bath)	1694	T.N.A., PROB 4/9777	Will also extant
4308	John MARKE senior, Mason of South Petherton	1723	DD/SP/1723/45	
4309	John MARKE the elder, Yeoman of South Petherton	1670	DD/SP/1670/5	
4310	Mary MARKE, Widow of Pitminster	1684	T.N.A., PROB 4/8746	Will. ex. 1685
4311	Nicholas MARKE of Taunton St. Mary Magdalene	1678	T.N.A., PROB 4/10448	Will also extant
4312	Andrew MARKES the elder, Yeoman of South Petherton	1670	DD/SP/1670/99	
4313	Elizabeth MARKES, Widow of Pitminster	1680	T.N.A., PROB 4/8268	Will also extant
4314	Francis MARKES, Yeoman of South Petherton	1681	DD/SP/1681/8	
4315	Mary MARKES, Widow of Dunster	1667	DD/SP/1667/77	
4316	Robert MARKES of Merriott	1714	DD/SP/442/15	Ad.ac.
4317	Elizabeth MARKS, Widow of Taunton	1725	DD/SP/1725/14	
4318	John MARKS of North Perrott	1626	D/D/cta/M8	Ad.ac.
4319	John MARKS, Husbandman of Fivehead	1640	DD/SP/1640/48	
4320	Mary MARLE of Cheddon Fitzpaine	1683	DD/SP/1683/47	Wife of John
4321	Christopher MARLER, Locksmith of Taunton St. Mary Magdalene	1684	DD/SP/1684/60	
4322	James MARLER of Ruishton	1642	DD/SP/1642/13	
4323	Katherine MARLER of Creech St. Michael	1674	DD/SP/1674/43	
4324	Richard MARLOWE, Clerk of Stockland Bristol	1647	DD/SP/1647/6	
4325	John MARRAKER, Clerk and parson of Wambrook	1591	W.S.H.C., P5/1591/53	Admon. bond, inv.
4326	Thamsen MARRE of Pitminster formerly of Stoke St. Mary	1675	DD/SP/1675/49	
4327	Giles MARRIN of Minehead	1691	DD/SP/1691/63	
4328	Robert MARRING of North Petherton	1675	DD/SP/1675/43	
4329	John MARSH, Yeoman of Shepton Montague	1628	D/D/ct/1/M14a	
4330	John MARSH, Yeoman of Trent	1686	T.N.A., PROB 4/5863	Will. ex. 1687
4331	Thomas MARSH of Chipstable	1667	DD/SP/1667/68	
4332	Thomas MARSH, Clothier of Weston (*sic*)	1743	T.N.A., PROB 3/42/8	
4333	Thomas MARSH, Esquire of Wellington	1780	DD/DP/10 OB6	
4334	William MARSH of Pyrland, Taunton St. James	1731	DD/SP/1731/35	
4335	John MARSHALL of Enmore	1639	DD/SP/1639/15	
4336	John MARSHALL, Husbandman of North Petherton	1665	DD/SP/1665/54	
4337	Judith MARSHALL of Chillington	1640	DD/SP/1640/43	

4338	Thomas MARSHALL, Gentleman of Taunton	1686	T.N.A., PROB 4/5862	Admon
4339	Thomas MARSHALL, Minister of the Gospel of Ilminster	1693/4	A/BVY/1	
4340	Judith MARSHALL of North Petherton	1641	DD/SP/1641/29	MARSHFIELD or MARSHWELL (*T.C.W.*)
4341	John MARSHE of Bruton	1625	D/D/cta/M10	Ad.ac.
MARSHFIELD see MARSHALL				
MARSHWELL see MARSHALL				
4342	William MARTEN of Wellington	1617	D/D/cta/M39	Ad.ac.
4343	Elizabeth MARTIN of Yeovil	1652	DD/SP/1652/8a	
4344	Elizabeth MARTIN of [no place]	1652	DD/SP/1652/8b	
4345	Fleming MARTIN, Widower of Bath	1800	T.N.A., PROB 31/1800/948	
4346	George MARTIN of Brompton Ralph	n.d.	DD/SP/17th Century/9	
4347	Joan MARTIN, Widow of Taunton St. Mary Magdalene	1693	DD/SP/1693/54	
4348	John MARTIN of Stogursey	1590	D/D/cta/M43	Ad.ac.
4349	John MARTIN of Lydeard St. Lawrence	1714	DD/SP/1714/16	
4350	Luke MARTIN, Yeoman of Cannington	1691	DD/SP/1691/80	
4351	Phillip MARTIN, Widow of Lyng	1637	DD/SP/1637/62	
4352	John MARTIN alias HARRIS of Stoke St. Mary	1691	DD/SP/1691/30	
4353	[missing] MARTIN alias MASON of Bratton, Minehead	1628	DD/SP/1628/14	
4354	John MARTINE of Stringston	1674	DD/SP/1674/48	
4355	Alexander MARTYEN of Shepton Mallet	1680	D/D/ct/1/M22	
4356	Elizabeth MARTYN, Widow of Creech St. Michael	1639	DD/SP/1639/36	
4357	George MARTYN of Cheddon Fitzpaine	1692	DD/SP/1692/10	
4358	George? MARTYN of Brompton Ralph	n.d.	DD/SP/Box 9	Fragment
MARTYN see GAYLERD				
4359	Ralph MARTYNE, Yeoman of Marston Magna	1678	T.N.A., PROB 4/5897	Will 1679. ex. 1679
4360	Ann MASCALL, Widow of Stogursey	1740	DD/SP/1740/3	
4361	Edmund MASCALL, Yeoman of Kingston Seymour	1634	D/D/cta/M11	Ad.ac.
4362	Henry MASCALL of Kingston Seymour	1619	D/D/cta/M23	Ad.ac.
4363	Joan MASCALL, Widow of Abbots Leigh	1690	B.A., 1690/25	Will also extant
4364	William MASCALL of Abbots Leigh	1666	B.A., 1666/35	Will also extant
4365	William MASEY of Chaffcombe	1664	DD/SP/1664/58	
4366	William MASEY, Gentleman of Bridgwater	1687	T.N.A., PROB 4/10475	Will 1688. ex. 1688

4367	Agnes MASON, Widow of Porlock	1676	DD/SP/1676/23	
4368	Philip MASON of Taunton St. Mary Magdalene	1685	DD/SP/1685/7	
MASON see MARTIN				
4369	Henrie MASTERS of Yeovil	1643	D/D/ct/1/M29	
4370	James MASTERS, Clerk of Bath	1667	D/D/cta/M26	Ad.ac. for a clergyman
4371	John MASTERS of Martock	n.d.	D/D/ct/1/M31	
4372	Nicholas MASTERS, Waggoner of Taunton St. Mary Magdalene	1685	DD/SP/1685/102	
4373	Thomas MASTERS of Ilchester	1620	D/D/cta/M2	Ad.ac.
4374	Thomas MASTERS of Ilchester	1620	D/D/cta/M3	Ad.ac.
4375	Thomas MASTERS, Yeoman of Goathurst	1648	DD/SP/1648/25	
MASTERS see WEAVER				
4376	Elias MATHEW of Whitestaunton	1670	DD/SP/1670/7	
4377	John MATHEW, Tanner of Hatch Beauchamp	1678	DD/SP/1678/1	
4378	John MATHEW, Victualler of Taunton St. Mary Magdalene	1729	DD/SP/1729/58	
4379	Katteron MATHEW, Widow of Fitzhead	1629	D/D/ct/1/M33a	
MATHEW see ATCASTLE				
4380	Christopher MATHEWS, Yeoman of Lyncombe and Widcombe	1679	D/D/ct/1/M34	
4381	George MATTOCK of Wells	1736	D/D/Cti 106	
4382	George MATTOCK of Wells	1736	D/D/Cti 58	
4383	John MATTOCKE of Trull	1684	DD/SP/1684/141	
4384	Reverend Richard MAUNDER, Clerk of Norton Malreward	1737	D/D/cta/M17	Ad.ac. and inv.
4385	Nicholas MAUNDRY of Puckington	1668	DD/SP/1668/43	
4386	Elizabeth MAUNDRY alias POLLARD, Widow of Taunton St. Mary Magdalene	1684	DD/SP/1684/102	
4387	John MAVERICK alias BULL of Trull	1645	DD/SP/1645/14	Names 6 children
4388	John MAXFIELD, Maltster of Kilmington	1788	T.N.A., PROB 31/1788/999	
4389	Richard MAY of Kewstoke	1687	D/D/cta/M18	Ad.ac.
4390	Samuel MAY of Uphill	1611	D/D/cta/M46	Ad.ac.
4391	Anne MAYE, Widow of Huish Champflower	1698	DD/SP/1698/36	
4392	Edward MAYE of Worle	1644	D/D/cta/M36	Ad.ac.
4393	Richard MAYE, Sergemaker of Taunton St. James	1685	DD/SP/1685/100	
4394	Hannah MAYES of Hillfarrance	1682	DD/SP/1682/43	

4395	Jane MAYES, Widow of Somerton	1729	D/D/cta/M16	Ad.ac.
4396	Michael MAYES of Hillfarrance	1682	DD/SP/1682/33	
4397	John MAYHO, Clothman of Chew (*sic*)	1495	T.N.A., PROB 2/97	Will T.N.A., PROB 11/10/11
4398	Thomas MAYNARD, Husbandman of Weston in Gordano	1588/9	D/D/ct/1/M41	
4399	William MAYNARD of North Stoke died at Upton in Bitton, Gloucestershire	1729	T.N.A., PROB 3/28/104	
4400	Thomas MAYNERD of Compton Martin	1601	D/D/cta/M47	Ad.ac.
4401	Joel MAYO, Yeoman of Norton St. Philip	1685	T.N.A., PROB 4/8692	Admon
4402	Sarah MAYO, Widow of Norton St. Philip	1686	T.N.A., PROB 4/16497	Will also extant
4403	Walter MAYOW of Croscombe	1482	T.N.A., PROB 2/10	
4404	Thomas MEACHAM, Yeoman of Combe St. Nicholas	1693	T.N.A., PROB 4/8255	Will also extant
4405	Andrew MEAD of Ilminster	1692	T.N.A., PROB 4/16343	Admon?
4406	Elizabeth MEADE of Drayton	1693	DD/SP/1693/68	
4407	Emblem MEADE, Widow of North Petherton	1673	DD/SP/1673/39	
4408	Jane MEADE, Widow of Fivehead	1683	DD/SP/1683/68	
4409	John MEADE, Carpenter of Wellington	1629	D/D/ct/1/M43	
4410	John MEADE of Taunton St. James	1666	DD/SP/1666/23	
4411	John MEADE of Lyng	1681	DD/SP/1681/86	
4412	Luce MEADE, Widow of Curry Mallet	1630	D/D/ct/1/M44	
4413	Mary MEADE, Widow of Lyng	1685	DD/SP/1685/12	
4414	Phillip MEADE of Fivehead	1646	DD/SP/1646/69	
4415	Sarah MEADE, Widow of Curry Mallet Note: Undated; appraised by Henry CANNICOTT and Robert DOLLEN	1630s	DD/SP/1632/33	
4416	Thomas MEADE, Yeoman of Drayton	1696	DD/SP/1696/15	
4417	Thomas MEADE the elder of Drayton	1678	DD/SP/1678/5	
4418	William MEADE, Grocer of Curry Rivel	1678	DD/SP/1678/6	
4419	William MEADE of Beercrocombe	1687	DD/SP/1687/45	
4420	George MEARE of Combwich, Otterhampton	1714	DD/SP/1714/29	
4421	Richard MEARE of Bradford	1683	DD/SP/1683/24	
4422	Sible MEARE of Nettlecombe	1673	DD/SP/1673/38	
4423	Edward MEECOE of Taunton St. Mary Magdalene	1683	DD/SP/1683/6	
4424	Joan MELHUISH, Widow of Brompton Regis	1716	DD/SP/1716/54	

4425	John MELHUISH senior, Weaver of Brompton Regis	1680	T.N.A., PROB 4/6840	Will also extant
4426	Robert MELHUISH, Yeoman of Brompton Regis	1734/5	D/D/Cti 60	
4427	William MELHUISH, Carpenter of Skilgate	1684	DD/SP/1684/26	
4428	Henry MELLIER alias MELLIAR, Yeoman of Pilton	1733	T.N.A., PROB 31/1733/715	With com.
4429	William MERCHANT of Wells St. Cuthbert	1598	D/D/cta/M40	Ad.ac.
4430	Joanna MEREDITH of Taunton St. Mary Magdalene Note: Admon, executrix? of John MEREDITH, also deceased	1677	T.N.A., PROB 4/6955	
4431	Robert MEREFEILD, Esquire of Crewkerne	1686	T.N.A., PROB 4/11216	Will also extant
4432	Agnes MEREFIELD of Merriott	1681	T.N.A., PROB 4/21969	Will 1681
4433	George MEREFIELD, Yeoman of Woolminstone, Crewkerne	1646	DD/SP/1646/79	
4434	John MEREFIELD of Nailsea	1689	T.N.A., PROB 4/6452	Admon
4435	William MERRETT of Bridgwater	1676	D/D/cta/M22	Ad.ac.
4436	Abraham MERRICK, Fuller of Taunton St. Mary Magdalene	1679	T.N.A., PROB 4/7937	Will also extant
4437	Edward MERRICK, Husbandman of Abbots Leigh	1681	B.A., 1681/54	Will also extant
4438	Martin MERRICK (MERUK) of Taunton	1639	DD/SP/1639/1	See *T.C.W.*
4439	John MERRIEN of Ashbeer, Stogumber	1666	DD/SP/1666/33	
4440	[missing] MERRILL, Milliner of Crewkerne	1697	DD/SP/1697/22	
4441	Mary MERRIOT, Widow of Compton Dundon	1679	T.N.A., PROB 4/22161	Admon; buried at Compton Dundon (Reg.)
4442	[missing] MERRY of Staplegrove	1673	DD/SP/1673/26	
4443	Bartholomew MERRY of Bicknoller	1666	DD/SP/1666/10	
4444	Giles MERRY, Yeoman of Crewkerne	1681	DD/SP/1681/111	
4445	Thomas MERRY of Bicknoller	1677	DD/SP/1677/5	
4446	John MESSITER of Wanstrow	1681	DD/CC/5342	
4447	John METFORD, Yeoman of Crewkerne	1671	DD/SP/1671/10	
4448	Charles MICHELL of Kilve	1684	T.N.A., PROB 4/8375	Will also extant
4449	Charles MICHELL, Bachelor of Windsor, Berkshire formerly of Friday Street, London and of St. Decumans, Somerset and of Aldermanbury, London	1807	T.N.A., PROB 31/1807/415	
4450	John MICHELL, Carpenter of Merriott	1669	DD/SP/1669/17	
4451	John MICHELL, Yeoman of Chedzoy	1670	DD/SP/1670/71	
4452	Leonard MICHELL, Husbandman of Wambrook	1639	W.S.H.C., P14/2	Inv. and will
4453	Margaret MICHELL, Spinster of Doniford, St. Decumans	1807	T.N.A., PROB 31/1807/991	

4454	Robert MICHELL of South Petherton	1610	DD/SP/1610/6	
4455	Thomas MICHELL of Lyng	1674	DD/SP/1674/33	
4456	Thomas MICHELL of Chedzoy	1680	DD/SP/1680/54	
4457	William MICHELL of Crewkerne	1608	D/D/cta/M34	Ad.ac.
4458	John MICHELL alias HADDEN of Merriott	1636	DD/SP/1636/21	See *T.C.W.*
4459	John MICHELL alias HALLET of Langport	1826	DD/LC/53/5	
4460	Alex MICHO of Taunton St. Mary Magdalene	1698	DD/SP/1698/6	
4461	Jane MIDDLE, Widow of Curry Mallet	1639	DD/SP/1639/10	
4462	Elezeas MIDDLETON of Taunton St. Mary Magdalene	1714	DD/SP/1714/18	
4463	Jane MIDDLETON, Widow of Cothelstone	1686	DD/SP/1686/24	
4464	John MIDDLETON of Bishops Lydeard	1587/8	D/D/ct/1/M53a	
4465	Ralph MIDDLETON of Drayton	1687	DD/SP/1687/17	
4466	Robert, James and Francis MIDDLETON of Ash Priors	1680	DD/SP/1680/89	
4467	Jane MIDELL of Hatch Beauchamp	1692	DD/SP/1692/3	
4468	Charles MILDON of Langford Budville	1672	DD/SP/1672/55	
4469	Charles MILDON of Langford Budville	1673	DD/SP/1673/25	
4470	Mary and Charles MILDON of Langford Budville	1678	DD/SP/1678/19	Children of Annis
4471	Florence MILES, Widow of Combe Florey	1640	DD/SP/1640/143	
4472	William MILES of Heathfield	1667	DD/SP/1667/69	
4473	William MILES of Taunton St. Mary Magdalene	1676	DD/SP/1676/39	Mentions shop contents
4474	David MILL, Esquire of Bath	1806	T.N.A., PROB 37/107	
4475	David MILL, Esquire of Bath	1807	T.N.A., PROB 31/1807/463	
4476	Ambrose MILLARD of Chewton Mendip	1622	D/D/cta/M32	Ad.ac.
4477	Hannah MILLARD of East Brent	1701	D/D/cta/M37	Ad.ac.
4478	Henry MILLARD of Compton Martin	1611	D/D/cta/M33	Ad.ac.
4479	Joan MILLARD of Compton Martin	1619	D/D/cta/M38	Ad.ac.
4480	Philip MILLARD of Bawdrip	1640	D/D/cta/M28	Ad.ac.
4481	Richard MILLARD, Miller of Compton Martin	1621	D/D/cta/M5	Ad.ac.
4482	William MILLARD, Innholder of Wells St. Cuthbert	1644	D/D/cta/M30	Ad.ac.
4483	Jane MILLER of Cheddon Fitzpaine	1710	DD/SP/1710/1	Probate, relict of William
4484	John MILLER of Crewkerne	1642	D/D/cta/M24	Ad.ac.
4485	Edward MILLERD of Barwick	1621	D/D/cta/M1	Ad.ac.
4486	John MILLES of Spaxton	1670	DD/SP/1670/19	

MILLES see MYLLS and MILLS				
4487	Christopher MILLS of Trull	1673	DD/SP/1673/32	
4488	Elizabeth MILLS of Bridgwater	1675	DD/SP/1675/88	
4489	Francis MILLS, Husbandman of Oake	1645	DD/SP/1645/36	
4490	George MILLS of Stogumber	1672	DD/SP/1672/17	
4491	John MILLS of Watchet, St. Decumans	1686	T.N.A., PROB 4/9526	Will also extant
4492	John MILLS of Durleigh	1694	DD/SP/1694/12	
4493	Joseph MILLS of Pitminster	1685	DD/SP/1685/109	
4494	Robert MILLS, Carpenter of Isle Brewers	1646	DD/SP/1646/61	
4495	Robert MILLS of Halse	1668	DD/SP/1668/60	
MILLS see MYLLS and MILLES				
4496	John MILLSHAM of Backwell	1619	D/D/cta/M31	Ad.ac.
4497	William MILMAN, Yeoman of Dillington, Ilminster	1695	T.N.A., PROB 5/2008	Will T.N.A., PROB 11/442, Sentence
4498	[missing] MILTON of Milverton ?	1638	DD/SP/1638/1	
	Note: Appraised by Peter MILTON, Natural Brother and Hercules COOK; damaged (*P.R.*)			
4499	Francis MILTON, Yeoman of Exton	1670	T.N.A., PROB 4/8561	Will also extant
4500	Grace MILTON, Spinster of Brompton Regis	1648	DD/SP/1648/43	
4501	Joane MILTON, Spinster of Brompton Regis	1642	DD/SP/1642/7	
4502	John MILTON, Husbandman of Brushford	1682	DD/SP/1682/4	
4503	John MILTON junior of Brushford	1673	DD/SP/1673/41	
4504	Justinian MILTON, Weaver of Milverton	1645	DD/SP/1645/62	
4505	Justinian MILTON junior of Milverton	1689	DD/SP/1689/43	
4506	Richard MILTON of Preston Bowyer, Milverton	1671	DD/SP/1671/2	
4507	Thomas MILTON of Upton	1682	DD/SP/1682/10	
4508	William MILTON of Brompton Regis	1639	DD/SP/1639/55	
4509	James MILVERTON, Miller of Winsham	1725	T.N.A., PROB 3/24/149	
4510	Humphry MINIVEE, Mercer of Crewkerne	1687	T.N.A., PROB 4/11895	Will. ex. 1688
4511	William MINSON, Tailor of Ilminster	1695	T.N.A., PROB 4/5888	Admon. ex. 1697
4512	[missing] MITCHELL of Dulverton	1694	DD/SP/1694/21	
4513	Francis MITCHELL, Husbandman of Little Puckington, Barrington	1678	DD/SP/1678/39	
4514	Francis MITCHELL of Ilminster	1737	T.N.A., PROB 3/36/46	Buried at Ilminster in 1735
4515	John MITCHELL of Lydeard St. Lawrence	1642	DD/SP/1642/41	

4516	John MITCHELL of Carhampton	1669	T.N.A., PROB 4/21928	Will 1670
4517	Martha MITCHELL, Widow of Dunster	1670	DD/SP/1670/10	
4518	Mary MITCHELL of Lyng	1696	D/D/cta/M19	Ad.ac.
4519	Stephen and Alice (wife) MITCHELL of Stocklinch Ottersey	1670	DD/SP/1670/45	
4520	Thomas MITCHELL junior of Merriott	1664	DD/SP/1664/49	
4521	Robert MOCKRIDGE of Thornfalcon	1681	DD/SP/1681/46	
4522	John MOFFAT of Ashbrittle	1716	DD/SP/1716/36	
4523	John MOGER, White yarn washer of Hewish, Crewkerne	1691	DD/SP/1691/52	
4524	Catherine MOGFORD, Widow of Minehead	1670	DD/SP/1670/66	
4525	Elizabeth MOGG, Widow of Chelwell, Cameley	1745	T.N.A., PROB 3/44/61	
4526	John MOGG of Shepton Montague	1645	D/D/ct/1/M62	
4527	Richard MOGG of Cameley	1740	D/D/Cti 57	
4528	William MOGG of Shepton Montague	1721	T.N.A., PROB 3/20/255	
4529	Barnabee MOGGRIDGE of Taunton St. James	1664	DD/SP/1664/12	
4530	Elizabeth MOGGRIDGE, Widow of Ashbrittle	1642	DD/SP/1642/8	
4531	Joan MOGGRIDGE, Widow of Sherston, North Petherton	1716	DD/SP/1716/59	
4532	Stephen MOGGRIDGE of [no place]	1680	DD/SP/1680/29	
4533	[missing] MOGGRIDGE ? of [no place]	1646	DD/SP/1646/28	
	Note: Female's inv. appraised by Edmund CANNYCOTT, Robert TRUMPE, Bartholomew SPILLER and John MOORE; Oliver MOGGRIDGE executor; damaged			
4534	Mary MOGRIDGE, Widow of Thornfalcon	1637	DD/SP/1637/37	
4535	Thomas MOGRIDGE, Innholder of Bridgwater	1680	DD/SP/1680/39	
4536	John MOHUN, Gentleman of South Petherton	1676	T.N.A., PROB 4/17069	Will also extant
4537	John MOLINS, Esquire of Charlton Horethorne	1743	T.N.A., PROB 31/1743/322	
4538	John MONTAGUE, Clerk of North Wootton?	1686	T.N.A., PROB 4/6891	Admon. ex. 1687
4539	George MOODY of Bath	1821	T.N.A., PROB 31/1821/556	
4540	William MOODY, Gentleman of Yatton	1674	T.N.A., PROB 4/17339	Will. ex. 1675
4541	Richard MOON, Innholder of Bedminster	1732	T.N.A., PROB 31/1732/511	With ad.ac.
4542	John MOONE of Middlezoy	1580/1	D/D/ct/1/M63	
4543	Marie MOONE, Singlewoman of Abbots Leigh and Tewkesbury, Gloucestershire	1611	B.A., 1611/56	
4544	Thomas MOONE of Charlton Mackrell	1588	D/D/cta/M15	Ad.ac.
4545	Andrew MOORE, Esquire of North Petherton	1746	T.N.A., PROB 31/1746/274	With ad.ac.

4546	Dorothy MOORE of Stogumber	1678	DD/SP/1678/2	
4547	Edmund MOORE of Isle Brewers	1648	DD/SP/1648/34	
4548	Henry MOORE of Bath	1667	D/D/cta/M27	Ad.ac.
4549	James MOORE of Sampford Brett	1664	DD/SP/1664/81	
4550	James MOORE, Clothier of Croscombe	1689	T.N.A., PROB 4/17982	Will also extant
4551	John MOORE of Curry Rivel	1671	DD/SP/1671/50	
4552	Mary MOORE, Widow of Milverton	1636	DD/SP/1636/58	
4553	Philip MOORE of [no place]	1719/20	DD/SF/15/2/35	Formerly DD/SF/3888
4554	Richard MOORE of Burnham on Sea	1677	D/D/cta/W33	Ad.ac.
4555	Robert MOORE, Esquire of Keynsham	1756	T.N.A., PROB 31/1756/438 and 1738/441	
4556	Thomas MOORE, Bachelor of West Coker	1680	T.N.A., PROB 4/6949	Admon
4557	Thomas MOORE, Clothier of Croscombe	1709	D/D/cta/M21	Ad.ac.
4558	Thomas MOORE of Chard	1736	D/D/Cti 59	
4559	Thomas MOORE senior, Husbandman of Caphays, Folke, Dorset, formerly of Holwell, Somerset	1728	W.S.H.C., P5/1728/75	Inv. and will
4560	Walter MOORE, Clothier of St. Decumans	1670	T.N.A., PROB 4/8462	Will also extant
4561	William MOORE, Joiner of Stogumber	1675	DD/SP/1675/66	
MOORE see COLLETT, MORSE				
4562	Robert MOOREMAN, Clerk of North Petherton	1681	DD/SP/1681/60	Late vicar
4563	John MORE of [no place]	1650	DD/SP/1650/3	
4564	Richard MORE, Weaver of Milverton	1689	DD/SP/1689/1	
4565	Thomas MORE, Husbandman of Brent Knoll	1584	D/D/cta/M44	Ad.ac.
4566	Mary MORELL of Moorlinch	1681	D/D/ct/1/M70	
4567	Henry MORETON, Gentleman of Kilton	1669	DD/SP/1669/48	
4568	Stephen MOREY alias WILLS of Otterford	1677	DD/SP/1677/74	
4569	Charles MORGAN, Coffeeman of Bath	1772	T.N.A., PROB 31/1772/157	
4570	Christopher MORGAN, Clothier of East Harptree	1619	D/D/ct/1/M72	
4571	Edward MORGAN of Milton Clevedon	1623	D/D/cta/M9	Ad.ac.
4572	Elizabeth MORGAN, Widow of Moorland, North Petherton	1672	DD/SP/1672/59	
4573	Eran MORGAN of Porlock	1695	DD/SP/1695/40	
4574	Gabriel MORGAN, Baker of Frome Selwood	1681	T.N.A., PROB 4/18957	Will 1681
4575	James MORGAN, Esquire of Pulteney Street, Bath	1811	T.N.A., PROB 37/127	Died at Kensington Gore

4576	John MORGAN of Stogursey	1672	DD/SP/1672/9	
4577	John MORGAN, Husbandman of Misterton	1683	DD/SP/1683/14	
4578	John MORGAN of Stogumber	1716	DD/SP/1716/4	
4579	Thomas MORGAN of Failand, Wraxall	1567	L.P.L., CM III/6	
4579a	Thomas MORGAN of Easton in Gordano	1726	T.N.A., PROB 31/1724/64 and 1724/65	
4580	William MORGAN, Gentleman of Wells	1674	T.N.A., PROB 4/10469	Will. ex. 1675
4581	William MORGAN, Mariner of Porlock	1714	DD/SP/1714/7	
MORGAN see AP MORGAN				
4582	Robert MORKERED, Joiner of Creech St. Michael	1707	DD/SP/1707/40	
4583	Henry MORLEY of Beercrocombe	1680	DD/SP/1680/66	
4584	Henry MORLEY of North Petherton	1682	DD/SP/1682/58	
4585	Roger MORLEY of Beercrocombe	1635	DD/SP/1635/50	
4586	Robert MORREN the elder, Yeoman of Knowle (*sic*)	1693	T.N.A., PROB 4/6914	Admon
4587	George MORRICE, Linen draper of Axbridge	1612	D/D/cta/M12	Ad.ac.
4588	Harry MORRICE of Clevedon	1591	D/D/cta/M45	Ad.ac.
4589	Edward MORRIS, Tailor of South Petherton	1685	DD/SP/1685/27	
4590	Elizabeth MORRIS, Widow of Bouden (*sic*)	1678	T.N.A., PROB 4/18079	Will 1679. ex. 1679
4591	Ellis MORRIS, Widow of South Petherton	1679	DD/SP/1679/15	
4592	Jane MORRIS of Milverton	1685	DD/SP/1685/76	
4593	Joan MORRIS, Spinster of Queen Camel	1621	D/D/cta/M13	Ad.ac.
4594	John MORRIS of Portishead	1644	D/D/cta/M35	Ad.ac.
4595	John MORRIS of South Petherton	1684	DD/SP/1684/124	
4596	John MORRIS of [no place]	1720	DD/SF/15/2/35	Formerly DD/SF/3888
4597	John MORRIS of 8 Bladud Buildings, Bath	1814	D/T/ba/50	Also possessions in Box, Wiltshire
4598	Robert MORRIS of Enmore	1664	DD/SP/1664/53	
4599	Robert MORRIS, Yeoman of Abbas Combe, Abbas and Temple Combe	1674	T.N.A., PROB 5/2002	
4600	Robert MORRIS, Fellmonger of North Petherton	1731	DD/SP/1731/29	
4601	William MORRISH of Goathurst	1713	DD/SP/1713/9	
4602	Thomas MORS of Porlock	1682	T.N.A., PROB 4/20438	Will. ex. 1683
4603	John MORSE, Husbandman of North Petherton	1640	DD/SP/1640/1	
4604	John MORSE of Bridgwater	1680	DD/SP/1680/18	

4605	Richard and Mary MORSE of Taunton St. James	1676	DD/SP/1676/11a+b	Notice withdrawing caveat
4606	William MORSE of South Brent	1620	D/D/cta/M4	Ad.ac.
4607	William MORSE alias MOORE, Maltster of Porlock	1684	T.N.A., PROB 4/6951	Will. ex. 1685
4608	John MORTIMER, Clothier of Beckington	1751	T.N.A., PROB 3/50/12	
4609	Richard MOSRUM, Husbandman of North Petherton	1665	DD/SP/1665/58	
4610	Jane MOSS, Widow of Beckington and Wingfield, Wiltshire	1738	W.S.H.C., P1/M/532	Inv. and will
4611	William MOUCHER of Hinton St. George	1737	DD/SP/1737/36	
4612	John MOULTON, Gentleman of Yarnfield, Maiden Bradley	1728	W.S.H.C., P2/M/952	Inv. and will
4613	John MOULTON, Widower of Nempnett Thrubwell	1840	T.N.A., PROB 31/1840/833	
4614	Joseph MOULTON of Yarnfield, Maiden Bradley	1691	W.S.H.C., P2/M/706	Inv. and will
4615	John MOUNTSHER, Innholder? of Bridgwater	1729	DD/SP/1729/61	
4616	John MOUNTSTEPHEN of Dunster	1799	T.N.A., PROB 31/1799/867	
4617	George MOUNTSTEVEN of Corfe	1687	DD/SP/1687/36	
4618	Jane MOUNTSTEVEN of Chedzoy	1680	DD/SP/1680/74	
4619	John MOUNTSTEVEN of Pitminster	1683	DD/SP/1683/76	
4620	Robert MOXHAM, Yeoman of Norton St. Philip	1721	T.N.A., PROB 3/20/1	
4621	Anthony MUDFORD the elder, Butcher of Thurlbear	1648	DD/SP/1648/50	
4622	Joan MUDFORD, Widow of Orchard Portman	1713	DD/SP/1713/15	
4623	Stephen MUDFORD, Husbandman of Stogursey	1690	DD/SP/1690/54	
4624	William MUDFORD of Merriott	1557	T.N.A., PROB 2/732	Will T.N.A., PROB 11/40/104
4625	James MULGROVE of Norton St. Philip	1588	D/D/cta/M42	Ad.ac.
4626	Laurence MULLENS of West Bagborough	1643	DD/SP/1643/44	
4627	John MULLFORD of Burnham on Sea	1642	D/D/cta/M29	Ad.ac.
4628	John MULLINGS senior of Cannington	1645	DD/SP/1645/28	
4629	Edmund MUNDAY of Durston	1693	DD/SP/1693/23	
4630	Edmund MUNDAY of Durston	1694	DD/SP/1694/23	
MUNDAY see CHEEKE				
4631	John MURFORD of Batheaston	1693	T.N.A., PROB 4/17366	Admon
4632	Hugh MURLY of Spaxton	1698	DD/SP/1698/43	
4633	Richard MURTON of Taunton St. James	1733	DD/SP/1733/16	
4634	Bartholomew MUSGRAVE of Bridgwater	1665	DD/SP/1665/24	
4635	Henry MUSGRAVE, Husbandman of North Petherton	1688	DD/SP/1688/9	
4636	John MUSGRAVE, Grocer of Taunton St. Mary Magdalene	1683	DD/SP/1683/73	

4637	Lawrence MUSGRAVE of Taunton St. Mary Magdalene	1680	DD/SP/1680/76	
4638	Mary MUSGRAVE, Spinster of Norton Fitzwarren	1672	DD/SP/1672/28	
4639	Mary MUSGRAVE, Widow of Stone, Exford	1784	T.N.A., PROB 31/1784/591	
4640	Thomas MUSGRAVE, Yeoman of Kingston St. Mary	1726	DD/SP/1726/25	
4641	Laurence MUSGROVE, Minister of Taunton St. James	1681	DD/SP/1681/50	
4642	Simon MUSGROVE, Worsted Comber of Creech St. Michael	1684	DD/SP/1684/82	
4643	Thomas MUSGROVE of Swell	1689	DD/SP/1689/34	
4644	George MUXFORD, Husbandman of Lydeard St. Lawrence	1674	DD/SP/1674/11	
4645	Hester MUXFORD of Lydeard St. Lawrence	1713	DD/SP/1713/13	
4646	Hester MUXFORD of Lydeard St. Lawrence	1713	DD/SP/442/8	Ad.ac.
4647	William MUXFORD, Husbandman of Lydeard St. Lawrence	1665	DD/SP/1665/29	
4648	William MUXFORD of Glastonbury St. Benedict	1733	B.A.L., Warner collection	
MYCHELL see HADDON				
4649	Joane MYLLS of Charlinch	1637	DD/SP/1637/32	
MYLLS see MILLS and MILLES				
4650	John NAISH, Grocer of Compton Martin	1683	T.N.A., PROB 5/3273	
4651	Joseph NAISH of Frome Selwood	1738	D/D/Cti 63	
4652	Madalen NAPPER of [no place]	1686	DD/SP/1686/28	
4653	Alice NASH of Abbots Leigh	1611	B.A., 1611/58	
4654	James NASH of Greinton	1747	T.N.A., PROB 31/1747/815	With ad.ac.
4655	John NASH of Burrington	1631	D/D/cta/N8	Ad.ac.
4656	Susanne NASH, Widow of Wells	1812	DD/WM/39	
4657	Francis NASHION, Husbandman of Kingston	1640	DD/SP/1640/114	
4658	Joan NATCOTT of Elworthy	1689	DD/SP/1689/44	
4659	Ann NATION of Cannington	1698	DD/SP/1698/14	
4660	Catherine NATION of Cannington	1678	D/D/cta/N11	Ad.ac.
4661	Christopher NATION, Cooper of Corfe	1688	DD/SP/1688/48	
4662	Christopher and Grace (his wife) NATION of Halse	1681	DD/SP/1681/56	
4663	Henry NATION, Tailor of Ash Priors	1680	DD/SP/1680/104	
4664	Thomasina NAYLE, Widow of Cothelstone	1675	DD/SP/1675/2	
4665	Francis NAYLER of Bridgwater	1683	DD/SP/1683/65	
4666	John NAYLER of Bridgwater	1691	DD/SP/1691/95	
4667	Alexander NEALE, Shoemaker of [no place]	1687	DD/SP/1687/27	

4668	Margery NEAT, Widow of Bath	1669	T.N.A., PROB 4/15441	Will 1669. ex. 1669
4669	John NEATHWAY, Husbandman of Clevedon	1591	D/D/cta/N12	Ad.ac.
4670	David NEEDES of Congresbury	1611	D/D/cta/N1	Ad.ac.
4671	Robert NELMES of Ham Green, Portbury	1609	B.A., 1609/56	
4672	Thomas NELMES of Portbury	1609	B.A., 1609/55	
4673	Margerie NETHERCOTT, Widow of Wembdon	1635	DD/SP/1635/41	
4674	William NETHERCOTT, Husbandman of Winsford	1685	DD/SP/1685/68	
4675	Peter NETHEY, Mariner of Brean	1823	D/B/AX/22.1–6	
4676	Alice NETHWAIE of Portbury	1594	D/D/cta/N13	Ad.ac.
4677	Christopher NETHWAIE of Bleadon	1625	D/D/cta/N4	Ad.ac.
4678	John NETHWAIE of Bleadon	1640	D/D/cta/N14	Ad.ac.
4679	[missing] NEW, Husbandman of Hamp, Bridgwater	1668	DD/SP/1668/64	
4680	John NEW, Innholder of Taunton St. Mary Magdalene	1681	DD/SP/1681/110	
4681	Joseph NEWBERRY of Ilchester	1686	T.N.A., PROB 4/21953	Admon, intestate
4682	Joseph NEWBERRY of Ilchester	1686	T.N.A., PROB 4/8564	Admon
4683	Robert NEWBERRY, Gentleman of Chard Borough	1740	T.N.A., PROB 3/39/3	Mentions books
4684	Robert NEWBERRY, Gentleman of Chard	1740	T.N.A., PROB 31/1740/50	
4685	Thomas NEWBERRY, Gentleman of Chard Borough and Town	1718	T.N.A., PROB 3/17/10	
4686	William NEWBERRY, Husbandman of Creech St. Michael	1666	DD/SP/1666/48	
4687	John NEWBERY of Wambrook	1589	W.S.H.C., P5/1588/44	Inv. and will
4688	Grace NEWBOROUGH of West Monkton	1720	DD/SP/1720/11	
4689	Roger NEWBOROUGH, Esquire of Berkley	1680	T.N.A., PROB 4/4649	Will 1680. ex. 1681
4690	Jeremiah NEWBROUGH, Yeoman of Creech St. Michael	1688	DD/SP/1688/47	
4691	Jerard NEWCOURT of Ivythorne, Street	1705	T.N.A., PROB 5/4961	
4692	William NEWLAND of Long Ashton	1620	D/D/cta/N2	Ad.ac.
4693	[missing] NEWMAN of North Cadbury	1781	W.S.H.C., 754/164	Inv. of household plate
4694	George NEWMAN, Gentleman of Charlton Musgrove	1681	T.N.A., PROB 4/8666	Will also extant
4695	James NEWMAN, Tobacconist of Bridgwater	1694	DD/SP/1694/18	
4696	John NEWMAN, Clerk of Compton Dando	1664	D/D/ct/1/N13	
4697	John NEWMAN, Husbandman of Curry Rivel	1669	DD/SP/1669/33	
4698	Richard NEWMAN of Evercreech Park, Evercreech and City of Westminster	1682	T.N.A., PROB 4/16795	Will. ex. 1683
4699	Thomas NEWMAN of Curry Rivel	1646	DD/SP/1646/4	

4700	William NEWMAN of Chewton Mendip	1683	T.N.A., PROB 4/5912	Will also extant
4701	William NEWMAN of Chewton Mendip	1690	T.N.A., PROB 5/5663	
4702	Richard NEWPORT alias PEARCE, Blacksmith of Sparkford	1625	D/D/cta/N3	Ad.ac.
4703	[missing] NEWTON of Milverton	1679	DD/SP/1679/59	Part only
4704	Joshua NEWTON of Charlton Mackrell	1720	DD/SF/15/2/35	Formerly DD/SF/3888
4705	Richard NEWTON, Yeoman of Taunton St. James	1700	DD/SP/1700/28	
4706	Thomas NEWTON of Yatton	1496	T.N.A., PROB 2/111	
4707	William NEWTON of Milverton	1676	DD/SP/1676/30	
4708	Robert NICCOLLS of Enmore	1635	DD/SP/1635/104	
4709	[missing] NICHOLAS of [no place]	1666	DD/SP/1666/26	
4710	Mrs Athaliah NICHOLAS of Taunton	1684	T.N.A., PROB 4/6885	Will. ex. 1685
4711	John NICHOLAS of Lyng	1684	DD/SP/1684/77	
4712	John NICHOLAS of Middle Elliscombe, Dunster	1746	DD/SP/1746/31	
4713	Dorothy NICHOLLS, Widow of Clapton, Cucklington	1685	T.N.A., PROB 4/2793	Admon
4714	Elizabeth NICHOLLS, Widow of Newman Street, Doulting	1677	T.N.A., PROB 4/19804	Will, relict and executrix of John NICHOLLS
4715	George NICHOLLS, Yeoman? of Catterton?	1680	T.N.A., PROB 4/7507	Will 1681. ex. 1681
4716	Thomas NICHOLLS, Gentleman of Clapton, Cucklington	1677	T.N.A., PROB 4/20039	Will 1677. ex. 1678
4717	Thomas NICHOLLS, Gentleman of Glastonbury	1735	T.N.A., PROB 31/1735/339	With ad.ac.
4718	John NICKLES of Pensford St. Thomas, Publow	1634	D/D/ct/1/N18	
4719	Wilmoth NICOLLS, Widow of Dulverton	1669	DD/SP/1669/47	
4720	Nicholas NICOLS of Cannington	1634	DD/SP/1634/32	See *T.C.W.*
4721	Mary Charlotte NICOLSON, Spinster of Axbridge formerly of Weston	1828	T.N.A., PROB 31/1828/1085	
4722	John NIX of Wells	1730	D/D/Cti 62	
4723	Number not used			
4724	Alce [missing] of West Bagborough	1638	DD/SP/1638/61	
4725	Alice NOARTH, Spinster of West Bagborough	1638	DD/SP/1638/70	Damaged; formerly DD/SP/1658/12
4726	John NORCOMBE, Singleman of Carhampton	1583	T.N.A., PROB 2/782	Will T.N.A., PROB 11/65/299
4727	Giles NORCROSSE of Rode	1611	D/D/cta/N10	Ad.ac.
4728	Anne NORMAN, Widow of Fiddington	1669	DD/SP/1669/81	
4729	Elizabeth NORMAN, Widow of Bridgwater	1689	DD/SP/1689/22	
4730	Gregory NORMAN of Cutcombe	1680	DD/SP/1680/73	

4731	James NORMAN of Watchet, St. Decumans	1748	DD/WO/36/4	
4732	John NORMAN of Ashbrittle	1645	DD/SP/1645/37	
4733	John NORMAN of Fiddington	1683	DD/SP/1683/18	
4734	John NORMAN of Winsford	1688	DD/SP/1688/12	
4735	John NORMAN, Husbandman of Dulverton	1697	DD/SP/1697/24	
4736	Mary NORMAN, Widow of Bridgwater	1680	DD/SP/1680/44	
4737	Robert NORMAN of Wellington	1615	D/D/ct/1/N24	
4738	Thomas NORMAN of Winsford	1635	DD/SP/1635/51	
4739	Thomas NORMAN, Yeoman of Wambrook	1672	W.S.H.C., P14/43	Inv. and will
4740	William NORMAN, Yeoman of Ashbrittle	1716	DD/SP/1716/19	
4741	[Male?] NORRIS of [no place]	1675	DD/SP/1675/28	
4742	George NORRIS, Potter of Donyatt	1684	DD/SP/1684/153	
4743	Giles NORRIS, Yeoman of Wayford	1717	DD/SP/1717/2	
4744	Hugh NORRIS of Wayford	1672	D/D/cta/N7	Ad.ac.
4745	Hugh NORRIS of St. Decumans	1676	T.N.A., PROB 4/2760	Admon. ex. 1678
4746	John NORRIS, Clothier ? of Frome	1676	T.N.A., PROB 4/17679	Admon
4747	Samuel NORRIS, Yeoman of Wayford	1717	DD/SP/1717/3–4	
4748	Edward NORTH of Chaffcombe	1640	DD/SP/1640/30	
4749	Edward NORTON of [no place]	n.d.	D/D/cta/N5	Ad.ac.
4750	Simon NORTON, Yeoman of Bicknoller	1588	D/D/cta/N9	Ad.ac.
4751	William NORTON of London	1594	DD/SAS/(A)/PD/81	
4752	William NORVALL, Yeoman of Churchill	1675	T.N.A., PROB 4/6944	Will also extant
4753	William NORVALL, Yeoman of Churchill	1676	T.N.A., PROB 4/8998	
	Note: Will 1675. Mentions Mary NORVALL, his widow, deceased.			
4754	James NOSSE of Heathfield	1687	DD/SP/1687/53	
4755	James NOSSE of Heathfield	1696	DD/SP/1696/34	
4756	Joan NOSSE of North Petherton	1621	D/D/cta/N6	Ad.ac.
4757	Joane NOSSE of [no place]	1581	D/D/ct/1/N30	Pvd 1581
4758	John NOSSE of Stawell, Moorlinch	1581	D/D/ct/1/N31	
4759	John NOSSE of Milverton	1646	DD/SP/1646/11	See will in DD/SP 106
4760	John NOSSE the elder of Heathfield	1681	DD/SP/1681/112	
4761	Robert NOSSE of Heathfield	1635	DD/SP/1635/2	
4762	William NOSSE of Buckland St. Mary	1637	DD/SP/1637/63	

4763	Roger NOSURNAME of Brockley	1587	D/D/cta/C28	Ad.ac.
4764	Grace NOTLEY of Chard	1733	D/D/Cti 61	
4765	Dorothy NOTT of Ashbrittle	1681	DD/SP/1681/18	
4766	Alexander NOWELL of Thurloxton	1666	DD/SP/1666/51	
4767	Mary, Ann, Joane, Alexander and Thomas NOWELL of [no place]	1684	DD/SP/1684/66	Children of Alexander senior
4768	Thomas NOWELL, Maltster of Thurloxton	1695	DD/SP/1695/30	
4769	Alice NUMAN, Widow of Bridgwater	1647	DD/SP/1647/18	
4770	John NUNNY of North Petherton	1700	DD/SP/1700/12	
4771	John NURCOMBE of Porlock	1646	DD/SP/1646/30	
4772	Nicholas NURCOMBE, Yeoman of Treborough	1685	DD/SP/1685/31	
4773	Alexander NURTON, Yeoman of Curry Rivel	1684	DD/SP/1684/96	
4774	Philip NURTON, Widow of Fivehead	1641	DD/SP/1641/49	
4775	Walter NURTON of Wrantage, North Curry	1589	D/D/ct/1/N35a	
4776	William NURTON of North Curry	1590	D/D/ct/1/N36	
4777	William NURTON of Ruishton	1691	DD/SP/1691/10	
4778	John NUTT, Clothier of Frome Selwood	1727	T.N.A., PROB 3/26/34	
4779	William NUTT of Creech St. Michael	1716	DD/SP/1716/6	
4780	John OAKE of Taunton St. Mary Magdalene	1685	DD/SP/1685/18	
4781	John OAKE of Bridgwater	1730	DD/SP/1730/10	
4782	Richard OARAM of Castle Cary	1630	D/D/cta/O4	Ad.ac.
4783	Hugh OARE, Yeoman of Buckland St. Mary	1646	DD/SP/1646/33	
4784	Joan ODIELL, Widow of Hinton St. George	1692	DD/SP/1692/31	
4785	William ODREY of Bridgwater	1664	DD/SP/1664/69	
4786	John OLAND of Blagdon	1630	D/D/cta/O1	Ad.ac.
4787	John OLAND of Blagdon	1630	D/D/cta/O2	Ad.ac.
4788	William OLAND, Yeoman of Stogursey	1739	DD/SP/1739/49	
4789	Edward OLD of Dinnington	1662?	DD/SP/1632/34	Undated; *T.C.W.*
4790	Johane OLD, Widow of Dinnington	1635	DD/SP/1635/21	
4791	William OLDINGE of Bagbury, Evercreech	1610	D/D/ct/1/O42	
4792	John OLDIS, Brassworker of Keynsham	1728	B.A., 1728/31	
4793	Cicilie OLDMAN, Widow of Crowcombe	1639	DD/SP/1639/37	
4794	Robert OLDMAN of West Bagborough	1685	DD/SP/1685/50	
4795	Thomas OLDMAN of West Bagborough	1695	DD/SP/1695/41	

4796	William OLDMAN, Husbandman of Crowcombe	1635	DD/SP/1635/125	
4797	John OLDMIXON of Oldmixon, Hutton and Bleadon	1679	T.N.A., PROB 4/6898	Will also extant
4798	Sarah OLDMIXON, Widow of Bridgwater	1689	DD/SP/1689/41	
4799	Edward OLFERD, Husbandman of Hambridge, Curry Rivel	1634	DD/SP/1634/15	
4800	Robert OLFORD, Hosier of Crewkerne	1664	DD/SP/1664/15	
4801	Roger OLFORD, Husbandman of Crewkerne	1692	DD/SP/1692/24	
4802	William OLFORD, Husbandman of Isle Abbotts	1664	DD/SP/1664/17	
4803	Elizabeth OLIFFE of Whitchurch	1664	D/D/cta/O5	Ad.ac.
4804	John OLIVER of Enmore	1672	DD/SP/1672/45	
4805	William ORAM of Baltonsborough	1596	D/D/cta/O7	Ad.ac.
4806	William ORAM of Cossington	1683	D/D/cta/O3	Ad.ac.
4807	George ORMSBY, Esquire of Bath formerly of Tobervaddy, Roscommon, Ireland	1813	T.N.A., PROB 31/1813/370	
4808	Roger OSBORNE, Dyer of Crewkerne	1644	DD/SP/1644/61	See *T.C.W.*
4809	Stephen OSBORNE, Sergemaker of Taunton St. James	1681	DD/SP/1681/72	
4810	Thomas OSLER of Curry Rivel	1680	DD/SP/1680/6	
4811	John OSMAN of North Petherton	1695	DD/SP/1695/39	
4812	Grace OSMOND, Widow of Otterford	1706	DD/SAS/C77/29	
4813	James OSMOND of Otterford	1684	T.N.A., PROB 4/8599	Will. ex. 1685
4814	Thomas OSMOND the elder of Stogumber	1680	DD/SP/1680/75	
4815	Martin OSMUND of Othery	1593	D/D/cta/O6	Ad.ac.
4816	Samuel OSTLER of Rydon, South Petherton	1783	T.N.A., PROB 31/1783/688	
4817	William OSTLER of South Petherton	1787	T.N.A., PROB 31/1787/537	With ad.ac.
4818	Alice OTHERY of Bridgwater	1674	DD/SP/1674/67	
4819	Androwes OVERTON of Queen Camel	1740	D/D/Cti 64	
4820	[missing] OWEN of [no place]	1638	DD/SP/1638/8	Anstice OWEN executrix; damaged
4821	David OWEN, Yeoman of Abbots Leigh	1728	B.A., 1729/28	Will also extant
4822	John OWEN of Milverton	1679	DD/SP/1679/37	
4823	Jonathan OWEN alias WOWEN of Bath	1726	T.N.A., PROB 31/1726/371 and 1726/372 and 1726/375	
4824	Andrew OWSLEY of Curry Rivel	1666	DD/SP/1666/28	
4825	Thomas PADDEN of Stringston	1716	DD/SP/1716/21	
4826	John PADDOCK of Othery	1725	D/D/cta/P29	Ad.ac. and inv.

4827	...... PADDON of Spaxton	1629	D/D/ct/1/P2	
4828	John PADDON the elder, Mason of Crowcombe	1640	DD/SP/1640/79	
4829	Mary PADDON of Cannington	1822	D/P/can/13/10/2	
4830	Leonard PAGE, Mariner of Bridgwater	1687	DD/SP/1687/23	
4831	Richard PAGE of Cannington	1687	DD/SP/1687/41	
4832	William PAGE, Grocer of Bridgwater	1672	T.N.A., PROB 4/5950	Admon
4833	John PAIN alias PAINE of Bridgwater	1805	T.N.A., PROB 31/1805/962	
4834	John PAINE of Taunton St. James	1664	DD/SP/1664/64	
4835	Richard PAINE of Westonzoyland	1620	D/D/cta/P11	Ad.ac.
4836	Sarah PAINE of Yarley, Wookey	1677	T.N.A., PROB 4/19584	Will also extant
PAINE see PAIN				
4837	John PAINTER of Old Cleeve	1783	T.N.A., PROB 31/1783/142	With ad.ac.
PAINTER see REYNEY				
4838	[Female] PALFREY of [no place]	1694	DD/SP/1694/35	Part missing
4839	Agnes PALFREY of Wambrook	1677	W.S.H.C., P14/44	Inv.
4840	John PALFREY of Wambrook	1673	W.S.H.C., P14/36	Admon. bond, inv.
4841	Simon PALFREY of Milverton	1634	DD/SP/1634/1	
4842	William PALFREY, Gentleman of Curry Rivel	1674	DD/SP/1674/36	
4843	Bartholomew PALL of Crewkerne	1670	DD/SP/1670/14	
4844	William PALLFRIE of Langford Budville	1632	D/D/cta/P15	Ad.ac. 1639?
4845	Jeremy PALLMER of Beckington	1676	T.N.A., PROB 4/4275	Will 1676
4846	Richard PALLMER of Dunster	1637	DD/SP/1637/23	
4847	...... PALMER of Locking ?	1634/5	D/D/ct/1/P9	Pvd 1634/5
4848	Ann PALMER of North Petherton	1646	DD/SP/1646/53	
4849	Benjamin PALMER, Innholder of Taunton St. Mary Magdalene	1723	DD/SP/1723/50	
4850	Henry PALMER the elder, Miller of Crewkerne	1636	DD/SP/1636/6	
4851	Henry PALMER the elder, Miller of Misterton	1670	DD/SP/1670/106	
4852	James PALMER, Yeoman of Emborough	1735	D/D/cta/P31	Ad.ac. and inv.
4853	John PALMER of Seavington St. Mary	1620	D/D/cta/P2	Ad.ac.
4854	John PALMER, Gentleman of Taunton	1647	DD/SP/1647/14	
4855	John PALMER of [no place]	1649	DD/SP/1649/72	
4856	John PALMER, Gentleman of Bridgwater	1665	D/D/cta/P49	Ad.ac.
4857	John PALMER of Wembdon	1669	DD/SP/1669/88	

4858	John PALMER, Yeoman of Crewkerne	1672	DD/SP/1672/50	
4859	John PALMER of Stawley	1720	DD/SP/1720/16	
4860	John PALMER, Yeoman of Preston Plucknett	1813	DD/CH/133/7	
4861	Mary PALMER, Widow of Locking	1638	D/D/cta/P1	Ad.ac.
4862	Robert PALMER of Taunton St. Mary Magdalene	1695	DD/SP/1695/23	
4863	Stephen PALMER of Paulton	1796	T.N.A., PROB 31/1796/460	With com.
4864	Thomas PALMER, Yeoman of Crewkerne	1665	DD/SP/1665/51	
4865	Thomas PALMER the younger, Yeoman of Crewkerne	1681	DD/SP/1681/12	
4866	William and Mary PALMER of Taunton	1727	DD/SP/442/81	Ad.ac.
4867	William PALMER the elder, Husbandman of North Petherton	1668	DD/SP/1668/3	
4868	Colonel PALMER of Aller Farm, Aller	1724	DD/AH Box 23/14	
4869	Simon PALMER alias GRINSLADE of Milverton	1680	DD/SP/1680/93	
4874	Humphry PARFITT, Yeoman of Dean, West Cranmore	1675	T.N.A., PROB 4/6948	Will also extant
4875	Owen PARFITT, Farmer of Downhead, Doulting	1686	T.N.A., PROB 5/3225	
4876	William PARFITT, Coalminer of Chewton Keynsham, Keynsham	1735	D/D/Cti 69	
4877	Avon PARIS of Whitestaunton	1695	DD/SP/1695/11	
4878	Henry PARIS of Chedzoy	1749	DD/SP/1749/33	
4879	William PARIS, Husbandman of Hatch Beauchamp	1693	DD/SP/1693/45	
4880	John PARKE of Isle Brewers	1668	DD/SP/1668/55	
4881	Gresigan PARKER, Widow of Taunton	1639	DD/SP/1639/46	
4882	John PARKER of Catcott	n.d.	D/D/ct/1/P25	
4884	Peter PARKER of West Monkton	1671	DD/SP/1671/25	
4885	Richard PARKER of Ubley	1684	T.N.A., PROB 4/8761	Will also extant
4883	William PARKER of [no place]	1616	D/D/cta/P3	Ad.ac.
4886	William PARKER, Yeoman of Pitminster	1690	T.N.A., PROB 5/5662	
PARKER see WEBB				
4887	John PARKIN of Bristol St. Nicholas died at Swainswick	1733	T.N.A., PROB 3/32/39	
PARKINS see PERKIN				
4888	Richard PARKS of Durston	1685	DD/SP/1685/96	
4889	Mary PAROMORE of Stoke Pero	1641	DD/SP/1641/21	
4890	Mary PARRAMORE of Porlock	1725	DD/SP/1725/10	
4891	Mary PARRAMORE of Porlock	1725	DD/SP/1725/9	
4892	Thomas PARRAMORE of Minehead	1716	DD/SP/1716/20	

4893	Henry PARRAT of Nynehead	1646	DD/SP/1646/65	
4894	Joan PARRAT, Widow of Spaxton	1697	DD/SP/1697/57	
PARRAT see PERRATT				
4895	Susanna PARRE of [no place]	1693	T.N.A., PROB 4/13155	Admon. ex. 1697
4896	Peter PARRIE of Stoke St. Gregory	1596	D/D/cta/P75	Ad.ac.
4897	David PARRIS, Carpenter of West Bagborough	1684	DD/SP/1684/107	
4898	Edmond PARRIS of Chard	1782	T.N.A., PROB 31/1782/407	
4899	Elizabeth PARRIS of Hatch Beauchamp	1668	DD/SP/1668/59	
4900	Thomas PARRIS of Hatch Beauchamp	1692	DD/SP/1692/2	
4901	Johan PARRYS, Widow of Merriott	1577	D/D/ct/1/P26	Pvd 1577
4902	Thomas PARRYS, Husbandman of Merriott	1577	D/D/ct/1/P27	
4903	John PARSLY, Husbandman of Puckington	1729	DD/SP/1729/45	
4904	[Male] PARSONS of [no place]	1694	DD/SP/1694/1	Part missing
4905	Agnes PARSONS of [no place]	1699	DD/SP/442/35	Ad.ac.
4906	Agnes PARSONS of Bishops Hull	1713	DD/SP/442/11	Ad.ac.
4907	Amy PARSONS, Spinster of Beercrocombe	1640	DD/SP/1640/34	
4908	Cornelius PARSONS of Trull	1682	DD/SP/1682/49	
4909	Edmond PARSONS of Sampford Arundel	1686	T.N.A., PROB 4/4531	Admon
4910	Edward PARSONS of Treborough	1674	DD/SP/1674/8	
4911	Edward PARSONS of Thorne St. Margaret	1695	DD/SP/1695/7	
4912	George PARSONS of Durleigh	1596	D/D/cta/P58	Ad.ac.
4913	George PARSONS of North Petherton	1645	DD/SP/1645/65	Damaged
4914	George PARSONS of Trull	1682	DD/SP/1682/48	
4915	George PARSONS, Husbandman of North Petherton	1683	DD/SP/1683/102	
4916	Henry PARSONS of Langford Budville	1681	DD/SP/1681/32	
4917	Henry PARSONS, Merchant of Sampford Arundel	1698	T.N.A., PROB 4/5971	Will, also as executor of his brother John
4918	Hugh PARSONS of Abbots Leigh	1671	B.A., 1671/6	
4919	James PARSONS of Bridgwater	1837	T.N.A., PROB 31/1837/1224	
4920	John PARSONS of Tickenham	1598	D/D/cta/P77	Ad.ac.
4871	John PARSONS of [no place]	1621	D/D/cta/P6	Ad.ac.
4921	John PARSONS of Kingston	1640	DD/SP/1640/100	
4922	John PARSONS of Chedzoy	1648	DD/SP/1648/55	

4923	John PARSONS, Weaver of Langford Budville	1664	DD/SP/1664/25	
4924	John PARSONS, Yeoman of Yatton	1764	T.N.A., PROB 31/1764/906	
4925	John PARSONS the elder of Bickenhall	1640	DD/SP/1640/4	
4872	Joseph PARSONS of Middlezoy	1648	D/D/cta/P7	Ad.ac.
4926	Margaret PARSONS, Widow of Charlinch	1721	DD/SP/1721/20	
4927	Marie PARSONS, Widow of Beercrocombe	1636	DD/SP/1636/25	
4928	Mary PARSONS of Hillfarrance	1635	DD/SP/1635/25	
4929	Mary PARSONS of Trull	1682	DD/SP/1682/47	
4930	Richard PARSONS, Mariner of Abbots Leigh	1641	B.A., 1641/38	Will also extant
4870	Robert PARSONS of [no place]	1635	D/D/cta/P5	Ad.ac.
4931	Robert PARSONS of Sampford Arundel	1690	DD/SP/1690/17	
4932	Thomas PARSONS of Middlezoy	1629	D/D/ct/1/P30	Pvd 1629
4933	Thomas PARSONS of Sampford Arundel	1669	DD/SP/1669/21	
4934	Thomas PARSONS of Bishops Hull	1713	DD/SP/442/12	Ad.ac.
4935	Thomas PARSONS of Bishops Hull	1713	DD/SP/442/7	Ad.ac.
4936	Thomas PARSONS of Bridgwater	1825	T.N.A., PROB 31/1825/997	
4937	William PARSONS, Gentleman of Slowcourt, West Camel	1674	T.N.A., PROB 4/8601	Will 1677. ex. 1678
4938	William PARSONS of West Camel	1677	T.N.A., PROB 5/5519	
4873	William PARSONS of Muchelney	1736	D/D/cta/P32	Ad.ac.
4939	William PARSONS, Mason of Montacute	1766	T.N.A., PROB 31/1766/309	
4940	Elizabeth PARTRIDGE of Misterton	1692	DD/SP/1692/6	
4941	John PARTRIDGE of North Perrott	1676	T.N.A., PROB 4/3555	Admon
4942	Walter PARTRIDGE of Compton Bishop	1775	T.N.A., PROB 31/1775/684	
4943	William PASMOORE of Taunton St. Mary Magdalene	1685	DD/SP/1685/15	
4944	Walter PASMORE of Withypool	1636	DD/SP/1636/17	See *T.C.W.*
4945	Christopher PASSIVELL of Taunton St. James	1666	DD/SP/1666/59	
4946	Isabell PATCH of Lower Stratton, South Petherton	1640	DD/SP/1640/87	
4947	Charlotte Josepha PATERSON, Widow of Bath formerly of Bombay, India	1813	T.N.A., PROB 31/1813/694	
4948	James PATERSON, Esquire, Lieutenant Colonel in service of the Honourable East India Company in the Establishment at Bombay of Bath	1813	T.N.A., PROB 31/1813/895	
4949	Joane PATRICKE, Widow of Minehead	1637	DD/SP/1637/67	

4950	Edward PATTEN, Yarnworker of Crewkerne	1700	DD/SP/1700/20	
4951	John PATTEN of Crewkerne	1677	DD/SP/1677/58	
4952	Betty PAUL, Spinster of Cossington	1851	T.N.A., PROB 37/1619	
4953	George PAUL of Hatch Beauchamp	1746	DD/SP/1746/29	
4954	Robert PAUL, Clerk of East Coker	1674	D/D/cta/P33	Ad.ac.
4955	William PAUL, Clerk of Crewkerne	1737	T.N.A., PROB 3/36/57	
4956	Anna PAULE of D......	1694	DD/SP/1694/32	
4957	Roger PAULE, Potter of Donyatt	1667	DD/SP/1667/28	
4958	Thomas PAULE of Hatch Beauchamp	1696	DD/SP/1696/37	
4959	Bernard PAULL of Winsham	1677	T.N.A., PROB 4/2812	Will also extant
4960	Mathew PAULL, Yeoman of North Perrott	1685	T.N.A., PROB 4/3835A	Will also extant
4961	Richard PAULL the elder, Yeoman of Barrington	1681	DD/SP/1681/10	
4962	Thomas PAWDY of Montacute	1623	D/D/cta/P9	Ad.ac.
4963	Amos PAWLETT, Esquire of Hinton St. George	1697	T.N.A., PROB 5/5020	Com. and return
4964	Richard PAYEN of Tickenham	1634	D/D/cta/P34	Ad.ac.
4965	Ann PAYNE of Weston Bampfylde	1740	D/D/cta/P31	Ad.ac. and inv.
4966	Ben PAYNE of Cannington	1713	DD/SP/1713/14	
4967	Elizabeth PAYNE, Widow of Bridgwater	1720	DD/SP/1720/8	
4968	Hugh PAYNE, Merchant of Minehead	1723	DD/SP/1723/34	
4969	John PAYNE, Husbandman of Abbots Leigh	1611	B.A., 1611/61	Will also extant
4970	John PAYNE of Taunton St. James	1665	DD/SP/1665/7	
4971	John PAYNE, Gentleman of Huntstile, Goathurst	1674	DD/SP/1674/31	
4972	Margaret PAYNE of Truddoxhill, Nunney	1619	D/D/ct/1/P48	
4973	Samuel PAYNE of Weston Bampfylde	1762	T.N.A., PROB 31/1762/721	
PAYNE see PAINE				
4974	John PEAKE, Miller of Stogumber	1675	DD/SP/1675/23	
4975	[missing] PEARCE of [no place]	1673	DD/SP/1673/14	Incomplete entry
4976	Alies PEARCE, Spinster of Staplegrove	1649	DD/SP/1649/79	
4977	Anne PEARCE, Widow of Abbots Leigh	1681	B.A., 1681/58	Will also extant
4978	Bartholomew PEARCE of Haygrove, Bridgwater	1669	DD/SP/1669/75	
4979	Bernard PEARCE, Shoemaker? of Taunton St. Mary Magdalene	1691	DD/SP/1691/57	
4980	Christian PEARCE of Minehead	1639	DD/SP/1639/32	

4981	Christian PEARCE of West Pennard	1735	D/D/Cti 70	
4982	James PEARCE of Minehead	1697	DD/SP/1697/12	
4983	Joane PEARCE, Widow of Staplegrove	1648	DD/SP/1648/67	
4984	John PEARCE of Seavington St. Mary	1682	DD/SP/1682/35	
4985	John PEARCE of Bicknoller	1713	DD/SP/1713/24	
4986	Richard PEARCE of West Monkton	1588	D/D/cta/P26	Ad.ac.
4987	Richard PEARCE of Selworthy	1685	DD/SP/1685/36	
4988	Robert PEARCE of Rodney Stoke	1685	D/D/cta/P35	Ad.ac.
4989	Robert PEARCE, Husbandman of Stoke (*sic*)	1683/4	D/D/ct/1/P53	
4990	Roger PEARCE of Milverton	1672	DD/SP/1672/46	
4991	William PEARCE of Westonzoyland	1676	D/D/cta/P36	Ad.ac.
4992	William PEARCE of [no place]	n.d.	D/D/cta/P27	Ad.ac.
PEARCE see NEWPORT				
4993	George PEARE the younger of Minehead	1685	DD/SP/1685/83	
4994	Ellen PEARS, Widow of Wambrook	1603	W.S.H.C., P5/1603/56	Will and inv.
4995	[missing] PEARSE, Blacksmith of [no place]	1664	DD/SP/1664/82	
4996	Benjamin PEARSE of Withypool	1684	DD/SP/1684/180	
4997	Ezra PEARSE, Clerk of North Curry	1731	T.N.A., PROB 3/30/113	
4998	Francis PEARSE of Withypool	1722	DD/SP/1722/33	
4999	Francis PEARSE of Withypool	1722	DD/SP/442/76	Ad.ac.
5000	John PEARSE, Gentleman of Winsford	1697	T.N.A., PROB 4/9651	Will also extant
5001	John PEARSE of Winsford	1731	DD/SP/1731/44	
5002	Nicholas PEARSE of Dulverton	1684	DD/SP/1684/67	
5003	Peter PEARSE, Clothier of Wells	1685	T.N.A., PROB 4/2840	Will also extant
5004	Richard PEARSE, Clerk of Nynehead	1681	DD/SP/1681/17	
5005	Robert PEARSE of Winsford	1684	DD/SP/1684/81	
5006	Thamsin PEARSE of Seavington St. Michael	1687	DD/SP/1687/7	
5007	Thomas PEARSE, Husbandman of Withypool	1686	DD/SP/1686/39	
5008	William PEARSE of Bathealton	1711	DD/SP/442/3	Ad.ac.
5009	Thomas PECKE the elder of Wells St. Cuthbert	1632	D/D/cta/P23	Ad.ac.
5010	Martin PEEKE of Thorney, Muchelney	1606	D/D/cta/P64	Ad.ac.
5011	David PEIRCE, Husbandman of Clatworthy	1683	DD/SP/1683/45	
5012	John PEIRCE of Creech St. Michael	1713	DD/SP/1713/4	

5013	John PEIRCE, Husbandman of Drayton	1730	DD/SP/1730/27	
5014	Margerie PEIRCE, Widow of Crowcombe	1645	DD/SP/1645/1	
5015	Roger PEIRCE, Rector of Dinnington	1691	DD/SP/1691/53	
5016	William PEIRCE of Withypool	1696	DD/SP/1696/21	
5017	John PEIRCE alias SMITH of Isle Brewers	1689	DD/SP/1689/6	
5018	Lucy PEIRS, Spinster of Bath	1763	T.N.A., PROB 31/1763/953	
5019	William PEIRS, Archdeacon of Taunton, D.D. of Wells and of Christian Malford, Wiltshire	1682	T.N.A., PROB 4/5946	Will also extant
5020	William PEIRS, Esquire of Baltonsborough	1765	T.N.A., PROB 31/1765/148	
5021	John PEIRSE, Gentleman of Churchill	1682	T.N.A., PROB 4/5962	Admon
5022	Thomas PENNY, Esquire of Bridgwater	1733	T.N.A., PROB 3/32/104	
5023	Thomas PENROSE of Bedminster	1724	T.N.A., PROB 3/23/115	
5024	Thomas PENROSE of Bedminster	1724	T.N.A., PROB 5/3873	
5025	Humfry PEPPERHILL, Husbandman of Crowcombe	1640	DD/SP/1640/108	
5026	Ales PEREN of Spaxton	1642	DD/SP/1642/25	
5027	William PERIAM of Bishops Hull	1729	T.N.A., PROB 3/28/58	
5028	William PERIAM of Bishops Hull	1729	T.N.A., PROB 31/1729/226	
5029	Zachariah PERIAM, Esquire of Milverton	1738	T.N.A., PROB 31/1738/741	With ad.ac.
5030	Zachariah PERIAM, Esquire of Milverton	1739	T.N.A., PROB 31/1739/126	With com.
5031	Mary PERIE, Spinster of Langford Budville	1639	DD/SP/1639/38	
5032	Richard PERIOTT of Milverton	1646	DD/SP/1646/36	
5033	John PERKIN the elder, Yeoman of Isle Abbotts	1637	DD/SP/1637/29	
5034	Alice PERKINS, Widow of Isle Abbotts	1666	DD/SP/1666/21	
5035	John PERRATT of Skilgate	1709	DD/SP/442/52	Ad.ac.
5036	Luce PERRATT of Ashbrittle	1635	DD/SP/1635/58	
5037	Thomas PERRATT of Skilgate	1704	DD/SP/442/63	Ad.ac.
5038	William PERRATT of North Newton, North Petherton	1676	DD/SP/1676/8	
5039	Christian PERRET of Staplegrove	1636	DD/SP/1636/15	
5040	William PERRET, Tailor of Oake	1691	DD/SP/1691/9	
5041	Samuel PERRIAM of Langford Budville	1684	DD/SP/1684/39	
5042	Thomas PERRIAM of Bishops Hull	1678	DD/SP/1678/25	
5043	Henry PERRIE of Wrington	1608	D/D/cta/P62	Ad.ac.
5044	Thomas PERRIE of Barrington	1677	DD/SP/1677/54	

5045	Bartholomew PERRIM of Spaxton	1641	DD/SP/1641/68	See *T.C.W.*
5046	Susan PERRIN of Spaxton	1644	DD/SP/1644/55	
5047	William PERROTT, Blacksmith of Langford Budville	1640	DD/SP/1640/109	
5048	Dorothy PERRY, Widow of Yarnfield, Maiden Bradley	1639	W.S.H.C., P2/P/364	Admon. bond, inv.
5049	John PERRY, Yeoman of Wellington	1717	DD/SF/9/3/16	Formerly DD/SF/1162
5050	Mary PERRY, Widow of Sampford Arundel	1685	DD/SP/1685/95	
5051	Richard PERRY of Middlezoy	1639	D/D/cta/P25	Ad.ac.
5052	Richard PERRY of Edgarley, Glastonbury	1729	D/D/cta/P37	Ad.ac. and inv.
5053	Thomas PERRY, Sergemaker of [no place]	1706	T.N.A., PROB 4/22702	Will 1706
5054	Thomasine PERRY, Widow of Durleigh	1691	DD/SP/1691/75	
5055	John PERRYAM, Yeoman of Butleigh Wootton, Butleigh	1640	D/D/cta/P54	Ad.ac.
5056	George PESTER, Free-mason of Taunton	1674	DD/SP/1674/53	
5057	Richard PESTER of North Petherton	1680	DD/SP/1680/101	
5058	Thomas PETER of Stocklinch Magdalene	1669	T.N.A., PROB 4/5949	Admon. ex. 1670
5059	John PETERS of Wells St. Cuthbert	1588	D/D/cta/P67	Ad.ac.
5060	Thomas PETERS, Shoemaker of Wells St. Cuthbert	1622	D/D/cta/P12	Ad.ac.
5061	William PETHER the elder, Butcher of Cannington	1640	DD/SP/1640/49	
5062	Gilbert PETRIE, Esquire of Bath formerly of Tobago, West Indies	1820	T.N.A., PROB 31/1820/799	
5063	Agnes PETTEN of Fivehead	1676/7	D/D/ct/1/P70	
5064	John PETTEN, Soapboiler of Bishops Hull	1769	T.N.A., PROB 31/1769/66	
5065	Roger PETTEN of Curry Rivel	1673	DD/SP/1673/30	
5066	[missing] PETTITT of [no place]	1695	DD/SP/1695/34	
5067	William PETTITT of Bridgwater	1685	DD/SP/1685/29	
5068	William PETTITT of Bridgwater	1699	DD/SP/442/34	Ad.ac.
5069	John PEYRES of Wambrook	1594	W.S.H.C., P5/1594/71	Will and inv.
5070	Sir Edward PHELIPS of Montacute	1700	DD/PH/226/17	
	Note: Inv. of the household goods, furniture, etc., prepared after the death of Sir Edward PHELIPS, with rooms named			
5071	Sir Robert PHELIPS of Montacute	1638	A/BIV/2	Transcript
5072	Eleanor PHELPS, Widow of Englishcombe	1733	D/D/Cti 67	
5073	Job PHELPS of Winsham	1719	T.N.A., PROB 3/18/95	
5074	John PHELPS, Mariner of Abbots Leigh	1646	B.A., 1646/35	
5075	John PHELPS, Merchant of Winsham	1702	T.N.A., PROB 4/22517	Will 1702?

5076	John Bryant PHELPS, Yeoman of Crewkerne	1827	T.N.A., PROB 31/1827/968	
5077	John PHELPS the elder, Husbandman of Stocklinch Magdalene	1639	DD/SP/1639/39	
5078	Richard PHELPS, Yeoman of Merriott	1669	DD/SP/1669/54	
5079	Robert PHELPS of Porlock	1670	DD/SP/1670/107	
5080	Robert PHELPS of Porlock	1670	DD/SP/1670/11	
5081	Robert PHELPS of Porlock	1678	DD/SP/1678/8	
5082	Walter PHELPS of Stocklinch Ottersey	1645	DD/SP/1645/13	See *T.C.W.*
5083	William PHELPS of Drayton	1714	DD/SP/1714/13	
5084	John PHILLIPPS, Husbandman of Orchard Portman	1688	DD/SP/1688/42	
5085	Robert PHILLIPPS of Weston [near Bath]	1591	D/D/cta/P73	
	Note: Ad.ac.; buried at Weston (near Bath) in 1591 (Reg.)			
5086	Thomas PHILLIPPS of Portbury	1668	D/D/cta/T16	Ad.ac.
5087	Magdalene PHILLIPS of Porlock	1685	DD/SP/1685/67	
5088	Margerie PHILLIPS of Drayton	1649	DD/SP/1649/78	
5089	Mary PHILLIPS of Drayton	1675	DD/SP/1675/26	
5090	Richard PHILLIPS of Queen Camel	1816	DD/BR/me/27	
5091	Thomas PHILLIPS of West Monkton	1668	DD/SP/1668/27	
5092	William PHILLIPS, Mercer of Glastonbury died at St. Clements Dane, Middlesex	1689	T.N.A., PROB 4/4581	Admon
5093	William? PHILLIPS of Pitminster?	1645	DD/SP/1645/12	Proved by Susanna, Widow
5094	Georg PHILPS of Luccombe	1667	DD/SP/1667/66	
5095	Henry PHILPS of Porlock	1684	DD/SP/1684/142	
5096	John PHILPS, Husbandman of Barrington	1690	DD/SP/1690/47	
5097	Mary PHILPS, Widow of Porlock	1684	DD/SP/1684/152	
5098	Matthew PHIPP of St. Clement Danes, Middlesex late of Bridgwater	1752	T.N.A., PROB 31/1752/55	With ad.ac.
5099	George PHIPPEN of Shepton Mallet	1668	D/D/cta/P53	Ad.ac.
5100	Abraham PHIPPS, Coalminer of Easton in Gordano	1767	B.A., 1767/CP	Widow's will
5101	Robert PHIPPS, Yeoman of Flax Bourton	1681	T.N.A., PROB 4/9859	Will also extant
5102	John PICKE of Thorney, Muchelney	1683	T.N.A., PROB 4/19758	Will also extant
5103	Thomas PICKE, Husbandman of Milverton	1681	DD/SP/1681/63	
5104	John PICKERINGE of Coley, Harptree (*sic*)	1626	D/D/ct/1/P84	
5105	John PICKHOLE of South Cheriton, Horsington	1693	DD/DNL/59	

5106	Elizabeth PIKE of Lydeard St. Lawrence	1664	DD/SP/1664/34	Wife of Lawrence
5107	Hugh PIKE of Stogumber	1634	D/D/cta/P22	Ad.ac.
5108	Robert PIKE of Crowcombe	1667	DD/SP/1667/8	
5109	Simon PIKE of Preston, Stogumber	1635	DD/SP/1635/85	
5110	John PIKES of [no place]	1646	DD/SP/1646/72	
5111	Alce PILE, Widow of Chedzoy	1645	DD/SP/1645/52	
5112	Margaret PILE, Widow of Creech St. Michael	1695	DD/SP/1695/6	
5113	Mary PILLE, Widow of Luxborough	1639	DD/SP/1639/31	
5114	William PINCHIN of Carlingcott, Camerton	1665	D/D/cta/P48	Ad.ac.
5115	William PINCKARD of Martock	1625	D/D/cta/P14	Ad.ac.
5116	Henry PINCKNEY of Bridgwater	1668	DD/SP/1668/65	
5117	John PINKER, Widower of Keynsham	1744	T.N.A., PROB 31/1744/395, 1744/491 and 1744/700	With ad.ac.
5118	John PINKER, Widower of Keynsham	1746	T.N.A., PROB 31/1746/224	
5119	John PINKER the younger, Butcher of Keynsham	1737	D/D/Cti 68	
5120	John PINN, Whitebaker of Taunton St. Mary Magdalene	1684	DD/SP/1684/123	
5121	Elizabeth PINNEY, Widow of Drayton	1677	DD/SP/1677/57	
5122	John PINNEY of Shepton Beauchamp	1689	DD/SP/1689/17	
5123	John PINNIE of Trull	1684	DD/SP/1684/165	
5124	Robert PINNIE of Drayton	1668	DD/SP/1668/67	
5125	John PIPPIN, Blacksmith of Crowcombe	1675	DD/SP/1675/7	
5126	William PIPPIN of Winsford	1679	DD/SP/1679/38	An indigent person who had reliefe
5127	John PITCHER of South Petherton	1684	DD/SP/1684/89	
5128	Richard PITHER of Thurloxton	1665	DD/SP/1665/42	
5129	George PITMAN of Chedzoy	1690	DD/SP/1690/10	
5130	George PITMAN of Isle Abbotts	1716	DD/SP/1716/12	
5131	James PITMAN of Isle Abbotts	1716	DD/SP/1716/18	
5132	John PITMAN of Charlton Musgrove	1641	D/D/cta/P56	Ad.ac.
5133	John PITMAN of Taunton St. James	1741	DD/SP/1741/14	
5134	Priscilla PITMAN, Spinster of Bridgwater	1735	D/D/cta/P40	Ad.ac. and inv.
5135	Robert PITMAN of Westonzoyland	1729	D/D/cta/P39	Ad.ac.
5136	John PITMAN alias PITTS of Isle Abbotts	1683	DD/SP/1683/103	

PITMAN see PITTS

5137	Mrs E.B. PITT of Trull	1875	D.H.C., 1044BaDD/2/13	
5138	Jane PITT of Clewer, Wedmore	1733	D/D/Pd/21	Possibly not proved
5139	Jonathan PITT, Esquire of Curry Rivel	1684	T.N.A., PROB 4/16110	Will also extant
5140	Richard PITT of Cricket Malherbie	1688	DD/GL/172	
5141	Samuel PITT, Esquire of Cricket Malherbie, died at Kensington, Middlesex	1729	T.N.A., PROB 31/1729/263	
PITT see APLEY, PYTT				
5142	Christopher PITTARD, Yeoman of Trent	1679	T.N.A., PROB 4/8276	Will 1679
5143	William PITTARD of Curry Rivel	1700	DD/SP/1700/9	
5144	Joan PITTERD of Bladon, Kingsbury Episcopi	1661	DD/PE/23	
5145	Henry PITTES of Ilminster	1702	T.N.A., PROB 4/25360	Will. ex. 1701
5146	John PITTMAN of Charlton Musgrove	1631	D/D/cta/P38	Ad.ac.
5147	Robert PITTMAN of Sandford Orcas	1619	D/D/cta/P61	Ad.ac.
5148	Robert PITTMAN of Holton	1642	D/D/cta/P57	Ad.ac.
5149	Elizabeth PITTS of Crewkerne	1669	DD/SP/1669/12	
5150	Elizabeth PITTS of Brislington	1676	T.N.A., PROB 4/21527	Will 1676. Daughter of James PITTS
5151	Robert PITTS of Chard	1676	D/D/cta/P41	Ad.ac.
5152	John PITTS alias PITMAN of Isle Abbotts	1668	DD/SP/1668/57	
PITTS see PITMAN				
5153	Joane PITWOOD of Dunster	1671	DD/SP/1671/39	
5154	Thomasine PLAICE, Widow of Withypool	1640	DD/SP/1640/5	
5155	Joane PLANT, Widow of Chillington	1635	DD/SP/1635/95	
5156	John PLAYCE of Portbury	1667	D/D/cta/P51	Ad.ac.
5157	William PLAYCE of Brompton Regis	1648	DD/SP/1648/47	
PLAYCE see PLAICE				
5158	Arthur PLAYER, Esquire of Hadspen, Pitcombe	1730	T.N.A., PROB 3/29/62	
5159	Henry PLAYER, Merchant of Bridgwater	1718	T.N.A., PROB 5/1902	
5160	Henry PLAYER of Bridgwater	1718	T.N.A., PROB 5/5692	
5161	John PLENTY, Yeoman of Pilton	1683	T.N.A., PROB 4/2454	Will also extant
5162	William PLENTY, Yeoman of Redhouse, Pilton	1690	T.N.A., PROB 4/12794	Will. ex. 1691
5163	Henry PLESE of Brompton Regis	1669	DD/SP/1669/35	
5164	Henry PLESE of Brompton Regis	1669	DD/SP/1669/37	
5165	John PLESE of Brompton Regis	1684	DD/SP/1684/69	

5166	Robert PLIMPTON of Shepton Mallet	1685	T.N.A., PROB 4/15453	Will 1678
PLIMPTON see HICKS				
5167	Thomas PLIMTON, Yeoman of Cricket Malherbie	1672	T.N.A., PROB 4/6953	Will also extant
5168	Agnes PLOWMAN, Widow of Minehead	1646	DD/SP/1646/94	
5169	Reverend John Warren PLOWMAN, Clerk of Stogursey	1803	T.N.A., PROB 31/1803/647	
5170	Richard PLUCKNETT of North Cadbury	1596	D/D/cta/P20	Ad.ac.
5171	William PLUCKNETT the elder of Charlton Horethorne	1634	D/D/cta/P19	Ad.ac.
5172	Robert PLUMLEY, Mendipman of East Harptree	1619	D/D/cta/P50	Ad.ac.
5173	Robert PLUMLIE of East Harptree	1619	D/D/ct/1/P98	
5174	Richard PLUMMER, Hosier of Leigh on Mendip	1684	T.N.A., PROB 4/2453	Will also extant
5175	Isaac POCKRIDGE of Rode	1705	T.N.A., PROB 4/22360	Admon
5176	Anne POCOCKE, Widow of Curry Rivel	1725	DD/SP/1725/1	
5177	Mary POCOCKE, Widow of Lyng	1645	DD/SP/1645/11	
5178	Robert POCOCKE senior, Husbandman of Lyng	1640	DD/SP/1640/129	
5179	Thomas POCOKE of Lyng	1680	DD/SP/1680/48	
5180	Robert PODDY of Langport Eastover, Langport	1682	T.N.A., PROB 4/4750	Will also extant
5181	Marmaduke PODGER, Cordwainer of Taunton St. Mary Magdalene	1696	DD/SP/1696/41	
5182	Robert PODGER, Cordwainer of Hambridge, Curry Rivel	1678	DD/SP/1678/59	
5183	Thomas PODGER of Swell	1755	DD/SP/1755/36	
5184	[missing] POGER, Widow of Curry Rivel	1714	DD/SP/1714/14	
5185	George POGER of Cricket Malherbie	1677	DD/SP/1677/85	
5186	William POGER of Bridgwater	1675	DD/SP/1675/72	
5187	Edmond POLE, Yeoman of Creech St. Michael	1681	DD/SP/1681/27	
5188	Henry POLE of Haydon, Taunton St. Mary Magdalene	1645	DD/SP/1645/51	
5189	John POLE, Husbandman of Creech St. Michael	1648	DD/SP/1648/44	
5190	John POLE of Ruishton	1695	DD/SP/442/31	Ad.ac.
5191	Nicholas POLE senior of Halse	1698	DD/SP/1698/21	
5192	Philippe POLE of Taunton St. Mary Magdalene	1612	DD/SP/1612/7	
5193	Thomas POLE, Yeoman of Creech St. Michael	1669	DD/SP/1669/93	
5194	Edward POLES of Bridgwater	1639	D/D/cta/P16	Ad.ac.
5195	Agnes POLLARD, Clothier of Holford	1690	DD/SP/1690/68	
5196	George POLLARD, Woolman of Taunton St. Mary Magdalene	1682	T.N.A., PROB 4/3229	Will 1682. ex. 1683

5197	George POLLARD of Kilve	1685	T.N.A., PROB 4/8353	Will also extant
5198	George POLLARD of Porlock	1691	DD/SP/1691/21	
5199	John POLLARD of Moorlinch	1647	D/D/cta/P59	Ad.ac.
5200	John and Elizabeth POLLARD of Porlock	1667	DD/SP/1667/24	
5201	Katherine POLLARD, Widow of Taunton St. James	1669	DD/SP/1669/34	
5202	Lewes POLLARD, Clothier of Holford	1689	DD/SP/1689/36	Reference to tools, etc
5203	Margaret POLLARD of [no place]	1729	DD/SP/1729/65	
5204	Richard POLLARD, Gentleman of Bicknoller	1638	D/D/cta/P18	Ad.ac.
5205	Stuckely POLLARD of Knighton, Stogursey	1729	DD/SP/1729/43	
POLLARD see MAUNDRY				
5206	Thomas POLLETT of Bridgwater	1588	D/D/cta/P69	Ad.ac.
5207	Charles POMEROY of Wells	1772	T.N.A., PROB 31/1772/381	With ad.ac.
5208	Jane POMROY, Widow of Wells	1771	T.N.A., PROB 31/1771/761	Formerly wife of Charles
5209	[missing] PONTER of Cannington	1721	DD/SP/1721/8	
5210	John POOL of Cannington	1636	DD/SP/1636/7	
5211	Anthony POOLE, Gentleman of Chillington	1699	T.N.A., PROB 4/8772	Will. ex. 1700
5212	Charles POOLE, Widower of Nether Stowey	1812	T.N.A., PROB 31/1812/131	
5213	Charles POOLE, Widower of Nether Stowey	1822	T.N.A., PROB 31/1822/1169	
5214	Dorothy POOLE, Widow of Seavington St. Mary	1691	DD/SP/1691/6	
5215	Edward and Mary POOLE of Angersleigh	1695	DD/SP/1695/24	
5216	George POOLE of Stringston	1680	DD/SP/1680/96	
5217	Henry POOLE of North Petherton	1670	DD/SP/1670/34	
5218	James POOLE of Cannington	1642	DD/SP/1642/30	
5219	Joan POOLE of Monksilver	1675	DD/SP/1675/65	
5220	Joan POOLE of Stogumber	1687	DD/SP/1687/20	
5221	John POOLE, Cordwainer of West Bagborough	1670	DD/SP/1670/105	
5222	John POOLE of East Quantoxhead	1672	DD/SP/1672/31	
5223	Mary POOLE of Monksilver	1637	DD/SP/1637/7	
5224	Mary POOLE of Norton Fitzwarren	1678	DD/SP/1678/80	
5225	Susanna POOLE, Widow of Stockland Bristol	1675	DD/SP/1675/61	
5226	Thomas POOLE of Chillington	1731	DD/SP/1731/10	
5227	Walter POOLE of Wembdon	1665	DD/SP/1665/25	
5228	[missing] POOLE alias HAYWARD of Porlock	1668	DD/SP/1668/36	

POOLE see HAYWARD				
5229	Mathew POOLL of Over Stowey	1681	DD/SP/1681/82	
5230	Edward POORE the elder, Gentleman of Ilton	1672	T.N.A., PROB 4/20563	Will also extant
5231	Elizabeth POORE of Ruishton	n.d.	D/D/cta/P76	Ad.ac.
5232	John POPE of Glastonbury St. John	1590	D/D/cta/P72	Ad.ac.
5233	Richard POPE, Carpenter of Westonzoyland	1629	D/D/ct/1/P118	
5234	Richard POPE of West Harptree	1749	D/D/Cti 107	
5235	Alexander POPHAM of Bourton on the Hill, Gloucestershire	1689	DD/POt/166	
5236	Alexander POPHAM of Wellington	1722	T.N.A., PROB 3/21/268	
5237	Edward POPHAM of Clavelshay, North Petherton	1735	DD/POt/167	
5238	Elizabeth POPHAM, Widow of Bridgwater	1693	DD/SP/1693/26	
5239	Joan POPHAM, Widow of Otterhampton	1629	D/D/ct/1/P122	
5240	Joan POPHAM, Widow of Otterhampton	1629	D/D/ct/1/P123	
5241	Richard POPHAM, Gentleman of West Quantoxhead	1664	DD/SP/1664/8	
5242	Silvester POPHAM, Gentlewoman of [no place]	1639	DD/SP/1639/50	
5243	Thomas POPHAM, Tailor of Cannington	1637	DD/SP/1637/20	
5244	William POPHAM of Wedmore	1663	DD/SAS/FA/161/18	
5245	William POPHAM of Horsey, Bridgwater	1674	DD/SP/1674/38	
5246	John POPLE senior, Husbandman of Stawell, Moorlinch	1644/5	D/D/ct/1/P124	
5247	Richard POPLE, Labourer of Curry Rivel	1647	DD/SP/1647/3	
5248	John PORCH of Meare	n.d.	D/D/cta/P78	Ad.ac.
PORCH see VICERY				
5249	Dorothy PORET, Spinster of St. George Hanover Square, Middlesex died at Bath	1743	T.N.A., PROB 31/1743/302	
5250	Thomas PORKER of Cannington	1683	DD/SP/1683/78	
5251	John PORLLING?, Yeoman of Yatton	1685	T.N.A., PROB 4/8456	Admon
5252	Adrian PORTER of North Petherton	1628	DD/SP/1628/16	See *T.C.W.*
5253	Ann PORTER, Widow of Thurloxton	1732	DD/SP/1732/15	
5254	Ann PORTER, Widow of Abbots Leigh	1773	B.A., 1773/CP	Will also extant
5255	Cicilie PORTER of North Petherton	1640	DD/SP/1640/125	
5256	Edward PORTER of Cannington	1640	DD/SP/1640/13	
5257	Elizabeth PORTER, Widow of Wrington	1687	T.N.A., PROB 4/20310	Will also extant
5258	George PORTER, Husbandman of Chadmead Corner, North Petherton	1673	DD/SP/1673/22	

5259	Henry PORTER of Kingsdon	1692	DD/SAS/C73/9	
5260	John PORTER of Watchet, St. Decumans	1581	D/D/ct/1/P129	
5261	John PORTER of Creech St. Michael	1634	DD/SP/1634/2	
5262	John PORTER of Taunton St. James	1675	DD/SP/1675/82	
5263	Margaret PORTER, Widow of Cannington	1640	DD/SP/1640/110	
5264	Rawleigh PORTER, Widow of Taunton St. James	1678	DD/SP/1678/62	Relict of J. PORTER
5265	Richard PORTER of Walton	1662	D/D/cta/P45	Ad.ac.
5266	Richard PORTER of Walton	1662	D/D/cta/P46	Ad.ac.
5267	Richard PORTER of Abbots Leigh	1682	B.A., 1682/35	
5268	Richard PORTER senior, Yeoman of North Petherton	1672	DD/SP/1672/11	
5269	Robert PORTER of West Monkton	1678	DD/SP/1678/58	
5270	Robert PORTER of Huntspill	1732	D/D/cta/P42	Ad.ac.
5271	Roger PORTER of North Petherton	1645	DD/SP/1645/56	
5272	Roger PORTER, Husbandman of North Petherton	1697	DD/SP/1697/45	
5273	Samuel PORTER of Galhampton, North Cadbury	1739	D/D/Cti 65	
5274	William PORTER of Wrington	1675	T.N.A., PROB 4/19941	Will. ex. 1676
5275	Dorothy PORTER alias STUDIER alias CHAPLIN of Taunton St. Mary Magdalene	1683	DD/SP/1683/31	Wife of Jasper, gentleman
5276	William PORTMAN, Knight of the Bath and Baronet of Orchard Portman	1690	*S.D.N.Q.* vol.13 p.320	
5277	Edward PORTNELL, Worsted Comber of North Petherton	1680	DD/SP/1680/95	
5278	Gabriel POSTILL of Chiselborough	1588	D/D/cta/P65	Ad.ac.
POTER see POTTER				
5279	Alice POTTER, Widow of Milverton	1664	DD/SP/1664/6	
5280	Charles POTTER, Esquire of [Blank] and St. Martin-in-the-Fields, Middlesex	1663	T.N.A., PROB 4/20246	Admon
5281	John POTTER, Yeoman of Elworthy	1640	DD/SP/1640/53	
5282	John POTTER, Yeoman of Pitminster	1683	DD/SP/1683/99	
5283	Michael POTTER, Yeoman of Whitestaunton	1682	T.N.A., PROB 4/8173	Will 1682, ex. 1683
5284	Richard POTTER of Stawley	1641	DD/SP/1641/6	Inv. shows POTER
5285	William POTTER, Husbandman of Cheddon Fitzpaine	1692	DD/SP/1692/19	
5286	Thomas POTTINGER of Martock	1668	D/D/cta/P52	Ad.ac.
5287	Earl POULETT of Hinton St. George	1819	DD/PT Box 9 H/452	

5288	William POUND of Abbots Leigh	1684	B.A., 1684/47	
5289	Phillippe POUNDE, Husbandman of Stockland Bristol	1627	D/D/ct/1/P131	
5290	[missing] POWELL, Widow of Taunton St. Mary Magdalene	1670	DD/SP/1670/8	
5291	Anthony POWELL of Milverton	1682	DD/SP/1682/45	
5292	John POWELL, Yeoman of Bathampton	1640	D/D/cta/P55	Ad.ac.
5293	John POWELL of Frome Selwood	1644	D/D/ct/1/P133	
5294	John POWELL of Porlock	1683	DD/SP/1683/42	
5295	Mary POWELL, Widow of Batheaston	1688	T.N.A., PROB 4/4308	Admon
5296	Richard POWELL, Clerk of Cannington	1684	DD/SP/1684/134	
5297	Robert POWELL, Gentleman of Wells	1664	D/D/cta/P47	Ad.ac.
POWELL see 1.				
5298	Thomas POWLE of Ashcott	1588	D/D/cta/P70	Ad.ac.
5299	Johan POWNDE, Spinster of Towbridge, Taunton St. James	1642	DD/SP/1642/14	
5300	Anthony POYDON, Yeoman of Whitelackington	1679	T.N.A., PROB 4/2770	Will. ex. 1681
5301	George POYER, Miller of Taunton St. Mary Magdalene	1672	DD/SP/1672/65	
POYLE see WHITE				
5302	Ralph POYNTING of West Harptree	1584	D/D/cta/P66	Ad.ac.
5303	Richard POYNTON of [no place]	1671	DD/SP/1671/24	
5304	Giles POYNTZ, Surgeon and Apothecary of Dunster	1732	T.N.A., PROB 31/1732/772	
5305	Elizabeth POYTON, Widow of Cannington	1635	DD/SP/1635/74	
5306	John POYTON, Clothier of Croscombe	1692	T.N.A., PROB 4/5937	Will also extant
5307	Philip POYTON, Clothier of Croscombe	1683	T.N.A., PROB 4/17567	Will also extant
5308	John PRANKARD of Langport	1822	T.N.A., PROB 31/1822/948	
5309	Anthony PRATT of Hamp, Bridgwater	1648	DD/SP/1648/52	
5310	Thomas PRATT junior of Taunton St. James	1716	DD/SP/1716/60	
5311	William PRATTENT the elder of Chew Magna	1638	D/D/cta/P17	Ad.ac.
5312	John PREIST of Crowcombe	1635	DD/SP/1635/15	
PRELAT see HOMET				
5313	Amos PRESTON, Gentleman of Glastonbury	1621	D/D/cta/P24	Ad.ac.
5314	Alice PREW of Shapwick	1622	D/D/cta/P13	Ad.ac.
5315	Francis PREW of Lyng	1674	DD/SP/1674/41	
5316	John PREWETT of Huntspill	1623	D/D/cta/P4	Ad.ac.
5317	Francis PRICE, Mariner of Bridgwater	1637	DD/SP/1637/70	

5318	Morgan PRICE of Minehead	1669	DD/SP/1669/9	
5319	Morgan PRICE of Minehead	1675	DD/SP/1675/41	
5320	Thomas PRICE alias AMERYE of Stogursey	1587	D/D/cta/P71	Ad.ac.
PRICE alias AMERYE				
5321	John PRICHARD, Innholder of Lower Weare, Weare	1673	T.N.A., PROB 4/19979	Will also extant
5322	John PRIDDIE, Yeoman of Kingston	1640	DD/SP/1640/92	
5323	Alexander PRIDDY of Kittisford	1697	DD/SP/1697/15	
5324	John PRIDDY of Thornfalcon	1679	DD/SP/1679/39	
5325	Richard PRIDDY, Sergeweaver of Milverton	1668	DD/SP/1668/8	
5326	Robert PRIEST of Pitminster	1691	DD/SP/1691/64	
5327	Ann PRIGG of Curry Rivel or Drayton	1657	DD/SP/1657/10	
5328	James PRIGG of Taunton St. Mary Magdalene	1689	DD/SP/1689/20	
5329	Joan PRIGG, Widow of Drayton	1731	DD/SP/1731/36	
5330	John PRIGG, Miller of Drayton	1681	DD/SP/1681/95	
5331	Richard PRIGG of Drayton	1671	DD/SP/1671/47	
5332	Richard PRIGG of Drayton	1673	DD/SP/1673/42	
5333	Samuel PRIGG, Clerk of Stanton Drew	1742	T.N.A., PROB 3/41/62	
5334	Thomas PRIGG of Drayton	1687	DD/SP/1687/6	
5335	Nicholas PRIGGE of Curry Rivel	1641	DD/SP/1641/34	
5336	Thomas PRIGGE, Clerk of Frome Selwood	1687	T.N.A., PROB 4/12086	Will 1686
5337	Dorothy PRINCE of Crewkerne	1669	DD/SP/1669/15	
5338	John PRINCE of West Monkton	1670	DD/SP/1670/91	
5339	John PRINCE, Apothecary? of Bridgwater	1725	DD/SP/1725/11	
5340	Edward PRING, Labourer of Langford Budville	1681	DD/SP/1681/30	
5341	James PRINGE of Staplegrove	1665	DD/SP/1665/6	
5342	Thomas PRIOR alias AMERIE of Stogursey	1588	D/D/cta/P79	Ad.ac.
5343	Thomas PRIOR alias AMRY of Stogursey	1678	DD/SP/1678/42	
5344	William PRISCOT of Luccombe	1635	DD/SP/1635/27	See *T.C.W.*
5345	Nicholas PRISCOTT of [no place]	1625	D/D/ct/1/P145	
5346	Hugh PRIST of Stogursey	1674	DD/SP/1674/15	
5347	Joane PROCKTER, Widow of Stoke St. Mary	1662	DD/SP/1662/30	
5348	Robert PROCKTER, Merchant of Taunton St. Mary Magdalene	1684	T.N.A., PROB 4/501	Will 1684

5349	William PROCKTER of Taunton St. Mary Magdalene	1687	DD/SP/1687/52	
PROCTER see ATCASTLE				
5350	Hugh PROILLE, Husbandman of Dunster	1644	DD/SP/1644/58	
5351	Joan PROLE of East Quantoxhead	1666	DD/SP/1666/76	
5352	John PROLE of Over Stowey	1690	DD/SP/1690/52	
5353	Mary PROLL, Widow of Dunster	1713	DD/SP/1713/42	
5354	George PROUSE of Dinnington	1714	DD/SP/442/14	Ad.ac.
5355	James PROUSE of Bradford	1677	DD/SP/1677/23	
5356	James PROVICE of Queen Charlton	1610	D/D/ct/1/P147	Buried at Queen Charlton
5357	John PROVIS of Shepton Mallet	1683	T.N.A., PROB 4/6946	Will also extant
5358	Richard PROVIS of Shepton Mallet	1684	D/D/cta/P43	Ad.ac.
5359	Hellena PROWSE, Widow of Spaxton	1683	T.N.A., PROB 4/10428	Will also extant
5360	James PROWSE of Norton Fitzwarren	1711	T.N.A., PROB 5/3205	
5361	John PROWSE, Esquire of Compton Bishop	1688	T.N.A., PROB 4/8771	Admon. ex. 1689
5362	Nicholas PROWSE, Clerk of Minehead	1666	DD/L/P30/110a	
5363	Robert PROWSE of Taunton	1645	DD/SP/1645/47	
5364	Mary PROWSE alias CADE of Taunton St. Mary Magdalene	1677	DD/SP/1677/4	
5365	John PRUETT of Otterhampton	1691	DD/SP/1691/68	
5366	Aaron PRYER, Clothmaker of Crewkerne	1704	DD/SP/442/61	Ad.ac.
PRYER see PRIOR				
5367	Bridget PRYNN of Swainswick	1634	D/D/cta/P21	Ad.ac.
5368	[missing] PRYOR, Mariner ? of Bridgwater	1689	DD/SP/1689/25	
	Note: Mentions 'One sea compass two bookes rule and glasse' valued at 10 shillings; damaged			
5369	George PRYOR, Clerk of Kilve	1593	D/D/cta/P74	Ad.ac. for a clergyman
5370	George PRYOR of Spaxton	1675	D/D/cta/P44	Ad.ac.
5371	Andrew PUDDIE of Lympsham	1626	D/D/cta/P8	Ad.ac.
5372	Jane PUDDY of Lympsham	1640	D/D/cta/P10	Ad.ac.
5373	Henry PULLEN, Innholder of Taunton St. Mary Magdalene	1672	DD/SP/1672/66	
5374	John PULLMAN of Taunton	1713	DD/SP/1713/37	
5375	William PULLMAN of Chard	1598	D/D/cta/P28	Ad.ac.
5376	Ambrose PULSFORD of Dulverton	1628	DD/SP/1628/15	
5377	Grace PULSFORD, Widow of Dulverton	1695	DD/SP/1695/4	
5378	Robert PULSFORD, Husbandman of Pitminster	1679	DD/SP/1679/14	

5379	Peter PUNTER of Minehead	1693	DD/SP/1693/61	
5380	Robert PUNTER of Minehead	1701	T.N.A., PROB 4/22730	Will also extant
5381	Catherine PURCHASE of West Monkton	1689	DD/SP/1689/9	
5382	Richard PURCHASE of West Monkton	1682	DD/SP/1682/2	
5383	John PURNELL of Farrington Gurney	1669	T.N.A., PROB 4/25589	Will also extant
5384	Isaac PUSSEY of Spaxton	1674	DD/SP/1674/37	
5385	William PUXLIE of Nailsea	1607	D/D/cta/P63	Ad.ac.
5386	Robert PUXTON of Holton	1687	T.N.A., PROB 4/9297	Admon
5387	Edmond PYKE of Moorlinch	1639/40	D/D/ct/1/P154	
5388	Edmund PYKE of Crewkerne	1681	DD/MR/70	
5389	Jarvis PYKE, Flaxman of Merriott	1667	DD/SP/1667/44	
5390	John PYKE of Huish Episcopi	1683	T.N.A., PROB 4/2762	Admon
5391	John PYKE of Stogumber	1708	DD/SP/442/55	Ad.ac.
PYKE see PIKE				
5392	[Male] PYLE of [no place]	n.d.	DD/SP/17th Century/10	Mentions Grace, relict
5393	Agnes PYLE, Widow of Ash Priors	1685	DD/SP/1685/60	
5394	Anthony PYLE of Ash Priors	1713	DD/SP/1713/41	
5395	Joan PYLE of Crowcombe	1685	DD/SP/1685/110	
5396	William PYLE of Ash Priors	1683	DD/SP/1683/61	
5397	Henry PYLE alias BAYLIE of Milverton	1637	DD/SP/1637/8	
5398	Thomas PYLEMAN of Otterhampton	n.d.	D/D/cta/P60	Ad.ac.
5399	Joan PYLLE, Widow of Dulverton	1692	DD/SP/1692/25	
5400	Amy PYNE, Widow of Curry Mallet	1693	T.N.A., PROB 4/25	Will also extant
5401	James PYNE of Taunton St. Mary Magdalene	1673	DD/SP/1673/13	
5402	John PYNE, Esquire of Pitney	1696	DD/CM/54	
5403	John PYNE, Esquire of Pitney	1696	T.N.A., PROB 4/1755	Will. ex. 1697
5404	John PYNE the elder, Esquire of Curry Mallet	1678	T.N.A., PROB 4/20023	Will also extant
5405	Jethrow PYNE (HIND) of Taunton St. Mary Magdalene	1683	DD/SP/1683/56	
5406	Francis PYNNY of Beercrocombe	1666	DD/SP/1666/77	
PYNNY see PINNIE				
5407	Robert PYTHER of Horsey, Bridgwater	1667	DD/SP/1667/16	
PYTHER see PITHER				
5408	John PYTMAN of Bridgwater	1741	DD/SP/1741/13	

5409	Priscilla PYTMAN, Spinster of Bridgwater	1735	D/D/Cti 66	
PYTMAN see PITMAN				
5410	Alice PYTT, Widow of West Bagborough	1647	DD/SP/1647/7	
5411	Mary PYTT, Widow of Isle Abbotts	1640	DD/SP/1640/56	
5412	John PYTTARD of Martock	1587	D/D/cta/P68	Ad.ac.
QUALE see LIGHTFOOTE				
5413	Hugh QUANTOCK of South Petherton	1697	DD/SP/1697/36	
5414	Richard QUARLE of Moorland, North Petherton	1646	DD/SP/1646/1	
5415	Henry QUARTLEY of Winsford	1665	DD/SP/1665/10	
5416	John QUARTLEY of Chipstable	1685	DD/SP/1685/65	
5417	Agnes QUARTLY, Spinster of Clatworthy	1642	DD/SP/1642/4	Damaged
5418	Nathaniel QUASH of Taunton	1675	T.N.A., PROB 4/20174	Admon
5419	Robert QUEAR of Creech St. Michael	1677	DD/SP/1677/28a+b	
5420	Edward QUICK, Blacksmith of Selworthy	1689	DD/SP/1689/5	Iron and steel bought at Bristol Fair
5421	John QUICK of Cannington	1662	D/D/cta/Q3	Ad.ac.
5422	John QUICK, Husbandman of Chedzoy	1669	DD/SP/1669/101	
5423	John QUICK, Husbandman of Chedzoy	1670	DD/SP/1670/18	
5424	John QUICK, Yeoman of Hindon, Minehead	1697	DD/SP/1697/32	
5425	Nicholas QUICK of Uphill	1638	D/D/cta/Q2	Ad.ac.
QUICK see DORRANT				
5426	Francis QUICKE, Yeoman of Stogumber	1670	T.N.A., PROB 4/8176	Will 1665
QUICKE see DORRANT				
5427	Jane QUINTE, Widow of Wellington	1629	D/D/ct/1/Q2a	
5428	Robert QUIRCK of Hindon, Minehead	1664	DD/SP/1664/60	
5429	John RACKSWORTHY of Milverton	1648	DD/SP/1648/41	
5430	Jonathan RADCLYFFE, Bachelor of Bath City died at St. Mary Islington, Middlesex	1663	T.N.A., PROB 4/8507	Admon
5431	Elizabeth RADFORD, Spinster of Chard	1677	T.N.A., PROB 4/12967	Admon. ex. 1679
5432	Elizabeth RADFORD, Spinster of Taunton St. Mary Magdalene	1686	DD/SP/1686/20	
5433	John RADFORD of Dunster	1635	DD/SP/1635/68	
5434	John RADFORD, Miller of Taunton St. James	1666	DD/SP/1666/67	
5435	Richard RADFORD, Husbandman of Mark	1678	T.N.A., PROB 4/10481	Will. ex. 1678
5436	Grace RAINSBURY, Widow of Langford Budville	1664	DD/SP/1664/26	

5437	John RAISON the elder, Husbandman of Stoke sub Hamdon	1629	D/D/ct/1/R4a	Pvd 1629
5438	Katherine RAKESWORTHY of Milverton	1648	DD/SP/1648/45	
5439	William RALFE, Yeoman of Wellington	1676	T.N.A., PROB 4/8544	Will also extant
5440	Agnes RALFRY, Widow of Wambrook	1628	W.S.H.C., P5/1628/77	Inv. and will
5441	Agnes RALPH, Spinster of North Petherton	1685	DD/SP/1685/106	
5442	Thomas RAMSTER, Innholder of Taunton St. Mary Magdalene	1684	DD/SP/1684/164	
5443	John RANDAL, Innholder of Frome Selwood	1730	D/D/cta/R35	Ad.ac.
5444	Giles RANDLE of West Coker	1833	T.N.A., PROB 31/1833/1935	
5445	Veranzio RANZZINI, Bachelor of Bath	1810	T.N.A., PROB 31/1810/1064	
5446	Edmund RATCLIFE of Bath St. James	1584	D/D/cta/R31	Ad.ac.
5447	Thomas RAULE of Porlock	1825	DD/RWL/7	
5448	Wilmot RAULE of Porlock	1768	DD/RWL/6	
5449	Philip RAWE of Curry Mallet	1646	DD/SP/1646/5	
5450	Richard RAWE, Woolen Draper of [no place]	1687	T.N.A., PROB 4/8234	Admon
5451	Anthony RAWES of West Bower, Bridgwater	1665	DD/SP/1665/14	
5452	Alice RAWLE, Widow of Oare	1640	DD/SP/1640/50	
5453	David RAWLE, Husbandman of Frome	1667	T.N.A., PROB 4/8011	Admon
5454	David RAWLE, Yeoman of Oare	1686	T.N.A., PROB 4/8738	Will also extant
5455	David RAWLE of Porlock	1721	DD/SP/1721/25	
5456	William RAWLE of Porlock	1666	DD/SP/1666/61	
5457	Edward RAWLE alias YEOND, Husbandman of Selworthy	1638	DD/SP/1638/59	
5458	Briant RAWLENS, Clothier of Donyatt	1680	DD/SP/1680/31	
5459	John RAWLENS, Butcher of Stolford, Stogursey	1693	DD/SP/1693/48	
5460	Mary RAWLENS alias WHELLER of Fivehead	1680	DD/SP/1680/46	
RAWLINGES see GLOVER				
5461	Thomas RAWLINGS junior, Tanner of Stogursey	1674	DD/SP/1674/16	
5462	Mary RAWLINS alias GLOVER of Stogursey	1639	DD/SP/1639/47	
5463	Daniel RAWLINSON of Chard	1701	T.N.A., PROB 4/22289	Will also extant
RAWLYNS see SIMONS				
5464	Edward RAY, Physician of Bridgwater	1676	DD/SP/1676/1	
5465	William RAYMNET of Winsford	1667	DD/SP/1667/36	
5466	Anne RAYMOND of Stogumber	1689	T.N.A., PROB 4/25575	Admon. ex. 1689
5467	Robert RAYMOND, Tanner of Milborne Port	1687	T.N.A., PROB 4/2246	Will 1687. ex. 1688

5468	George RAYMUND of Marston Magna	1747	DD/SAS/FA/165	
5469	Henry RAYNES of [no place]	1601	D/D/cta/R28	Ad.ac.
5470	William RAYNES of [no place]	1581	D/D/cta/R22	Ad.ac.
5471	Ralph RAYNIE alias PAYNTER of Bridgwater	1622	D/D/cta/R2	Ad.ac.
5472	Hugh RAYNOLD of Oake	1670	DD/SP/1670/69	
5473	Anthony RAYNOLDS of Taunton	1666	DD/SP/1666/14	
5474	Thomas RAYNOLES of Horsey, Bridgwater	1640	DD/SP/1640/14	
5475	James REACH, Clothier of Taunton St. Mary Magdalene	1691	T.N.A., PROB 4/8662	Will 1691. ex. 1692
5476	John READ of Shepton Montague	1677	T.N.A., PROB 5/5652	
5477	William READ of East Brent	1611	D/D/cta/R27	Ad.ac.
5478	John READE, Yeoman of Kenn	1680	T.N.A., PROB 4/8419	Will also extant
5479	Lettice READE of Cathanger, Fivehead	1641	DD/SP/1641/41	See *T.C.W.*
5480	Robert READE of [no place]	1628/9	D/D/ct/1/R15	
5481	Samuel READE of Wells	1687	T.N.A., PROB 4/8471	Admon
5482	Joane READE alias MACEY of West Monkton	1666	DD/SP/1666/54	
5483	Thomas REASON of Spaxton	1716	DD/SP/1716/53	
5484	William REASON of Spaxton	1689	DD/SP/1689/30	
5485	Avery REDHILL of Enmore	1683	DD/SP/1683/90	
5486	Charles REDING of Over Stowey	1731	DD/SP/1731/13	
5487	John REDMAN, Yeoman of Priddy	1682	T.N.A., PROB 4/8650	Admon. ex. 1683
5488	John REDMAN of Langford, Churchill	1687	T.N.A., PROB 4/21167	Will also extant
5489	Elizabeth REED of [no place]	1619	D/D/cta/R9	Ad.ac.
5490	Richard REED, Husbandman of Taunton St. James	1690	DD/SP/1690/18	
5491	Thomas REED senior of Bridgwater	1745	DD/SP/1745/25	
5492	William REED of Cheddon Fitzpaine	1679	DD/SP/1679/44	
5493	Joane REED alias GADD, Widow of Cheddon Fitzpaine	1681	DD/SP/1681/58	
5494	Joan REED alias KENT, Widow of Luccombe	1682	DD/SP/1682/38	
5495	Henry REEDE of Cannington	1669	DD/SP/1669/41	
5496	William REEDE of Cannington	1686	T.N.A., PROB 4/6011	Will 1686
5497	Agnes REEVE, Spinster of North Petherton	1636	DD/SP/1636/26	
5498	George REEVE, Goldsmith of Bath	1676	T.N.A., PROB 4/4377	Will 1676
5499	John REEVE, Yeoman of Shearston, North Petherton	1667	DD/SP/1667/96	
5500	George REEVES of Taunton St. Mary Magdalene	1681	DD/SP/1681/65	

5501	James REEVES, Victualler of Taunton	1731	DD/SP/1731/26	
5502	John REEVES of Chedzoy	1641	DD/SP/1641/14	
5503	Mary REEVES of Chedzoy	1641	DD/SP/1641/15	
5504	Thomas REEVES of Taunton St. Mary Magdalene	1675	DD/SP/1675/29	Mentions a house in North Street
5505	William REEVES of Abbots Leigh	1636	B.A., 1636/48	Will
5506	Amy RENDALL, Widow of Bridgwater	1638	DD/SP/1638/63	
5507	Henry? RENDALL of Selworthy	1635	DD/SP/1635/42	
5508	John RENDALL, Husbandman of Creech St. Michael	1634	D/D/ct/1/R18	
5509	John RENDALL of Ham, Creech St. Michael	n.d.	D/D/cta/R17	Ad.ac.
5510	Simon RENDHALL, Gentleman and Widower of Litton	1842	T.N.A., PROB 37/1200	With com.
5511	Giles RENDLE of Oare	1685	DD/SP/1685/92	
5512	John RENDLE of East Harptree	1627	D/D/ct/1/R20	
5513	Noah RENDOLL of [no place]	1645	DD/SP/1645/16	
5514	Edward REVENHILL, Gentleman of Wellington	1682	DD/DP/36/5	
5515	Frances REW, Spinster of Bishops Hull	1674	DD/SP/1674/62	
5516	Jane REW, Widow of Lydeard St. Lawrence	1672	DD/SP/1672/1	
5517	John REWE of Kittisford	1640	DD/SP/1640/95	
5518	Edward REYNEY alias PAINTER, Innholder of Bridgwater	1680	DD/SP/1680/97	
REYNEY see PAINTER				
5519	Samuel REYNOLDS of Taunton	1690	T.N.A., PROB 4/9463	Will 1690
5520	John RICE of Monksilver	1675	DD/SP/1675/16	
5521	Lewis RICE of Minehead	1691	DD/SP/1691/65	
5522	William RICE of East Brent	1590	D/D/cta/R34	Ad.ac.
5523	William RICE of Bawdrip	1612	D/D/cta/R12	Ad.ac.
5524	William RICE of Monksilver	1668	DD/SP/1668/11	
5525	Christian RICH of Seavington St. Mary	1667	DD/SP/1667/98	
5526	Dynah RICH, Widow of Crewkerne	1670	DD/SP/1670/57	
5527	Edward RICH of Over Stowey	1667	T.N.A., PROB 4/1829	Will also extant
5528	Elizabeth RICH of Over Stowey	1681	DD/SP/1681/48	
5529	Grace RICH, Singlewoman of Lydeard St. Lawrence	1677	DD/SP/1677/61	
5530	Hannah RICH, Widow of Over Stowey	1723	DD/DR/70/(pt.1)	
5531	Johanna RICH, Spinster of St. Decumans	1675	T.N.A., PROB 4/13306	Admon
5532	Samuel RICH, Clerk of Woodbridge, Holwell	1705	T.N.A., PROB 5/5329	

5533	Samuel RICH the elder of Over Stowey	1683	DD/SP/1683/7	
5534	Susanna RICH of Lydeard St. Lawrence	1700	DD/SP/1700/24	
5535	Thomas RICH of Lydeard St. Lawrence	1677	T.N.A., PROB 4/21768	Will also extant
5536	Thomas RICH, Yeoman of Lydeard St. Lawrence	1685	DD/SP/1685/112	See DD/SP 1686/3a
5537	Ellinor RICHARDS of Donyatt	1635	DD/SP/1635/62	
5538	George RICHARDS of Glastonbury St. John	1735	D/D/Cti 73	
5539	George RICHARDS junior of Norton Fitzwarren	1679	DD/SP/1679/13	
5540	Goddard RICHARDS, Esquire, Colonel in service of the Honourable East India Company of Bath	1835	T.N.A., PROB 31/1835/1888	
5541	John RICHARDS of Cannington	1635	DD/SP/1635/75	
5542	John RICHARDS of Heathfield	1696	DD/SP/1696/17	
5543	Nicholas RICHARDS of Luxborough	1690	DD/SP/1690/38	
5544	Nicholas RICHARDS of Middle Chinnock	1703	T.N.A., PROB 4/22563	Admon. ex. 1704
5545	Nicholas RICHARDS of Cutcombe	1743	DD/SP/1743/21	
5546	Susanna RICHARDS, Widow of Cutcombe	1721	DD/SP/1721/6	
5547	Thomas RICHARDS of East Brent	1623	D/D/cta/R4	Ad.ac.
5548	William RICHARDS of West Buckland	1766	DD/RC Box 2	
5549	William RICHARDS of West Buckland	1831	DD/RC Box 1	
5550	William RICHARDS of Martock?	1877	DD/X/BUT/1	
5551	Robert RICKARD of Creech St. Michael	1670	DD/SP/1670/77	
5552	William RICKARD the younger of North Petherton	1670	DD/SP/1670/40	
5553	Deanes RICKARDS, Widow of [no place]	1648	DD/SP/1648/60	
5554	Walter RICKETT, Carpenter of North Petherton	1714	DD/SP/1714/25	
5555	George RICKMAN, Clothier of Chard	1689	T.N.A., PROB 4/8395	Will 1689
5556	Philip RIDDLER of Dunster	1646	DD/SP/1646/74	
5557	Anthonie RIDDOTT, Miller of Street	1617	D/D/ct/1/R30	
5558	Hugh RIDEN of Burnham on Sea	1623	D/D/cta/R3	Ad.ac.
5559	Walter RIDEOUT of Stoford, Barwick	1681	T.N.A., PROB 4/9078	Will also extant
5560	John RIDGE of Bicknoller	1639	D/D/cta/R1	Ad.ac.
5561	William RIDGE of Goathurst	1687	DD/SP/1687/65	
5562	Israel RIDGWAY of Cannington	1684	DD/SP/1684/61	
5563	Agnes RIDLER of Cutcombe	1634	DD/SP/1634/22	
5564	Angus RIDLER of Porlock	1672	DD/SP/1672/37	

5565	Christine RIDLER of Cutcombe	1697	DD/SP/1697/65	
5566	Christopher RIDLER, Husbandman of Porlock	1723	DD/SP/1723/47	
5567	David RIDLER of Porlock	1665	DD/SP/1665/13	
5568	John RIDLER of Cutcombe	1733	DD/SP/1733/18	
5569	Nicholas RIDLER of Cutcombe	1635	DD/SP/1635/101	
5570	Richard RIDLER of Cutcombe	1664	DD/SP/1664/47	
5571	Richard RIDLER of Stoke Pero	1668	DD/SP/1668/12	
5572	William RIDLER of Porlock	1688	DD/SP/1688/10	
5573	William RIDLER of Selworthy	1743	DD/SP/442/85	Ad.ac. by Robert PHELPS
5574	Anne RIDOUT, Widow of Stoford, Barwick	1691	T.N.A., PROB 4/2270	Will also extant
5575	William RIDOUT, Yeoman of Horsington	1670	T.N.A., PROB 4/3856	Will also extant
5576	Thomas Medlycott RIGGS of [no place]	1737-1739	DD/S/BT/24/3/26–31	Ad.ac.
5577	Richard RIMMELL, Yeoman of Frome Selwood	1707	W.S.H.C., P25/1707/2	
	Note: the will was made at Frome, Somerset, but the inv. was taken at Westbury, Wiltshire			
5578	Richard RINGE, Miller of Coley Mill, East Harptree	1636/7	D/D/ct/1/R33	
5579	Benjamin RISDEN of Taunton St. James	1703	T.N.A., PROB 4/22504	Will. ex. 1702?
5580	Mr Benjamin RISDON of Taunton St. James	1703	T.N.A., PROB 4/22822	Will also extant
5581	William RISDON of Stockland Bristol	1732	DD/SP/1732/7	
5582	John RITCH of East Lydford	1635	D/D/cta/R6	Ad.ac.
5583	[missing] RITCHE of [no place]	1635	D/D/cta/R7	
	Note: Ad.ac.; mixed up with a document for Lawrence CARYE of Wellington			
5584	Henry RITHERDON of Langford Budville	1666	DD/SP/1666/55	
5585	John RITHERDON of Bradford	1609	DD/SF/11/1/30	Formerly DD/SF/102
5586	Nicholas RITHERDON of Langford Budville	1645	DD/SP/1645/42	
5587	William RITHERDON, Gentleman of Langford Budville	1662	DD/SAS/HV/50	
5588	Nicholas RITHERTON, Yeoman of Bradford	1685	DD/SP/1685/48	
5589	Edward ROACH, Shipwright of Abbots Leigh	1674	B.A., 1674/37	Will also extant
5590	Henry ROACH, Mariner of Abbots Leigh	1678	T.N.A., PROB 4/6338	Will 1679. ex. 1679
5591	Hugh ROACH, Shipwright of Abbots Leigh	1669	B.A., 1669/60	Will also extant
5592	Hugh ROACH, Shipwright of Abbots Leigh	1712	B.A., 1712/40	Will also extant
5593	Jane ROACH, Widow of Clapton in Gordano	1736	D/D/Cti 72	

5594	Thomas ROACH, Husbandman of Abbots Leigh	1623	B.A., 1623/54	Will also extant
5595	Mary ROBBINS, Widow of Bath	1772	T.N.A., PROB 31/1772/287	
5596	Alice ROBERTS of Bridgwater	1690	DD/SP/1690/61	
5597	Fernando? ROBERTS of [no place]	1667	DD/SP/1667/39	Proved by Edith, Widow
5598	Francis ROBERTS, Innholder of Axbridge	1735	D/D/Cti 74	
5599	John ROBERTS, Gentleman of Bridgwater	1666	DD/SP/1666/29	
5600	John ROBERTS of Cannington	1678	DD/SP/1678/13	
5601	Jonathan ROBERTS of Minehead	1795	T.N.A., PROB 31/1795/513	
5602	Thomas ROBERTS, Gentleman of Wells	1688	T.N.A., PROB 4/15737	Will also extant
5603	William ROBERTS of Brompton Ralph	1667	DD/SP/1667/94	
5604	William ROBERTS of Bridgwater	1691	DD/SP/1691/11	
5605	Richard ROBINCE of Nynehead	1670	DD/SP/1670/44	
5606	[missing] ROBINS of Walcot	1673-1684	D/D/cta/R8	
	Note: Ad.ac.; temp Bishop Peter MEWS			
5607	Amey ROBINS of Langford Budville	1688	DD/SP/1688/38	
5608	Gregory ROBINS, Carpenter of Chipstable	1683	DD/SP/1683/79	
5609	Henry ROBINS of Buckland St. Mary	1731	DD/SP/1731/28	
5610	John ROBINS of Hutton	1666	D/D/cta/R15	Ad.ac.
5611	John ROBINS of Dulverton	1681	DD/SP/1681/53	
5612	Richard ROBINS of Kingston Seymour	1705	D/D/cta/R23	Ad.ac.
5613	Thomas ROBINS of Weare	1646	D/D/cta/R13	Ad.ac.
5614	William ROBINS of Bathwick	1591	D/D/cta/R20	Ad.ac.
5615	William ROBINS of Dulverton	1700	DD/SP/1700/14	
5616	Andrew ROBINSON, Innholder of Chard	1689	DD/X/SN/6	
5617	Hannah ROBINSON, Spinster of Chard	1717	DD/SP/1717/1	
5618	John ROBINSON of Abbots Leigh	1672	B.A., 1672/46	
5619	Richard ROBINSON, Butcher of Bridgwater	1689	DD/SP/1689/45	
5620	Ruth ROBINSON, Widow of Abbots Leigh	1687	B.A., 1687/53	Will also extant
5621	Ann ROBINSON alias SHIRLEY of Pulteney Street, Bath	1812	T.N.A., PROB 37/194	
5622	Alice ROBYNSON of Langford Budville	1640	DD/SP/1640/80	
5623	John ROCETER the elder, Yeoman of Oake	1641	DD/SP/1641/38	
ROCETER see ROSSITER				

5624	Henry ROCH, Yeoman of Abbots Leigh	1618	B.A., 1618/60	Will also extant
5625	Thomas ROCKE of Baltonsborough	1667	D/D/cta/R14	Ad.ac.
5626	Edward RODBARD of Merriott	1885	DD/SB/53/4	
5627	John RODBURD of Stratton, South Petherton	1669	DD/SP/1669/13	
5628	John RODFORD, Carrier of Glastonbury St. John	1611	D/D/cta/R32	Ad.ac.
5629	Nicholas RODMAN, Yeoman of Churchill	1680	T.N.A., PROB 4/4768	Admon
5630	John RODWAY of Wellow	1644	D/D/cta/H62	Ad.ac.
5631	Edward ROE, Husbandman of Capton, Stogumber	1680	DD/SP/1680/21	
5632	Nathaniel ROE, Fuller of Bishops Hull	1681	DD/SP/1681/3	
5633	Phillip ROE, Yeoman of Clatworthy	1686	DD/SP/1686/41	
5634	William ROE of Walton	1642	D/D/ct/1/R45	
5635	Martin ROGER of Clatworthy	1686	DD/SP/1686/42	
5636	..... ROGERS of Frome	n.d.	D/D/ct/1/R46	
5637	Alice ROGERS of Stoke St. Mary	1634	DD/SP/1634/8	
5638	Andrew ROGERS of Frome Selwood	1682	T.N.A., PROB 4/17333	Will also extant
5639	Edward ROGERS of Enmore	1683	DD/SP/1683/34	
5640	Henry ROGERS of Dunwear, Bridgwater	1667	DD/SP/1667/9	
5641	John ROGERS of [no place]	1594	D/D/cta/R10	Ad.ac.; Bath area
5642	John ROGERS of Weston (near Bath)	1594	D/D/cta/R30	Ad.ac.
5643	John ROGERS of Bridgwater	1688	DD/SP/1688/45	Reference to provisions, brick, etc.
5644	John ROGERS, Yeoman of West Compton, Pilton	1690	DD/X/LLH/2	
5645	Richard ROGERS of Axbridge	1677	T.N.A., PROB 4/18521	Admon
5646	Richard ROGERS of Doulting	1587/8	D/D/cta/R33	Ad.ac.
5647	Thomas ROGERS of East Town, Tolland	1690	DD/SP/1690/66	
5648	Thomas ROGERS of East Town, Tolland	1709	DD/SP/442/54	Ad.ac.
5649	Thomas ROGERS, Cordwainer of Bruton	1734	D/D/Cti 71	
5650	William ROGERS of Crewkerne	1717	DD/SP/442/20	Ad.ac.
5651	William ROGERS of East Bower, Bridgwater	1737	DD/SP/1737/34	
ROGERS see TICE				
5652	Richard ROGGERR, Husbandman of Taunton St. Mary Magdalene	1691	DD/SP/1691/2	
5653	Arthur ROLEY of Taunton St. Mary Magdalene	1684	DD/SP/1684/114	
5654	Sir Francis ROLLE, Knight of Shapwick	1686	T.N.A., PROB 4/19632	Will. ex. 1687

5655	James ROOBENS, Weaver of Buckland St. Mary	1641	DD/SP/1641/55	
5656	Benedict ROOD of Chedzoy	1723	DD/SP/1723/39	
5657	James ROOD of Bridgwater	1689	DD/SP/1689/40	
5658	Thomas ROOD, Chandler of Bridgwater	1683	DD/SP/1683/16	
5659	John ROODE of Street	1689	DD/LTR/3	
5660	Thomas ROOK of Ivythorn, Street	1730	D/D/cta/R21	Ad.ac.
5661	Edmund ROOKE of Staple Fitzpaine	1660	DD/SP/1660/13	
5662	Elinor ROOKE of Thornfalcon	1640	DD/SP/1640/117	
5663	John ROOKE of North Petherton	1646	DD/SP/1646/68	
ROPER see SILKENS				
5664	Henry ROSE of St. Luke, Middlesex died at Bath	1734	T.N.A., PROB 31/1734/202	
5665	John ROSITER of Ash Priors	1687	DD/SP/1687/22	
5666	Andrew ROSS, Innholder of Taunton St. Mary Magdalene	1695	DD/SP/1695/19	
5667	James ROSSE the elder, Esquire of Moorhayes, Charlton Musgrove	1671, 1678	T.N.A., PROB 4/514	Admon. Two inventories
5668	Abel ROSSITER, Miller of Cheddon Fitzpaine	1687	DD/SP/1687/31	
5669	Christopher ROSSITER of Kingstone	1730	DD/SP/1730/15	
5670	Dorothy ROSSITER, Widow of Halse	1694	DD/SP/1694/27	
5671	Joel ROSSITER, Tailor of Hillfarrance	1669	DD/SP/1669/91	
5672	Mathahia ROSSITER of Taunton St. Mary Magdalene	1691	DD/SP/1691/71	
5673	Elizabeth ROSSITER alias LISSANT of Taunton St. Mary Magdalene	1681	DD/SP/1681/92	
ROSSITER see ROCETER				
5674	Ann ROSWELL of Lydeard St. Lawrence	1679	DD/SP/1679/49	
5675	[missing] ROUNSEVALL alias CARTER of Oake	1646	DD/SP/1646/14	
5676	Henry ROUSE of North Cadbury ?	1616-1626	D/D/cta/R11	
	Note: Ad.ac.; temp Bishop Arthur LAKE; mixed up with an account relating to the Taunton area			
5677	John ROUTLEY, Yeoman of Hapcott, Minehead	1666	DD/SP/1666/36	
5678	Margaret ROUTLEY, Widow of Dunster	1731	DD/SP/1731/43	
5679	Henry ROW, Yeoman of Porlock	1679	DD/SP/1679/5	
5680	Thomas ROWCLIFFE, Clerk of Hardington Mandeville	1736	D/D/cta/R18	Ad.ac. and inv.
5681	George ROWE of Taunton	1686	T.N.A., PROB 4/6880	Admon
5682	John ROWE of Taunton St. Mary Magdalene	1594	D/D/cta/R25	Ad.ac.

5683	John ROWLAND of Langford Budville	1698	DD/SP/1698/1	
5684	Edmund ROWLIE of Meare	1625	D/D/cta/R5	Ad.ac.
5685	Edmund ROWLIE of [no place]	1625	D/D/cta/T10a	Ad.ac.
5686	Adam ROWSELL of Isle Abbotts	1636	DD/SP/1636/59	
5687	George ROWSELL the elder, Miller of Coombe, Crewkerne	1678	DD/SP/1678/84	
5688	Robert ROWSWELL senior, Husbandman of Shepton Beauchamp	1637	DD/SP/1637/38	
5689	Thomas ROWSWELL of Dunkerton	1603	D/D/cta/R29	Ad.ac.
5690	Elizabeth ROY of Christchurch, Southampton died at Shepton Mallet	1752	T.N.A., PROB 31/1752/578	Wife of Samuel ROY
5691	Elizabeth ROY of Christchurch, Southampton died at Shepton Mallet	1753	T.N.A., PROB 31/1753/11	Wife of Samuel ROY
5692	William ROYSE of Kingsbury (*sic*)	1683	T.N.A., PROB 4/20853	Admon
5693	William RUDDUCK, Gentleman of West Coker	1686	T.N.A., PROB 4/9934	
5694	John RUDMAN the elder, Tanner of Churchill	1678	T.N.A., PROB 4/10585	Will also extant
5695	Anthony RUGG of Taunton St. Mary Magdalene	1681	DD/SP/1681/108	
5696	Anthony RUGG of Taunton St. Mary Magdalene	1683	DD/SP/1683/57	
5697	George RUGG, Husbandman of Stocklinch Ottersey	1683	DD/SP/1683/53	
5698	John RUGG of Weston Bampfylde	1607	D/D/cta/R26	Ad.ac.
5699	John RUGG, Clerk of Cannington	1707	D/P/can/13/10/1	
5700	William RUMNEY of Portbury	1620	D/D/cta/R24	Ad.ac.
5701	Jeffery RUMNY, Yeoman of Walton	1680	D/D/ct/1/R64	
5702	Nicholas RUMPSON of Wembdon	1668	DD/SP/1668/5	
5703	Alice RUMSEY, Widow of Cannington	1665	DD/SP/1665/39	
5704	Richard RUMSEY, Carpenter of Cannington	1664	DD/SP/1664/23	
5705	Thomas RUSBACH, Bachelor of Bath formerly of Gloucester, Gloucestershire	1790	T.N.A., PROB 31/1790/413	
5706	Christopher RUSCOMBE, Yeoman of Spaxton	1695	DD/SP/1695/31	
5707	John RUSCOMBE, Yeoman of Stogursey	1690	DD/SP/1690/72	
5708	William RUSCOMBE, Gentleman of Cannington	1720	DD/SP/1720/24	
5709	John RUSH, Yeoman of Baltonsborough	1735	T.N.A., PROB 3/34/50	
5710	John RUSH the elder of Baltonsborough	1681	T.N.A., PROB 4/8409	Will 1681
5711	John RUSHCOMBE, Yeoman of Spaxton	1688	DD/SP/1688/56	

5712	James RUSHE, Yeoman of Baltonsborough	1604	D/D/ct/1/R66	
5713	James RUSHE, Gentleman of Baltonsborough	1668	T.N.A., PROB 4/6014	Will 1670. ex. 1670
5714	Edward RUSSELL of Hamp, Bridgwater	1674	DD/SP/1674/44	
5715	Henry RUSSELL of Hinton St. George	1683	DD/SP/1683/81	
5716	Jane RUSSELL of Cheddon Fitzpaine	1683	DD/SP/1683/46	Wife of William
5717	John RUSSELLS, Gentleman of South Petherton	1637	DD/SP/1637/44	
5718	Joan RUTLEY of Milverton	1690	DD/SP/1690/3	
5719	Mary RUTTER, Spinster of Witcombe (*sic*) and Corsham, Wiltshire	1710	W.S.H.C., P29/R5	
	Note: Will; nuncupative; died at her sister's house, in Corsham			
5720	Roger RUTTER of Ashbrittle	1646	DD/SP/1646/39	
5721	Gregory RYALL of Lyng	1684	DD/SP/1684/71	
5722	John RYALL, Bachelor of Henstridge	1737	T.N.A., PROB 31/1737/672 and 1737/673	With com.
5723	Elizabeth S...... of Stogursey	1639	DD/SP/1639/40	Damaged
5724	William S....... of [no place]	1641	DD/SP/1641/45	Damaged
5725	John SABINE of Bath City formerly of Tewin, Hertfordshire, died at Bristol	1776	T.N.A., PROB 31/1776/538	
5726	Elizabeth SAFFIN, Widow of Stogumber	1639	DD/SP/1639/28	
5727	Elizabeth SAFFIN, Widow of Stogumber	1681	DD/SP/1681/78	
5728	Mary SAFFIN of Porlock	1723	DD/SP/1723/46	
5729	Robert SAFFIN, Gentleman of Cutcombe	1685	DD/SP/1685/5	
5730	Thomas SAFFIN of Cutcombe	1670	DD/SP/1670/98	
5731	Briget SAGE of Luccombe	1641	DD/SP/1641/22	
5732	Francis SAGE of Cameley	1625	D/D/cta/S26	Ad.ac.
5733	Joseph SAGE, Butcher of Chew Magna	1733	D/D/Cti 77	
5734	Thomas SALE of Wellington	1607/8	D/D/ct/1/S4	
5735	William SALISBURY, Yeoman of Shepton Beauchamp	1698	DD/SP/1698/39	
5736	Henry SALLWAY of Fivehead	1635	D/D/cta/G9	Ad.ac.
5737	Ann SALMON of West Coker	1682	DD/NNE/c1048/8	
5738	Anne SALMON, Widow of Wells	1681	T.N.A., PROB 4/612	Will 1681
5739	James SALMON of Blackers Hill Farm, Chilcompton	1685	T.N.A., PROB 4/9503	Will. ex. 1686
5740	John SALMON, Husbandman of Marksbury	1610	D/D/cta/S37	Ad.ac.

5741	John SALMON of Marksbury	1610	D/D/cta/S38	Ad.ac.
5742	Thomas SALMON of Bath	1677	T.N.A., PROB 4/6850	Will 1677
5743	William SALSBURIE, Husbandman of Shepton Beauchamp	1648	DD/SP/1648/24	
5744	Elliott SALTER, Captain in HMS Navy (*sic*) of Bath	1793	T.N.A., PROB 31/1793/328	With ad.ac.
5745	Jeram SALTER of Staple Fitzpaine	1641	DD/SP/1641/37	
5746	John SALTER, Yeoman of Chilton, Moorlinch	1738	D/D/cta/S71	
	Note: Ad.ac. and inv.; the date is taken from his date of death in 1738			
5747	Robert SALTER, Weaver of West Buckland	1737	D/D/cta/S82	Ad.ac., 1740 and inv., 1737
5748	Francis SALWAY, Yeoman of Isle Brewers	1675	DD/SP/1675/13	
5749	Francis SALWAY, Yeoman of Fivehead	1689	DD/SP/1689/3	
5750	Henry SALWAY of Fivehead	1677	DD/SP/1677/89a+b	Releases by administrators
5751	Henry SALWAY, School Master of [no place]	1678	DD/SP/1678/4	
5752	John SALWAY of Curry Rivel	1665	DD/SP/1665/53	
5753	Margaret SALWAY, Widow of Fivehead	1678	DD/SP/1678/3	
5754	John SAM, Husbandman of Curry Mallet	1634	DD/SP/1634/25	
5755	Ezra SAMBORNE, Yeoman of Stowey	1666	DD/SAS/C82/43	
5756	Mary SAMBORNE of Nunney	1692	D/D/cta/S73	Ad.ac.
5757	Momely SAMBORNE of Nunney	1692	D/D/cta/S72	Ad.ac.
5758	William SAMBORNE, Esquire of Paulton	1670	T.N.A., PROB 4/10393	Will also extant
5759	Maudley SAMBOURNE, Esquire of Timsbury	1679	T.N.A., PROB 4/15718	Will also extant
5760	Christian SAMFORD, Widow of Old Cleeve	1678	T.N.A., PROB 4/10378	Will also extant
SAMMIS see SAMMYS				
5761	John SAMMYS alias SAMMIS, Yeoman of Moorland, Westonzoyland	1675	T.N.A., PROB 5/4958	
5762	Emma SAMPSON of Milborne Port	1593	D/D/cta/S42	Ad.ac.
5763	George SAMPSON, Gentleman of Middle Lambrook, Kingsbury Episcopi	1682	T.N.A., PROB 4/619	Will 1682
5764	Isott [Male] SAMPSON of South Petherton	1697	DD/SP/1697/7	
5765	Sarah SAMPSON of Staplegrove	1680	DD/SP/1680/82	
5766	Andrew SANDER of Porlock	1637	DD/SP/1637/56	
5767	Antony SANDERS of Abbots Leigh	1620	B.A., 1620/81	Will also extant
5768	Henry SANDERS, Shipwright of Abbots Leigh	1665	B.A., 1665/51	Will also extant
5769	Joan SANDERS, Widow of Milverton	1673	DD/SP/1673/12	

5770	Joanne SANDERS, Widow of Dunster	1645	DD/SP/1645/60	See *T.C.W.*
5771	John SANDERS, Shipwright of Abbots Leigh	1687	B.A., 1687/55	Will also extant
5772	John SANDERS, Victualler of Taunton St. Mary Magdalene	1690	DD/SP/1690/21	
5773	Phillip SANDERS, Mariner of Abbots Leigh	1665	B.A., 1665/53	Will also extant
5774	Simon SANDERS, Miller of Milverton	1676	DD/SP/1676/5	
5775	Valentine SANDERS of Chewton Keynsham, Keynsham	1669	T.N.A., PROB 4/9087	Will also extant
5776	William SANDERS of [no place]	n.d.	D/D/cta/Blank/42	
	Note: Damaged ad.ac.; mentions his wife and two young children; rent to Sir John SYDENHAM			
5777	Christopher SANDFORD of Thorne St. Margaret	1676	DD/SP/1676/35	
5778	Edward SANDFORD, Esquire of Bath formerly of Shrewsbury, Shropshire	1821	T.N.A., PROB 31/1821/412	
5779	Benjamin SANFORD, Bachelor of Nynehead	1659	DD/SF/11/1/55	Formerly DD/SF/794
5780	Henry SANFORD, Esquire of [no place]	1841	DD/SF/11/1/189	Formerly DD/SF/1710
5781	Henry SANFORD of Nynehead	1659/60	DD/SF/11/1/56	Formerly DD/SF/796
5782	John SANFORD, Gentleman of Taunton	1698	DD/SP/1698/49	
5783	John SANFORD, Esquire of [no place]	*c.*1700	DD/SF/11/1/109	Formerly DD/SF/291
5784	William SANFORD, Bachelor of Nynehead	1659	DD/SF/11/1/54	Formerly DD/SF/795
5785	William SANFORD of Nynehead	1718/19	DD/SF/11/1/127	Formerly DD/SF/1766
5786	Banjamin SANGER of Lopen	1720	DD/SP/1720/27	
5787	Thomas SANSOME of Westonzoyland	1641	D/D/cta/S47	Ad.ac.
5788	John SARTAIN, Victualler of Bath	1738	D/D/Cti 87	
5789	John SATCHELL of Taunton St. James	1721	DD/SP/1721/31	
5790	Mathew SATCHELL of Norton Fitzwarren	1637	DD/SP/1637/64	See *T.C.W.*
5791	Samuel SATCHELL of Taunton St. Mary Magdalene	1690	T.N.A., PROB 4/10411	Admon, intestate
5792	Samuel SATCHELL of Taunton St. James	1696	DD/SP/1696/40	
5793	Mary SATCHFIELD, Widow of Long Ashton	1656	B.A., 1656/1	Will also extant
5794	Richard SATELL of Halberton, Devon	1652	DD/SP/1652/7	Possessions in Weare in Huish Episcopi
SAUNDARS see TAYLAR				
5795	Amos SAUNDERS of Martock	1626	D/D/cta/S1	Ad.ac.
5796	Dorothy SAUNDERS of East Quantoxhead	1635	DD/SP/1635/59	
5797	Edward SAUNDERS, Yeoman of Nempnett Thrubwell	1736	D/D/Cti 83	
5798	Elizabeth SAUNDERS, Widow of Abbots Leigh	1669	B.A., 1669/65	Will also extant
5799	Hannah SAUNDERS, Spinster of Abbots Leigh	1719	B.A., 1719/40	Will also extant

5800	Isaac SAUNDERS of Taunton St. Mary Magdalene	1666	DD/SP/1666/71	
5801	James SAUNDERS, Saddler of Cudworth	1630	DD/SX/78/2	
5802	Joan SAUNDERS of Shuttern, Taunton	1725	DD/SP/1725/24	Wife of John, a Saddler
5803	John SAUNDERS of Axbridge	1600	D/D/cta/S55	Ad.ac.
5804	John SAUNDERS of Walcot	1638	D/D/cta/S2	Ad.ac.
5805	John SAUNDERS of Taunton	1668	DD/SP/1668/56	
5806	John SAUNDERS, Glover of Taunton St. Mary Magdalene	1683	DD/SP/1683/25	
5807	John SAUNDERS the elder, Hosier of Frome Selwood	1683	T.N.A., PROB 4/18319	Admon
5808	Robert SAUNDERS, Yeoman of Walcot	1673	D/D/cta/S74	Ad.ac.
5809	Susanna SAUNDERS of Chewton Keynsham, Keynsham	1676	T.N.A., PROB 4/6856	Admon. ex. 1677
5810	Thomas SAUNDERS of Weston (*sic*)	1669	D/D/cta/S48	Ad.ac.
5811	Valentine SAUNDERS of Chewton Keynsham, Keynsham	1677	T.N.A., PROB 4/20518	Will 1669
5812	William SAUNDERS of Odcombe	1583	D/D/cta/S4	Ad.ac.
5813	William SAUNDERS of North Petherton	1639	D/D/cta/S3	Ad.ac.
5814	William SAUNDERS of Taunton	1668	DD/SP/1668/42	
SAUNDERS see TAYLER, VICARY				
5815	Edward SAVAGE of Wells	1604	D/D/cta/S65	Ad.ac.
5816	John SAVAGE of Taunton St. Mary Magdalene	1675	DD/SP/1675/53	
5817	Mary SAVAGE of Combe Florey	1683	DD/SP/1683/50	Wife of William
5818	Thomas SAVAGE of Combe Florey	1664	DD/SP/1664/28	
5819	William SAVAGE, Gentleman of Combe Florey	1685	T.N.A., PROB 4/8480	Admon
SAVAGE see HEMBOROW				
5820	Joan SAVEDGE, Widow of Abbots Leigh	1695	B.A., 1695/36	Will also extant
5821	John SAVEDGE, Shipwright of Abbots Leigh	1691	B.A., 1691/41	Will also extant
5822	Emily SAVERY, Spinster and Bastard of Shepton Mallet	1835	T.N.A., PROB 31/1835/1819	
5823	Katheren SAVIDGE of Taunton St. Mary Magdalene	1635	DD/SP/1635/93	See *T.C.W.*
5824	Mary SAVIDGE, Widow of Mudgeley, Wedmore	1680	T.N.A., PROB 4/21539	Will. ex. 1681
5825	Margaret SAVOR of Hillfarrance	1683	DD/SP/1683/37	
5826	Thomas SAVORY of Pill Bridge, Ilchester	1685	T.N.A., PROB 4/16740	Admon
5827	Joan SAVYDGE, Widow of Abbots Leigh	1624	B.A., 1624/61	Will also extant
5828	Grace SAW, Widow of Bath	1678	T.N.A., PROB 4/16152	Admon
5829	Thomas SAWIER of Banwell	1588	D/D/cta/S45	Ad.ac.
5830	Thomas SAWTELL of Stoke St. Gregory	1763	DD/SAS/PR/95	

5831	Joane SAWTLE of Curry Rivel	1646	DD/SP/1646/21	
5832	John SAWTLE of Curry Rivel	1667	DD/SP/1667/42	
5833	William SAWTLE of Curry Rivel	1670	DD/SP/1670/23	
SAWYER see SAYER				
5834	Hugh SAYER of Uphill	1598	D/D/cta/S39	Ad.ac.
5835	Phillippe SAYER of Leigh on Mendip	1682	D/D/ct/1/S26	
5836	Sarah SAYER, Widow of Spaxton	1730	DD/SP/1730/4	
5837	Henry SAYWARD of Cannington	1667	DD/SP/1667/22	
5838	Richard SCADDEN senior of Pitminster	1635	DD/SP/1635/118	
5839	Joane SCADDIN of Nynehead	1629	D/D/ct/1/S28a	
5840	Elizabeth SCADDING, Widow of Angersleigh	1638	DD/SP/1638/38	
5841	John SCADDING of Angersleigh	1640	DD/SP/1640/146	
5842	Simon SCADDING of Angersleigh	1638	D/D/cta/S29	Ad.ac.
5843	Joan SCADING, Widow of Pitminster	1670	DD/SP/1670/95	
5844	Robert SCADING, Tanner of Pitminster	1681	DD/SP/1681/13	
5845	Ann SCAFFORD of Walton in Gordano	1737	D/D/Cti 89	
5846	Thomas SCORE, Husbandman of North Petherton	1670	DD/SP/1670/42	
5847	Robert SCORE alias WILLIAMS of Stockland Bristol	1640	DD/BR/rd/2	
5848	Francis SCOTT of West Pennard	1827	DD/FS Box 38	
5849	James SCOTT of Treborough	1717	DD/SP/442/23	Ad.ac.
5850	John SCOTT of Milborne Port	1775	T.N.A., PROB 31/1775/290	
5851	Marmaduke SCOTT of Drayton	1713	DD/SP/1713/22	
5852	Mary SCOTT, Widow of Minehead	1677	DD/SP/1677/33	
5853	Robert SCOTT of [no place]	1756	DD/YB/89	
5854	Thomas SCOTT of [no place]	1681	T.N.A., PROB 4/25640	Admon. ex. 1681
5855	William SCOTT of Minehead	1684	DD/SP/1684/155	
5856	William SCOTT, Mariner of Minehead	1693	DD/SP/1693/13	
5857	Daniel SCRACE, Bachelor, gentleman of Bath	1828	T.N.A., PROB 31/1828/1031	With ad.ac.
5858	Anne SEAGER, Widow of Pitminster	1682	DD/SP/1682/14	
5859	Anne SEAGER, Spinster of Pitminster	1683	DD/SP/1683/19	
5860	Leonard SEAGER of Pitminster	1640	DD/SP/1640/120	
5861	Nicholas SEAGER of Stocklinch Ottersey	1684	DD/SP/1684/91	
5862	Catherine SEALEY, Widow of Creech St. Michael	1745	DD/SP/1745/26	

5863	Giles SEALEY of Lilstock	1637	DD/SP/1637/59	
5864	Joan SEALEY, Widow of Bridgwater	1731	DD/SP/1731/12	
5865	John SEALEY of Kilve	1684	DD/SP/1684/83	
5866	Mary SEALEY of Over Stowey	1635	DD/SP/1635/105	See *T.C.W.*
5867	Nicholas SEALEY of Dulverton	1635	DD/SP/1635/91	
5868	Richard SEALEY of [no place]	n.d.	DD/SP/Box 11	
5869	William SEALEY of Kilve	1666	DD/SP/1666/44	
5870	William SEALEY of North Petherton	1714	DD/SP/1714/3	
5871	William SEALEY junior, Sergeweaver of Hillfarrance	1682	DD/SP/1682/17	
5872	Frances SEALY, Widow of Bridgwater	1718	T.N.A., PROB 3/17/59	
5873	Richard SEALY of Creech St. Michael?	n.d.	DD/SP/17th Century/11	Mentions Joanna, relict
5874	Simon SEALY of Spaxton	1639	D/D/ct/1/S31	
5875	Edmund SEAMAN the elder of Bishops Lydeard	1685	T.N.A., PROB 4/6120	Admon
5876	John SEARLE of Wellington	1629	D/D/ct/1/S33	
5877	John SEARLE of Ashcott	1669	D/D/cta/S50	Ad.ac.
5878	Nicholas SEARLE of Kittisford	1690	DD/SP/1690/79	
5879	Edward SEARLLE of Ashbrittle	1642	DD/SP/1642/37	
5880	John SEARY, Clerk of Lullington	1622	D/D/cta/S21	Ad.ac. for a clergyman
5881	Thomas SEDGBOROWE of Chipstable	1642	DD/SP/1642/9	
5882	Andrew SEDGBURROW, Blacksmith of Dulverton	1666	DD/SP/1666/41	
5883	Ann SEELEY alias HILLARD, Merchant? of Taunton	1683	T.N.A., PROB 4/19910	Admon, wife of Joseph HILLARD
5884	Robert SEELY, Gentleman of Odcombe	1681	T.N.A., PROB 5/498	Will T.N.A., PROB 11/371, Sentence
5885	Henry SELLECK of West Monkton	1646	DD/SAS/C432/21	
5886	Joane SELLECK, Spinster of Lydeard St. Lawrence	1668	DD/SP/1668/10	
5887	John SELLECK of Lydeard St. Lawrence	1697	DD/SP/1697/25	
5888	Thomas SELLECK of North Petherton	1646	DD/SP/1646/23	
5889	William SELLECKE of Oake	1660	DD/SP/364	
5890	William SELLICK of Oake	1690	DD/SP/1690/75	
5891	Henry SELLWAY of Chewton Mendip	1737	D/D/Cti 85	
5892	James SELLY of Minehead	1735	DD/SP/1735/27	
5893	William SENIOR of Chedzoy	1742	DD/SP/1742/17	
5894	William SERGEANT of Meare	1601	D/D/cta/S33	Ad.ac.
5895	Robert SERLE, Gentleman of Sherston, North Petherton	1640	DD/SP/1640/104	

5896	William SERLE, Esquire of Bradford	1726	T.N.A., PROB 3/25/146	
5897	Elizabeth SESSE of Taunton St. James	1716	DD/SP/1716/3	
5898	Isabel SEVALL of Portbury	1620	D/D/cta/S16	Ad.ac.
5899	John SEVIE of Shepton Mallet	1625	D/D/cta/S18	Ad.ac.
5900	Mary SEVIER, Widow of Bedminster	1785	T.N.A., PROB 31/1785/176	
5901	Thomas SEVIER of East Brent	1710	D/D/cta/S75	Ad.ac.
5902	John SEWARD, Yeoman of Wambrook	1685	W.S.H.C., P14/61	Inv. and will
5903	Richard SEWARD of Wambrook	1626	W.S.H.C., P5/1626/45	Com., inv. and will
5904	Robert SEWARD, Husbandman of Wambrook	1633	W.S.H.C., P5/1633/51	Com., inv., will
SHALGROVE see GREENE				
5905	John SHALLISH, Miller of Over Stowey	1690	DD/SP/1690/20	
5906	John SHAPCOTT of Wiveliscombe	1703	T.N.A., PROB 5/1906	Admon
5907	Joane SHAPLAND, Widow of Exford	1666	DD/SP/1666/11	
5908	John SHAPTEN of Langford Budville	1721	DD/SP/1721/1	
5909	Thomas SHARLOCK, Husbandman of Lopen	1642	DD/SP/1642/35	
5910	John SHARLOCKE, Yeoman of Lopen	1681	DD/SP/1681/66	
5911	Thamasan SHARLOCKE, Spinster of Lopen	1642	DD/SP/1642/36	
5912	Christopher SHARP of Taunton St. Mary Magdalene	1681	DD/SP/1681/57	
5913	John SHARP of Milverton	1686	DD/SP/1686/4	
5914	Jonathon SHARP of Taunton St. Mary Magdalene	1691	DD/SP/1691/42	
5915	Mary SHARP, Widow of Milverton	1698	DD/SP/1698/3	
5916	Emanuel SHARPE, Clerk of Taunton St. Mary Magdalene	1679	T.N.A., PROB 4/11887	Will also extant
5917	Thamsen SHARPE, Widow of Cothelstone	1641	DD/SP/1641/99	Damaged
5918	Henry SHATOKE of Stogumber	1646	DD/SP/1646/29	
5919	Elizabeth SHATTOCK, Widow of Taunton St. James	1645	DD/SP/1645/49	
5920	John SHATTOCK, Husbandman of Crowcombe	1685	DD/SP/1685/88	
5921	Robert SHATTOCK of Dunwear, Bridgwater	1640	DD/SP/1640/15	
5922	William SHATTOCK of Milverton	1690	DD/SP/1690/64	
5923	Henry SHATTOCKE of Staplegrove	1638	DD/SP/1638/31	
5924	Henry SHATTOCKE, Clothier of Norton Fitzwarren	1678	DD/SP/1678/72	
5925	Henry SHATTOCKE senior of West Monkton	1665	DD/SP/1665/2	
5926	John SHATTOCKE of Staplegrove	1630	DD/SP/1630/18	
5927	John SHATTOCKE of Staplegrove	1687	DD/SP/1687/18	

5928	John SHATTOCKE the elder of Norton Fitzwarren	1637	DD/SP/1637/3	
5929	Robert SHATTOCKE of Dunwear, Bridgwater	1640	DD/SP/1640/15	
5930	William SHATTOCKE the second, Husbandman of West Bagborough	1637	DD/SP/1637/39	
5931	Richard SHEARES of Minehead	1689	T.N.A., PROB 4/4067	Admon
5932	Thomas SHEAVALIER of South Petherton	1666	DD/SP/1666/60	
5933	John SHEPHEARD of South Brent	1635	D/D/cta/S13	Ad.ac.
5934	Thomas SHEPHERD, Esquire of Heightly, Chudleigh, Devon formerly of Butcombe Court, Somerset	1818	T.N.A., PROB 31/1818/255	With ad.ac.
5935	George SHEPPARD of Othery	1625	D/D/cta/S11	Ad.ac.
5936	James SHEPPARD of Chew Magna	1735	D/D/Cti 75	
5937	John SHEPPARD of Wrington	1630	D/D/cta/S76	Ad.ac.
5938	John SHEPPARD of South Brent	1635	D/D/cta/S10	Ad.ac.
5938a	John SHEPPARD, Yeoman of Knightcott, Banwell	1689	DD/SAS/G1740/5/4/3	
5939	John SHEPPARD of Croscombe	n.d.	D/D/cta/S62	
	Note: Ad.ac.. Exhibited before William HUGHES (d.1738), Chancellor of Bath and Wells			
5940	Joseph SHEPPARD junior of Kewstoke	1767	A/AKH/8/4	
5941	Robert SHEPPARD of Taunton	1603	D/D/cta/S35	Ad.ac.
5942	Thomas SHEPPARD, Butcher of Stawell, Moorlinch	1629	D/D/ct/1/S59	
SHEPPARD see SORE				
5943	Giles SHERLOCK of Ilchester	1739	D/D/cta/S77	Ad.ac. and inv.
5944	William SHERLOCK, Yeoman of Crewkerne	1686	DD/SP/1686/13	
5945	Elizabeth SHERMAN, Widow of Otterhampton	1678	DD/SP/1678/54	
5946	John SHERMAN, Groom of Hestercombe, Kingston St. Mary	1698	DD/SP/1698/29	
5947	Richard SHERMAN of Combwich, Otterhampton	1674	DD/SP/1674/50	Reference to a share in *The David* of Bridgwater
5948	Samuel SHERRY of Taunton St. Mary Magdalene	1679	DD/SP/1679/25	
5949	Anne SHERWOOD of Pitminster	1723	DD/SP/1723/35	
5950	Edward SHERWOOD, Carver of Durston	1714	DD/SP/1714/8	
5951	Frances SHERWOOD, Widow of Kingston St. Mary	1730	DD/SP/1730/26	
5952	Jacob SHERWOOD, Yeoman of Pitminster	1667	DD/SP/1667/53	
5953	John SHERWOOD of Bath	1620	D/D/cta/S34	Ad.ac.
5954	John SHERWOOD of Enmore	1630s	DD/SP/1632/36	Undated; Elizabeth relict

5955	Robert SHERWOOD of Durston	1684	DD/SP/1684/167	
5956	Robert SHERWOOD of Durston	1685	DD/SP/1685/56a	
5957	Henry SHIPARD of Bridgwater	1716	DD/SP/1716/57	
5958	William SHIPTON of Taunton St. Mary Magdalene	1685	DD/SP/1685/13	
SHIRLEY see ROBINSON				
5959	Hugh SHOARD, Gentleman of Yarnfield, Maiden Bradley	1731	W.S.H.C., P2/S/1339	Inv. and will
5960	Anthony SHOLLER, Bachelor of Combe Florey	1681	DD/SP/1681/37	
5961	Jane SHOOEBROOKE of Durston	1687	DD/SP/1687/21	
5962	Joseph SHORNEWAY of Brompton Ralph	1681	DD/SP/1681/62	
5963	John SHORNY, Sergemaker of Stogursey	1696	DD/SP/1696/43	
	Note: With covering letter to Mr. SOUTHIE register at the Free School, Taunton			
5964	[missing] SHORT of [no place]	1690	D/D/cta/E1	
	Note: Ad.ac.; two children of the deceased named SHORT and the account was made by Hester EVANS			
5965	Benjamin SHORT, Sergemaker of Taunton St. James	1681	DD/SP/1681/90	
5966	Walter SHORT, Cole Miner of Mells	1717	D/D/cta/S78	Ad.ac.
5967	William SHORT of Midsomer Norton	1629	D/D/ct/1/S66a	
5968	Hugh SHOTT, Yeoman of Hele, Bradford on Tone	1729	DD/SP/1729/56	
5969	Christopher SHOTTOCKE of Taunton St. James	1638	DD/SP/1638/58	See *T.C.W.*
5970	William SHOTTOCKE of Dulverton	1677	DD/SP/1677/36	
5971	George SHOVE of Bridgwater	1690	DD/SP/1690/41	
5972	John SHUES, Husbandman of Middlezoy	1628	D/D/ct/1/S69	
5973	John SHURTT of Hill, Kilve	1680	DD/SP/1680/94	
5974	Thomas SHURTT of Kilve	1681	DD/SP/1681/20	
5975	William SHURTT of Kilve	1681	DD/SP/1681/19	
5976	John SHUTE, Gentleman of Hinton Charterhouse	1735	D/D/Cti 82	
5977	Mary SHUTE, Widow of Monkton Combe	1771	T.N.A., PROB 31/1771/460	
5978	Robert and Julian (Wife) SHUTT of Stogursey	1670	DD/SP/1670/73	
5979	Edward SIBLEY, Barber of Bathealton	1695	DD/SP/1695/2	
5980	[missing] SIBLY of [no place]	1692	DD/SP/1692/20	Incomplete
5981	John SIBLY, Blacksmith of Bathealton	1690	DD/SP/1690/29	
5982	Robert SIDERFIN the elder, Yeoman of East Linch, Timberscombe	1688	DD/MAL/14/1	
5983	Laurence SILK of West Monkton	1691	DD/SP/1691/41	

5984	Edward SILKE of Stockland Bristol	1737	DD/SP/1737/33	
5985	Sampson SILKE, Baker of Pensford St. Thomas, Publow	1676	T.N.A., PROB 4/1331	Admon
5986	David SILKENS alias ROPER of Stogursey	1670	DD/SP/1670/74	
5987	Robert SILLIVEN of Minehead	1693	DD/SP/1693/14	
5988	Thomas SILLIVON, Carpenter of Lyng	1667	T.N.A., PROB 4/15748	Will also extant
5989	Henry SILVER, Edge tool maker of Bedminster	1741	T.N.A., PROB 31/1741/590	With ad.ac.
SILVESTER see GAWLER				
5990	Joane SIMES, Widow of Shepton Beauchamp	1648	DD/SP/1648/35	
5991	Thomas SIMES, Woolen Draper of Axbridge	1682	T.N.A., PROB 4/9746	
5992	Elizabeth SIMMONS of Wells	1678	D/D/cta/S79	Ad.ac.
5993	John SIMON the elder of Coat, Martock	1629	D/D/ct/1/S71a	
5994	John SIMONS of [no place]	n.d.	DD/SP/17th Century/12	Appraised? by John RAWLYNS
5995	William SIMONS, Clothier of Hillfarrance	1681	T.N.A., PROB 4/3887	Will. ex. 1682
5996	Anne SIMPSON, Widow of Bath	1808	T.N.A., PROB 31/1808/850	
5997	William SIMSON of Taunton St. Mary Magdalene	1691	T.N.A., PROB 4/22016	Admon
5998	Joan SINGER alias SMITH of Buckland Dinham	1691	T.N.A., PROB 4/2759	Will 1691
5999	Richard SINGLE, Woolen Draper of Barrington	1669	DD/SP/1669/55	
6000	Thomas SINGLE of Puckington	1634	D/D/cta/S28	Ad.ac.
6001	John SINNINEY of Kingston	1675	DD/SP/1675/3	
6002	Elizabeth SKEETE, Spinster of Bath	1793	T.N.A., PROB 31/1793/546	
6003	John SKELLEN, Husbandman of South Petherton	1635	DD/SP/1635/112	
6004	John SKILLING of Seavington St. Michael	1713	DD/SP/1713/27	
6005	Ann SKINNER of Chipstable	1678	DD/SP/1678/48	
6006	Elizabeth SKINNER, Spinster of Trull	1668	DD/SP/1668/21	
6007	Joseph SKINNER of Stogumber	1697	DD/SP/1697/61	
6008	George SKONE of Edinburgh, Scotland died at Bath	1734	T.N.A., PROB 31/1734/424	
6009	William SKOTT, Husbandman of Butleigh	1601	D/D/ct/1/S76	
6010	John SKRINE the elder of Bathford	1675	DD/BR/cc/2	Pvd Wells 1676
6011	Joseph SKRINE of Bathford	1670	D/D/cta/S80	Ad.ac.
6012	William SKRINE of Bathford	1689	T.N.A., PROB 4/8682	Will 1689
6013	Stephen SKURRAY of Beckington	1762, 1767	DD/RG/60	
6014	William SLACK, Esquire of Bathwick	1846	T.N.A., PROB 37/1387	

6015	William SLADDON, Tanner of Milverton	1691	DD/SP/1691/25	
6016	David SLADE, Yeoman of Norton Fitzwarren	1732	DD/SP/1732/8	
6017	John SLADE, Coverlet weaver of Wambrook	1627	W.S.H.C., P5/1626/19	Admon. bond, com., inv.
6018	John SLADE, Draper of Butleigh	1740	D/D/cta/S29a	Ad.ac. and inv.
6019	John SLADE, Draper of Butleigh	1740	D/D/cta/S81	Ad.ac. and inv.
6020	Mary SLADE, Widow of Taunton St. Mary Magdalene	1678	T.N.A., PROB 4/4589	Will also extant
6021	Samuel SLADE of Taunton St. Mary Magdalene	1675	DD/SP/1675/10	
6022	Tremor SLADE, Husbandman of Wayford	1664	DD/SP/1664/54	
6023	[Male] SLAPE of [no place]	1694	DD/SP/1694/7	
6024	Agnes SLAPE of Donyatt	1636	DD/SP/1636/38	
6025	Emanuel SLAPE of Norton Fitzwarren	1691	DD/SP/1691/24	
6026	Ralph SLAPE the elder of Norton Fitzwarren	1683	T.N.A., PROB 4/18024	Will. ex. 1684
6027	Tristram SLAPE of Stoke St. Mary	1688	DD/SP/1688/3	
6028	William SLAPE, Yeoman of Donyatt	1636	DD/SP/1636/37	
6029	Robert SLATFORD, Esquire of North Brewham	1723	T.N.A., PROB 3/22/76	
6030	James SLEDMAN of [no place]	1720	DD/SF/15/2/35	Formerly DD/SF/3888
6031	William SLEW, Husbandman of High Ham	1720	DD/SF/15/2/35	Formerly DD/SF/3888
6032	Ann SLOCOMBE of St. Decumans	1747	D/D/Ppb 81	
6033	Hugh SLOCOMBE, Shoemaker of Minehead	1734	DD/SP/1734/22	
6034	Humphrey SLOCOMBE of Over Stowey	1677	DD/SP/1677/77	
6035	Joane SLOCOMBE, Spinster of Runnington	1687	DD/SP/1687/56	
6036	Johane SLOCOMBE, Widow of Durston	1648	DD/SP/1648/51	
6037	John SLOCOMBE of Durston	1677	DD/SP/1677/71	
6038	Mary SLOCOMBE, Spinster of Runnington	1687	DD/SP/1687/55	
6039	Robert SLOCOMBE of Huish Champflower	1637	DD/SP/1637/47	
6040	Robert SLOCOMBE of Wilton	1671	DD/SP/1671/46	
6041	Thomas SLOCOMBE, Husbandman of Creech St. Michael	1681	DD/SP/1681/2	
6042	Walter SLOCOMBE of Cannington	1638	DD/SP/1638/28	
6043	Walter SLOCOMBE, Gunsmith of Dunster	1676	DD/SP/1676/52	
6044	Hugh SLOPER of Woolverton	1675	T.N.A., PROB 4/22017	Admon
6045	Henry SLY of Bath St. Peter and St. Paul	1664	D/D/cta/S63	Ad.ac.
6046	John SMALCOMBE, Feltmaker of Bath	1686	T.N.A., PROB 4/6132	Will 1687. ex. 1687
6047	Andrew SMALCORNE of Whitestaunton	1716	DD/SP/1716/35	Buried at Whitestaunton 1715

6048	Anthony SMALE, Weaver of Milverton?	1700	DD/SP/1700/26	Parish missing but assessors of Milverton
6049	Edward SMALE of [no place]	1695	DD/SP/1695/1	
6050	Margaret SMALE, Widow of Thurloxton	1641	DD/SP/1641/30	
6051	Richard SMALE of Chilton (*sic*)	1639	D/D/cta/S15	Ad.ac.
6052	Agnis SMALLE alias HOOPER of Bridgwater	1640	DD/SP/1632/37	Undated; *T.C.W.*
6053	Grace SMART, Widow of South Petherton	1714	DD/SP/1714/22	
6054	Lucy SMART, Widow of Shockerwick, Bathford	1736	D/D/Cti 84	
6055	William SMART of Enmore	1688	DD/SP/1688/35	
6056	Alice SMITH, Widow of Lydeard St. Lawrence	1645	DD/SP/1645/26	
6057	Ann SMITH, Widow of Bath	1779	T.N.A., PROB 31/1779/498	
6058	Ann Papwell SMITH, Widow of Combhay formerly of Bath	1837	T.N.A., PROB 31/1837/1447	
6059	Anne SMITH, Widow of Frome Selwood	1685	T.N.A., PROB 4/6919	Will also extant
6060	Arthur SMITH, Clothier of Chard	1685	T.N.A., PROB 4/12123	Admon
6061	Cuthbert SMITH of Hinton St. George	1685	DD/SP/1685/25	
6062	Daniel SMITH, Doctor of Physic of Bath late of Bristol	1779	T.N.A., PROB 31/1779/497	
6063	Deborah SMITH, Spinster of Norton Fitzwarren	1745	T.N.A., PROB 31/1745/464	
6064	Deborah SMITH, Spinster of Norton Fitzwarren	1746	T.N.A., PROB 31/1746/171	
6065	Ebenezer SMITH, Printer of Bath St. James	1830	T.N.A., PROB 31/1830/940	
6066	Edward SMITH of Minehead	1677	T.N.A., PROB 4/25194	Will. ex. 1677
6067	Edward SMITH of Taunton	1681	DD/SP/1681/107	
6068	Elinor SMITH, Widow of Merriott	1669	DD/SP/1669/22	
6069	Francis SMITH of Taunton	1635	DD/SP/1635/133	
6070	George SMITH of Isle Brewers	1681	DD/SP/1681/42	
6071	Griffin SMITH, Clerk of Kelston	1681	T.N.A., PROB 4/8244	Will also extant
6072	Henry SMITH of East Chinnock	1612	D/D/cta/S36	Ad.ac.
6073	Henry SMITH of Hawkridge	1642	DD/SP/1642/20	
6074	Henry SMITH, Tallow Chandler of Frome Selwood	1676	T.N.A., PROB 4/21052	Will also extant
6075	Henry SMITH of Frome Selwood	1684	T.N.A., PROB 4/8521	
	Note: Will 1676, goods left unadministered by Jayne SMITH, relict			
6076	Hugh SMITH of Long Ashton	1581	B.A., AC/F8/1–6	
6077	Sir Hugh SMITH of Long Ashton	1680	B.A., AC/F8/1–7	
6078	Sir Hugh SMITH, Baronet, K.B. of Long Ashton	1681	T.N.A., PROB 4/21434	Will also extant

6079	James SMITH of Bishops Lydeard	1641	T.N.A., PROB 2/730	Will T.N.A., PROB 11/186/230
6080	Joan SMITH, Widow of Bristol	1560	B.A., AC/F8/1–8	
6081	Joan SMITH of Taunton St. Mary Magdalene	1671	DD/SP/1671/6	
6082	Joan SMITH of Otterford	1786	DD/MA/13/9–19	
6083	Joane SMITH of Taunton St. Mary Magdalene	1684	DD/SP/1684/131	Wife of John
6084	John SMITH of Bristol	1557	B.A., AC/F8/1–9	
6085	John SMITH of Bishops Lydeard	1587	D/D/cta/S44	Ad.ac.
6086	John SMITH of Taunton	1593	D/D/cta/S41	Ad.ac.
6087	John SMITH of West Chinnock	1623	D/D/cta/S7	Ad.ac.
6088	John SMITH, Yeoman of Wedmore	1679	D/P/wed/23/11	
6089	John SMITH of Ruishton	1679	DD/SP/1679/17	
6090	John SMITH of Nettlecombe	1680	DD/SP/1680/10	
6091	John SMITH, Carpenter of Brompton Ralph	1684	DD/SP/1684/137	
6092	John SMITH, Woolen Draper of Frome Selwood	1685	T.N.A., PROB 4/6055	Will also extant
6093	John SMITH of Taunton	1688	T.N.A., PROB 4/6097	Admon
6094	John SMITH of Luccombe	1700	DD/SP/1700/4	
6095	John SMITH the elder of Crewkerne	1635	DD/SP/1635/81	
6096	Jone SMITH, Widow of Hillfarrance	1630s	DD/SP/1632/38	
	Note: Undated; appraised by William JACOB and Michael WASHER			
6097	Joyce SMITH, Widow of Frome Selwood	1684	T.N.A., PROB 4/2782	Admon
6098	Joyce SMITH of Frome Selwood	1684	T.N.A., PROB 5/3272	
6099	Mathew SMITH of Long Ashton	1583	B.A., AC/F8/1–10	
6100	Miles SMITH of Bath	1737	T.N.A., PROB 31/1737/842	With Commissioners account
6101	Milo SMITH of Bath City	1736	T.N.A., PROB 3/35/75	Mentions cloth etc.
6102	Milo SMITH, Mercer of Bath	1736	T.N.A., PROB 31/1736/189, 1736/248 and 1736/390	With account in T.N.A., PROB 31/1740/539
6103	Richard SMITH, Innholder? of Taunton St. Mary Magdalene	1670	DD/SP/1670/53	Of an inn named the Swan
6104	Richard SMITH of Thornfalcon	1675	DD/SP/1675/91	
6105	Richard SMITH, Yeoman of Milverton	1677	DD/SP/1677/83	
6106	Richard SMITH of Buckingham, Buckinghamshire died at Taunton	1695	T.N.A., PROB 4/17501	Admon
6107	Robert SMITH of Taunton St. Mary Magdalene	1685	DD/SP/1685/78	
6108	Robert SMITH the younger, Yeoman of Crewkerne	1648	DD/SP/1648/40	

6108a	Robert SMITH the younger of Frome Selwood	1661	DD/SAS/S2062/1	
6109	Thomas SMITH, Shoemaker of Taunton	1639	DD/SP/1639/67	
6110	Thomas SMITH of Seaborough	1661	DD/SP/1661/14	
6111	Thomas SMITH, Hosier of Crewkerne	1686	T.N.A., PROB 4/10551	Admon. ex. 1687
6112	Thomas SMITH of Ilchester	1732	T.N.A., PROB 31/1732/191	
6113	Thomas SMITH of Otterford	1768	DD/MA/13/8	
6114	Truth SMITH, Widow of Ashcott	1679	T.N.A., PROB 4/17891	Admon
6115	William SMITH of Lillsdon, North Curry	1590	D/D/ct/1/S99a	
6116	William SMITH of Long Ashton	1619	D/D/cta/S60	Ad.ac.
6117	William SMITH of Norton Fitzwarren	1671	DD/SP/1671/17	
6118	William SMITH of Taunton	1679	DD/SP/1679/10	
6119	William SMITH, Yeoman of South Petherton	1681	DD/SP/1681/9	
6120	William SMITH, Gentleman of Seaborough	1693	T.N.A., PROB 4/8730	Will also extant
6121	William SMITH of Milborne Port	1744	T.N.A., PROB 3/43/39	
6122	William SMITH of Milborne Port	1744	T.N.A., PROB 31/1744/380	
6123	Sara SMITH formerly HONE, Widow of Taunton	1815	T.N.A., PROB 31/1815/952	
SMITH see PEIRCE, SINGER, WORNELL				
6124	Johane SMITHE, Widow of Taunton St. Mary Magdalene	1636	DD/SP/1636/31	
6125	John SMITHFIELD of Wellow	1619	D/D/cta/S61	Ad.ac.
6126	Edmund SMOCKE of Minehead	1635	DD/SP/1635/113	
6127	Alexander SMYTH of Minehead	1635	DD/SP/1635/119	
6128	Florence SMYTH, Widow of Ashton Court, Long Ashton died at Heath House, Stapleton, Gloucestershire	1852	T.N.A., PROB 37/1671	
6129	Robert SMYTH, Husbandman of Comeytrowe, Trull	1635	DD/SP/1635/134	
6130	John SMYTHE of Queen Camel	1558/9	DD/SF/11/1/5–6	Formerly DD/SF 1004–1005
6131	Thomas SMYTHE of Stawell, Moorlinch	1581	D/D/ct/1/S111	
6132	William SMYTHE of Queen Camel	1561	DD/SF/11/1/18	Formerly DD/SF/1007
6133	Charles SNAPE of Wootton Courtenay	1730	T.N.A., PROB 3/29/147	
6134	[missing] SNELLINGE of Minehead ?	1638	DD/SP/1638/30	
	Note: Alice SNELLINGE his widow; mentions 14 debtors from Minehead			
6135	James SNOOKE senior, Husbandman of Pitminster	1677	DD/SP/1677/62	
6136	Andrew SNOW of Porlock	1693	DD/SP/1693/20	
6137	John SNOW of Hamp, Bridgwater	1664	DD/SP/1664/44	

6138	Margaret SNOW of Stoke Pero	1672	DD/SP/1672/38	
6139	Thomas SNOW of Taunton St. James	1684	DD/SP/1684/68	
SNOW see JACOB, JACOBS				
6140	Peter SOAPER, Yeoman of Dinnington	1678	DD/SP/1678/50	
6141	Richard SOAPER of hinton St. George	1640	DD/SP/1640/142	
6142	Gregory SOG of Minehead	1731	DD/SP/1731/31	
6143	John SOMERHAYES of Wellington	1732	T.N.A., PROB 3/31/6	
6144	Robert SOMERS of Middlezoy	1621	D/D/cta/S19	Ad.ac.
6145	Walter SOMERS, Yeoman of Pensford St. Thomas, Publow	1700	T.N.A., PROB 4/17050	Will also extant
6146	Nicholas SOMERSETT, Miller of Dinnington	1695	DD/SP/1695/16	
6147	Julyan SOPER of Stawell, Moorlinch	1581	D/D/ct/1/S124	
6148	Thomas SORE alias SHEPPARD of Chew Magna	1621	D/D/cta/S12	Ad.ac.
6149	[missing] SORRAGE alias HAGLEY, Yeoman of Chipstable	1716	DD/SP/1716/27	
6150	Anthony SOUTHCOT of Porlock	1670	DD/SP/1670/17	
6151	Thomasin SOUTHCOTT, Widow of Chipstable	1688	DD/SP/1688/39	
6152	Richard SOUTHEY the elder of Wellington	1670	T.N.A., PROB 4/8454	Will also extant
SOUTHEY see THURSTON, WARRE				
SOUTHIE see SHORNY				
6153	[missing] SOUTHWOOD of Monksilver	1671	DD/SP/1671/16	
6154	John SOUTHWOOD of Crowcombe	1681	DD/SP/1681/14	
6155	Katherine SOUTHWOOD of Pitminster	1734	DD/MT/5/iv	
6156	Michael SOUTHWOOD of [no place]	1620	DD/MT/64	
6157	Peter SOUTHWOOD of Pitminster	1691	DD/MT/61	
6158	Thomas SOWTHEY junior of Milverton	1685	DD/SP/1685/86	
6159	Anne SPARKE, Widow of Fivehead	1713	DD/SP/1713/31	
6160	Edward SPARKE, Roper of Minehead	1688	DD/SP/1688/11	
6161	Elizabeth SPARKE, Widow of Abbots Leigh	1671	B.A., 1671/40	Will also extant
6162	John SPARKE of Porlock	1675	DD/SP/1675/62	
6163	John SPARKE, Yeoman of Pitminster	1678	DD/SP/1678/33	
6164	Peter SPARKE, Yeoman of Buckland St. Mary	1676	DD/SP/1676/34	
6165	William, minor SPARKE of Luccombe	1697	DD/SP/1697/35	
6166	Hugh SPARKES of Abbots Leigh	1682	B.A., 1692/38	
6167	John SPARKES, Blacksmith of Porlock	1639	DD/SP/1639/64	

6168	John SPARKES, Yeoman of Keynsham	1734	D/D/Cti 78	
6169	William SPARKES, Shipwright of Abbots Leigh	1726	B.A., 1726/30	Died at sea
6170	Mary SPARKS, Widow of Keynsham	1736	D/D/Cti 86	
6171	Elizabeth SPARROW, Widow of Abbots Leigh	1674	B.A., 1674/39	Will also extant
6172	Henry SPARROW, Husbandman of Abbots Leigh	1672	B.A., 1672/52	Will also extant
6173	Richard SPARROWE of Abbots Leigh	1618	B.A., 1618/67	Will also extant
6174	William SPEARING, Woolen Draper of Axbridge	1691	T.N.A., PROB 4/11485	Will 1691
6175	John SPEEKE, Gentleman of Bath	1670	T.N.A., PROB 4/10193	Admon
6176	John SPEER of Trull	1680	T.N.A., PROB 4/17633	Will also extant
6177	Agnes SPENCER of Crewkerne	1646	DD/SP/1646/35	See *T.C.W.*
6178	John SPENCER, Mason of Abbas Combe, Abbas and Temple Combe	1622	D/D/cta/S32	Ad.ac.
6179	William SPENCER of Cheddar	1661	DD/SAS/FA/161/1	
6180	Henry SPENDER, Glover of Yeovil	1697	T.N.A., PROB 4/21707	Will also extant
6181	Henry SPENDER of Yeovil	1697	T.N.A., PROB 5/4956	
6182	John SPENSER, Yeoman of Huntspill	1689	DD/ALN Box 1	
6183	John SPICER alias GOODMAN of Milverton	1673	DD/SP/1673/37	
6184	Hugh SPILLER of Ilminster	1728	DD/CHG/48	
6185	Hugh SPILLER the elder of Donyatt	1679	DD/CHG/48	
6186	John SPIRRING, Husbandman of West Harptree	1632	D/D/ct/1/S128a	
6187	John SPOORE, Yeoman of North Petherton	1692	DD/SP/1692/4	
6188	Hester SPORIE of Porlock	1645	DD/SP/1645/66	
6189	Bartholomew SPORRYER of Porlock	1635	DD/SP/1635/69	See *T.C.W.*
6190	Launcelot SPORRYER of Dunster	1725	DD/SP/1725/20	
6191	Henry SPRAGUE of Minehead, lived in Waterford, Ireland	1690	DD/SP/1690/53	
	Note: He lived in Waterford, Ireland and his children were sent to the Grandmother Elizabeth BAKER in Minehead			
6192	John SPRAKE of Taunton	1664	DD/SP/1664/55	
6193	John SPRAKE of Taunton	1689	T.N.A., PROB 4/4590	Will 1687
6194	John SPREAT, Gentleman of Nynehead	1734	T.N.A., PROB 3/33/9	
6195	John SPREAT, Gentleman of Nynehead	1734	T.N.A., PROB 31/1734/51	
6196	William SPREAT of Stogursey	1666	DD/SP/1666/45	
6197	Richard SPREATT, Gentleman of Taunton St. Mary Magdalene	1697	DD/SP/1697/5	
6198	Ann SPROUTING, Widow of Bridgwater	1678	DD/SP/1678/17	
6199	Robert SPRUDE of Congresbury	1581	D/D/ct/1/S134	

6200	Daniel SPURLE, Innholder of Stogumber	1694	DD/SP/1694/3	
6201	Elizabeth SPURRIER, Widow of Oare	1679	DD/SP/1679/8	
6202	Henry SPURRIER, Blacksmith of Luccombe	1680	DD/SP/1680/28	
6203	Peter SPURRIER of Porlock	1667	DD/SP/1667/5	
6204	Peter SPURRIER, Bachelor of Oare	1762	T.N.A., PROB 31/1762/766	With ad.ac. 31/1762/300
6205	Henry SPURRYER, Tanner of Selworthy	1721	DD/SP/1721/7	
6206	William SPYRYNG of Litton	1558	T.N.A., PROB 2/330	Will T.N.A., PROB 11/42B/19
6207	Ann SQUIER, Widow of Shepton Beauchamp	1628/9	D/D/ct/1/S140	
6208	Gregorie SQUIER of Isle Abbotts	1635	DD/SP/1635/54	
6209	Sebastian SQUIRE, Barber of Taunton St. Mary Magdalene	1695	DD/SP/1695/37	
6210	David SQUIRLE of Winsford	1675	DD/SP/1675/11	
6211	John SQUYRES of Lyng	1730	DD/SP/1730/24	
6212	Agnes STABBS of Taunton St. Mary Magdalene	1641	DD/SP/1641/4	Damaged
6213	Joan STABBS of Taunton St. James	1677	DD/SP/1677/44	
6214	Nicholas STABBS of Taunton	1667	DD/SP/1667/80	
6215	John STACEY, Husbandman of North Petherton	1681	DD/SP/1681/24	
6216	John STACIE of North Petherton	1685	DD/SP/1685/99	
6217	William STACIE of North Curry	1589	D/D/ct/1/S142a	
6218	William STACIE, Cordwainer of North Petherton	1684	DD/SP/1684/93	
6219	George STACY of Enmore	1635	DD/SP/1635/109	
6220	Richard STACY, Husbandman of North Petherton	1652	DD/SP/1652/9	
6221	Walter STACYE the elder of Marsh, Horsington	1678	DD/DNL/151	
6222	Emlin STAGG, Widow of Cheddon Fitzpaine	1683	DD/SP/1683/4	
6223	Jane STAINER, Widow of Ham Green, Easton in Gordano	1690	B.A., 1690/42	Will also extant
6224	Thomas STALKER, Bachelor of Bath City	1755	T.N.A., PROB 3/54/14	
6225	Thomas STALKER, Bachelor of Bath	1755	T.N.A., PROB 31/1755/118 and 1755/325	
6226	Gyles STALLENDGE of Creech St. Michael	1684	DD/SP/1684/172	
6227	Robert STALLENGE of Bishops Lydeard	1639	D/D/cta/S17	Ad.ac.
6228	Henry STANDARD, Husbandman of Fivehead	1640	DD/SP/1640/88	
6229	John STANDARD of Lyng	1730	DD/SP/1730/16	
6230	Edward STANDARS of Fivehead	1693	DD/SP/1693/44	
6231	Elizabeth STANDERD the younger of North Petherton	1635	DD/SP/1635/43	

6232	Francis STANDERWICK, Yeoman of Combe St. Nicholas	1677	T.N.A., PROB 4/20758	Admon
6233	Richard STANDERWICK of Broadway	1675	DD/SP/1675/92	
6234	Richard STANDERWICK of Bickenhall	1678	DD/SP/1678/88	
6235	Alexander STANDFAST of Dunwear, Bridgwater	1666	DD/SP/1666/74	
6236	Dorothy STANDFAST, Widow of Tolland	1640	DD/SP/1640/93	See *T.C.W.*
6237	John STANDFAST of Lydeard St. Lawrence	1640	DD/SP/1640/61	
6238	John STANDFAST of Lydeard St. Lawrence	1669	DD/SP/1669/27	
6239	John STANDFAST of Withycombe	1670	DD/SP/1670/12	
6240	Thomas STANDFAST, Yeoman of Cheddon Fitzpaine	1675	DD/SP/1675/1	
6241	Thomas STANDFAST of Cheddon Fitzpaine	1692	DD/SP/1692/26	See also D/P/che.f. 2/1/2
6242	Cornelius STANTON of Taunton	1557	T.N.A., PROB 2/306	Will T.N.A., PROB 11
6243	Edward STAPLE of South Brent	1629	D/D/ct/1/S144a	
6244	Leonard STAPLE, Hosier of Wambrook	1665	W.S.H.C., P5/1665/77	Inv. and will
6245	Sarah STAPLE, Widow of Thornfalcon	1684	DD/SP/1684/72	
6246	Thomas STAPLE of Wambrook	1590	W.S.H.C., P5/1590/53	Inv., tuition bond, will
6247	Thomas STAPLE, Husbandman of Wambrook Note: Admon. bond, com., inv., letter	1648	W.S.H.C., P5/1647/15	
6248	Thomas STAPLETON, Blacksmith of High Ham	1735	D/D/Cti 76	
6249	Aaron STARK of Chard	1781	DD/WL/11	
6250	Hugh STARKE, Husbandman of Cricket St. Thomas	1635	DD/SP/1635/34	
6251	Hugh STARKE of Taunton St. Mary Magdalene	1681	DD/SP/1681/59	Lists shop contents and creditors
6252	Richard STARKEY, Yeoman of Durleigh	1720	DD/SP/1720/25	
6253	Ann STARR, Widow of Curry Rivel	1682	DD/SP/1682/46	
6254	Edward STARR of Yeovil	1692	T.N.A., PROB 5/5776	
6255	Edward STARRE of Yeovil	1671	T.N.A., PROB 5/3222	
6256	Richard START, Mercer of Porlock	1720	DD/SP/1720/12	Detailed list of cloths
6257	Robert STAWELL the elder of Cothelstone	*c*.1500	T.N.A., PROB 2/461	
6258	Thomas STAYNER of Stogumber	1683	T.N.A., PROB 4/8834	Will also extant
6259	William STAYNER, Shipwright of Abbots Leigh	1641	B.A., 1641/50	
6260	Ann STAYNINGS, Singlewoman of Selworthy	1682	DD/SP/1682/51	
6261	John STAYNINGS of Winsford	1634	DD/SP/1634/19	
6262	Ambrose STEARE, Yeoman of Sampford Arundel	1698	DD/SP/1698/32	
6263	Andrew STEARE of Taunton St. Mary Magdalene	1669	DD/SP/1669/51	

6264	Lawrence STEAVANS of Hillfarrance	1716	DD/SP/1716/56	
STEAVENS see STEPHENS				
6265	George STEDMAN, Gentleman of Downside, Midsomer Norton	1686	T.N.A., PROB 4/1991	Will. ex. 1687
6266	Henry STEEDS of Combhay	1738	D/D/Cti 88	
6267	John STEEVEN of Stogumber	1640	DD/SP/1640/145	
6268	Richard STEEVENS, Husbandman of Lydeard St. Lawrence	1683	DD/SP/1683/39	
6269	Roger STEEVENS, Singleman of Brompton Regis	1667	DD/SP/1667/60	
6270	William STEEVENS of Lydeard St. Lawrence	1685	DD/SP/1685/46	
STEMBRIDGE see SWEETING (Elizabeth)				
6271	Sarah STENNER, Widow of Williton, St. Decumans	1810	T.N.A., PROB 31/1810/1189	
6272	Elizabeth STENTON, Widow of Isle Abbotts	1639	DD/SP/1639/48	
6273	Robert STEPHEN junior of Brompton Regis	1675	DD/SP/1675/71	
6274	[missing] STEPHENS of Lydeard St. Lawrence	1667	DD/SP/1667/41	Proved by Mary, Widow
6275	[missing] STEPHENS of Taunton?	1673	DD/SP/1673/16	
	Note: Incomplete entry, mentions timber and standings in Taunton			
6276	Henry STEPHENS, Gentleman of Stogursey	1680	DD/SP/1680/87	
6277	John STEPHENS, Clothier of Holford	1681	DD/SP/1681/38	
6278	Richard STEPHENS of Goathurst	1684	DD/SP/1684/17	
6279	Simon STEPHENS, Victualler of Taunton St. Mary Magdalene	1729	DD/SP/1729/64	
6280	Thomas STEPHENS, Husbandman of Brompton Ralph	1666	DD/SP/1666/37	
6281	Thomas STEPHENS of Crowcombe	1700	DD/SP/442/39	Ad.ac.
6282	William STEPHENS of West Monkton	1689	DD/SP/1689/47	
6283	William STEPHENS of Lower Marsh, Kingston St. Mary	1730	DD/SP/1730/12	
STEPHENS see STEEVENS, STEVENS, etc				
6284	Joane STEVANS, Widow of Weston-super-Mare	1638/9	D/D/ct/1/S150	
6285	Robert STEVEN of Brompton Regis	1642	DD/SP/1642/21	
6286	Alice STEVENS of Buckland St. Mary	1680	DD/SP/1680/4	
6287	Christian STEVENS of Brompton Regis	1611	D/D/cta/S58	Ad.ac.
6288	Francis STEVENS, Bachelor of Easton in Gordano	1719	T.N.A., PROB 3/18/257	
6289	Lawrence STEVENS of Hillfarrance	1717	DD/SP/442/25	Ad.ac.
6290	Robert STEVENS of [no place]	1620	D/D/ct/1/S152	Pvd 1620
6291	Thomas STEVENS of Pitcombe	1622	D/D/cta/S20	Ad.ac.
6292	Thomas STEVENS of Pitcombe	1622	D/D/cta/S22	

6293	Thomas STEVENS of Crowcombe	1673	DD/SP/1673/27	
6294	Thomas STEVENS, Yeoman of Langford Budville	1674	DD/SP/1674/24	
6295	Thomas STEVENS of Crowcombe	1700	DD/SP/1700/8	
6296	William STEVENS, Yeoman of Milverton	1680	DD/SP/1680/100	
6297	Daniel STEWART of Taunton	1804	T.N.A., PROB 31/1804/1029	With ad.ac.
6298	David STEWART of Taunton St. Mary Magdalene	1802	T.N.A., PROB 31/1802/11	
6299	Bess STEYNINGS of [no place]	n.d.	DD/WO/57/3	
6300	Joane STIBBS, Widow of Stockland Bristol	1681	DD/SP/1681/54	
6301	John STIBS of Nunney	1677	D/D/ct/1/S157	
6302	Isabel STIDMAN of Ashwick	1595	D/D/cta/S40	Ad.ac.
6303	Mary STILINGE, Widow of North Petherton	1641	DD/SP/1641/74	
6304	Robert STILL of Wellington	1589	D/D/cta/S46	Ad.ac.
6305	Ambrose STIRGES of Moorlinch	1666	D/D/cta/S52	Ad.ac.
6306	Richard STITCHELL, Minister of Isle Brewers	1684	DD/SP/1684/136	
6307	John STOAD of Curry Rivel	1700	DD/SP/1700/2	
6308	John STOAKS of Chelwood	1735	D/D/Cti 81	
6309	Elizabeth STOATE of Selworthy	1641	DD/SP/1641/77	See *T.C.W.*
6310	Henry STOATE, Carpenter of Exford	1684	DD/SP/1684/163	
6311	Thomas STOATE of Withypool	1684	DD/SP/1684/85	
6312	John STOCK, Drugget maker of Rode	1722	T.N.A., PROB 3/21/105	
6313	John STOCKE, Yeoman of Sidcot, Winscombe	1670	T.N.A., PROB 4/4466	Will also extant
6314	William STOCKE the younger of Porlock	1683	DD/SP/1683/38	
6315	George STOCKER, Woolen Draper of Ilminster	1686	T.N.A., PROB 4/8971	Admon
6316	Joseph STOCKER, Mercer of Wiveliscombe	1679	T.N.A., PROB 4/20722	Will also extant
6317	Mary STOCKER of Chilcompton	1670	T.N.A., PROB 5/5269	
6318	William STOCKER, Gentleman of Chilcompton	1723	T.N.A., PROB 3/22/125	
6319	Andrew STOCKHAM of East Quantoxhead	1704	DD/SP/442/62	Ad.ac.
6320	Robert STOCKMAN, Sheargrinder of Taunton St. Mary Magdalene	1670	DD/SP/1670/70	
6321	John STOCKS of Luccombe	1680	DD/SP/1680/85	
6322	Elizabeth STODDEN, Widow of Pitminster	1695	DD/SP/1695/29	
6323	Elizabeth STODDEN, Widow of The Three Chalks Inn, Stogursey	1737	DD/SP/1737/37	

6324	George STODDEN of Selworthy	1674	DD/SP/1674/6	
6325	John STODDEN, Bachelor of Selworthy	1640	DD/SP/1640/62	
6326	John STODDEN of North Petherton	1681	DD/SP/1681/28	
6327	Robert STODDEN, Bachelor of Selworthy	1638	DD/SP/1638/29	
6328	William STODDEN, Tanner of Selworthy	1635	DD/SP/1635/6	See *T.C.W.*
6329	Christian STODDEN alias BLACKFORD, Widow of Selworthy	1640	DD/SP/1640/6	
6330	Lewis STODDEN alias BLACKFORD of Selworthy	1640	DD/SP/1640/148	
6331	John STODGELL of North Petherton	1668	DD/SP/1668/13	
6332	Mary STODGELL of North Petherton	1668	DD/SP/1668/18	
6333	Nicholas STODGELL senior, Husbandman of Creech St. Michael	1676	DD/SP/1676/20	
6334	Nicholas STOGELL junior of North Petherton	1676	DD/SP/1676/21	
6335	John STOKES of Winscombe	1663	D/D/cta/S49	Ad.ac.
6336	Jonas STOKES of Hinton Blewett	1707	D/D/cta/S67	Ad.ac.
6337	Samuel STOKES, Gentleman of Tickenham	1752	T.N.A., PROB 3/51/11	
6338	William STOKHAM, Husbandman of East Quantoxhead	1667	DD/SP/1667/83	
6339	Agnes STOLE, Widow of Berrow	1633/4	D/D/ct/1/S163a	
6340	Joan STOLEY, Widow of Porlock	1674	DD/SP/1674/19	
6341	Augustine STONE of Sampford Arundel	1666	DD/SP/1666/15	
6342	Avis STONE of Cannington	1634	DD/SP/1634/42	
6343	Christopher STONE, Husbandman of Milverton	1689	DD/SP/1689/33	
6344	Elizabeth STONE of Poleshill, Milverton	1670	DD/SP/1670/101	
6345	Elizabeth STONE, Widow of Cannington	1675	DD/SP/1675/45	
6346	Elizabeth STONE, Stockingmaker of Stoke St. Michael	1742	D/D/cta/S68	
	Note: Ad.ac. and inv.; died in 1742			
6347	George STONE, Miller of Failand, Wraxall	1629	D/D/ct/1/S165	
6348	George STONE of Chipstable	1720	DD/SP/1720/14	
6349	George STONE of Chipstable	1720/1	DD/SP/442/69	Ad.ac.
6350	Giles STONE of Withycombe	1644	DD/SP/1644/60	
6351	Henry STONE, Yeoman of Cannington	1637	DD/SP/1637/57	
6352	Joan STONE, Widow of Clatworthy	1697	DD/SP/1697/69	
6353	Joane STONE of Stogursey	*c*.1590	D/D/cta/S5	Ad.ac.
6354	John STONE of Shapwick	1665	D/D/cta/S53	Ad.ac.
6355	John STONE of Rodway, Cannington	1671	DD/SP/1671/40	

6356	John STONE of Raddington	1683	DD/SP/1683/95	
6357	John STONE of Upton	1692	T.N.A., PROB 4/9308	Will also extant
6358	John STONE, Husbandman of Curry Rivel	1731	D/D/Cti 80	
6359	Mary STONE, Widow of Ashbrittle	1694	T.N.A., PROB 4/21694	Will 1695. ex. 1695
6360	Nicholas STONE, Clothier of Langford Budville	1697	T.N.A., PROB 4/13302	Will also extant
6361	Nicholas STONE senior of Banwell	1664	T.N.A., PROB 5/3075–6	PROB 5/314
6362	Radegan STONE, Widow of Chipstable	1634	DD/SP/1634/16	
6363	Richard STONE, Husbandman of West Monkton	1640	DD/SP/1640/44	
6364	Richard STONE of Bridgwater	1667	DD/SP/1667/27	
6365	Richard STONE of Bruton	1728	T.N.A., PROB 3/27/59	
6366	Robert STONE, Husbandman of Oake	1664	DD/SP/1664/2	
6367	Robert STONE of Chipstable	1728	A/EEN/42	
6368	Robert STONE of Brushford	1766	T.N.A., PROB 31/1766/511	
6369	Robert Yeoman STONE of Sampford Brett	1785	T.N.A., PROB 31/1785/823	
6370	Samuel STONE of Wiveliscombe	1677	T.N.A., PROB 4/6103	Admon
6371	Stephen STONE of Taunton St. Mary Magdalene	1690	DD/SP/1690/45	
6372	Thomas STONE of Otterhampton	1620	D/D/cta/S6	Ad.ac.
6373	Thomas STONE of Ashbrittle	1684	T.N.A., PROB 4/17324	Admon
6374	Thomas STONE of Bridgwater	1695	DD/SP/1695/9	
6375	Thomasin STONE, Widow of Ashbrittle	1684	DD/SP/1684/105	
6376	[missing] STONE? of [no place]	1694	DD/SP/1694/17	Incomplete, mentions John STONE, nephew
6377	George STORIE of Nyland, Glastonbury	1623	D/D/cta/S23	Ad.ac.
6378	Edmund STORKE of Lyng	1689	DD/SP/1689/23	
6379	John STOT of Exford	1664	DD/SP/1664/41	
6380	John STOUER of Curry Mallet	1637	DD/SP/1637/41	
STOUER see STOWER				
6381	William STOURTON, Yeoman of Isle Brewers	1691	DD/SP/1691/4	
6382	Mary STOWELL, Singlewoman of West Monkton	1688	DD/SP/1688/28	
6383	Peter STOWELL, Mason of Taunton St. James	1637	DD/SP/1637/48	See *T.C.W.*
6384	Thomas STOWELL of Bridgwater	1673	DD/SP/1673/21	
6385	Matthew STOWER of Glastonbury	1728	D/D/Cti 79	
6386	Roger STOWER of Walton	1639	D/D/cta/S31	Ad.ac.

6387	Walter STOWEY of Winsford	1636	DD/SP/1636/18	
6388	Joan STOWLEY, Singlewoman of Luccombe	1699	DD/SP/1699/2	
6389	Margery STRACEY, Widow of Creech St. Michael	1679	DD/SP/1679/45	
6390	Robert STRACEY, Yeoman of Creech St. Michael	1679	DD/SP/1679/46	
6391	Hodges STRACHEY of Sutton Court, Stowey	1746	DD/SH/79/10/31	
6392	John STRACHEY of Sutton Court, Stowey	1675	DD/SH/79/9 c/2480	
6393	Francis Adams STRADLING of Chedzoy	1844	DD/S/ST/13	
6394	Mary STRADLING of Wembdon	1829	DD/S/ST/14	
6395	Isott STRANG of Dulverton	1640	DD/SP/1640/73	
6396	John STRANGE of Sampford Brett	1687	DD/SP/1687/38	
6397	Joseph STRANGE of Sampford Brett	1729	DD/SP/1729/49	
6398	Mary STRANGE alias EDWARDS, Spinster of Milverton	1685	DD/SP/1685/59	
6399	Giles STRANGEWAYS of Compton Dundon	n.d.	T/PH/dst 1	Extract only
6400	Giles STRANGWAIES of [no place]	1720	DD/SF/15/2/35	Formerly DD/SF/3888
6401	Giles STRANGWAYS, Esquire of Charlton Adam	1678	T.N.A., PROB 4/497	Will ex. 1678
6402	William STRAWBRIDGE of Cannington	1720	DD/SP/1720/21	
6403	Elizabeth STREET, Widow of Angersleigh	1684	DD/SP/1684/115	
6404	John STREET junior of Minehead	1669	DD/SP/1669/31	
6405	Michael STREET of East Quantoxhead	1635	DD/SP/1635/44	
6406	William STREET of Kilve	1698	DD/SP/1698/45	
STRETTINGER see ELSWORTHY				
6407	[missing] STRICK of [no place]	1811, 1812	DD/PL/52/c/463	
6408	Thomas STRICKLAND, Blacksmith of Barrington	1680	DD/SP/1680/63	
6409	John STRIDE, Mercer of Dunster	1713	DD/SP/1713/25	
6410	William STRIDE of Bruton	1683	T.N.A., PROB 4/6308	Will 1683
6411	Gabriel STRINGER of Stowell	1723	D/D/cta/S69	Ad.ac.
6412	Reverend Thomas STRINGER, Clerk of Chard	1794	T.N.A., PROB 31/1794/793	
6413	James STRODE, Merchant of Shepton Mallet	1684	T.N.A., PROB 4/8739	Will also extant
6414	Martha STRODE, Widow of Fonthill, West Cranmore	1729	T.N.A., PROB 31/1729/512	
6415	Thomas STRODE of Maperton and Shepton Mallet	1697	T.N.A., PROB 4/19652	Will 1697. ex. 1698
6416	William STRODE, Esquire of Somerton	1500	T.N.A., PROB 2/165	Will T.N.A., PROB 11/12/113
6417	William STRODE of Hardington Mandeville	1825	T.N.A., PROB 31/1825/337	

6418	Ann STRONG, Widow of Hinton St. George	1729	DD/SP/1729/51	
6419	Elizabeth STRONG of Wootton Courtenay	1629	D/D/ct/1/S176a	
6420	George STRONG, Tailor of Taunton	1669	DD/SP/1669/92	
6421	George STRONG the elder of Watchet, St. Decumans	1634	D/D/cta/S9	Ad.ac.
6422	Henry STRONG of Carhampton	1670	T.N.A., PROB 4/15461	Will 1669. ex. 1670
6423	Hugh STRONG of Wootton Courtenay	1668	DD/SP/1668/37	
6424	John STRONG, Joiner of Wootton Courtenay	1683	DD/SP/1683/44	
6425	Charles STROUD(E) of Butleigh	1737	D/D/cta/S70	
	Note: Ad.ac. and inv.; died in 1737			
6426	Edward STROUDE of Fivehead	1686	DD/SP/1686/31	
6427	Roger STROWDE of Fivehead	1639	DD/SP/1639/16	
6428	Elizabeth STUCKEY, Widow of Chaffcombe	1725	DD/SP/1725/4	
6429	Henry STUCKEY of South Petherton	1696	DD/SP/1696/3	
6430	John STUCKEY of Curry Rivel	1731	DD/SP/1731/9	
6431	John STUCKEY the elder of Dinnington	1669	DD/SP/1669/26	
6432	Katerne STUCKEY, Widow of Compton Durville, South Petherton	1648	DD/SP/1648/59	
6433	Paschia STUCKEY of Barrington ?	1630s	DD/SP/1632/39	
	Note: Undated; goods bequeathed to Maria STUCKEY his daughter (Reg.)			
6434	Thomas STUCKEY, Husbandman of Barrington	1688	DD/SP/1688/29	
6435	William STUCKEY, Husbandman of Crewkerne	1646	DD/SP/1646/10	
6436	William STUCKEY of Curry Rivel	1684	DD/SP/1684/21	
6437	George STUDDIER the elder of Enmore	1640	DD/SP/1640/83	
STUDIER see PORTER				
6438	George STUDYER of Enmore	1677	DD/SP/1677/72	
6439	William STURREDGE of Bath	1622	D/D/cta/S25	Ad.ac.
6440	John STURTON of Isle Brewers	1681	DD/SP/1681/41	
6441	Thomas STURTON, Brazier of South Petherton	1683	T.N.A., PROB 4/8495	Admon
6442	John STUTT of Bradford	1677	DD/SP/1677/38	
6443	Roger STYLE of [no place]	1623	D/D/cta/S14	Ad.ac.
6444	Henry SUGAR of Charlton Adam	1611	D/D/cta/S64	Ad.ac.
6445	Henry SUGAR of Charlton Adam	1611	D/D/cta/S66	Ad.ac.
6446	William SUGG, Thatcher of Yeovil	1629	D/D/cta/S27	Ad.ac.

6447	George SULLEY the elder, Yeoman of Nettlecombe	1669	DD/SP/1669/97	
6448	Alice SULLY, Widow of Withiel Florey	1640	DD/SP/1640/7	
6449	Anthony SULLY, Butcher of Staplegrove	1665	DD/SP/1665/15	
6450	Bennony SULLY of North Petherton	1713	DD/SP/1713/6	
6451	Caleb SULLY, Tailor of Cutcombe	1694	DD/SP/1694/10	Reference to materials, spices, etc.
6452	Henry SULLY of Kingston St. Mary	1716	DD/SP/1716/33	
6453	John SULLY of Cutcombe	1692	DD/SP/1692/30	
6454	John SULLY, Clerk of Crowcombe	1700	DD/SP/1700/21	
6455	John SULLY, Clerk of Crowcombe	1700	DD/SP/1700/25	
6457	John SULLY, Clerk of Crowcombe	1700/1	DD/SP/442/38	Ad.ac.
6458	Thomas SULLY of Winsford	1661	DD/SP/1661/15	
6459	Thomas SULLY, Blacksmith of Goathurst	1684	DD/SP/1684/76	
6460	William SULLY of Stogumber	1678	DD/SP/1678/29	
6461	William SULLY, Yeoman of Withiel Florey	1690	DD/SP/1690/39	
6462	Elizabeth SULLY (SELLY), Widow of Nettlecombe	1671	DD/SP/1671/21	
SULLY see JEFFORD				
6463	Josias SUMERILL, Blacksmith of Nettlecombe	1721	DD/SP/1721/17	
6464	John SUMERTON, Clothier of Taunton	1649	DD/SP/1649/70	
6465	Thomas SURFILL of Hillfarrance	1684	DD/SP/1684/133	
6466	Thomas SUTTON, Husbandman of Queen Camel	1623	D/D/cta/S24	Ad.ac.
6467	William SWAINE of Winscombe	1600	D/D/cta/S54	Ad.ac.
6468	William SWAINE, Yeoman of Seavington St. Mary	1685	DD/SP/1685/61	
6469	William SWAINE of [no place]	1693	DD/SP/1693/72	
6470	John SWAN of Enmore	1635	DD/SP/1635/110	
6471	William SWAYNE of East Brent	1666	D/D/cta/S51	Ad.ac.
6472	John SWEATLAND of Frome Selwood	1704	T.N.A., PROB 4/22638	Will also extant
6473	John SWEET the elder of Middle Chinnock	1681	T.N.A., PROB 4/6952	Will also extant
SWEETE see BINGHAM				
6474	Elizabeth SWEETING of Staplegrove	1689	DD/SP/1689/38	
	Note: Moiety of the goods now belonging to Elizabeth STEMBRIDGE, minor			
6475	Elizabeth SWEETING of Kilve	1690	DD/SP/1690/33	
6476	Giles SWEETING of Bicknoller	1691	DD/SP/1691/83	
6477	Henry SWEETING, Yeoman of Crowcombe	1688	DD/SP/1688/16	

6478	Henry SWEETING the younger, Yeoman of Elworthy	1670	DD/SP/1670/114	
6479	Henry SWEETING the younger, Yeoman of Elworthy	1670	DD/SP/1670/72	
6480	Hugh SWEETING junior of Stogumber	1685	DD/SP/1685/87	
6481	John SWEETING, Yeoman of Crowcombe	1697	DD/SP/1697/27	
6482	John SWEETING of Crowcombe	1706	DD/SP/442/60	Ad.ac.
6483	Lewes SWEETING of Bishops Lydeard	1687	T.N.A., PROB 4/21049	Will 1687
6484	Lewis SWEETING, Yeoman of Stogursey	1721	DD/SP/1721/15	
6485	Susannah SWEETING of Stogumber	1731	DD/SP/1731/34	
6486	Henry SWEETTING junior of Elworthy	1671	DD/SP/1671/42	
6487	Thomas SWETTING, Clothier of Tolland	1677	DD/SP/1677/75	
6488	Mary SWINERTON the elder of Taunton St. Mary Magdalene	1692	D/D/cta/S57	Ad.ac.
6489	Antipas SWINNERTON the elder, Wool-stapler of Taunton St. Mary Magdalene	1680	T.N.A., PROB 4/9058	Will also extant
6490	Humphrey SYDENHAM of Dulverton	1692	T.N.A., PROB 5/4959	
6491	Joan SYDENHAM of Cannington	1499	T.N.A., PROB 2/160	Will T.N.A., PROB 11/11/35
6492	Mary SYDENHAM, Mistress of Oake	1666	DD/SP/1666/63	
6493	William SYDENHAM of Dulverton	1692	DD/SP/1692/8	
6494	[missing] SYLLY of [no place]	1670	DD/SP/1670/115	
6495	John SYME, Husbandman of Mark	1619/20	D/D/ct/1/S187	
6496	Henry SYMES the elder, Woolen Draper of Axbridge	1686	T.N.A., PROB 4/8977	Will 1687. ex. 1687
6497	John SYMES of Mathews Field, Bridgwater	1691	DD/SP/1691/12	
6498	John SYMES, Merchant of Bridgwater	1716	DD/SP/1716/34	
6499	Stephen SYMES, Husbandman of Wambrook	1640	W.S.H.C., P14/1	Inv., note of probate, will
6500	Steven and Alice SYMES, Husbandman of Wambrook	1641	W.S.H.C., P5/1641/82	Admon. bond, inv.
6501	Thomas SYMES of South Petherton	1605	D/D/cta/S59	Ad.ac.
6502	William SYMES of Westonzoyland	1607	D/D/ct/1/S191	
6503	William SYMES of Asker[swell], Dorset died at Glastonbury Note: Admon, goods unadministered by Anne his relict, also deceased	1668	T.N.A., PROB 4/11186	
6504	William SYMES, Clothier of Shepton Mallet	1691	T.N.A., PROB 4/7657	Will 1691. ex. 1692
6505	Judith SYMMONS, Spinster of Churchill	1688	T.N.A., PROB 4/19221	Admon
6506	Elizabeth SYMONDS, Widow of Wembdon	1670	DD/SP/1670/39	
6507	John SYMONDS of Portbury	1719	DD/X/WI 4 c/2608	
6508	John SYMONDS, Gentleman of Portbury	1722	T.N.A., PROB 3/21/150	

6509	Francis SYMONS of Stogursey	1690	DD/SP/1690/81	
6510	John SYMONS of East Brent Court, East Brent	1581	D/D/ct/1/S193	
6511	John SYMONS of Otterhampton	1690	DD/SP/1690/37	
6512	John SYMONS of Winford	1697	DD/SP/1697/14	
6513	John SYMONS, Husbandman of Stogursey	1731	DD/SP/1731/8	
6514	Thomas SYMONS, Tanner of Shurton, Stogursey	1691	DD/SP/1691/58	
6515	William SYMONS alias BUTCHER of Horsey, Bridgwater	1680	DD/SP/1680/70	
6516	John SYMS of Wick St. Lawrence	1639	D/D/cta/S30	
	Note: Ad.ac.; see burial register for 30 January 1638/9			
6517	John TACHELL, Yeoman of West Coker	1694	T.N.A., PROB 4/6191	Will also extant
6518	Mary TACHELL of West Coker	1690	T.N.A., PROB 4/19935	Will also extant
6519	Thomas TAGG, Innkeeper of Bath	1736	D/D/cta/T18	Ad.ac. and inv.
6520	William TAGG, Widower of Bath	1766	T.N.A., PROB 31/1766/678	
6521	George TAIGHLER the elder of Old Cleeve	1629	D/D/ct/1/T2a	
6522	Andrew TAILLER, Fuller of Selworthy	1637	DD/SP/1637/16	
6523	John TAILLER of Isle Brewers	1640	DD/SP/1640/51	
TAILLER see TAYLER				
6524	John TALBOT of Ilton	1678	T.N.A., PROB 4/18817	Will also extant
6525	John TALBOT, Yeoman of Bathealton	1698	DD/SP/1698/42	
6526	Dorothy TALBOTT, Spinster of Sutton Mallet, Moorlinch	1667	D/D/cta/T17	Ad.ac.
6527	Thomas TALBOTT, Yeoman of Butleigh	1612	D/D/ct/1/T3	
6528	William TALBUTT, Baker of South Brewham	1629	D/D/ct/1/T5a	
6529	James TAMPSON of Ruishton	1632/3	DD/SP/1632/25	
6530	William TANNAR, Mariner of Minehead	1667	DD/SP/1667/62	
6531	Alice TANNER of Portishead	1591	D/D/cta/T43	Ad.ac.
6532	Benjamin TANNER, Draper of Frome	1741	T.N.A., PROB 3/40/21	Mentions drapery etc.
6533	Benjamin TANNER of Frome	1741	T.N.A., PROB 31/1741/197	
6534	Henry TANNER, Yeoman of Kingston Seymour	1675	T.N.A., PROB 4/11927	Will also extant
6535	Henry TANNER of Taunton	1701	T.N.A., PROB 4/22559	Admon
6536	Lawrence TANNER of Lyng	1694	DD/SP/1694/8	
6537	Lydden TANNER of Dulverton	1758	T.N.A., PROB 3/57/18	
6538	Lyddon TANNER, Gentleman of Dulverton	1767	T.N.A., PROB 31/1767/254	
6539	Richard TANNER of Kingston Seymour	1640	D/D/cta/T15	Ad.ac.

6540	Thomas TANNER of Blackford, Wedmore	1661	DD/SAS/FA/161/16	
6541	Giles TANTON, Innholder of Combwich, Otterhampton	1675	DD/SP/1675/63	
6542	Giles TANTON, Innholder of Combwich, Otterhampton	1675	DD/SP/1675/64	
6543	Richard TANTON junior of West Monkton	1661	DD/SP/1661/18	
6544	Thomas TAPPER of North Petherton	1686	DD/SP/1686/16	
6545	John TAPSCOTT, Husbandman of Cutcombe	1664	DD/SP/1664/42	
6546	John TAPSCOTT of Cutcombe	1694	DD/SP/1694/20	
6547	Robert TAPSCOTT of Minehead	1691	DD/SP/1691/88	
6548	John TARR, Dealer of Porlock	1725	DD/SP/1725/12	
6549	John TARR alias HURLY of West Bagborough	1642	DD/SP/1642/29	
TARR see HAWKINS				
6550	Thomas TATCHELL junior, Cordwainer of South Petherton	1696	DD/SP/1696/13	
6551	William TATCHELL, Husbandman of Ash (Aishe), Martock	1629	D/D/ct/1/T9a	
6552	George TAUNTON of Yeovil	1634	D/D/ct/1/T10	
6553	Richard TAUNTON of West Monkton	1674	DD/SP/1674/1	
6554	Roger TAUNTON, Husbandman of West Monkton	1635	DD/SP/1635/28	
6555	William TAUNTON of West Monkton	1674	DD/SP/1674/51	
6556	Katherine TAYLAR alias SAUNDARS of Swell	1648	DD/SP/1648/68	See *T.C.W.*
6557	Amey TAYLER, Widow of Fivehead	1678	DD/SP/1678/81	
6558	Dorothy and Frances TAYLER of Bridgwater and Wembdon	1665	DD/SP/1665/19	
6559	John TAYLER, Gentleman of North Petherton	1683	DD/SP/1683/55	
6560	John TAYLER the elder of West Monkton	1670	DD/SP/1670/1	
6561	Richard TAYLER of Cannington	1672	DD/SP/1672/40	
6562	Richard TAYLER the elder of Crewkerne	1669	DD/SP/1669/76	
6563	Robert TAYLER of Stogursey	1629	D/D/ct/1/T16b+16c	Pvd 1629
6564	Robert TAYLER of Hillfarrance	1635	DD/SP/1635/114	See *T.C.W.*
6565	Robert TAYLER, Weaver of Luccombe	1684	DD/SP/1684/11	
6566	Thomas TAYLER of Taunton St. James	1666	DD/SP/1666/16	
6567	Thomas TAYLER of Ruishton	1688	DD/SP/1688/5	
6568	Thomas TAYLER the elder of Bridgwater	1683	DD/SP/1683/35	
6569	Willmoth TAYLER, Widow of Porlock	1634	DD/SP/1634/26	
6570	John TAYLER alias SAUNDERS of Swell	1634	DD/SP/1634/23	
6571	Anne TAYLOR, Widow of Crewkerne	1693	DD/SP/1693/41	

6572	Anne TAYLOR of Marston Magna	1693	T.N.A., PROB 5/4700	
6573	Benjamin TAYLOR, Yeoman of Trull	1723	DD/SP/1723/48	
6574	Edward TAYLOR of Swell	1699	DD/SP/442/33	Ad.ac.
6575	Francis TAYLOR, Yeoman of Hatch Beauchamp	1740	DD/SP/1740/6	
6576	Giles TAYLOR of Lilstock	1693	DD/SP/1693/35	
6577	Joan TAYLOR, Spinster of Luccombe	1677	DD/SP/1677/86	
6578	Johan TAYLOR the younger, Widow of Weston (near Bath)	1628	D/D/ct/1/T21	
6579	John TAYLOR of Chilton Cantelo	1683	T.N.A., PROB 4/18395	Will also extant
6580	John TAYLOR of Bridgwater	1708	DD/SP/442/56	Ad.ac.
6581	John TAYLOR, Husbandman of Stoke St. Mary	1716	DD/SP/1716/45	
6582	John TAYLOR of Langford Budville	1723	DD/SP/1723/49	
6583	Marmaduke TAYLOR, Mercer of Ilminster	1687	T.N.A., PROB 4/8751	Admon. ex. 1688?
6584	Reynoll TAYLOR of West Monkton	1724	DD/SP/1724/58	
6585	Richard TAYLOR of West Monkton	1676	DD/SP/1676/4	
6586	Richard TAYLOR of West Monkton	1716	DD/SP/1716/30	
6587	Thomas TAYLOR of West Coker	1680	T.N.A., PROB 5/3259	
6588	William TAYLOR, Husbandman of Cutcombe	1691	DD/SP/1691/50	
6589	John TAYLOUR, Victualler of Isle Brewers	1664	DD/SP/1664/45	
6590	William TAYLOUR, Weaver of Oake	1648	DD/SP/1648/57	
6591	Christopher TEAGUE of Minehead	1685	DD/SP/1685/69	
6592	Gawen TEAL, Yeoman of Cannington	1738	DD/SP/1738/44	
6593	Thomas TEAST of Easton in Gordano	1675	T.N.A., PROB 4/8910	Will also extant
6594	John TEDBALL of Huntspill	1740	D/D/cta/T21	Ad.ac. and inv.
6595	John TELLEY, Yeoman of Curry Rivel	1716	DD/SP/1716/28	
6596	John TEMPLEMAN, Butcher of Donyatt	1696	DD/SP/1696/7	
6597	Thomas TEMPLEMAN, Yeoman of Merriott	1693	DD/SP/1693/5	
6598	Alexander TEMPLER of North Petherton	1687	DD/SP/1687/54	
6599	English TEMPLER of Bradford	1635	DD/SP/1635/52	
6600	Jacob TEMPLER, Baker of Taunton	1645	DD/SP/1645/31	
6601	John TEMPLER of Lyng	1678	DD/SP/1678/85	
6602	Katherine TEMPLER of Dunster	1678	T.N.A., PROB 4/13277	Will. ex. 1679
6603	Grace TERRELL, Widow of Porlock	1678	DD/SP/1678/68	
6604	William TERRELL of Minehead	1645	DD/SP/1645/39	

6605	Mary TERRY, Widow of Bath	1798	T.N.A., PROB 31/1798/482	
6606	Francis TETT of Hinton St. George	1690	DD/SP/1690/15	
6607	Robert THACHER, Clerk of East Pennard	1611	D/D/cta/T37	Ad.ac.
6608	John THATCHER of Blagdon	1717	D/D/cta/T19	Ad.ac.
6609	Mary THATCHER of Taunton St. Mary Magdalene	1690	DD/SP/1690/49	
6610	Peter THATCHER, Clerk of Queen Camel	1625	D/D/cta/T1	Ad.ac. for a clergyman
6611	Thomas THETCHER of East Harptree	1620	D/D/ct/1/T29	
6612	Peter THICK of Wincanton	1623	D/D/cta/Q1	Ad.ac.
6613	Alice THOMAS, Widow of Stawley	1636	DD/SP/1636/1	
6614	Edward THOMAS of Pitminster	1690	DD/SP/1690/85	
6615	Gabriell THOMAS of Angersleigh	1665	DD/SP/1665/47	
6616	George THOMAS, Gentleman of Marsh Court, Wincanton	1686	T.N.A., PROB 4/8679	Will also extant
6617	Grace THOMAS of North Petherton	1640	DD/SP/1632/40	Undated; *T.C.W.*
6618	Griffith THOMAS, Husbandman of Brompton Regis	1683	DD/SP/1683/51	
6619	Honor THOMAS, Widow of Westbury	1661	DD/SAS/FA/161/21	
6620	Honour THOMAS, Widow of Luccombe	1685	DD/SP/1685/38	Widow of John
6621	John THOMAS, Husbandman of Milverton	1638	DD/SP/1638/55	
6622	John THOMAS, Yeoman of Trull	1678	DD/SP/1678/65	
6623	John THOMAS, Weaver of Stogursey	1681	DD/SP/1681/22	
6624	John THOMAS of North Petherton	1687	DD/SP/1687/59	
6625	John THOMAS, Husbandman of Compton Bishop	1690	T.N.A., PROB 4/12846	Will also extant
6626	John THOMAS, Tailor of Brompton Regis	1697	DD/SP/1697/70	
6627	John THOMAS of Shapwick	1738	D/D/Cti 93	
6628	Matthew THOMAS of Charlinch	1670	DD/SP/1670/43	
6629	Morgan THOMAS of Frome Selwood	1641	D/D/cta/T14	Ad.ac.
6630	Nicholas THOMAS of Milverton	1679	DD/SP/1679/6	
6631	Richard THOMAS, Clerk of Muchelney	1619	D/D/cta/T29	Ad.ac. for a clergyman
6632	Robert THOMAS, Mason of Langford Budville	1680	DD/SP/1680/33	
6633	Robert THOMAS, Husbandman of Kittisford	1688	DD/SP/1688/27	
6634	Robert THOMAS senior of Trull	1672	DD/CT/1	
6635	Samuel THOMAS, Clerk of Chard	1694	T.N.A., PROB 5/2013	Vicar of Chard, 1681–1692, non-juror
6636	Thomas THOMAS, Sailor of Walton	1618	D/D/cta/W54	Ad.ac.
6637	Thomasin THOMAS, Widow of Barrow Gurney	1686	T.N.A., PROB 4/13300	Will 1686

6638	William THOMAS of Coley, East Harptree	1633	D/D/ct/1/T37	
6639	William THOMAS of Creech St. Michael	1646	DD/SP/1646/6	
6640	Reverend William THOMAS of Ubley	1667	DD/BR/gi/2	
6641	William THOMAS, Barber of Dulverton	1682	DD/SP/1682/54	
6642	William THOMAS junior, Yeoman of Trull	1680	DD/SP/1680/57	
6643	James THOMAS alias GOD of Stogursey	1640	DD/SP/1640/16	
6644	Robert THOMAS alias HIER of Otterhampton	1638	DD/SP/1638/24	
THOMAS see HYER				
6645	Katherine THOMPSON, Widow of Wells	1731	T.N.A., PROB 31/1731/131	
6646	Richard THOMPSON, Husbandman of Orchard Portman	1698	DD/SP/1698/30	
6647	Nicholas THOMSON, Widow of Taunton St. Mary Magdalene Magdalene	1716	DD/SP/1716/37	
6648	Agnes THORNE of Withiel Florey	1675	DD/SF/11/1/75	Formerly DD/SF/1059
6649	Arthur THORNE junior, Blacksmith of Bradford	1684	DD/SP/1684/36	
6650	Bartholomew THORNE, Husbandman of Chilton (*sic*)	1640	DD/SP/1640/57	
6651	George THORNE of Stogursey	1639	D/D/cta/T9	Ad.ac.
6652	George THORNE of Exford	1641	DD/SP/1641/78	See *T.C.W.*
6653	George THORNE the elder of Portishead	1662	D/D/cta/T31	Ad.ac.
6654	Henry THORNE of Kilton	1731	DD/SP/1731/30	
6655	John THORNE, Yeoman of South Petherton	1671	DD/SP/1671/36	
6656	John THORNE, Yeoman of Crowcombe	1677	DD/SP/1677/29	
6657	John THORNE of South Petherton	1682	T.N.A., PROB 4/11316	Will. ex. 1683
6658	John THORNE of Cannington	1706	DD/SP/1706/39	
6659	Mary THORNE of Exford	1646	DD/SP/1646/70	
6660	Richard THORNE of Treborough	1675	DD/SP/1675/70	
6661	Richard THORNE of Kilve	1697	DD/SP/1697/20	
6662	Robert THORNE of Withycombe	1702	DD/SP/442/42	Ad.ac.
6663	Robert THORNE, Yeoman of Ilminster	1728	T.N.A., PROB 3/27/163	
6664	Thomas THORNE of Chilton (*sic*)	1642	DD/SP/1642/11	
6665	Thomas THORNE of Lyng	1642	DD/SP/1642/38	
6666	William THORNE of Bridgwater	1641	DD/SP/1641/92	
6667	William THORNE of Withycombe	1680	DD/SP/1680/49	
6668	[missing] THORNE? of [no place]	1639	D/D/cta/T2	

	Note: Ad.ac.; fragment mentions Jane THORNE their daughter			
6669	Elizabeth THORNLEY, Widow of Bath	1729	D/D/cta/T20	Ad.ac.
6670	Johane THRASHER alias HILL, Widow of Puckington	1648	DD/SP/1648/36	
6671	Anthony THRESHEAR of Rode	1682	DD/PL/21/c/463	
6672	Edward THRUSTON of West Buckland	1758	DD/MT/70	
6673	Malachi THRUSTON, Doctor of Physic of Nynehead	1701	T.N.A., PROB 4/22819	Admon, late a lunatic
6674	Margery THRUSTON, Widow of West Buckland	1685	T.N.A., PROB 4/6155	Admon
6675	Edward THRUSTONE, Gentleman of West Buckland	1675	T.N.A., PROB 4/10363	
	Note: Admon, goods left unadministered by his widow Margaret administrix			
6676	Malachi THURSTON of Nynehead	1701	T.N.A., PROB 5/5696	
6677	Robert THURSTON of Wootton Courtenay	1693	DD/SP/1693/56	
	Note: Addressed to Mr. Southey at the Fountaine Tavern, Taunton			
6678	Malachi THURSTON alias THURSTONE of Nynehead	1701	T.N.A., PROB 5/690	Admon 1702
6679	Robert THUSTON, Tanner of Wootton Courtenay	1664	DD/SP/1664/3	
6680	Edward TIBBETT of Dundry	1600	D/D/cta/T40	Ad.ac.
6681	Richard TIBBETT of Farleigh Hungerford	1638	D/D/cta/T5	Ad.ac.
6682	Thomas TIBBOTT, Blacksmith of Filton alias Whitchurch	1678	T.N.A., PROB 4/6991	Will also extant
6683	John TICE, Clerk of Seavington Abbot, Seavington St. Mary	1667	DD/SP/1667/45	
6684	[missing] TICE alias ROGERS, Clothworker of Bruton	1688	T.N.A., PROB 4/10462	Will 1688
6685	Thomas TICE alias ROGERS, Bachelor of Bruton	1684	T.N.A., PROB 4/11910	Will 1683. ex. 1684
6686	William TIES, Clerk of Donyatt	1623	DD/SAS/C59/16	
6687	Robert TILLER, Husbandman of Corfe	1686	DD/SP/1686/26	
6688	Anne TILLEY of Lyncombe and Widcombe	1691	T.N.A., PROB 5/410	Admon 1692
6689	Mary TILLEY, Widow of Marston Bigot	1684	T.N.A., PROB 4/10520	Admon
6690	Richard TILLEY of Marston Bigot	1689	T.N.A., PROB 4/6868	Will 1684
6691	Gillian TILLIE of Abbots Leigh	1625	B.A., 1625/80	
6692	Robert TILLIE of Chewton Mendip	1619	D/D/cta/T36	Ad.ac.
6693	John TIRRELL, Yeoman of Dunster	1674	DD/SP/1674/30	
6694	John TISSE of Isle Abbotts	1637	DD/SP/1637/10	
6695	John TIVER of North Petherton	1691	DD/SP/1691/13	
6696	Richard TIVER of North Petherton	1684	DD/SP/1684/53	
6697	Agnes TIZARD, Spinster of Merriott	1698	DD/SP/1698/37	
6698	Ann TIZARD of Merriott	n.d.	D/D/cta/T34	Ad.ac.

6699	Joan TOLBUTT of Milverton	1702	DD/SP/1702/36	
6700	Daniel TOLE, Butcher of Lyng	1682	DD/SP/1682/41	
6701	Thomas TOLEMAN of East Lambrook, Kingsbury Episcopi	1634	D/D/ct/1/T43	Pvd 1634
6702	Hugh TOLLER of West Monkton	1680	DD/SP/1680/51	
6703	Dorothy TOMAS, Gentlewoman of Nynehead	1629	D/D/ct/1/T44	
TOMAS see THOMAS				
6704	John TOMLYN of Upton Noble	1638	D/D/cta/T7	Ad.ac.
6705	Robert TOMMAS, Husbandman of Curry Mallet	1679	DD/SP/1679/11	
6706	Francis TOMS, Husbandman of Abbots Leigh	1625	B.A., 1625/81	Will also extant
6707	Faith TOMSON of Brompton Ralph	1638	DD/SP/1638/33	
6708	Margaret TOMSON of Taunton St. Mary Magdalene	1684	DD/SP/1684/112	Wife of Samuel
6709	Nicholas TOMSON the elder, Yeoman of Middlezoy	1670	T.N.A., PROB 4/2063	Will also extant
6710	Ann TOOGOOD, Widow of Milborne Port	1618	D/D/cta/T33	Ad.ac.
6711	Catherine TOOGOOD of Milverton	1691	DD/SP/1691/51	
6712	John TOOGOOD, Yeoman of Milverton	1642	DD/SP/1642/10	
6713	John TOOGOOD, Yeoman of Bickenhall	1688	DD/SP/1688/26	
6714	William TOOGOOD of Milverton	1634	DD/SP/1634/36	
TOOGOOD see DRUER, TUOGOOD				
6715	Bartholomew TOOKER of Glastonbury	1690	D/D/cta/T22	Ad.ac.
6716	John TOOKER, Carrier of Chard	1694[?]	T.N.A., PROB 4/8759	Admon?
6717	Robert TOOKER, Miller of Nettlecombe	1687	DD/SP/1687/39	
6718	Nicholas TOOMBS of Long Ashton	1670	T.N.A., PROB 4/12255	Will also extant
6719	Edward TOPP of Nether Stowey and Stockton, Wiltshire	1741	T.N.A., PROB 3/40/132	
6720	Daniel TOR of Winsford	1643	DD/SP/1643/47	
6721	George TORR of Winsford	1666	DD/SP/1666/49	
6722	John TORR, Husbandman of Ash Priors	1671	DD/SP/1671/48	
6723	[missing] TORR alias HEARLY of West Bagborough	1677	DD/SP/1677/65	
6724	[missing] TORR alias HEATHFIELD, Yeoman of Crowcombe	1694	DD/SP/1694/5	
6725	Leonard TORRINGTON of Old Cleeve	1629	D/D/ct/1/T47a	
6726	Thomas TOURK of [no place]	1630s	DD/SP/1632/31	Undated
6727	Nicholas TOVEY, Mariner of Easton in Gordano	1675	T.N.A., PROB 4/9425	Will 1675
6728	John TOWELL of Exton	1681	DD/SP/1681/93	
6729	Andrew TOWGOOD, Yeoman of Yarnfield, Maiden Bradley	1648	W.S.H.C., P2/T/216	Com., inv., will

6730	John TOWGOODE the elder of Crewkerne	1642	DD/SP/1642/43	
6731	John TOWILL, Merchant of Watchet, St. Decumans	1686	T.N.A., PROB 4/17387	Admon
6732	Elianor TOWILLS of Nether Stowey	1685	T.N.A., PROB 4/9041	Will. ex. 1686
6733	Mary TOWILLS of Trull	1673	DD/SP/1673/18	
6734	Edmond TOWLE of Dulverton	1687	DD/SP/1687/10	
6735	Richard TOWMAN of Bathealton	1667	DD/SP/1667/31	
6736	Robert TOWNING of Curry Mallet	1695	DD/SP/1695/5	
6737	Thomas TOWNING senior, Husbandman of Curry Rivel	1675	DD/SP/1675/77	
6738	John TOWTE, Yeoman of Brushford	1676	DD/SP/1676/51	
6739	John TRACY the elder of Chedzoy	1681	DD/SP/1681/109	
6740	Joan TRASK, Widow of Merriott	1730	DD/SP/1730/29	
6741	Christopher TRATT, Yeoman of Pitminster	1679	DD/SP/1679/41	
6742	John TRATT, Yeoman of Buckland St. Mary	1725	DD/SP/1725/21	
6743	Peter TRATT, Yeoman of North Petherton	1684	DD/SP/1684/179	
6744	Richard TRATT of Buckland St. Mary	1713	DD/SP/442/9	Ad.ac.
6745	Simon TRATT, Yeoman of North Petherton	1725	DD/SP/1725/17	
6746	Thomas TRATT of North Petherton	1646	DD/SP/1646/54	
6747	Thomas TRATT senior, Husbandman of North Petherton	1697	DD/SP/1697/68	
6748	Joane TRATT alias BEARD, Widow of Bishops Lydeard	1644	DD/SP/1644/67	
6749	Sir Thomas TRAVEL, Knight of Milborne Wick (Milbourn Week), Milborne Port but died in St. Martin-in-the-Fields, Middlesex	1726	T.N.A., PROB 31/1726/100	With ac.
6750	Mary TRAVERSE of Curry Rivel	1680	DD/SP/1680/90	
6751	William TRAWAYE, Blacksmith of Ashbrittle	1693	DD/SP/1693/38	
6752	William TREABLE, Gentleman of Langford Budville	1686	DD/SP/1686/32	
6753	Alice TREBLE, Spinster of Brompton Ralph	1637	DD/SP/1637/68	
6754	William TREBLE of Combe Florey	1692	DD/SP/1692/12	
6755	Hugh TREBYLL, Gentleman of Combe Florey	1681	T.N.A., PROB 4/6160	Will also extant
6756	Martha TRELAWNEY, Widow of South Petherton	1738	DD/SP/1738/45	
6757	John TREMAYLL of Cannington	1535	DD/S/WH/115	Rooms given
6758	Thomas TRENCHARD of Woolverton	1557	T.N.A., PROB 2/305	Will T.N.A., PROB 11/33/20
6759	Henry TRENT, Bachelor of St. Andrew, Holborn, London died at Ilchester	1674	T.N.A., PROB 4/6183	Admon. ex. 1675

6760	Nicholas TRESSER of Huish (*sic*)	1580	T.N.A., PROB 2/779	Will T.N.A., PROB 11/62/421
6761	Thomas TREVELIAN, Yeoman of Litton	1682	T.N.A., PROB 4/19849	Admon
6762	Elizabeth? TREVELYAN of Nettlecombe	1691	T.N.A., PROB 4/12186	Will also extant
6763	John TREVELYAN of [no place]	1563	DD/WO/16/7	
6764	Lady Mary TREVELYAN of Nettlecombe	1689	DD/WO/40/5	
6765	John TREVILLIAN of Kingsbury Episcopi	1664	D/D/cta/T32	Ad.ac.
6766	Richard TREVILLIAN, Gentleman of Middleney, Drayton	1680	T.N.A., PROB 4/8595	Will. ex. 1681
6767	Katherine TREVILLION, Widow of Ilton	1629	D/D/cta/T4	Ad.ac.
6768	Elizabeth TREWMAN of Portbury	1682	D/D/cta/T24	Ad.ac.
6769	Jane TRIGGS, Spinster of Bridgwater	1676	DD/SP/1676/29	
6770	John TRIPP of Shipham	1677	T.N.A., PROB 4/20189	Will also extant
6771	Margery TRIPP of Chew Stoke	n.d.	D/D/ct/1/T53	Temp Elizabeth
6772	Roger TRIPP, Yeoman of Compton Bishop	1678	T.N.A., PROB 4/6867	Admon. ex. 1679
6773	Thomas TRISTER of Drayton	1640	DD/SP/1640/101	
6774	John TRISTRAM, Clerk of Barrington	1619	D/D/cta/T27	Ad.ac.
6775	John TRISTRAM of Dulverton	1605/6	D/D/ct/1/T54a	
6776	Charles TROBRIDGE of Winsford	1731	DD/SP/1731/41	
6777	Chris TROTT of Taunton St. Mary Magdalene	1692	DD/SP/1692/18	
6778	Hugh TROTT of Spaxton	1693	DD/SP/1693/34	
6779	Joan TROTT of Bradford	1680	DD/SP/1680/41	
6780	John TROTT, Woolcomber of Crowcombe	1664	DD/SP/1664/67	
6781	John TROTT of South Bradon, Puckington	1685	DD/SP/1685/71	
6782	John TROTT of Bradford	1687	T.N.A., PROB 4/6901	Will 1688. ex. 1688
6783	Richard TROTT of Yeovil died at Ilchester	1733	T.N.A., PROB 31/1733/732	
6784	Richard TROTT, Widower of Yeovil died at Ilchester	1734	T.N.A., PROB 3/33/28	
6785	Richard TROTT of Yeovil died at Ilchester	1734	T.N.A., PROB 31/1734/148	
6786	Robert TROTT of Taunton St. Mary Magdalene	1730	DD/SP/1730/19	
6787	Simon TROTT of Spaxton	1676	DD/SP/1676/38	
6788	William TROTT of Chilton (*sic*)	1668	DD/SP/1668/20	
6789	William TROTT senior of [no place]	1686	T.N.A., PROB 4/11136	Will 1686
6790	Alice TROWBERIGE of Minehead	1691	DD/SP/1691/47	
6791	Edmund TROWBRIDGE of Kilmersdon	1711	DD/MY/1	
6792	Margaret TROWBRIDGE of Kilmersdon	1731	DD/MY/1	

6793	James TROWD, Husbandman of West Buckland	1619	D/D/cta/F18	Ad.ac.
6794	James TROWD of West Buckland	1619	D/D/cta/T28	Ad.ac.
6795	Richard TRUCKWELL of Brompton Ralph	1678	DD/SP/1678/16	
6796	John TRUMP of Staple Fitzpaine	1684	DD/SP/1684/143	
6797	Michael TRUMP of Staple Fitzpaine	1684	DD/SP/1684/129	
6798	Michael TRUMP, Blacksmith of Curland	1695	DD/SP/1695/36	
6799	David TRUTCH of Spaxton	1645	DD/SP/1645/7	
6800	Richard TRUTCH, Blacksmith of Spaxton	1741	DD/SP/1741/10	
6801	Lavinia TUCK of Bicknoller	1731	DD/SP/1731/15	
6802	[missing] TUCKER of Wick St. Lawrence ?	1632	D/D/cta/T25	
	Note: Ad.ac.; mentions sons William and Thomas			
6803	Edmond TUCKER of Lyng	1681	DD/SP/1681/29	
6804	Hannah TUCKER, Widow of Cossington	1736	D/D/Cti 91	
6805	Henry TUCKER, Husbandman of North Petherton	1648	DD/SP/1648/30	
6806	John TUCKER of West Bradley	1619	D/D/cta/T35	Ad.ac.
6807	John TUCKER of Exford	1646	DD/SP/1646/9	
6808	John TUCKER of Stogumber	1689	DD/SP/1689/2	
6809	John TUCKER, Yeoman of Brean	1735	D/D/Cti 90	
6810	John TUCKER of Huntspill	1826	DD/UK/39	
6811	John TUCKER the elder of Nailsea	1667	D/D/cta/T30	Ad.ac.
6812	Nicholas TUCKER of Buckland St. Mary	1692	DD/SP/1692/37	
6813	Sarah TUCKER, Widow of West Monkton	1687	DD/SP/1687/61	
6814	Thomas TUCKER of Somerton	1610	D/D/cta/T38	Ad.ac.
6815	Tristram TUCKER of Spaxton	1640	DD/SP/1640/84	
6816	William TUCKER of [no place]	1601	D/D/cta/T8	Ad.ac.
6817	William TUCKER of Pitminster	1689	DD/SP/1689/32	
6818	William TUCKER, Yeoman of Yatton	1711	T.N.A., PROB 5/3203	
6819	Edmund TUCKIE of [no place]	1613	D/D/cta/T3	Ad.ac.
6820	William TUCKYE of Kewstoke	1612	D/D/cta/T39	Ad.ac.
6821	Joane TUDBALL, Widow of Exford	1693	T.N.A., PROB 4/21263	Will 1668
6822	John TUDBALL, Yeoman of Huish Champflower	1735	T.N.A., PROB 3/34/112	
6823	John TUDBALL, Yeoman of Huish Champflower	1735	T.N.A., PROB 31/1735/544	
6824	Thomas TUDBALL of Hillfarrance	1690	DD/SP/1690/82	

6825	Clement TUDWAY of Wells	1815	DD/TD/48/10	
6826	John TUFF, Mercer of Buckland St. Mary	1690	DD/SP/1690/71	
6827	William TUFF, Husbandman of Misterton	1713	DD/SP/1713/38	
6828	Katrene TUOGOOD of Oake	1646	DD/SP/1646/84	See *T.C.W.*
TUOGOOD see TOOGOOD				
6829	David TUPWELL, Yeoman of Cannington	1675	DD/SP/1675/79	
6830	John TURBERVILL, Esquire of Tolland	1678	T.N.A., PROB 5/5131	Probably of Gaulden Manor
6831	John TURBERVILLE, Esquire of Tolland	1678	T.N.A., PROB 4/9008	Admon. ex. 1679
6832	Elizabeth TURKE, Widow of Bicknoller	1634	DD/SP/1634/37	
6833	Elizabeth TURKE, Widow of Stogumber	1648	DD/SP/1648/64	
6834	Joseph TURKE of Vellow, Stogumber	1667	DD/SP/1667/70	Proved by Elizabeth, Widow
6835	James TURKS, Yeoman of Marston Bigot	1738	D/D/Cti 92	
6836	Edward TURLE the elder of Taunton St. James	1666	DD/SP/1666/64	
6837	Anthony TURNER of Stowey	1584	D/D/cta/T44	Ad.ac.
6838	Chrispian TURNER, Husbandman of Langford Budville	1685	DD/SP/1685/80	
6839	Henry TURNER, Sergemaker of Taunton St. Mary Magdalene			
6840	John TURNER of Taunton St. James	1593	D/D/cta/T42	Ad.ac.
6841	John TURNER of North Petherton	1690	DD/SP/1690/83	
6842	Peter TURNER, Yeoman of Cudworth	1813	T.N.A., PROB 31/1813/484	
6843	Richard TURNER of Goathurst	1734	DD/SP/1734/24	
6844	Thomas? TURNER of Broomfield?	1670	DD/SP/1670/113	
6845	John TURRELL, Tanner of Dulverton	1683	DD/SP/1683/98	
6846	William TUTCHEN, Woolen Weaver of South Petherton	1640	DD/SP/1640/135	
6847	Joan TUTHILL of West Monkton	1673	DD/SP/1673/23–24	
6848	William TUTT of Creech St. Michael	1638	DD/SP/1638/50	
6849	Andrew TUTTEN of Charlinch	1674	DD/SP/1674/49	
6850	Bartholomew TUTTLE of Curry Rivel	1667	DD/SP/1667/2	
6851	Marmaduke TUTTLE of Curry Rivel	1683	DD/SP/1683/13	
6852	Thomas TUTTLE of Curry Rivel	1695	DD/SP/1695/28	
6853	William TUTTON of Meare	1679	T.N.A., PROB 4/6915	Will also extant
6854	William TUTTON of Henton, Wookey	n.d.	DD/SAS/FA/131/33	
6855	John TWOES the elder of Wellington	1678	T.N.A., PROB 4/6839	Will also extant
6856	Julia TWYCROSS, Widow of Bath	1815	T.N.A., PROB 31/1815/752	

6857	Ann TWYFORD, Spinster of Charlton, Kilmersdon?	1772	T.N.A., PROB 31/1772/680	With account
6858	Thomas TYCE, Sergeweaver of North Petherton	1662	DD/SP/1662/26	
6859	Johane TYDDER, Widow of Stogursey	1629	D/D/ct/1/T74	
6860	John TYDDER alias LEWES, Hosier ? of Stogursey	1587	D/D/cta/T45	Ad.ac.
6861	John TYKE of East Brent	1585	D/D/ct/1/T75	
6862	Gregory TYLDED of Minehead	1675	DD/SP/1675/80	
6863	Thomas TYLER of Bedminster	1684	T.N.A., PROB 4/12105	Will 1685. ex. 1685
6864	Walter TYLER of Wick St. Lawrence	1633	D/D/cta/T26	
	Note: Ad.ac.; see burial register for 1 December 1598			
6865	Susan TYLIE, Widow of Cold Ashton, Gloucestershire	n.d.	D/D/ct/1/T81	
6866	Philip TYMEWELL of Taunton St. Mary Magdalene	1686	T.N.A., PROB 4/6889	Admon
6867	William TYNDALE alias HOLLIDAY of Bath	1815	T.N.A., PROB 31/1815/959	
6868	Daniel TYNDALL, Cordwainer of Batheaston	1738	D/D/Cti 94	
6869	Edward TYNTE of Chelvey	1630	DD/S/WH/101	Rooms given
6870	Benjamin TYRE, Yeoman of Shepton Mallet	1638	D/D/cta/T6	Ad.ac.
6871	Sir Charles TYRELL, Baronet of Thornton, Buckinghamshire died at Bath	1749	T.N.A., PROB 3/48/24	
6872	John UNCH of South Brent	1672	D/D/cta/U1	Ad.ac.
6873	John UPCOTE of Abbots Leigh	1704	B.A., 1704/34	Will also extant
6874	George UPCOTT of Stogumber	1685	DD/SP/1685/21	
6875	Joan UPCOTT, Widow of Brompton Regis	1676	DD/SP/1676/22	
6876	William UPCOTT of Brompton Regis	1670	DD/SP/1670/13	
6877	Agnes UPHAM, Widow of West Monkton	1683	DD/SP/1683/26	
6878	Benjamin UPHAM of Brompton Regis	1687	DD/SP/1687/2	
6879	Christopher UPHAM of Elworthy	1642	DD/SP/1642/39	
6880	Joan UPHAM of Brompton Regis	1677	DD/SP/1677/6	
6881	Joane UPHAM of Brompton Ralph	1670	DD/SP/1670/35	
6882	John UPHAM, Husbandman of [no place]	1646	DD/SP/1646/64	
6883	John UPHAM, Yeoman of Huish Champflower	1713	DD/SP/1713/33	See also DD/SP/442(10)
6884	John UPHAM of Huish Champflower	1713	DD/SP/442/10	Ad.ac.
6885	Thomas UPHAM of West Monkton	1666	DD/DP/65/1	
6886	Thomas UPHAM of West Monkton	1675	DD/SP/1675/85	
6887	John UPHILL of Edgarley, Glastonbury	1728	D/D/cta/U2	Ad.ac.

6888	John UPHILL of Glastonbury St. John	1737	D/D/cta/U3	Ad.ac. and inv.
6889	Agnes UPPHILL, Widow of Marston Magna	1625	D/D/cta/T10	Ad.ac.
6890	Henry UPPINGTON, Yeoman of Dulverton	1720	DD/WO/10/14/11	
6891	George UPTON, Gentleman of Fitzhead	1690	T.N.A., PROB 4/13056	Will also extant
6892	Nathaniel UPTON of Fitzhead	1694	T.N.A., PROB 4/4193	Admon
6893	Edward URCH, Gentleman of Mudgeley, Wedmore	1697	T.N.A., PROB 4/18673	Will also extant
URCH see UNCH				
6894	William URCHE alias FRY, Yeoman of Sandford, Winscombe and Hill Deverill, Wiltshire	1612	W.S.H.C., P5/1612/41	Two inventories, will
6895	Ames URVIN, Weaver of Crewkerne	1684	DD/SP/1684/118	
6896	Lewse URVINE of North Petherton	1635	DD/SP/1635/8	See *T.C.W.*
6897	Elizabeth USHER, Widow of Bath	1768	T.N.A., PROB 31/1768/24	With account
6898	Robert UTTERMARE of Curry Mallet	1643	DD/SP/1643/48	
6899	Richard VAGG of Batcombe	1611	D/D/cta/V9	Ad.ac.
6900	John VALACOTT of Sampford Brett	1640	DD/SP/1640/103	
6901	John VALENTINE, Fellmonger of Dulverton	1700	T.N.A., PROB 4/7558	Admon
6902	Marrien VALENTINE, Widow of Dulverton	1684	DD/SP/1684/65	
6903	John VALLENTINE, Fellmonger of Dulverton	1700	T.N.A., PROB 5/5786	
6904	John VARNEY of Stogursey	1667	DD/SP/1667/86	
6905	George VATER of Exford	1740	DD/SP/1740/7	
6906	William VATER of Stoke Pero	1638	DD/SP/1638/12	
6907	Virgill VAUGHAN, Gentleman of Paulton	1631	D/D/cta/V1	Ad.ac.
6908	Thomas VAX of Compton, South Petherton	1646	DD/SP/1646/55	
6909	Joane VEALE, Spinster of Chew Magna	1642	D/D/ct/1/V9	
6910	Roger VEISYE of Croscombe	1588	D/D/cta/V8	Ad.ac.
6911	Adam VELLETT, Sergemaker of Taunton St. James	1670	DD/SP/1670/33	
6912	Isaac VELVIN of Taunton St. James	1683	DD/SP/1683/11	
6913	Elizabeth VEN of Withiel Florey	1702	DD/SP/1702/37	See burial register for Withiel Florey
6914	Grace VEN, Widow of Brompton Regis	1675	DD/SP/1675/35	
6915	Grace VEN, Widow of Brompton Regis	1675	DD/SP/1675/68	
6916	Joane VEN of Upton	1667	DD/SP/1667/61	
6917	John VEN of Brompton Regis	1640	DD/SP/1640/8	
6918	John VEN of Skilgate	1687	DD/SP/1687/3	

6919	Richard VEN of Stogumber	1639	DD/SP/1639/27	
6920	[missing] VENN, Husbandman ? of Lydeard St. Lawrence ?	1668	DD/SP/1668/4	
	Note: Estates in Lydeard St. Lawrence, Bishops Lydeard, Bathealton and Taunton, appraised by Henry WOOLCOTT, Thomas WHITE senior, George WOOLCOTT junior, Lawrence SANDERS, Thomas CRIDLAND and Richard MUXFORD; Christian VENN relict; damaged			
6921	Emblen VENN of Lydeard St. Lawrence	1683	DD/SP/1683/3	
6922	Jane VENN of Lydeard St. Lawrence	1674	DD/SP/1674/23	
6923	Joane VENN of Lydeard St. Lawrence	1683	DD/SP/1683/2	
6924	Johan VENN, Spinster of Upton	1646	DD/SP/1646/56	
6925	John VENN, Husbandman of Brompton Regis	1646	DD/SP/1646/27	See *T.C.W.*
6926	Patience VENN, Spinster of Brompton Regis	1690	DD/SP/1690/23	
6927	Susanna VENN alias WATTS of North Petherton	1701	DD/SP/1701/34	
6928	Cicelie VENNE, Widow of Kilve	1637	DD/SP/1637/21	
6929	Anne VENNER, Widow of Bathealton	1680	DD/SP/1680/22	
6930	Domony VENNER of Taunton St. Mary Magdalene	1716	DD/SP/1716/47	
6931	John VENNICOTT of Dunwear, Bridgwater	1666	DD/SP/1666/56	
6932	William VERMAN of Huntspill	1664	D/D/cta/V5	Ad.ac.
6933	Robert VERNAM of Bath St. Michael	1621	D/D/cta/T13	Ad.ac.
6934	Edward VERRIER of Durston	1696	DD/SP/1696/44	
6935	Jonathon VERRIER of North Petherton	1743	DD/SP/1743/19	
6936	Nicholas VERYER of Lillesdon, North Curry	1590	D/D/ct/1/V13	
6937	Katherin VEYSEY of Nynehead	1640	DD/SP/1640/42	Inventory shows VOYSEY
6938	Agnes VICARS, Widow of Brompton Regis	1697	DD/SP/1697/23	
6939	John VICARY, Clothier of Staplegrove	1669	DD/SP/1669/99	
6940	Philip VICARY of Exton	1675	DD/SP/1675/12	
6941	Richard VICARY of [no place]	1665	DD/SP/1665/46	
6942	Robert VICARY of Dunster	1728	DD/SP/1728/36	
6943	Susan VICARY of Wootton Courtenay	1680	DD/SP/1680/99	
6944	William VICARY of Taunton St. James	1666	DD/SP/1666/32	
6945	John VICARY alias SAUNDERS of Wilton or Taunton St. Mary Magdalene	n.d.	DD/SP/17th Century/13	Fragment
6946	John VICCARY, Yeoman of Minehead	1688	T.N.A., PROB 4/16007	Will also extant
6947	Sarah VICERY née BEAKS alias PORCH of Wells	1829	DD/FS Box 47	
6948	John VICKARY, Clothier of Stogumber	1692	T.N.A., PROB 4/8661	Will. ex. 1693

6949	Edward VICKERMAN of Bedminster	1830	T.N.A., PROB 31/1830/989	And com.
6950	Joan VICKERS, Widow of Baltonsborough	1627	D/D/cta/T12	Ad.ac.
6951	Agnes VIELL, Widow of South Petherton	1629	D/D/ct/1/V15a	
6952	Francis VIGARS, Excise Officer of Crewkerne	1685	DD/SP/1685/104	
6953	Richard VIGOR, Yeoman of Lullington	1676	T.N.A., PROB 4/10392	Will also extant
6954	Robert VIGOR of Hemington	1634	D/D/cta/T11	Ad.ac.
6955	John VILDEW of Ashbrittle	1636	DD/SP/1636/42	
6956	Abraham VILDUE, Husbandman of West Bagborough	1665	DD/SP/1665/38	
6957	Ann VILE, Widow of Isle Abbotts	1688	DD/SP/1688/7	
6958	Edmond VILE, Husbandman of Bridge, South Petherton	1670	DD/SP/1670/52	
6959	Edmund VILE, Husbandman of Drayton	1731	DD/SP/1731/7	
6960	John VILE, Husbandman of Isle Abbotts	1682	DD/SP/1682/25	
6961	John VILE of South Harp, South Petherton	1688	DD/SP/1688/49	
6962	Joseph VILE of Isle Abbotts	1672	DD/SP/1672/13	
6963	Robert VILE, Soapboiler of Sell [Sea?], Ilminster	1731	T.N.A., PROB 3/30/4	
6964	William VILE, Husbandman of Isle Abbotts	1677	DD/SP/1677/21	
6965	Walter VILLIERS, Coronet in Regiment of Dragoons under Brigadier General KERR and Bachelor of Ilchester	1730	T.N.A., PROB 31/1730/155	
6966	Nicholas VILLIS, Fisherman of Stogursey	1681	DD/SP/1681/47	
6967	Frances VILLOWS of Cannington	1675	DD/SP/1675/42	
6968	Henry VINCENT, Potter of Wanstrow	1633	D/D/ct/1/V17	
6969	James VINCENT, Yeoman of Knowle St. Giles	1730	T.N.A., PROB 3/29/216	Buried at Knowle St. Giles
6970	John VINCENT of Glastonbury	1729	D/D/cta/V2	Ad.ac.
6971	Thomas VINCENT of Otterford	1650	DD/SP/1650/2	
6972	William VINCENT, Husbandman of Wambrook Note: Admon. bond, com., two inventories	1666	W.S.H.C., P14/19	
6973	Joseph VINEING of Wells	n.d.	D/D/cta/V7	Ad.ac.
6974	John VIRGIN of North Petherton	1684	DD/SP/1684/57	
6975	Thomas VIRROCK, Carpenter of Bedminster	1586	D/D/ct/1/V20	
6976	William VOWKS of Mark	1706	T.N.A., PROB 5/4985	
6977	Grace VOWLES of West Pennard	n.d.	D/D/cta/V6	Ad.ac.
6978	Mary VOWLES of Blagdon	1704	D/D/cta/V3	Ad.ac.

VOYSEY see VEYSEY

6979	[missing] W—- alias FRENCH of Creech St. Michael?	n.d.	DD/SP/17th Century/4	
	Note: Mentions 'his right in A house and backside in Creech late Robert Bunckombes'			
6980	Richard WADE of Chew Magna	1647	D/D/cta/W27	Ad.ac.
6981	Thomas WADE, Yeoman of Failand, Wraxall	1680	T.N.A., PROB 4/1018	Will also extant
6982	Annes WADHAM of West Hatch	1581	D/D/ct/1/W5	
6983	Thomas WADHAM of Ashbrittle	1677	DD/SP/1677/24	
6984	James WADMAN of Horsington	1806	T.N.A., PROB 31/1806/621	
6985	Mary WADMAN, Widow of Horsington	1806	T.N.A., PROB 31/1806/765	
6986	Reverend William WAINHOUSE of [no place]	1797	DD/DP/21	
6987	Thomas WAKLEY, Doctor of Physic of Chaffcombe	1689	T.N.A., PROB 4/6911	Admon
6988	Thomas WALDEN of Ilminster	1718	T.N.A., PROB 3/17/12	
6989	Giles WALDRON of Langridge	1590	D/D/cta/W77	Ad.ac.
6990	Robert WALDRON senior, Husbandman of Staple Fitzpaine	1697	DD/SP/1697/50	
6991	Thomas WALFERD junior of Bincombe, Over Stowey	1716	DD/SP/1716/61	
6992	Alexander WALFORD of Stogursey	1665	D/D/cta/W31	Ad.ac.
6993	Elizabeth WALFORD, Spinster of Stringston	1687	DD/SP/1687/40	
6994	Richard WALFORD, Mason of Stogursey	1729	DD/SP/1729/54	
6995	Walter WALFORD, Husbandman of Fiddington	1685	DD/SP/1685/40	
6996	John WALKER, Parson of Langridge	1581	D/D/ct/1/W7	Pvd 1581
6997	Thomas WALKER of [no place]	1669	DD/WHb/3088	
6998	Edeth WALL, Widow of Broadway	1639	DD/SP/1639/65	
6999	George WALL of Exton	1691	DD/SP/1691/77	
7000	Walter WALL of Huntspill	1638	D/D/cta/W17	Ad.ac.
7001	Thomas WALLE of East Brent	1665	D/D/cta/W32	Ad.ac.
7002	Richard WALLEN of Wick, Wells	1658	DD/SAS/FA/161/26	
7003	Joseph WALLINGTON of Somerset and Berkshire	1692	T.N.A., PROB 4/6247	Admon. ex. 1693
7004	Thomas WALLIS, Gentleman of Portbury	1675	T.N.A., PROB 4/15123	Will also extant
7005	Thomas WALLIS, Mariner of Easton in Gordano	1694	T.N.A., PROB 4/19557	Admon
7006	Thomas WALLIS, Innholder of Taunton	1712	D/D/cta/W34	Ad.ac.
7007	William WALLIS, Apothecary of Yeovil	1751	T.N.A., PROB 31/1751/550	
7008	Francis WALLRON, Esquire of Langridge	1613	G.A., D1799/F208	
7009	Nicholas WALLS of Walcot	1808	T.N.A., PROB 31/1808/240	
7010	John WALLYS the elder, Yeoman of High Ham	1588	D/D/cta/W80	Ad.ac.

7011	Anne WALROND, Widow of South Petherton	1671	DD/SP/1671/12	
7012	Henry WALROND of Ilminster	1720	DD/LC/53/3	
7013	John WALSH of Fivehead	1670	DD/SP/1670/3	
7014	John WALSH, Gentleman and Physician of Taunton St. James	1682	T.N.A., PROB 4/8674	Will also extant
7015	Nicholas WALSH, Yeoman of Chard	1624	D/D/ct/1/W15	
7016	John WALSHMAN of Spaxton	1636	DD/SP/1636/49	
7017	Gregory WALTER of Curry Mallet	1665	DD/SP/1665/56	
7018	Henry WALTER of Fromefield, Frome	1747	T.N.A., PROB 3/46/24	
7019	John WALTER of Abbas Combe, Abbas and Temple Combe	1729	DD/SE/40/2	
7020	Peter WALTER, Yeoman of Wyke Champflower, Bruton	1690	DD/SAS/C127/8	
7021	Peter WALTER, Clothier of Bathford	1719	T.N.A., PROB 3/18/98	
7022	Richard WALTER, Clothier of Woolard, Publow	1690	T.N.A., PROB 4/10335	Will also extant
7023	William WALTER of Bruton	1584	D/D/cta/W36	Ad.ac.
7024	William WALTER the elder of Lyng	1685	DD/SP/1685/51	
7025	John WALTER alias HOSIER of Wells St. Cuthbert	1628	D/D/cta/W10	Ad.ac.
7026	Robert WALTERS of Curry Rivel	1636	D/D/cta/W13	Ad.ac.
7027	George WALTHAM, Soapmaker of Crowcombe	1685	DD/SP/1685/58	
7028	Richard WALTHAM, Clothier of Milverton	1684	DD/SP/1684/158	
7029	Barnard WARD of Taunton St. Mary Magdalene	1671	DD/SP/1671/30	
7030	John WARD of Brompton Regis	1693	DD/SP/1693/67	
7031	Marmaduke WARD of Curry Rivel	1666	DD/SP/1666/30	
7032	Thomas WARD of Berrow	1631	D/D/cta/W37	Ad.ac.
7033	William WARD alias WARE senior of Durston	1674	DD/SP/1674/69	
WARD alias WARE, WARR				
7034	John WARE of Brompton Regis	1670	DD/SP/1670/109	
7035	Walter WARE of Marston Magna	1620	D/D/cta/W4	Ad.ac.
7036	William WARE, Clothier of Croscombe	1691	T.N.A., PROB 4/18191	Admon, intestate
WARE see WEARE				
7037	Robert WARFIELD of Meare	1730	D/D/cta/W38	Ad.ac.
7038	Christopher WARMAN of Taunton St. James	1668	DD/SP/1668/28	
7039	John WARMAN of Dunster	1697	DD/SP/1697/19	
7040	Thomasin WARMAN, Widow of Otterhampton	1636	DD/SP/1636/57	
7041	Thomas WARR the younger of Yatton	1639	D/D/cta/W3	Ad.ac.

7042	William WARR junior of Wiveliscombe	1676	DD/DP/3 OB5	
7043	William WARR alias WARD junior of Durston	1668	DD/SP/1668/9	
7044	Alice WARRE of Heathfield	1669	DD/SP/1669/89	
7045	Charles WARRE of Stoke Pero	1696	DD/SP/1696/35	
	Note: With letters to Mr. John SOUTHEY at the Fountain Tavern, Taunton			
7046	Humphrey WARRE of [no place]	1628	DD/SP/1628/13	
7047	Thomas WARRE, Esquire of Shepton Beauchamp	1686	T.N.A., PROB 5/1904	Will T.N.A., PROB 11/382
7048	William WARRE, Joiner of Wiveliscombe	1677	DD/DP/3/5	
7049	William WARRE, Yeoman of Selworthy	1697	DD/SP/1697/33	
7050	Elizabeth WARREN, Singlewoman of Kittisford	1693	DD/SP/1693/66	
7051	George WARREN of North Petherton	1640	DD/SP/1640/17	See *T.C.W.*
7052	George WARREN, Husbandman of North Petherton	1665	DD/SP/1665/23	
7053	Mary WARREN, Widow of Spaxton	1721	DD/SP/1721/10	
7054	Naboth WARREN, Husbandman of Wambrook	1667	W.S.H.C., P14/23	Admon. bond, inv.
7055	Samuel WARREN of Orchard Portman	1730	DD/SP/1730/23	
7056	Tobias WARREN, Husbandman of Worle	1611	D/D/cta/W62	Ad.ac.
7057	Tristram WARREN of Crewkerne	1666	DD/SP/1666/13	
7058	William WARREN of Pitminster	1690	DD/SP/1690/1	
7059	Robert WARRIN, Butcher? of North Petherton	1697	DD/SP/1697/43	Two butchers standings in Taunton
7060	George WARRY, Gentleman of Chard	1783	T.N.A., PROB 31/1783/505/2	
7061	Christian WASHER, Widow of Luxborough	1640	DD/SP/1640/40	
7062	John WASHER of Treborough	1640	DD/SP/1640/111	
7063	Katherine WASHER, Widow of Oake	1677	DD/SP/1677/73	
7064	William WASHFORD, Maltster of Bridgwater	1725	DD/SP/1725/5	
7065	John WASON of [no place]	n.d.	D/D/cta/W35	Ad.ac.
7066	Joseph WASON of Frome Selwood	1683	T.N.A., PROB 4/6887	Admon
7067	Thomas WASON, Yeoman of East Pennard	1688	DD/BR/hk/5	
7068	Mary WASON?, Widow of Frome Selwood	1688	T.N.A., PROB 4/2466	Admon
7069	William WASTELL of Hinton Blewett	1587	D/D/cta/W55	Ad.ac.
7070	Robert WASTFIELD, Gallipot maker of Brislington	1677	T.N.A., PROB 4/6221	Will 1677
7071	John WASTLYNN of Lydeard (*sic*)	1591	D/D/ct/1/W33	
7072	George WATERMAN of Kingstone	1690	DD/SP/1690/4	
7073	Philip WATERMAN of Thornfalcon	1632	DD/SP/1632/20	

7074	Steven WATERMAN of Bridgwater	1640	DD/SP/1640/18	
7075	Thomas WATERMAN, Sergemaker of Bridgwater	1698	DD/SP/1698/50	
7076	William WATERMAN of Kingston St. Mary	1716	DD/SP/1716/49	
7077	George WATKIN of West Quantoxhead	1691	DD/SP/1691/90	
7078	Edward WATKINS, Gentleman of Cannington	1635	DD/SP/1635/53	
7079	George WATKINS, Fuller of Bridgwater	1700	DD/SP/1700/5	
7080	John WATS, Tanner of Selworthy	1661	DD/SP/1661/20	
7081	Robert WATSON, Innholder of Bridgwater	1756	DD/SP/442/86	Ad.ac. and inv.
7082	Sarah WATTES of Shepton Mallet	1648	D/D/cta/W28	Ad.ac.
7083	Ann WATTS, Widow of Frome	1835	T.N.A., PROB 31/1835/205	Formerly wife of James WATTS
7084	Cressett WATTS, Spinster of North Petherton	1700	DD/SP/1700/17	
7085	Edmund WATTS, Gentleman of Brindsey, Congresbury	1683	T.N.A., PROB 4/3846	Admon
7086	Henry WATTS, Seaman of Bridgwater	1669	DD/SP/1669/7	
7087	Hugh WATTS, Gentleman of Cucklington	1729	T.N.A., PROB 3/28/30	
7088	John WATTS of Shepton Mallet	1625	D/D/cta/W1a	Ad.ac.
7089	John WATTS, Yeoman of Shepton Mallet	1638	D/D/cta/W14	Ad.ac.
7090	John WATTS of Bodden, Doulting	1682	T.N.A., PROB 4/6265	Will 1683. ex. 1683
7091	John WATTS of Bishops Hull	1693	DD/SP/452	
7092	Thomas WATTS of Batcombe and Sedgehill, Wiltshire	1612	W.S.H.C., P2/W/226	Damaged inv.
7093	William WATTS of Shepton Mallet	1684	D/D/cta/W39	Ad.ac.
WATTS see VENN				
7094	John WAY, Husbandman of Wambrook	1686	W.S.H.C., P14/66	Inv. and will
7095	John WAY, Tailor of Dunster	1695	DD/SP/1695/14	
7096	Joseph WAY, Sergemaker of Ilminster	1724	T.N.A., PROB 3/23/206	
7097	Richard WAY of Brompton Ralph	1703	DD/SP/442/65	Ad.ac.
7098	Robert WAY, Cooper of Brompton Ralph	1684	DD/SP/1684/178	
7099	Thomas WAY of Pitminster	1671	DD/SP/1671/41	
7100	William WAY, Husbandman of Brompton Ralph	1684	DD/SP/1684/177	
7101	William WAY of Trull	1700	DD/SP/1700/11	
7102	Thomas WAYLANDE of Frome Selwood	1592	D/D/cta/W79	Ad.ac.
7103	Edward WAYMOUTH of Buckland St. Mary	1692	DD/SP/1692/22	
7104	Ann WEALDRON of Curry Rivel	1731	DD/SP/1731/3	
7105	John WEARE of South Petherton	1687	DD/SP/1687/47	

7106	John WEARE the elder, Yeoman of South Harp, South Petherton	1678	DD/SP/1678/75	
7107	Thomas WEARE of Milverton	1677	DD/SP/1677/10	
7108	Thomas WEARE or WARE of Milverton	1677	T.N.A., PROB 5/3220	
7109	John WEAVER of [no place]	n.d.	DD/SP/17th Century/14	
	Note: Appraised by John GENTLE and Henry GOOLD			
7110	Margaret WEAVER, Yeoman of Curry Rivel	1713	DD/SP/1713/10	
7111	John WEAVER alias MASTERS, Yeoman of Curry Mallet	1672	DD/SP/1672/18	
7112	Richard WEAVER alias MASTERS of Hatch Beauchamp	1668	DD/SP/1668/38	
7113	Joane WEAY of Bishops Hull	1640	DD/SP/1640/58	
7114	Richard WEAY of Clatworthy	1681	T.N.A., PROB 4/4498	Will also extant
7115	Alice WEBB, Widow of Wambrook	1632	W.S.H.C., P5/1632/51	
	Note: Appointment of guardian, inv., tuition bond, will			
7116	Edmund WEBB, Husbandman of Crowcombe	1639	DD/SP/1639/66	
7117	Elizabeth WEBB, Widow of West Cranmore	1741	D/D/cta/W42	Ad.ac. and inv.
7118	Joane WEBB of Langridge	1581	D/D/ct/1/W47	
7119	John WEBB of Drayton	1684	DD/SP/1684/46	
7120	John WEBB of Cutcombe	1685	DD/SP/1685/42	
7121	John WEBB of Ilminster	1687	T.N.A., PROB 4/20502	Admon
7122	Laurence WEBB, Gunmaker of Bridgwater	1637	DD/SP/1637/52	
7123	Martha WEBB, Widow of Wincanton	1779	T.N.A., PROB 31/1779/450	Formerly wife of Simon
7124	Peter WEBB, Clerk of Winsford	1724	T.N.A., PROB 3/23/71	Rector of Winsford
7125	Richard WEBB, Gentleman of Cricket Malherbie	1784	T.N.A., PROB 5/2816	
7126	Richard WEBB, Farmer and Widower of Cricket Malherbie	1787	T.N.A., PROB 31/1787/472	
7127	Robert WEBB, Mercer of Ilminster	1679	T.N.A., PROB 4/16227	Will. ex. 1680
7128	Thomas WEBB of Wambrook	1575	W.S.H.C., P5/1574/15	Admon. bond, inv.
7129	Thomas WEBB of Glastonbury	1611	D/D/cta/W63	Ad.ac.
7130	Thomas WEBB, Gunsmith of Havyat, Wrington	1686	D/D/cta/W41	Ad.ac.
7131	Thomas WEBB senior of Bridgwater	1690	DD/SP/1690/16	
7132	William WEBB of Chew Stoke	n.d.	D/D/cta/W43	Ad.ac. and inv.
7133	William WEBB alias PARKER, Husbandman of East Harptree	1625	D/D/ct/1/W51	
7134	Joan WEBBE of Shepton Mallet	1619	D/D/cta/W52	Ad.ac.
7135	John WEBBE of Axbridge	1633	D/D/cta/W40	Ad.ac.

7136	John WEBBE of Clapton	1694	T.N.A., PROB 4/2404	Will also extant
7137	Richard WEBBE the elder of Bathford	1639	D/D/cta/W1	Ad.ac.
7138	Abraham WEBBER of Gillingham, Kent died at Bath	1766	T.N.A., PROB 31/1766/438	
7139	Arthur WEBBER of Minehead	1646	DD/SP/1646/88	
7140	Arthur WEBBER, Husbandman of Woolcomb, Minehead	1676	DD/SP/1676/49	
7141	Daniel WEBBER of Taunton St. Mary Magdalene	1682	DD/SP/1682/55	Hannah relict
7142	David WEBBER of Selworthy	1675	DD/SP/1675/81	
7143	Edward WEBBER of Exton	1686	DD/SP/1686/30	
7144	Elizabeth WEBBER of Wellington	1676	T.N.A., PROB 4/15215	Will also extant
7145	Gertrude WEBBER, Widow of Brompton Regis	1687	DD/SP/1687/58	
7146	James WEBBER of Brompton Ralph	1730	DD/SP/1730/13	
7147	Jane WEBBER, Widow of Clatworthy	1692	DD/SP/1692/14	
7148	John WEBBER, Husbandman of Exton	1635	DD/SP/1635/26	
7149	John WEBBER of Huish Champflower	1688	DD/SP/1688/1	
7150	John WEBBER of Stogumber	1713	DD/SP/1713/21	
7151	John WEBBER senior of Brompton Regis	1683	DD/SP/1683/71	
7152	Peter WEBBER of Brompton Regis	1635	DD/SP/1635/106	See *T.C.W.*
7153	Phillip WEBBER of Clatworthy	1681	DD/SP/1681/105	
7154	Robert WEBBER, Husbandman of Halse	1672	DD/SP/1672/2	
7155	Thomas WEBBER, Tailor of Brompton Regis	1669	DD/SP/1669/98	
7156	Thomas WEBBER of Luxborough	1671	DD/SP/1671/19	
7157	Thomas WEBBER of Bathealton	1689	DD/SAS/PD/49	
7158	Thomas WEBBER, Gentleman of Rhode, North Petherton	1690	DD/SP/1690/43	
7159	William WEBBER of Cutcombe	1675	DD/SP/1675/90	
7160	William WEBBER, Farmer of North Petherton	1846	DD/TCM/21/18	
7161	John WEDLAKE of Luccombe	1680	DD/SP/1680/16	
7162	Eleanor WEECH of High Ham	1663	D/D/cta/W57	Ad.ac.
7163	Ursula WEECH, Widow of St. Michaelchurch	1674	DD/SP/1674/17	
7164	James WEEKES of Taunton St. Mary Magdalene	1664	DD/SP/1664/75	
7165	Robert WEEKES, Tanner of Wootton Courtenay	1664	DD/SP/1664/4	
7166	Susane WEEKES of Spaxton	1642	DD/SP/1632/41	Undated; *T.C.W.*
7167	Richard WEIGHT of Long Ashton	1728	D/D/cta/A25	Ad.ac. and inv.
7168	Mary WEITHER of Heathfield	1637	DD/SP/1637/12	

7169	William WELBORNE of Chard	1612	DD/HI/457	
7170	Elizabeth WELCH, Widow of Shapwick	n.d.	D/D/cta/W26	Ad.ac.
7171	Robert WELCH of Stoke St. Mary	1681	DD/SP/1681/103	
7172	Thomas WELCH of St. Decumans	1803	T.N.A., PROB 31/1803/503	
7173	James WELDON, Esquire of Bath	1800	T.N.A., PROB 31/1800/98 and PROB/1800/128	
7174	Simon WELFORD of Wells St. Cuthbert	1620	D/D/cta/W6	Ad.ac.
7175	Elioner WELLES of [no place]	1635	DD/SP/1635/55	
7176	Joan WELLICKE of Lydeard St. Lawrence	1639	DD/SP/1639/56	
7177	Hugh WELLMAN, Yeoman of Ilminster	1686	T.N.A., PROB 4/19705	Admon
7178	Richard WELLMAN, Husbandman of Misterton	1683	DD/SP/1683/91	
7179	Thomas WELLMAN of Cudworth	1686	T.N.A., PROB 4/9522	Admon
7180	Ellinor WELMAN, Widow of Closworth	1676	T.N.A., PROB 4/6278	Admon
7181	Philip WELSCHE of Badgworth	1628	D/D/cta/W11	Ad.ac.
7182	James WELSH, Clerk of Compton Bishop	1604	D/D/ct/1/W58	
7183	Thomas WELSH, Gentleman of Compton Bishop	1676	T.N.A., PROB 4/8647	Admon. ex. 1677
7184	Isott WELSHMAN, Widow of Elworthy	1648	DD/SP/1648/56	
7185	James WELSHMAN of Crowcombe	1689	DD/SP/1689/26	
7186	James WELSHMAN of West Buckland	1691	DD/SP/1691/66	
7187	Richard WELSHMAN, Husbandman of Nynehead	1674	DD/SP/1674/60	
7188	George WELSHOW of Crowcombe	1696	DD/SP/1696/28	
7189	Emma WERE, Spinster and Bastard of Nowers, Wellington formerly of Uffculm, Devon	1818	T.N.A., PROB 31/1818/1040	
7190	Thomas WERNALL junior, Woolcomber of Taunton St. James	1713	DD/SP/1713/44	
7191	Bartholomew WESCOMBE of Stogursey	1639	D/D/ct/1/W66	
7192	Mary WESCOMBE of Nether Stowey	1755	DD/MDW/18	With ad.ac.
7193	Robert WESCOMBE of Hillfarrance	1635	DD/SP/1635/56	
7194	William WESCOMBE of Fiddington	1639	DD/SP/1639/3	See *T.C.W.*
7195	William WESCOMBE of Nether Stowey	1755	DD/MDW/18	
7196	Henry WESCOTT of Kingston	1673	DD/SP/1673/9	
7197	Robert WESCOTT of South Petherton	1620	D/D/cta/W5	Ad.ac.
7198	William WESCOTT of Wootton Courtenay	1673	DD/SP/1673/5	
7199	Anne WEST of Isle Abbotts	1678	DD/SP/1678/87	

7200	Charles Baldwin WEST, Widower of Crowcombe	1817	T.N.A., PROB 31/1817/984	
7201	Edward WEST, Yeoman of Trull	1641	DD/SP/1641/83	
7202	Edward WEST, Worsted Comber of Taunton St. Mary Magdalene	1681	DD/SP/1681/104	
7203	Joane WEST, Widow of Bridgwater	1681	DD/SP/1681/21	
7204	Joane WEST of Ash Priors	1721	DD/SP/442/28	Ad.ac.
7205	Joane WEST of Ash Priors	1721	DD/SP/442/72	Ad.ac.
7206	Robert WEST of Chillington	1646	DD/SP/1646/34	
7207	Simon WEST, Watchmaker of Taunton St. Mary Magdalene	1695	DD/SP/1695/35	
7208	Elizabeth WESTAVIE of Porlock	1674	DD/SP/1674/52	
7209	Elizabeth WESTCOMBE of Stogursey	1744	DD/MDW/18	
7210	Robert WESTCOMBE of Milverton	1690	DD/SP/1690/28	
7211	Andrew WESTCOTT, Innholder of South Petherton	1730	DD/SP/1730/25	
7212	John WESTCOTT of South Petherton	1665	DD/SP/1665/28	
7213	John WESTCOTT, Husbandman of Wootton Courtenay	1676	DD/SP/1676/33	
7214	John WESTCOTT senior of Wootton Courtenay	1669	DD/SP/1669/42	
7215	Philip WESTCOTT, Apothecary, Bachelor of Taunton St. Mary Magdalene	1733	T.N.A., PROB 3/32/101	
7216	Thomesine WESTCOTT, Widow of South Petherton	1640	DD/SP/1640/59	
7217	William WESTCOTT, Weaver of Selworthy	1683	DD/SP/1683/23	
7218	William WESTCOTT of Luccombe	1723	DD/SP/1723/38	
7219	William WESTCOTT the younger, Husbandman of Wooton Courtenay	1668	DD/SP/1668/47	
7220	Philip WESTCOTTS, Apothecary of Taunton	1733	T.N.A., PROB 31/1733/418	
7221	Richard WESTERN of Bishops Hull	1685	DD/SP/1685/41	
7222	Jenny WESTON of [no place]	*c.*1775	DD/WHh/1107	
7223	Gabriell WESTOVER of Taunton	1645	DD/SP/1645/18	
7224	Johan WESTREN of Porlock	1638	DD/SP/1638/13	
7225	Ellinor WESTRON of Luxborough	1641	DD/SP/1641/57	
7226	Robert WEY the elder, Husbandman of Dunster	1646	DD/SP/1646/44	
7227	Thomas WHAITE of Donyatt	1724	DD/SP/1724/60	
7228	William WHAITE of Broadway	1647	DD/SP/1647/17	
7229	William WHAITE of Broadway	1647	DD/SP/1647/19	

7230	Elizabeth WHARTON, Spinster of Bath	1738	T.N.A., PROB 3/37/15	
7231	Elizabeth WHARTON, Spinster of Bath	1738	T.N.A., PROB 31/1738/110 and 1738/147	
7232	Robert WHATLEY, Cardmaker of Frome Selwood	1684	T.N.A., PROB 4/6217	Will also extant
7233	Attowill WHEADON senior, Tanner of Wootton Courtenay	1721	DD/SP/1721/23	
7234	John WHEADON of Spaxton	1681	DD/SP/1681/81	
7235	Anne WHEDDON of Withiel Florey	1698	DD/SP/1698/9	
7236	Frances WHEDDON of Withycombe	1701	DD/SP/442/41	Ad.ac.
7237	Hugh WHEDDON of Wootton Courtenay	1720	DD/SP/1720/7	
7238	Richard WHEDDON of Watchet, St. Decumans	1730	T.N.A., PROB 3/29/223	
7239	Richard WHEDDON of Watchet, St. Decumans	1734	T.N.A., PROB 31/1734/139	With account
7240	Florence WHEDON, Widow of Stogursey	1647	DD/SP/1647/13	
7241	Richard WHELLEGG of North Petherton	1639	D/D/ct/1/W74	
7242	James WHELLER, Husbandman of Drayton	1730	DD/SP/1730/28	
7243	John WHELLER, Husbandman of Swell	1693	DD/SP/1693/69	
7244	Christopher WHELLER alias COPP of Swell	1669	DD/SP/1669/40	
WHELLER see RAWLENS				
7245	Charity WHELLICKE, Widow of Milverton	1693	DD/SP/1693/49	
7246	John WHEREAT, Yeoman of Haygrove, Woolverton	1746	T.N.A., PROB 3/45/67	
7247	Dorothy WHETCOMBE of Taunton St. James	1629	D/D/ct/1/W75	Pvd 1629
7248	Richard WHETCOMBE of Taunton St. Mary Magdalene	1721	DD/SP/1721/2	
7249	John WHETHAM, Clothier of Taunton	1686	T.N.A., PROB 4/4511	Will also extant
7250	Richard WHIDDEN, Yeoman of Watchet, St. Decumans	1660	T.N.A., PROB 2/666	Exhibited 1660
7251	George WHIPPEY, Yeoman of Puxton	1668	T.N.A., PROB 4/8663	Will. ex. 1669
7252	John WHIPPEY of Filton alias Whitchurch, Whitchurch	1671	DD/CCHg/22	
7253	Christian WHIPPIE of Walton	1619	D/D/cta/W53	Ad.ac.
7254	John WHIPPIE of Whitchurch	1589	D/D/cta/W81	Ad.ac.
7255	John WHIPPIE, Ship Carpenter of Abbots Leigh	1636	B.A., 1636/62	See 1636/62b for a caveat
7256	John WHIPPIE, Yeoman of Filton alias Whitchurch	1671	DD/BR/da/6	
7257	Thomas WHIPPIE, Yeoman of Whitchurch	1687	T.N.A., PROB 4/15619	Will also extant
7258	Arthur WHITCH, Husbandman of Creech St. Michael	1671	DD/SP/1671/23	
WHITCH see WEECH				
7259	Robert WHITCHURCH of Frome	1738	T.N.A., PROB 31/1738/452	

7260	William WHITCHURCH of Frome Selwood died in the Fleet Prison, London	1750	T.N.A., PROB 3/49/16	
7261	Alice WHITE, Widow of South Harp, South Petherton	1636	DD/SP/1636/30	
7262	Alles WHITE, Widow of Culbone	1641	DD/SP/1641/23	
7263	Andrew WHITE, Gentleman of Creech St. Michael	1647	DD/SP/1647/1	
7264	Christopher WHITE of Beercrocombe	1685	DD/SP/1685/108	
7265	Edward WHITE, Yeoman of Angersleigh	1664	DD/SP/1664/63	
7266	Edward WHITE of Wrington	1735	D/D/Cti 96	
7267	Francis WHITE, Yeoman of Skilgate	1685	T.N.A., PROB 4/8041	Will. ex. 1686
7268	Francis WHITE of Bath	1693	T.N.A., PROB 4/11329	Admon
7269	Gregory WHITE, Yeoman of Combe Florey	1664	DD/SP/1664/33	
7270	Henry WHITE the younger, Yeoman of Ash Priors	1664	DD/SP/1664/77	
7271	Honour WHITE, Widow of Selworthy	1684	DD/SP/1684/171	
7272	Ignatus WHITE of Curry Mallet	1723	DD/SP/1723/51	
7273	John WHITE, Yeoman of South Harp, South Petherton	1623	D/D/ct/1/W83	
7274	John WHITE of Brompton Regis	1635	DD/SP/1635/35	
7275	John WHITE of Shepton Mallet	1641	D/D/cta/W29	Ad.ac.
7276	John WHITE of Hamp, Bridgwater	1675	DD/SP/1675/18	
7277	John WHITE of Selworthy	1675	DD/SP/1675/5	
7278	John WHITE, Yeoman of North Petherton	1722	DD/SP/442/78	Ad.ac.
7279	John WHITE, Yeoman of Ubley	1734	D/D/Cti 99	
7280	Martha WHITE of Wells	1791	T.N.A., PROB 31/1791/631	Wife of Isaac WHITE
7281	Richard WHITE of [no place]	1674	DD/SP/1674/3	
7282	Robert WHITE of Greenore, Chewton Mendip	n.d.	D/D/cta/W61	Ad.ac.
7283	Thomas WHITE of Creech St. Michael	1645	DD/SP/1645/10	
7284	Thomas WHITE of Dommet, Buckland St. Mary	1679	DD/SP/1679/9	
7285	William WHITE of Creech St. Michael	1676	DD/SP/1676/43	
7286	William WHITE, Mariner of Bridgwater	1725	DD/SP/1725/18	
7287	William WHITE the elder of Curry Rivel	1640	DD/SP/1640/89	Transcript in File 4 No. 26
7288	Philip WHITE alias POYLE of [no place]	1640	D/D/cta/W25	Ad.ac.
WHITE see KNIGHT				
7289	Katherine WHITEFIELD, Widow of Winsford	1617	D/D/ct/1/W87a	
7290	Robert WHITEFIELD of Cutcombe	1640	DD/SP/1640/121	Or WHITFILL

7291	Abraham WHITEHEAD, Carpenter of Dulverton	1693	DD/SP/1693/3	
7292	Thomas WHITEHEAD of [no place]	1648	D/D/cta/W2	Ad.ac.
7293	Thomas WHITEHEAD of Bruton	1690	T.N.A., PROB 4/4554	Will 1691. ex. 1691
7294	Gregory WHITEHEARE of Dulverton	1681	DD/SP/1681/15	
7295	William WHITEHOUSE of Abbots Leigh	1617	B.A., 1617/68	
7296	Francis WHITEING of Bath St. James	1638	D/D/cta/W15	Ad.ac.
7297	Eliza WHITENOLE, Widow of Crewkerne	1684	DD/SP/1684/23	
7298	William WHITEWOOD of Frome Selwood	1664	D/D/cta/W59	Ad.ac.
7299	Christopher WHITEYEAR, Husbandman of Thorne St. Margaret	1676	DD/SP/1676/6	
7300	John WHITFIELD of Chelsea, Middlesex died at Bath	1724	T.N.A., PROB 31/1724/507	
WHITFILL see WHITEFIELD				
7301	John WHITHEAD, Husbandman of Chedzoy	1642	DD/SP/1642/42	
7302	Maria WHITHERS of Wells died at Staplegrove	1834	T.N.A., PROB 37/905	
WHITING see WHYTING				
7303	Henry WHITINGE of Long Ashton	1678	T.N.A., PROB 4/13209	Will. ex. 1679
7304	Robert WHITINGE of Bedminster and Long Ashton	1679	D/D/ct/1/W94	
7305	Richard WHITNELL of Bradford	1684	DD/SP/1684/109	
7306	Henry WHITROW of Stoke St. Mary	1667	DD/SP/1667/57	
7307	Mary WHITTEAR, Widow of Dulverton	1688	DD/SP/1688/23	
7308	Joan WHITTING of Nailsea	1624	D/D/cta/W8	Ad.ac.
7309	Edward WHITTINGSTOWE of Doulting	1597	D/D/cta/W71	Ad.ac.
7310	William WHITTINGTON, Gentleman of Weston [near Bath]	1696	T.N.A., PROB 4/4155	Will also extant
7311	Nicholas WHITTOCKE of Pensford St. Thomas, Publow	1612	D/D/cta/W65	Ad.ac.
7312	Mary WHITTOOKE of Frome Selwood	1691	T.N.A., PROB 4/6881	Will also extant
7313	Anne WHYNNELL alias BOLER of Chard	1680	T.N.A., PROB 4/19868	Admon
WHYNNELL alias BOLER				
7314	Samuel WHYTING alias WHITING, Mariner of Shepton Mallet and H.M.S. *Burford* and *Combustion* Fireship	1785	T.N.A., PROB 31/1785/485	
7315	Joan WICKHAM of Stogursey	1693	DD/SP/1693/6	
7316	Richard WICKHAM, Yeoman of Stogursey	1698	DD/SP/1698/46	
7317	Richard WICKHAM, Yeoman of Fiddington	1714	DD/SP/1714/15	
7318	Charles WIDCOMBE of Chewton Mendip	n.d.	D/D/cta/W49	Ad.ac. and inv.
7319	John WIDDICOMBE of Stoke St. Gregory	1634	D/D/cta/W12	Ad.ac.

7320	Joan WIDLAKE of Cutcombe	1639	DD/SP/1639/2	
7321	John WIDLAKE, Husbandman of Throat, Luxborough	1716	DD/SP/1716/46	
7322	John WIDLAKE, Husbandman of Throat, Luxborough	1717	DD/SP/442/21	Ad.ac.
7323	Lawrence WIDLAKE of Cutcombe	1662	DD/SP/1662/23	
7324	Naomy WIDLAKE, Widow of Luccombe	1683	DD/SP/1683/74	
7325	Thomas WIDLAKE of Cutcombe	1681	DD/SP/1681/31	
7326	Richard WIEECH of Durston	1679	DD/SP/1679/54a	
7327	William WIET of Buckland St. Mary	1648	DD/SP/1648/48	
7328	George WIETT, Milliner of Over Stowey	1636	DD/SP/1636/11	
7329	John WIETT of Buckland St. Mary	1677	DD/SP/1677/70	
7330	Arthur WIGGINS, Labourer of Keynsham	1733	D/D/Cti 104	
7331	Joseph WIGHTMAN, Major General of St. James Westminster, Middlesex died at Bath	1722	T.N.A., PROB 31/1722/583	
7332	Joseph WILCOX of Beckington	1810	D/P/bec/23/4	
7333	Thomas WILCOX, Tailor of Donyatt	1686	DD/SP/1686/11	
WILCOX see ANDREWES				
7334	John WILD, Gentleman of Combe Florey	1625	DD/SP/1625/9	
7335	John WILD, Gentleman of Combe Florey	1682	DD/CH Box 47	
7336	Thomas WILKENS of Nempnett Thrubwell	1667	T.N.A., PROB 5/3243	
7337	Roger WILKES of Westonzoyland	1639	D/D/cta/C13a	Ad.ac.
7338	Alexander WILKINGS of Broadway	1687	DD/SP/1687/12	
7339	Edward WILKINS of Nempnett Thrubwell	1669	T.N.A., PROB 4/6917	Will 1669. ex. 1670
7340	Morris WILKINS of Taunton St. James	1684	DD/SP/1684/59	
7341	Philippa WILKINS of Chillington	1634	DD/SP/1634/10	See *T.C.W.*
7342	Richard WILKINS of West Harptree	1686	T.N.A., PROB 4/7963	Will also extant
7343	Hugh WILKINSON, Esquire of Bath formerly of Calcutta, India	1824	T.N.A., PROB 31/1824/1065	
7344	John WILKINSON, Clerk of Thorne Coffin	1664	D/D/cta/W58	Ad.ac. for a clergyman
7345	Christopher WILLCOX of East Brent	1598	D/D/cta/W21	Ad.ac.
7346	John WILLCOX, Yeoman of Drayton	1695	DD/SP/1695/20	
7347	Mary WILLCOX, Widow of Winford	1738	D/D/Cti 103	
7348	William WILLCOX of Chewton Mendip	1598	D/D/cta/W69	Ad.ac.
7349	Thomas WILLETT, Yeoman of Blagdon	1629/30	D/D/ct/1/W112	
7350	John WILLEY of Old Cleeve	1634	D/D/ct/1/W113	

7351	[Male] WILLIAMS of [no place]	1694	DD/SP/1694/31	
7352	[missing] WILLIAMS of [no place]	*c*.1667	D/D/cta/Blank/51	
	Note: Damaged ad.ac.; mentions the tutorship of Sarah WILLIAMS			
7353	Anthony WILLIAMS senior of Curry Mallet	1693	DD/SP/1693/36	
7354	Ben WILLIAMS of West Quantoxhead	1714	DD/SP/1714/2	
7355	David WILLIAMS, Shipbuilder of Bridgwater	1786	DD/HC Box 138	Bankrupt
7356	Edward WILLIAMS, Blacksmith of Selworthy	1684	DD/SP/1684/9	
7357	Henry WILLIAMS, Mariner of Bridgwater	1697	DD/SP/1697/38	
7358	James WILLIAMS of Taunton St. Mary Magdalene	1594	D/D/cta/W20	Ad.ac.
7359	James WILLIAMS of Trull	1679	DD/SP/1679/51	
7360	James WILLIAMS of Brushford	1721	DD/SP/1721/4	
7361	Jerome WILLIAMS of Curry Mallet	1669	DD/SP/1669/32	
7362	Joan WILLIAMS of Dodington	1684	DD/SP/1684/40	
7363	Joan WILLIAMS, Widow of Sherborne, Dorset formerly of South Cheriton, Horsington	1700	W.S.H.C., P5/1700/48	Inv. and will
7364	Joan WILLIAMS, Widow of Spaxton	1713	DD/SP/1713/36	
7365	Joane WILLIAMS, Widow of Brompton Regis	1640	DD/SP/1640/63	
7366	John WILLIAMS of East Coker	1612	D/D/cta/W66	Ad.ac.
7367	John WILLIAMS, Blacksmith of Bedminster	1675	T.N.A., PROB 4/10224	Will 1675
7368	John WILLIAMS of Over Stowey	1677	DD/SP/1677/9	
7369	John WILLIAMS of West Monkton	1678	DD/SP/1678/51	
7370	John WILLIAMS, Tailor of Minehead	1680	DD/SP/1680/71	
7371	John WILLIAMS of Withypool	1691	DD/SP/1691/76	
7372	John WILLIAMS, Rector of Abbas and Temple Combe	1692	*S.D.N.Q.* vol.28 p.39	
7373	John WILLIAMS, Clerk of South Cheriton, Horsington	1693	DD/DNL/151	Printed in *S.D.N.Q.* vol.26 p.185
7374	Nathaneil WILLIAMS senior of Exton	1681	DD/SP/1681/73	
7375	Nathaniel WILLIAMS of Luxborough	1706	DD/SP/442/59	Ad.ac.
7376	Richard WILLIAMS of Luxborough	1678	DD/SP/1678/35	
7377	Richard WILLIAMS of Brompton Regis	1707	DD/SP/442/57	Ad.ac.
7378	Richard WILLIAMS of Over Stowey	1630s	DD/SP/1632/42	
	Note: Undated; appraised by John and Robert SLOCOMBE			
7379	Robert WILLIAMS of Bridgwater	1691	DD/SP/1691/74	
7380	Simon WILLIAMS of Minehead	1675	DD/SP/1675/94	

7381	Thomas WILLIAMS of Chard	1674	T.N.A., PROB 4/2777	Will 1674
7382	Thomas WILLIAMS, Innholder of Taunton St. Mary Magdalene	1683	DD/SP/1683/63	
7383	Thomas WILLIAMS, Husbandman of Withypool	1693	DD/SP/1693/15	
7384	William WILLIAMS of Kingston Seymour	1588	D/D/cta/W75	Ad.ac.
WILLIAMS see SCORE				
7385	James WILLIE of Cutcombe	1669	DD/SP/1669/90	
7386	Katherine WILLIE of Otterford	1693	T.N.A., PROB 4/8408	Will also extant
7387	Robert WILLIE of Kewstoke	1639	D/D/cta/W18	Ad.ac.
7388	Thomas WILLIES, Yeoman of South Petherton	1667	DD/SP/1667/46	
7389	Edward WILLIS of Clevedon	1640	D/D/cta/W30	Ad.ac.
7390	George WILLIS, Yeoman of Easton in Gordano	1734	T.N.A., PROB 31/1734/430	with account
7391	Humphry WILLIS of St. Andrews, Glamorgan died at Woolavington	1687	T.N.A., PROB 4/8060	Admon, died at Woollavington
7392	Mary WILLIS, Widow of Exmouth, Devon formerly of Eversley, Southampton afterwards of Belvedere, Bath	1810	T.N.A., PROB 31/1810/620	
7393	Thomas WILLIS of Clutton	1599	D/D/cta/W68	Ad.ac.
7394	William WILLIS of Taunton St. Mary Magdalene	1681	DD/SP/1681/70	
7395	Thomas WILLIS [WILLIE?] of Otterford	1692	T.N.A., PROB 4/6954	Will also extant
7396	John WILLMOTT of Nailsea	1590	D/D/cta/W76	Ad.ac.
7397	John WILLMOTT of Nailsea	1590	D/D/cta/W78	Ad.ac.
7398	Odes WILLMOTT senior, Yeoman of Stoke St. Gregory	1679	T.N.A., PROB 4/2416	Will also extant
7399	Richard WILLMOTT of West Dowlish, Dowlish Wake	1737	T.N.A., PROB 3/36/47	
7400	Richard WILLMOTT the younger, Sergemaker of Rapps, Broadway	1730	T.N.A., PROB 31/1730/251	
7401	Agnes WILLOUGHBY of [no place]	1620	DD/56/3, 57/11	
7402	Richard WILLOUGHBY of [no place]	1602	DD/WO/40/5	
7403	Richard WILLOUGHBY of [no place]	1602	DD/WO/56/3	
7404	Thomas WILLOUGHBY of Berkley	1703	DD/OB/107	
7405	Gilbert WILLS of [no place]	1641	DD/SP/1641/36	
7406	Hugh WILLS, Tailor of Merriott	1677	DD/SP/1677/17	
7407	Thomas WILLS, Yeoman of Chewton Mendip	*c.*1740	D/D/cta/W44	Ad.ac. and inv.
WILLS see MOREY				

7408	Elizabeth WILLSON, Widow of Whitchurch	1634	D/D/cta/W16	Ad.ac.
7409	Avice WILLY of South Petherton	1671	DD/SP/1671/11	
7410	Richard WILLY, Clothier of Lopen	1678	DD/SP/1678/32	
7411	William WILLY, Husbandman of Over Stratton, South Petherton	1696	DD/SP/1696/25	
7412	Thomas WILMOT of Stogursey	1676	DD/SP/1676/25	With release by sister
7413	William WILMOT, Yeoman of Portishead	1735	D/D/Cti 101a-b	
7414	Charles WILMOTT, Yeoman of Weston in Gordano	1735/6	D/D/Cti 102	
7415	Edward WILMOTT of West Dowlish, Dowlish Wake	1688	T.N.A., PROB 4/19883	Will also extant
7416	John WILMOTT of Fivehead	1714	DD/SP/1714/1	
7417	John WILMOTT of Fivehead	1714	DD/SP/1714/19	
7418	Richard WILMOTT the younger, Sergemaker of Rapps, Broadway	1730	T.N.A., PROB 3/29/84	
7419	Edmond WILSHEERE of Lyng	1668	DD/SP/1668/16	
7420	John WILSHERE of Weston (near Bath)	1626	D/D/ct/1/W124	
7421	William WILSHIERE of Wellow	1702	D/D/cta/W45	Ad.ac.
7422	Thomas WILSON, Yeoman of Dulverton	1716	DD/SP/1716/2	
7423	William WILTON, Stockingmaker of Bruton	1734	D/D/cta/W46	Ad.ac. and inv.
7424	Sarah WIMPEW of Midsomer Norton	1695	D/D/cta/W47	Ad.ac.
7425	Thomas WIN alias WRIGHT, Blacksmith of North Petherton	1713	DD/SP/1713/16	
7426	Charlotte Katherine WINDSOR, Widow of Taunton formerly of Long Croft, Herts. then of New Hampton, Middx.	1836	T.N.A., PROB 31/1836/1610	
7427	Thomas WINNE of Middlezoy	1629	D/D/ct/1/W127a	
7428	Richard WINNIATT of Bedminster	1815	T.N.A., PROB 31/1815/596	
7429	John WINSLADE of North Petherton	1683	DD/SP/1683/17	
7430	William WINSLADE the elder, Husbandman of North Petherton	1642	DD/SP/1642/19	
7431	John WINSOR of Misterton Note: Admon. ex. 1691, died intestate about the age of 16	1690	T.N.A., PROB 4/11563	
7432	Charles WINTER of Watts House, Bishops Lydeard	1836	DD/LP/3	
7433	James WINTER, Yeoman of Treborough	1672	DD/SP/1672/35	
7434	James WINTER of Court House, Bishops Lydeard	1830	DD/LP/3	
7435	Joan WINTER of Halse	1698	DD/SP/1698/8	Wife of John
7436	John WINTER of Sampford Brett	1639	DD/SP/1639/21	See *T.C.W.*
7437	John WINTER of Bridgwater	1674	DD/SP/1674/63	

	Note: Mentions a share in *The Speedwell* and *The Langport* 'Friggott'			
7438	John WINTER, Sergemaker of Langford Budville	1690	T.N.A., PROB 4/18421	Will also extant
7439	John WINTER of Brompton Ralph	1716	DD/SP/1716/50	
7440	John WINTER of Ilchester	1740	T.N.A., PROB 3/39/94	
7441	John WINTER of Old Cleeve	1783	T.N.A., PROB 31/1783/757	
7442	Mary WINTER of Mudford	1670	T.N.A., PROB 4/20433	Admon
7443	Mary WINTER, Widow of Stogursey	1725	DD/SP/1725/7	
7444	Richard WINTER of Halse	1677	DD/SP/1677/14	
7445	Simon WINTER, Cook of Langford Budville	1639	DD/SP/1639/17	
7446	Thomas WINTER of Sampford Brett	1639	DD/SP/1639/49	
7447	Thomas WINTER, Butcher of Tolland	1665	DD/SP/1665/22	
7448	William WINTER of Enmore	1640	DD/SP/1640/54	
7449	John WINTERHAY of Glastonbury St. John	n.d.	D/D/cta/W48	Ad.ac.
7450	Josias WINTERHAY of [no place]	1687	DD/SP/1687/64	
7451	John WINTLE, Widower of Bath	1799	T.N.A., PROB 31/1799/507	
7452	John WINTLE, Widower of Bath formerly of St. Margaret's Hill, Southwark, Surrey afterwards of Hatton Street, Middlesex	1799	T.N.A., PROB 37/249	Declaration
7453	Thomas WINWOOD, Clerk of Langford Budville	1640	DD/SP/1640/115	
7454	James WIPPLE of Raddington	1683	DD/SP/1683/10	
7455	William WIPPLE of Stogumber	1639	DD/SP/1639/29	See *T.C.W.*
7456	John WISE of [no place]	1584	D/D/cta/W22	Ad.ac.
7457	William WITCH of Bridgwater	1646	DD/SP/1646/43	
7458	John WITHER, Mason of Brompton Regis	1638	DD/SP/1638/14	
7459	William WITHER of Over Stowey	1665	DD/SP/1665/40	
WITHER see WEITHER				
7460	George WITHERALL of Drayton	1694	DD/SP/1694/16	
7461	Roger WITHERALL, Smith of Dinnington	1686	DD/SP/1686/12	
7462	Robert WITHEREDGE of [no place]	1601	D/D/cta/W19	Ad.ac.
7463	Emma WITHERS of Taunton St. James	1641	DD/SP/1641/90	
7464	Humfry WITHERS of Over Stowey	1640	DD/SP/1640/85	See *T.C.W.*
7465	John WITHERS of Goathurst	1682	DD/SP/1682/16	
7466	Mary WITHERS of Taunton St. Mary Magdalene	1669	DD/SP/1669/4	
7467	Thomas WITHERS the elder, Husbandman of Heathfield	1664	DD/SP/1664/83	

7468	Edward WITHICOMBE of Holford	1680	DD/SP/1680/69	
7469	John WITHICOMBE, Yeoman of Bradwood, Carhampton	1700	T.N.A., PROB 4/6903	Will 1700
7470	John WODDALL of Congresbury	1597	D/D/cta/W70	Ad.ac.
7471	Sir Jacob WOLFE, Baronet of Hammett Street, Taunton	1809	T.N.A., PROB 31/1809/474	
7472	Richard and Cicely WOLFORD of Glastonbury St. John	1591	D/D/cta/W60	Ad.ac.
7473	Richard and Cisily WOLFORD of Glastonbury	1591	D/D/cta/W72	Ad.ac.
7474	Blanch WOLLASTON, Widow of Bath	1819	T.N.A., PROB 31/1819/662	
7475	George WOOD, Grocer of Bridgwater	1685	T.N.A., PROB 4/20362	Will 1686. ex. 1686
7476	Joan WOOD, Widow of Dulverton	1693	DD/SP/1693/27	
7477	John WOOD of Luccombe	1688	DD/SP/1688/22	
7478	John WOOD, Carrier of Milverton	1729	DD/SP/1729/42	
7479	John WOOD of [no place]	1630s	DD/SP/1632/43	Undated and damaged; mentions several skins
7480	Marjery WOOD, Widow of Kingston	1670	DD/SP/1670/90	
7481	Peter WOOD of Isle Brewers	1647	DD/SP/1632/44	Undated; *T.C.W.*
7482	Robert WOOD of Cutcombe	1664	DD/SP/1664/31	
7483	Thomas WOOD of Chewton Mendip	1662	D/D/cta/W56	Ad.ac.
7484	Thomas WOOD of Kittisford	1689	DD/SF/11/2/12	Formerly DD/SF/3134
7485	Tristram WOOD, Gentleman of Kittisford	1669	T.N.A., PROB 4/6212	Will. ex. 1670
7486	William WOOD of Withiel Florey	1673	DD/SP/1673/20	
7487	William WOOD, Bachelor of Exford	1716	DD/SP/1716/40	
7488	William WOOD of Exton	1716	DD/SP/442/19	Ad.ac.
7489	William WOODALL the elder, Miller of Nynehead	1686	DD/SF/11/1/90	Formerly DD/SF/2095
7490	Mary WOODBORN of East Chinnock	1763	D/P/chin.e./13/10/2	
7491	Henry WOODBORNE of Curry Rivel	1592	D/D/cta/W73	Ad.ac.
7492	[missing] WOODBOURNE of Curry Rivel	1687	D/D/cta/W51	Ad.ac.
7493	Josiah WOODCOCKE of Taunton	1668	DD/SP/1668/24	
7494	George WOODFORD of West Buckland	1629	D/D/ct/1/W136a	
7495	John WOODHOUSE of [no place]	1668	DD/X/PLY/6	
7496	John WOODHOUSE, Yeoman of Creech St. Michael	1720	DD/SP/1720/9	
7497	Robert WOODHOUSE, Yeoman of North Petherton	1729	DD/SP/1729/59	
7498	John WOODLAND of Durleigh	1693	DD/SP/1693/9	
7499	John WOODLAND, Widower of Huntspill	1737	D/D/cta/W50	Ad.ac. and inv.

7500	Charles WOODMAN junior of Pitminster	1694	DD/SP/1694/25	See also D/P/pit 2/1/1
7501	Phillip WOODROW, Bargeman of Lyng	1645	DD/SP/1645/50	
7502	Roger WOODS of [no place]	1565/6	DD/SF/11/1/11	Formerly DD/SF 808
7503	John WOODWARD of Donyatt	1681	DD/SP/1681/74	
7504	William WOODWARD of Chard	1625	D/D/cta/W9	Ad.ac.
7505	William WOODWARD of Donyatt	1675	DD/SP/1675/60	
7506	William WOODWARD, Tailor of Donyatt	1686	DD/SP/1686/10	
7507	Thomas WOODYATES the elder, Clothier of Nunney	1675	T.N.A., PROB 4/16104	Will also extant
7508	John WOOKEY of Hinton Blewett	1695	T.N.A., PROB 4/25504	Will. ex. 1695
7509	William WOOKEY of Bridgwater	1675	DD/SP/1675/19	
7510	George WOOLCOTT the elder, Clothier of Tolland	1683	DD/SP/1683/89	
7511	Naboth WOOLCOTT of Elworthy	1680	DD/SP/1680/12	
7512	Robert WOOLCOTT, Clothier of Williton, St. Decumans	1677	T.N.A., PROB 4/1352	Will also extant
7513	[Male] WOOLFREY of [no place]	1694	DD/SP/1694/28	Part missing
7514	John WOOLFREY, Husbandman of Fivehead	1693	DD/SP/1693/73	
7515	John WOOLFREY of Drayton	1742	DD/SP/1742/16	
7516	Conant WOOLLCOTT of Nettlecombe	1664	DD/SP/1664/61	
7517	William WOOLLCOTT, Weaver of Langford Budville	1670	DD/SP/1670/28	
7518	Robert WOOLLFALL, Clerk of Wanstrow	1612	D/D/cta/W64	Ad.ac. for a clergyman
7519	Henry WOOLLMINGTON of Barwick	1623	D/D/cta/W7	Ad.ac.
7520	John WOOLMINGTON senior, Yeoman of Wambrook	1641	W.S.H.C., P5/1641/104	Inv. and will
7521	Julian WOOLMINGTON of Ash, Martock	1629	D/D/ct/1/W141	
7522	Richard WOOLMINGTON of Wambrook	1599	W.S.H.C., P5/1599/40	Admon. bond, inv.
7523	Ann WOOTTEN of Langford Budville	1685	DD/SP/1685/6	
7524	Christopher WOOTTEN, Blacksmith of Langford Budville	1688	DD/SP/1688/50	
7525	Christopher WOOTTON, Blacksmith of Langford Budville	1675	DD/SP/1675/34	
7526	Ralph WORNELL alias SMITH, Blacksmith of Trull	1682	DD/SP/1682/36	
7527	John WORSLEY, Chapman of Bath City	1745	T.N.A., PROB 3/44/47	
7528	John WORTH, Esquire of Luccombe	1730	D.H.C., 49/9/1/645	
7529	Richard WORTH, Gentleman of Somerset	1637	D.H.C., 49/9/1/641	
7530	John WORTHY senior of Swell	1691	DD/SP/1691/34	
7531	Richard WORTHY of Drayton	1731	DD/SP/1731/21	
7532	Robert WOTWAY of Horsey, Bridgwater	1674	DD/SP/1674/55	

WOWEN see OWEN				
7533	Robert WRAIGHT, Mariner of Wellington and Bristol	1754	B.A., 1754/27	Will also extant
7534	[missing] WRAPPER of [no place]	1696	DD/SP/1696/1	
7535	Ann WRAXAL, Widow of Portbury	1736	D/D/Cti 100	
7536	Richard WRAYFORD of Kingstone	1697	DD/SP/1697/47	
7537	Anne WRENCH, Widow of [no place]	1682	T.N.A., PROB 4/15720	Admon
7538	William WRENCHE of Witcombe ?	1591	D/D/cta/W74	Ad.ac.
7539	Absolom WRENTMORE, Innholder of Glastonbury	1728	D/D/Cti 98	
7540	John WRENTMORE of Taunton	1634	DD/SP/1634/27	
7541	John WRENTMORE of Taunton	1648	DD/SP/1648/27	
7542	Sandy WRENTMORE, Gentleman of Axbridge	1681	T.N.A., PROB 4/21723	Admon with com.
WRENTMORE see BAND				
7543	John WRIGHT of Dunster	1670	DD/SP/1670/67	
7544	John WRIGHT the younger, Mercer of Dunster	1679	T.N.A., PROB 4/10554	Will also extant
7545	Samuel WRIGHT of Bath	1717	T.N.A., PROB 5/5685	
7546	Uriah WRIGHT of North Petherton	1697	DD/SP/1697/42	
WRIGHT see WIN				
7547	Sir John WROTH, Baronet of North Petherton	1677	T.N.A., PROB 4/20498	Will. ex. 1678
7548	Sampson WROTH, Clockmaker of Taunton St. Mary Magdalene	1714	DD/SP/1714/10	
7549	Daniel WYATT of Combe St. Nicholas	1797	DD/BD/36	
7550	Francis WYATT, Weaver of Trull	1678	DD/SP/1678/66	
7551	Francis WYATT, Weaver of Trull	1678	DD/SP/1678/90	
7552	James WYATT, Yeoman of Queen Charlton	1727	D/D/Cti 97	
7553	John WYATT of Pitminster	1668	DD/SP/1668/53	
7554	John WYATT of Taunton St. James	1669	DD/SP/1669/74	
7555	John WYATT of Taunton St. James	1670	DD/SP/1670/29	
7556	James WYBORNE senior of Dunster	1678	DD/SP/1678/46	
7557	Thomas WYCHEFFEILLD of Chapel Allerton	1557	T.N.A., PROB 2/291	Will T.N.A., PROB 11/38/20
7558	John WYLD, Gentleman of Combe Florey	1683	T.N.A., PROB 4/9511	Will also extant
7559	Jane WYLKES of Stocklinch Ottersey	1634	DD/SP/1634/38	
7560	John WYMPEW of Nunney	1646	D/D/cta/W82	Ad.ac.
7561	Barbara WYNDHAM of [no place]	1704-	DD/WY/10/7/2	

		1706		
	Note: Formerly DD/WY Box 185; wife of Sir Wadham WYNDHAM			
7562	Edmond WYNDHAM, Esquire of Kentsford, St. Decumans	1697	T.N.A., PROB 4/8417	Will. ex. 1698
7563	Edmund WYNDHAM of Kentsford, St. Decumans	1697	DD/WO/53/1	
7564	Sir Edward WYNDHAM, Baronet of Orchard Wyndham, St. Decumans	1696	T.N.A., PROB 4/6863	Admon
7565	Dame Frances WYNDHAM of Orchard Wyndham, St. Decumans	1697	DD/WY/11/2/2	Formerly DD/WY/20/37
7566	Sir Francis WYNDHAM, Baronet of Trent	1676	T.N.A., PROB 4/6248	Will also extant
7567	Mary WYNDHAM of Kentsford, St. Decumans	1697	DD/WO/56/3	Goods removed from Kentsford, St. Decumans
7568	Thomas WYNDHAM, Esquire of Witham Friary	1690	T.N.A., PROB 4/6282	Will also extant
7569	Sir William WYNDHAM of Orchard Wyndham, St. Decumans	1683	DD/WY/11/2/1	Formerly DD/WY Box 20 no. 38
7570	Mrs WYNTER of Bath	1691	G.A., D1799/F17	
7571	William YANDALL of Clatworthy	1724	DD/SP/442/79	Ad.ac.
7572	Anne YANDLE, Widow of North Petherton	1671	DD/SP/1671/8	
7573	Julian YARD of Clevedon	1591	D/D/cta/Y3	Ad.ac.
7574	Thomas YARD, Gentleman of Staple Fitzpaine	1685	DD/SP/1685/8	
7575	Thomas YARD senior, Gentleman of Staple Fitzpaine	1669	DD/SP/1669/23	
7576	Uriah YAW of Milverton	1685	DD/SP/1685/94	
7577	Betty YEA, Spinster of Bishops Hull	1794	T.N.A., PROB 31/1794/293	With account
7578	David YEA, Esquire of Wiveliscombe died at Taunton	1794	T.N.A., PROB 31/1794/289	
7579	Master John YEADLE, Clerk of Bruton	1688	T.N.A., PROB 4/8257	Will 1688
7580	Mary YEADLE, Spinster of Westonzoyland	1624	D/D/ct/1/Y24a	
7581	John YEALD, Husbandman of Westonzoyland	1604	D/D/ct/1/Y25a	
7582	Richard YEANDLE of Raddington	1732	DD/SP/1732/10	
7583	Edward YEATS, Weaver of Hillfarrance	1645	DD/SP/1645/53	See *T.C.W.*
7584	Symon YEAW of Enmore	1667	DD/SP/1667/21	Reference to property in Otterhampton
7585	Rebecca YEEM of Withycombe	1672	DD/SP/1672/39	
7586	William YELVERTON of Donyatt	1679	T.N.A., PROB 4/8262	Admon
7587	Andrew YENDALL, Husbandman of Skilgate	1640	DD/SP/1640/41	
7588	Francis YENDALL of Oake	1680	DD/SP/1680/86	
7589	Katherine YENDALL, Widow of Exton	1642	DD/SP/1642/31	
7590	Joane YENDLE of Skilgate	1629	D/D/ct/1/Y30a	

7591	Thomas YENDLE, Husbandman of Skilgate	1637	DD/SP/1637/17	
7592	Thomas YENDLE of Skilgate	1667	DD/SP/1667/6	
7593	John YEOMAN of Glastonbury St. John	1728	D/D/Cti 105	
7594	John YEOMANS of [no place]	1740	D/D/cta/Y1	Ad.ac.
7595	John YEOND of Selworthy	1678	DD/SP/1678/89	
YEOND see RAWLE				
YEVEN see EWEN				
7596	John YEWENS of Taunton St. James	1666	DD/SP/1666/68	
7597	Peter YOND of Taunton St. James	1693	DD/SP/1693/50	
7598	Thomas YORCK alias FRANCK of Winford	1625	D/D/cta/W24	Ad.ac.
7599	James YORKE of East Harptree	1738	DD/HI/211	
7600	Walter YOUD, Yeoman of Selworthy	1669	DD/SP/1669/59	
7601	Edward YOUENS, Weaver of Dunster	1645	DD/SP/1645/44	
7602	Anne YOUNG, Widow of Trent	1674	T.N.A., PROB 4/8732	Will. ex. 1675
7603	Arthur YOUNG of Fivehead	1678	DD/SP/1678/73	
7604	Edith YOUNG, Widow of Abbots Leigh	1625	B.A., 1625/93	Will also extant
7605	Elizabeth YOUNG of Shapwick	1738	D/D/Cti 95	
7606	Francis YOUNG of Clatworthy	1691	DD/SP/1691/35	
7607	Francis YOUNG of Greinton	1711	D/D/cta/Y2	Ad.ac.
7608	John YOUNG of Rowberrow	1823	DD/HB/35	
7609	Josephine YOUNG, Yeoman of Stogursey	1712	DD/SP/1712/3	
7610	Nicholas YOUNG of Combe Florey	1716	DD/SP/442/22	Ad.ac.
7611	William YOUNG, Yeoman of Merriott	1629	D/D/ct/1/Y38a	
7612	Edward YOUNGE of Taunton St. James	1674	DD/SP/1674/9	
7613	James YOUNGE of Fivehead	1716	DD/SP/1716/52	
7614	Mary YOUNGE of Rowberrow	1629	D/D/ct/1/Y36	
7615	Nicholas YOUNGE, Gentleman of Combe Florey	1716	DD/SP/1716/51	
7616	Richard ZEALIE of Burrington	1621	D/D/cta/W23	Ad.ac.
7617	Bridgitt ZEALLY of Holford	1648	DD/SP/1648/54	
ZEALLY see SEALY				
7618	John ZELLACKE of Tolland	1588	D/D/cta/Z1	Ad.ac.

INDEX OF PARISH, CITY, COUNTY AND COUNTRY NAMES

(Note: This index has been arranged using C.R. Humphrey-Smith's *The Phillimore atlas and index of parish registers*).

INDEX OF OCCUPATIONS

INDEX OF SOCIAL DESCRIPTIONS

INDEX OF PERSONAL NAMES

(These are in addition to the main series of records in this handlist starting at page 1)